SUBMARINE

SUBMARINE STORIES

STORIES

Recollections from the Diesel Boats

EDITED BY PAUL STILLWELL

NAVAL INSTITUTE PRESS
Annapolis, Maryland

Naval Institute Press
291 Wood Road
Annapolis, MD 21402

This book has been brought to publication with the
generous assistance of Everett Weaver.

Library of Congress Cataloging-in-Publication Data
    Submarine stories : recollections from the diesel boats /
edited by Paul Stillwell.
        p. cm.
    Includes index.
    ISBN-13: 978-1-59114-841-8 (alk. paper)
    ISBN-10: 1-59114-841-3 (alk. paper)
      1. Submarines (Ships)—United States—History.
2. United States. Navy—Submarine forces—History.
I. Stillwell, Paul, 1944–
V858.S73 2007
359.9'330973—dc22

                                2006033777

Printed in the United States of America on acid-free paper

14 13 12 11 10 09 08 07   9 8 7 6 5 4 3 2

First printing

Dedicated to Slade Cutter,
a great submariner and
a great friend

Contents

Preface xi

Acknowledgments xiii

1. **Parks and the *Pompano*** 1
   Capt. Slade D. Cutter, USN (Ret.)

2. **The President Takes a Plunge** 10
   Theodore Roosevelt

3. **World War I** 13
   Vice Adm. Paul F. Foster,
   U.S. Naval Reserve (Ret.)

4. **Submarine School** 25
   Adm. Stuart S. Murray, USN (Ret.)

5. **Beginning of the S-Boats** 31
   Vice Adm. George C. Dyer, USN (Ret.)

6. **Building the Submarine Base at
   Pearl Harbor** 36
   Adm. Stuart S. Murray, USN (Ret.)

7. **Early Command** 42
   Rear Adm. George W. Bauernschmidt,
   Supply Corps, USN (Ret.)

8. **Loss of the *S-51* and *S-4*** 47
   Adm. Robert L. Dennison, USN (Ret.)

9. **Far East Duty** 51
   Rear Adm. Ernest M. Eller, USN (Ret.)

10. **R-Boat Service** 58
    Rear Adm. Edward K. Walker, USN (Ret.)

11. **Oddball S-Boat** 62
    Rear Adm. William D. Irvin, USN (Ret.)

12. **Developing the Fleet Boats** 67
    Adm. Stuart S. Murray, USN (Ret.)

13. **Submarine Tender** 72
    Rear Adm. George W. Bauernschmidt,
    Supply Corps, USN (Ret.)

14. **Submarine Detailing** 75
    Rear Adm. John F. Davidson, USN (Ret.)

15. **Developing the Torpedo Data
    Computer** 77
    Rear Adm. Edward K. Walker, USN (Ret.)

16. **The *Squalus* Rescue** 80
    Chief Machinist's Mate William Badders,
    USN (Ret.)

17. **Encounters with Corpses** 85
    Rear Adm. Charles A. Curtze, USN (Ret.)

18. **Another View on the *Squalus*** 91
    Capt. Robert L. Evans, USN (Ret.)

19. **Grandstand Seat at Pearl Harbor** 94
    Vice Adm. Lawson P. Ramage, USN (Ret.)

20. **Disaster at Cavite** 98
    Rear Adm. Norvell G. Ward, USN (Ret.)

21. **Escape from the Japanese** 101
    Chief Ship's Clerk, CWO-2, Cecil S. King,
    USN (Ret.)

22. **Reservists at Submarine School** 104
    Vice Adm. Eugene P. Wilkinson,
    USN (Ret.)

23. ***Drum* at War** 107
    Rear Adm. Maurice H. Rindskopf,
    USN (Ret.)

24. **Breakers Ahead!** 113
    Capt. Edward L. Beach, USN (Ret.)

25. **Battle of Midway** 118
    Rear Adm. Roy S. Benson, USN (Ret.)

26. **Peril at Fifty Fathoms** 120
    Billy A. Grieves

27. **Sub Sailors' Liberty** 124
    James B. O'Meara

28. **Surface Action** 128
    Capt. Paul R. Schratz, USN (Ret.)

29. **Stern Skipper** 132
    Rear Adm. Julian T. Burke Jr., USN (Ret.)

30. **Special Missions** 136
    Rear Adm. Norvell G. Ward, USN (Ret.)

31. **Scouting the Gilbert Islands** 141
    Rear Adm. William D. Irvin, USN (Ret.)

32. **Saga of a *Sculpin* Survivor** 146
    Chief Motor Machinist's Mate George
    Rocek, USN (Ret.)

33. **Aide to Admiral King** 153
    Capt. Robert E. Dornin, USN (Ret.)

34. **Crossing the Equator** 156
    Rear Adm. Julian T. Burke Jr., USN (Ret.)

35. **Black Submariner** 158
    Chief Interior Communications
    Electrician Hosey Mays, USN (Ret.)

36. **Wolf Pack Operations** 163
    Vice Adm. Lawson P. Ramage, USN (Ret.)

37. **Rescuing POWs** 170
    Rear Adm. Robert W. McNitt, USN (Ret.)

38. **Enemy Rescue** 174
    James B. O'Meara

39. **New Bride, New Boat** 177
    Cdr. John D. Alden, USN (Ret.)

40. **Abandoning the *Darter*** 183
    Vice Adm. Eugene P. Wilkinson,
    USN (Ret.)

41. **Dodging Mines and Praying** 186
    Rear Adm. Julian T. Burke Jr., USN (Ret.)

42. **Not Enough Fish** 191
    Capt. William F. Calkins,
    U.S. Naval Reserve (Ret.)

43. **SubPac Operations** 195
    Rear Adm. Norvell G. Ward, USN (Ret.)

44. **The Postwar Naval Reserve** 200
    Capt. Richard B. Laning, USN (Ret.)

45. **Submarines and Ice** 205
    Dr. Waldo K. Lyon

46. **Missiles at Sea**   212
    Vice Adm. Eugene P. Wilkinson,
    USN (Ret.)

47. **Fire in the** *Cochino*   216
    Rear Adm. Roy S. Benson, USN (Ret.)

48. **Hot New Guppy**   220
    Capt. Paul R. Schratz, USN (Ret.)

49. **Those Disastrous Pancake Diesels**   227
    Adm. Harold E. Shear, USN (Ret.)

50. **Photo Reconnaissance**   232
    Vice Adm. Joe Williams Jr., USN (Ret.)

51. **The Whale-Shaped** *Albacore*   235
    Capt. Harry A. Jackson, USN (Ret.)

52. **Firing the Regulus**   239
    Rear Adm. Norvell G. Ward, USN (Ret.)

53. **Tangling with the Soviets**   242
    Vice Adm. Joe Williams Jr., USN (Ret.)

54. **Angles and Dangles**   246
    Adm. Harry D. Train II, USN (Ret.)

55. **A Few Days in October**   254
    Chief Surface Ordnance Technician,
    CWO-4, Jerry E. Beckley, USN (Ret.)

56. **A Submariner's Memories**   260
    Wayne L. Miller

57. **Last of the B-Girls**   267
    Master Chief Machinist's Mate Charles E.
    Wormwood III, USN (Ret.)

58. **End of an Era**   274
    Cdr. Andrew Wilde, USN

Sources of Chapters   281
Index   285

Preface

IN THE YEAR 2000, when the terms *Y2K* and *millennium* appeared frequently in the news media, much less fanfare accompanied the centennial of the U.S. Navy's submarine force. Those 2000 terms were a passing fad; the submarine service is still with us, as it has been for more than one hundred years.

During that time technological development has been amazing, beginning with the USS *Holland*, commissioned on 12 October 1900. She was 53 feet, 10 inches long, displaced seventy-four tons, and had a designed depth of 100 feet. She was powered by a 45-horsepower gasoline engine, had a top speed of eight knots, and carried three torpedoes. The newest nuclear-powered attack submarine, the USS *Hawaii*, goes into commission in 2007. She is 377 feet long and displaces nearly eight thousand tons. Even bigger are the ballistic missile submarines, 560 feet long and displacing more than eighteen thousand tons, comparable to World War II heavy cruisers. Current submarines' weapons capabilities include torpedoes, mines, cruise missiles, and nuclear-armed ballistic missiles—the latter capable of causing monumental damage thousands of miles from submerged launching sites.

The intermediate generations of submarines—between the tiny *Holland* and the nuclear-powered behemoths of today—were the diesel boats. The first one, USS *F-1*, entered active service in the U.S. Navy in 1912; the last diesel attack boat, USS *Blueback*, left the fleet in 1990; and the experimental USS *Dolphin* was decommissioned in 2006. These ever-more-modern craft were in operation throughout nearly all of the twentieth century. Just as the technology was developing, so too were the men who went to sea in those diesel boats. They learned to adapt to boats that could dive deeper than their predecessors, go faster, shoot farther, and stay underwater longer. Submariners are volunteers who constitute a special breed. They are also prone to the same habit as their counterparts throughout other branches of the Navy: they like to tell sea stories.

This volume contains a few dozen selected sea stories from those special individuals. In many cases the tales provide material that is not contained in official records. These recollections are culled from several sources; most of them are from oral histories conducted under the auspices of the U.S. Naval Institute. And that is the great value of oral history; it preserves memories that otherwise would be lost. My intent in assembling this collection is both to inform and entertain. Above all, these stories illustrate the human aspects of serving in diesel boats: the training, operations in peacetime and war, liberty exploits, humorous sidelights, and the special feelings of bonding and camaraderie that grow among shipmates. When I began doing oral history work for the Naval Institute, the first submariner I interviewed was Slade Cutter, a legendary skipper in World War II. His story begins this book.

Acknowledgments

B Y ITS VERY NATURE, this is a book that relies on the contributions of many individuals. I would like to mention a few who may not be so obvious. One is Everett "Tuck" Weaver, a submariner who was an officer on board the highly accomplished *Barb* during World War II. Some years ago he facilitated the publication of Rear Adm. Gene Fluckey's book *Thunder Below* by the University of Illinois Press. Now he has provided a generous financial contribution that has allowed a substantial increase in the number of illustrations used in *Submarine Stories*.

Thanks go to Dot Abbott of the special collections at the United States Naval Academy's Nimitz Library; she was helpful in supplying material for this book, as she has been on many occasions in the past. Charles Hinman and Nancy Richards of the *Bowfin* memorial at Pearl Harbor were extremely pleasant and accommodating when I visited the museum. They made available a number of files and gave me leads that put me in touch with former *Bowfin* crew member Hosey Mays. Dr. Robert Mays, the submariner's son, provided useful topics for me to pursue in interviewing his dad.

Capt. Brent Greene, former skipper of the nuclear submarine *Hyman G. Rickover*, and his wife Debbie are longtime friends. They put me in touch with Admiral Rickover's widow Eleonore, who supplied a photo of her husband as executive officer of the *S-48*. Rick Connole, another good friend, is both a son and stepson of submariners. His father, David Connole, was killed when the *Trigger* was lost near the end of World War II. Rick's mother then married Roy Benson, a previous skipper of the *Trigger*. Rick spent a holiday weekend scanning photos from the collections of both Connole and Benson for use in this book. Other members of submarine families who supplied pictures were Ingrid Beach, widow of Capt. Edward L. Beach; Elizabeth Ann "Sitta" Schafer, daughter of Rear Adm. Bub Ward; and Susan Williams, daughter of Vice Adm. Joe Williams.

Dr. Tom Grassey of the Naval War College has long been interested in the naming of U.S. Navy ships; he guided me to Capt. William Calkins's delightful memoir on submarine naming during World War II. A similar tip came from Capt. Grayson Merrill, a missile pioneer who has long championed the role of Regulus-armed submarines during the Cold War. He pointed me toward Chief WO Jerry Beckley's account of the *Grayback* during the Cuban Missile Crisis, and Bob Harmuth put me in touch with Beckley.

Cdr. Andrew Wilde and Lt. Cdr. John Vlattas of the Navy's last active diesel submarine, the *Dolphin*, were gracious hosts when I visited their boat at the Point Loma submarine facility in San Diego. They gave me a friendly, hands-on tour that included the engine room, berthing areas, and other spaces on board the truly cramped diesel submarine. Master Chief Joe Eller, the chief of the boat, joined us in sharing a conversation over "bug juice" and coffee at the submarine's small mess table.

Bob Cressman, head of the Ship Histories Branch of the Naval Historical Center, made available the files of the USS *Blueback*, the last diesel-powered attack boat. That in turn led to a productive interview with Master Chief Charles Wormwood, the submarine's last chief of the boat. R. G. Grant of the Oregon Museum of Science and Industry was helpful in providing material about the current condition of the *Blueback*.

Many other individuals helped in the process of rounding up the photos. I am indebted to Capt. Tim Wooldridge, a retired naval aviator who has done an enormous amount of volunteer work to benefit the Naval Institute's photo archive. His assistant, Janis Jorgensen, is a retired Naval Reserve officer who does a splendid job in serving customers of the institute's photo collection. Sandy Schlosser has put in thousands of volunteer hours on that collection. All of the above have benefited from the dedicated service of Patty Maddocks and Dawn Stitzel, who in years past headed the photo library.

I first encountered Ed Finney, a photo specialist at the Naval Historical Center, more than forty years ago, when we were in the same company at Navy boot camp in Great Lakes, Illinois. Ed patiently went through drawers full of photo cards to guide me to old submarine pictures. Bill King did double service in recommending that I interview his dad, Chief WO Cecil King, and Bill also provided a photo. Dr. Tom Hone, whom I first came to know in the 1970s, is one of the foremost experts on the history of the U.S. Navy between the world wars; he supplied pictures from his collection. Adm. Harry Train, Vice Adm. Dennis Wilkinson, Rear Adm. Bob McNitt, Rear Adm. Mike Rindskopf, Rear Adm. Julian Burke, Cdr. John Alden, and Chief WO Jerry Beckley generously provided pictures from their scrapbooks to illustrate their recollections.

Ruth Cutter, widow of Slade Cutter, put me in touch with Jim O'Meara, who was enthusiastic about contributing to this book. He supplied copies of articles he had written for *Polaris*, the newsletter of the World War II SubVets organization, and provided illustrations. Gale Munro of the Navy Art Collection in Washington, D.C., was helpful, as she has been many times in the past. Carl LaVO, author of *Back from the Deep*, the superb book on the *Sculpin* and *Squalus/Sailfish*, put me in touch with George Rocek, who supplied pictures to go with his chapter.

A serendipitous addition to the book came in the form of Wayne Miller's deck-plates view of submarine life. One day I happened to be at the Navy Media Center in Anacostia, D.C., and was waiting in a staff lounge for an upcoming appointment. In came Miller to heat up a bag of popcorn during a break in his work at the center. While the microwave did its job, Miller and I chatted about his submarine service, and he invited me to his home so we could put his recollections into a tape recorder.

Dr. Jack Sweetman, a retired Naval Academy history professor, is a friend of many years. In the course of his work on a book about the Navy's landing at Veracruz, Mexico, in 1914, he had come to know Vice Adm. Paul F. Foster, a participant in that operation. Jack recommended that I take a look at Foster's Columbia University oral history, which contained information on his role as a World War I submariner. Foster was not only a courageous naval officer but also a delightful storyteller, so I was pleased to add his chapter. The man who interviewed Foster for Columbia University was Dr. John T. Mason Jr., a friend and mentor of mine. He was my predecessor in running the Naval Institute's oral history program; many of the chapters in this book come from his interviews.

Another tip on long-ago submarine experiences came from Cdr. Jerry Hendrix, a member of the Naval Institute's editorial board. Jerry is a student of the presidency of Theodore Roosevelt and guided me to a letter that Roosevelt had written about his 1905 visit to the USS *Plunger*.

On the Naval Institute Press staff I am indebted to acquisitions editor Eric Mills, who provided steady encouragement as this book was coming together. A special note of thanks goes to Karin Kaufman, who as copy editor capably backstopped my efforts as the book moved forward to publication. The volume's excellent index is the work of Anne-Marie Downey; Jessica Schultheis has been most friendly and helpful as the book's production editor. Barbara Werden executed the splendid look of the book, both the overall design and the individual page layouts.

Finally, I truly appreciate the love and support of my wife Karen and our sons James, Robert, and Joseph.

SUBMARINE STORIES

1

Parks and the *Pompano*

CAPT. SLADE D. CUTTER,
USN (RET.)

The name Slade Cutter evokes great respect among the submariners who served in World War II. He was a man's man, physically big, an athlete who had been a great football player and boxer at the United States Naval Academy in the early 1930s. He served on active duty for some thirty years after graduating from the academy and seemed to want to live down his athletic prowess. Instead, he preferred to be assessed as the professional naval officer he was. His wartime record in command of the submarine *Seahorse* was superb. He stood high among skippers in terms of ships sunk, and he was awarded four Navy Crosses for valor. Perhaps his most appealing quality was his sense of modesty; while others with lesser achievements crowed about themselves, he preferred to avoid the spotlight. Here is his account of the experiences that made him into a successful submariner.

I WAS WITH LT. CDR. LEW PARKS for three years in the USS *Pompano*. He took command of the submarine in April 1939, about a year after I graduated from Naval Submarine School. We were supposed to be qualified in submarines within one year after graduation or else the skipper was supposed to explain why not to the Bureau of Navigation. One year with Parks went by; two years went by, and I still wasn't qualified. Neither were Penrod Schneider and Dave Connole, my two closest contemporaries in the boat. By 1941, we were pretty unhappy, but there was a reason for the delay.

Parks explained to us that as soon as an officer was qualified for his dolphins, he was pulled off that submarine and sent to new construction.

This great prewar shot by Tai Sing Loo shows the *Pompano*'s crew gathered forward of the superstructure on the teak-wood deck. Lt. Cdr. Lew Parks is front row center; Lt. (j.g.) Slade Cutter, still without dolphins on his chest, is second from left in the front row. *Tai Sing Loo photo from Naval Institute Photo Archive*

The empty billets were then filled with Naval Reservists, and he didn't like Reservists. So Parks said, "If I don't qualify you guys, you won't get pulled off. We're going to war, and I want to be ready." He just poured stuff into us, worked our tails off, but he wouldn't qualify us. "The bureau will never check up on us," he said. He was right; the bureau didn't check. But I was bothered because my peers from other boats were going around with submarine pins, and here I was with a clean chest. It kind of hurt my ego.

Despite all this, one of the luckiest breaks I got was going to the *Pompano* under Parks. He taught me to be a submariner. He was an outstanding teacher because he was very demanding, and in that environment, we were all highly motivated. He was a great leader, and the war was coming on. When the *Matsuta Maru* or one of the other big ships came in from Japan, he used to send me, as the *Pompano*'s torpedo officer and fire control officer, down to the docks at Aloha Tower in Honolulu to look them over. He wanted me to see if there were any features on those ships that would help estimate their courses if we ever encountered them at sea.

As the war got closer, it wouldn't have done a bit of good to complain about not getting our submarine qualification, so we kept quiet. Then one day, for some reason, our division commander or someone else apparently said, "You've got to qualify these people or else." So Parks made arrangements for a target: twelve to twenty-five knots, zigzagging. She was the old destroyer *Litchfield*, and we were going to fire exercise torpedoes at her. Parks had taught us how to solve approach problems in our heads. We never used what was called an "is-was," an instrument to get the distance to the track, the gyro angles, and things like that. We couldn't even use the stadimeter in the periscope to estimate range.

For this test our division commander, Cdr. Merrill Comstock, came along to observe. Parks said to us, "I don't want you to do anything except say, 'Make the tubes ready,' and then, 'Fire.' You can say, 'Come right or left' so many degrees by the compass, but don't give a course."

Penrod Schneider was first to fire, and he missed. The target zigged on him just as he fired—a tough break. Then Connole fired; he got a hit. I fired, and I got a hit. And Parks, showman that he was, said, "Make ready another tube for Mr. Schneider."

Schneider fired another one, and he got a hit. Commander Comstock was sitting there, but he didn't know what the hell had gone on, because the division commanders in those days were unfamiliar with modern fire control equipment. All he knew was that the target signaled back hits, so it was pretty obvious that we were qualified for our dolphins. Normally, you'd get qualified in submarines and then, a year or so later, you'd get qualified for command. But Parks was a showman. He turned to Comstock while we were all right there, and he said, "Commodore, I think these officers are ready to be qualified for command, too, don't you?"

And after our show, the division commander had to agree we were ready. We were qualified for command the same day we qualified for submarines. That was Parks's moment of glory too. And he deserved it, because he had worked our butts off, and he taught us all these things. We had learned everything from him, not from Submarine School. His training helped me a great deal later on in the war. It helped me sink ships.

Along with the training the officers and crew received to prepare us for war, the *Pompano* got some improvements. In late 1941 our division of submarines was sent to Mare Island Navy Yard in California to get degaussing gear installed and to get the conning tower doors removed. Believe it or not, we had glass windows in our conning towers, and they were taken out and welded shut with steel. We also had some work done on our diesel engines, which were perpetually giving us problems. We were at Mare Island for two months, and then we left about the first of December to return to Pearl Harbor in company with the *Pollack* and *Plunger*.

On the morning of 7 December, at about five minutes after eight o'clock, a radioman came up through the conning tower and reached up and handed the officer of the deck a dispatch that read "Air raid on Pearl Harbor. This is no drill." On board were two lieutenant commanders we were bringing out to take command of submarines. Like Parks, they had served in China,

and they got talking about the Japanese: "That's just like those yellow bastards. [As readers know, such remarks were typical at that time.] They'd do something like that." They believed the dispatch right away. So we rigged ship for dive.

We had been scheduled to arrive at the entrance buoys in Pearl Harbor that morning at six o'clock, which would have put us right there at the time of the attack. But the *Pompano* had experienced engine trouble, and that had held the other submarines back too. So we weren't due in until that afternoon. We were 135 miles from Pearl Harbor, northeast of it on the great circle route from San Francisco, when we were attacked by Japanese aircraft. We couldn't get under, because to make as much speed as we could, we had pumped out all our variable ballast. As a result, when the dispatch came in, Parks said, "Rig ship for dive and compensate. Get the water back in so we can dive."

Before we could dive, we were strafed by the first wave of planes. The other submarines went under. We weren't damaged. Norman Ives was the division commander by then, and Parks sent a message to him over the radio: "You should tell Pearl Harbor we were attacked by enemy aircraft."

Ives replied, "They've got too much on their mind." And it was a good thing, I guess, because if anything had been sent after the enemy, it would have been sunk. After a while, we got a message to proceed to Lahaina Roads, submerge, and stay submerged until the following night, when we could surface and would receive a message telling us what to do. The Submarine Force commander told us to meet the *McFarland*, the destroyer that escorted the three of us into Pearl Harbor on 9 December.

When we got into port, there were many people on the dock, but we couldn't get anyone to handle our lines. It was like they were all in a daze. Fortunately, we got some help from a former *Pompano* torpedoman's mate named Russell Reed, whom the captain had put in the brig when we left Pearl to go to Mare Island for the overhaul. I don't recall what he had done wrong; he was always doing something bad ashore. Parks had disqualified him from submarine duty, and he was through. When we got back, two months later, Reed was on the dock, and he was the one guy who handled the lines. They had let him out of the brig. So he came back on board, requalified for submarine duty.

Also on the dock was an ensign named Thomas Patrick McGrath, who had been brigade commander at the Naval Academy and a football player. In fact, I'd gotten to know him when I was an assistant coach. All he had on were a pair of khaki shorts, open sandals, and a .45-caliber automatic. When his ship, the battleship *California*, was sunk, all of his clothes were lost. He had been sleeping up in the submarine base grounds with a lot of other survivors. He knew I was in the *Pompano* and came on board. I invited him to the wardroom to have lunch with us, and he said, "I want to go out on the first ship that's going out after those bastards."

The skipper, who was in his cabin just aft of the wardroom, came out and said, "Young man, do you mean that?"

"Yes, sir," said McGrath.

With that, Parks got up and went to headquarters. He wasn't gone fifteen minutes before he returned. "Son, you are a member of the *Pompano* crew."

On the eighteenth of December, we left Pearl Harbor on our first war patrol. On the morning of the twentieth, we were sighted by a PBY patrol plane, obviously from Pearl Harbor. We were then about six hundred miles out, I guess. We dove, because a submarine was fair game.

About two o'clock that afternoon, I was below when the diving alarm went, and shortly after, wham! wham! wham!—three bombs. The carrier *Enterprise* was then at sea, and I learned later that Lt. Cdr. Hallsted Hopping, leader of a section of aircraft from the carrier, had mistakenly bombed us. The aircraft came out of a cloud. We hadn't seen them and didn't have any radar then. The bombs they dropped landed on the far side, but they were close enough to open seams in our main ballast tanks, which were carrying fuel oil, so we left a trail of oil wherever we went for the rest of the patrol.

After that experience, we continued our journey. We didn't dive for a number of days. Other submarines, practically all of them, would stay submerged all day and run on the surface only at night. Of course, that practice stopped very soon, because it took too long to get to the patrol area, staying submerged all day then getting up at night. Parks didn't pay attention to the other submarines; off he went. We steered west toward Ponape and Truk in the Caroline Islands, headquarters of the Japanese fleet. And while we were heading for Truk, we were diverted to Wake Island, because the U.S. Navy hadn't gotten any word from Wake and wanted to see if the Japanese were there.

When we arrived, the Japanese were on Wake. Parks, of course, got in really close to look it over, and he saw the Japanese and their flag flying over the Pan Am building and all that sort of stuff. He was going at dead slow speed. It was a flat, calm sea, and we had just a little bit of periscope up. We started to go down below periscope depth, so Parks said, "Bring her up, bring her up, goddamn it, bring her up." He didn't want to speed up, so he said, "Put a bubble in negative tank."

However, instead of blowing water out of the negative tank, the auxiliary man had his hand on the crank for the bow buoyancy tank. He was cranking the high-pressure air and looking at the negative tank gauge, and nothing was happening. So he gave it more and gave it more. He was blowing bow buoyancy by mistake. The next thing we knew, we were on the surface, four hundred yards off the beach at Wake Island. We vented bow buoyancy in a hurry and went all ahead full. We got under, and fortunately nothing happened to us, because the Japanese weren't looking for enemy submarines.

We didn't have enough fuel to make it to Truk. You see, everything, including fuel consumption, was theoretical before the war. They never tested these things. They never sent submarines that far to see if they could really do it. So as soon as we started on patrol, Parks kept a graph on our fuel consumption (also on our food). Well, he knew we couldn't possibly get to

Ponape and Truk and then get back to Pearl Harbor. No way, even if the tank hadn't been leaking.

So instead, we went down to Wotje Atoll in the Marshall Islands. Our job was to reconnoiter for Vice Adm. William Halsey's carrier raid on 1 February 1942, the first offensive action against the enemy. We reconnoitered Wotje then cleared out of there. The carrier task force came in the day after we sent our report. I don't know how much damage they did, but the raid boosted the morale of our forces and the people back home.

One of our tasks during this patrol to the Marshalls was to attack any enemy ships we could. On 12 January, off Wotje, we fired at the *Yawata*, a big transport. She was a luxury liner before the war. We reported sinking her because we didn't know what a torpedo hit sounded like. We heard the hits and saw the splash of water, so Parks assumed she was going to sink. When we came up after the depth-charge attack, there was no *Yawata* around. She had just bailed out, that's all; she hadn't been hurt at all. Two duds bounced against her and caused the splashes along the side that Parks had taken to be hits.

Parks almost made a nervous wreck out of me with his desire to patrol close to the beach, especially since our charts were from about 1895. Whenever we closed in on Wotje, I would have the listening gear lowered, and we would stop every now and then along the way and listen. We could hear the reef, and when we got close, we wouldn't go any farther. We would always be pretty close to where Parks wanted to be each morning, because he didn't want to run in submerged; he wanted to be there.

One day the Japanese had two destroyers out that we thought were looking for us. I don't know whether they were looking for us, but they were patrolling the entrance. So Parks maneuvered all day long, trying to get in position to hit them, but they never settled down enough to allow us a good firing position. I was operating the torpedo data computer, and the captain was up in the conning tower. Finally, in desperation, he decided to shoot. We fired two torpedoes, and both of them prematured. Next I heard from Parks, "Range twelve hundred yards, speed twenty-five, angle on the bow two degrees port, stand by." I put on the solution light: "Fire!"

About this time, Parks said over the loud-speaker system, "Slade, did you ever have so much fun before with your clothes on?" I'll never forget it.

Well, I wasn't worrying about having fun—clothes on or off—at that stage of the game. Looking at the torpedo data computer, here was this target at twelve hundred yards, and it would be over us in a minute or so. It came, and it delivered the first depth charge we'd ever heard. I didn't know what they sounded like. A barrage came over, and I knew what it was like to face death, right then, because we heard the water rushing through the superstructure. As we learned later, that is normal, but we thought we had been holed. So I thought, That's the end; you don't feel anything. We realized very shortly that we hadn't been holed. And then it was a matter of maneuvering to get away from the destroyer. We abandoned the conning tower, and to this day I can see Lew Parks on the annunciator controls and the wheel in the control room. He maneuvered the submarine around, all ahead full, starboard back full, and port ahead full to cut down the turning circle to evade these guys up above dropping their depth charges.

Then he shifted to hand steering to reduce our submarine's noise. Two men turned the steering wheel by hand. Well, that was our baptism of depth charges. And apparently, Parks thoroughly enjoyed it. He was having a hell of a time. This was what he had been waiting and preparing for. (After that experience, every time we went out on patrol, one of the pre-patrol training exercises was to have a destroyer drop one or two depth charges a hundred yards away so everybody could hear what they sounded like.)

A number of the prewar skippers turned out to be cautious when depth charges began falling around them. Parks, who had graduated from the Naval Academy in 1925, was exceptional among his contemporaries for his sense of bravery and aggressiveness. He could have been a top skipper at age fifty, and it's just a crime that he didn't command a good sub with good torpedoes,

because he would have made a killing.

After we got back from the Marshalls and spent some time in the shipyard at Pearl, the next patrol we made was to the South China Sea between Hong Kong and the Philippines. When we were off Wake, an enemy plane sighted us. He came in and dropped one bomb, and we went down to about 250 feet. In the after battery compartment we had two toilets, and the discharge for them went through the ballast tank outboard; air pressure would blow out the waste. Well, where this went through the hull was a flange with a gasket, and the rascals in the shipyard had put in a split gasket. They had done that because it was easier to put on; they didn't have to take the toilet out, so they just cut it and slipped it around there. But a split gasket won't hold under pressure; it opens. So we were down there, and water was coming into the after battery compartment. It was a serious situation, and we had to do something about it. We were not far off Wake, at night, on the surface, and we were unable to dive because we had to remove the pipe going through the hole and put a blank flange over the hole with the proper gasket. We had only one toilet for all the crew after that, which was a problem too.

While we were on the surface, a motor machinist's mate by the name of Herbert Calcaterra, known as "Chainfall" because you didn't need a chainfall with him on board, helped me saw through that tough Monel discharge line with a hacksaw blade held in our hands with a rag. He was strong as an ox, and I was pretty husky in those days too. We were putting all we could into it, motivated because we couldn't dive and were in enemy-controlled waters. Finally we cut through it, they put on the correct flange, and we went on our way. (Calcaterra was killed later in the year while manning a deck gun and had a destroyer escort named for him.)

From there we went out in the South China Sea. We were on the surface one night when we picked up a contact. We shut off our engines and put our stern toward it. We didn't want to be picked up, but the contact saw us and turned toward us. We turned away, and it turned toward us again. Parks sent for me to man the .50-caliber machine gun we had aft. "Put it on them," he said.

We made another course change, and the target turned toward us again. Parks said, "Let him have it"—his way of saying "Commence fire"— so I pulled the trigger. I guess this thing was about three hundred yards away. It was a fishing boat, stack aft, and the bridge was aft—a good size, probably twenty men aboard. After that first burst of probably fifty rounds, a guy held up a lantern to show the rising sun on the boat's flag. He thought we were Japanese. Once again the captain said, "Let them have it," so I opened up again, and this time I just kept firing. Finally the boat caught fire. I guess the tracers set off the fuel or something, and it burned, and we got out of there. A fisherman had held the lantern. That's one of the terrible things of war. He was harmless, and he thought we were friends. He was probably coming over to exchange information. I was quite upset after I found out what the target was. But it didn't bother Parks. Fishermen were also the enemy. "Don't worry about that," he said. "They're feeding them, and they are fair game."

We didn't run into many contacts on that patrol, so it was a frustrating time. Parks did achieve some of the early sinkings of the war: the nine-hundred-ton tanker *Tokyo Maru* on 25 May 1942 and the eight-thousand-ton *Atsuta Maru* on 30 May. I should mention that at this point Parks had gotten away from his prewar practice of keeping his attack techniques a secret from fellow submariners. Once the war began, he shared everything; it all came in his patrol reports. It was a new ball game. In fact, in order to impress people, Parks did a lot of things one probably wouldn't consider too prudent. For instance, he didn't let us make our trim dives when we began our patrols because he wanted to keep Dave Connole, the diving officer, on his toes.

After those sinkings in late May, we came back from our second war patrol. We stopped at Midway Island in early June, right after the Battle of Midway. We picked up a Japanese prisoner there and transported him to Pearl Harbor to wind up the patrol. As we came in, we met the destroyer *Litchfield*, the flagship of Submarine Squadron Four. The skipper was a classmate of Parks, and the exec was a classmate of mine. By then I was the *Pompano*'s executive officer. I was up on the bridge, and the skipper was down below. The skipper of the destroyer got on the voice radio. We were just batting the breeze back and forth, and I mentioned we had a prisoner aboard.

He said, "Mike Fenno [off the submarine *Trout*] came in here last week, and he had a prisoner aboard. It took an hour and a half before they could get the Marines over to take the prisoner off, and they wouldn't let anybody aboard

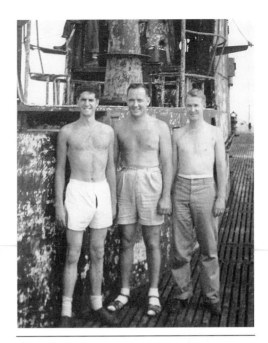

Three of the Pompano's officers pose on deck while on war patrol. Left to right: Ralph Pleatman, Slade Cutter, and David Connole. *Courtesy of Rickart Connole*

until the prisoner was removed. I'll call [the signal tower] with my thirty-six-inch searchlight and tell them you have a prisoner aboard, and they'll meet you down there."

I said, "Fine, thank you very much, sir."

I called down and told the captain that I had exchanged messages with the *Litchfield* and her skipper was going to inform harbor control that we had a prisoner on board. The next thing I knew, up came Parks, face covered with lather and wearing only sandals and a towel wrapped around his waist. And, boy, was he fit to be tied. He really ripped me up one side and down the other. "What the hell do you mean by doing that?" he said.

I said, "Captain, what would you have done?"

"That has nothing to do with it," he said. "Do I interfere with your operating the internal mechanism of this ship?"

"No, sir." He didn't either; he never bothered me a bit.

"I don't expect you to interfere with the external affairs of the ship. That's my responsibility."

Even though he had orders and was due to be detached shortly after our arrival in Pearl, he was still the captain of the *Pompano*, and he guarded his prerogatives. Ashore, we were on a first-name basis, Lew and Slade, after all these years. That night we got drunk, as we always did after coming in from patrol. I finally said, "Lew, what the hell would you have done?"

Then he gave me the same thing: "God damn it, that isn't the point." He would have done the same thing I did, of course, but the point was that I had overstepped my bounds. You would think he would have overlooked it since he was leaving for the States shortly, but that's the way he was. It was good training.

The next day, in the afternoon, we were in the officers' club at Pearl. Lew bought one or two cases of beer and passed it around. He was in a very expansive mood. So everybody had some beer, and he had plenty to drink, too, of course, as the day passed into evening. There were two Army second lieutenants there; they had been enlisted men just before the war hit, and now they were officers. One of them had been on board our ship because he was a friend of our cook.

We were trying to get a ride out to the Royal Hawaiian Hotel, where we went for rest and recreation. Parks and his wife lived in the Diamond Head area, beyond the Royal Hawaiian. But we couldn't find any transportation, and there was a curfew in Honolulu at night. Then one of these Army guys spoke up and said, "Well, that's the trouble with the Navy. You have no morale. Here we are, just second lieutenants, and we have a command car."

But the lieutenants made two mistakes: They stayed in the bar and they left the keys in the command car. So several of us, including Parks, Tommy Thomas, Dave Connole, and me, got in. Since Parks was the skipper, he got behind the wheel. The car had about five speeds ahead, and the reverse was somewhere in there. We kept inching ahead as Parks tried to find the reverse gear, and we went right through the hedge in front of the officers' club.

Finally, he got the car into reverse, backed out into the street, and went out on the highway into Honolulu, onto Dillingham Boulevard. Parks managed to get the thing into high gear. As we approached town, we saw some streetlights up over the road. Tommy Thomas was in the back seat. The curtains were up in this command car, and there was a rifle and a bandolier of ammunition in back. The bandolier held common, tracer, and armor-piercing bullets. Armor piercing was black, common had nothing on the nose of the bullets, and the tracers were red.

Thomas said, "See if those are the same as the Navy's, Slade." I was sitting in the front seat, and he handed me the rifle and the shells. So I loaded them. And what the hell was I going to shoot at? Well, I tried to hit those streetlights, I remember, as we drove through. None of us could have seen the tracer, anyway. Then we got into town, and right as we made the turn onto Beretania Street, we saw the Dole Pineapple water tower, painted like a big pineapple. That was a good target, I thought, so whammo, whammo, as we were going by.

The next thing we knew, a green Marine car with MPs in it pulled up alongside and motioned us over. The Navy yard was changing shifts, and there was lot of traffic. As you come to Beretania and King, one street goes along the waterfront, and the other goes the other way; it's about a forty-five-degree angle. We were in the left-hand lane, and the Marines were to the left of us, so we went up Beretania, and the only place they could go was up King Street. Gee, they couldn't get us.

So we got to the Aloha Tower, and the territorial guards were stationed there. They stopped us, and Parks took out his wallet. I don't know what he showed them—his Elks membership card or whatever—but that was enough for these guys, and they waved us through. We thought if we went in there, we would be safe. But I was worried about those damn Marines after us. I said, "Captain, let's get out of here."

"No, we'll not get out of here," Parks said. It was beneath his dignity to abandon the car and walk to the Royal Hawaiian from Aloha Tower. It was pretty far, about four or five miles, I guess, along the Ala Wai, the yacht basin. So we just drove down to the Aloha Tower and turned left and went on out the Ala Wai, along the waterfront. I hadn't been able to spot my shots yet, but now we had a yacht basin with these white balls for anchors, and I could spot them in the water. Boy, here I was. We were going along and whammo, whammo.

The next thing I knew, we were up over the curb and into a palm tree. And there was this same Marine Jeep and another Marine vehicle. There were three Marines in all, and they came out with guns drawn. We put our hands up. Parks said, "Don't shoot. We're not mad." They loaded us into the paddy wagon, and down to the police station we went. We got into the station, and there was a cordon of cops there, and they just walked us right through. All this gunfire in town, and here were the dangerous characters that did it.

A friend of mine, Dusty Dornin, who was a Naval Academy classmate and a submariner, had somehow heard about what happened to us, so he called and talked to the sergeant or whoever it was and offered to bring down bread and water to us.

The sergeant said to Dornin, "You come down here, and we'll lock you up too."

Then followed a couple of coincidences. The military governor was in charge of Honolulu. He was a graduate of West Point, a colonel, and he was a neighbor of Parks across the street out in Diamond Head. The federal prosecuting attorney was John Parks, the skipper's brother. Of course, Parks got hold of his brother, who got hold of the other guy. So these birds at the police station were in a quandary; they wanted to let us go, but they didn't know how to do it. Eventually, after we produced the shells as evidence, they let us go, subject to being recalled the next day.

Parks left; he was going back to the States. The next day, Thomas, who succeeded him as skipper of the *Pompano*, had to go down to the station, and they gave him a bad time because we had gotten away without punishment. It made the shore patrol officer very mad. He wanted to make an example of us, and he said if he ever caught us again, we would pay for it. "Parks is no longer around," he said, "and you won't have the protection of his brother and the provost marshal." So we got out of it, and we were very careful from then on in Honolulu.

But, you know, we didn't give a damn. In those days, I didn't care at all what happened. I didn't expect to survive the war; I don't think anybody did, really. Normally, these incidents would happen just after we came in from patrol. We would let off steam, get unwound, and then we would settle down and be reasonable.

2

The President Takes a Plunge

THEODORE ROOSEVELT

For many years the United States celebrated Navy Day on 27 October because future President Teddy Roosevelt was born on that date in 1858. He was an adventurous individual, as he demonstrated in many ways, including during his service as assistant secretary of the navy at the outset of the Spanish-American War and as a cavalry officer in Cuba during that same conflict. As president he was widely known as a champion for a strong fleet of battleships. He sent the Great White Fleet on a voyage around the world from 1907 to 1909 to demonstrate the nation's growing prowess as a naval power. But even before that voyage, he also evinced an interest in submarines. In 1905 he made a dive in the USS *Plunger*, the Navy's second submarine. She had been commissioned in September 1903, three years after the *Holland* had been the first. Roosevelt reported afterward, "Never in my life have I had such a diverting day . . . nor so much enjoyment in so few hours." The following is an excerpt from a letter the president wrote on 28 August 1905 to Charles Joseph Bonaparte, who was then secretary of the navy.

I HAVE BECOME GREATLY interested in submarine boats. They are in no sense substitutes for above-water torpedo boats, not to speak of battleships, cruisers, and the like, but they may on certain occasions supplement other craft, and they should be developed. Now there are excellent old-style naval officers of the kind who drift into positions at Washington who absolutely decline to recognize this fact and who hamper the development of the submarine boat in every way. One of the ways they have done it

This is the primitive USS *Plunger*, in which President Teddy Roosevelt made a dive when the twentieth century was yet young. *Naval Institute Photo Archive*

has been by the absurd and worse than absurd ruling that the officers and men engaged in the very hazardous, delicate, difficult and responsible work of experimenting with these submarine boats are not to be considered as on sea duty. I felt positively indignant when I found that the men on the *Plunger*, who incur a certain risk every time they go down in her and who have to be trained to the highest point as well as to show iron nerve in order to be of any use in their positions, are penalized for being on the *Plunger* instead of being in some much less responsible and much less dangerous position on a cruise in a big ship. I find that the officers, for instance, have no quarters on board and yet none on shore, and the Auditor for the Navy Department has refused to allow commutation for such quarters while the Navy Department has refused to allow the men

such quarters, servants or mess outfits. Of course this is monstrous. There should be a cook, steward and mess outfit allowed for each submarine vessel, and where possible—in almost every case it would be possible—quarters should be allowed for the officers. The regulations should provide that the services of officers attached to submarines should be considered as service on ships on the cruise. The case of the enlisted men, in whom I am even more interested, should be met by the embodiment in the regulations of certain changes as follows:

(a) That enlisted men serving on submarines under acting appointments as Chief Petty Officers, having finished their one-year probation and having been found professionally, mentally and morally qualified by a proper board of officers from ships other than those on which they are serving, shall receive permanent appointments in their ratings irrespective of service on cruising vessels.

(b) Enlisted men serving in submarines may be advanced in rating without regard to the compliment of the vessel.

PAY FOR SUBMARINE MEN

(a) That enlisted men regularly detailed for instruction in submarine boats but not having qualified shall receive five dollars per month in addition to the pay of their rating.

(b) Enlisted men serving with submarine boats and having been reported by their commanding officers to the Navy Department as qualified for submarine torpedo-boat work, shall receive ten dollars per month in addition to the pay of their rating.

(c) Enlisted men serving with submarine torpedo boats having been reported by their commanding officers to the Navy Department as qualified for submarine torpedo-boat work shall receive one dollar in addition to their pay for each day during any part of which they shall have been submerged in a submarine boat while underway.

In November of that year, three months after his letter, Roosevelt issued an executive order that gave additional pay to enlisted submariners. His other suggestions were incorporated into Navy Regulations in May 1907.

3

World War I

VICE ADM. PAUL F. FOSTER,
U.S. NAVAL RESERVE (RET.)

The first combat action for U.S. submarines came in World War I, when the Navy's undersea arm was still young. As this chapter demonstrates, it was very much a time of experimentation and development. Foster was a recognized leader who had served throughout his first-class year at the Naval Academy as the brigade commander, the top-ranking midshipman in the class of 1911. He went immediately to sea duty in the battleship *Utah*. In April 1914 the Navy and Marine Corps intervened at Veracruz, Mexico, during a period of unrest in that country. Foster led a company of sailors from the *Utah* in combat operations ashore. For his actions in that landing, Foster received the Medal of Honor. The following stories are taken from *The Reminiscences of Paul F. Foster* (April 1970) in the Oral History Collection of Columbia University.

I N THE LATE AUTUMN of 1914 I was detached from the *Utah*, in which I had served approximately three years, and ordered to submarine duty. I was assigned to one of the K-boats then operating in Long Island Sound.

The most important feature of that period of service was a visit of the division of K-boats in which I was serving to New London, [Connecticut], to make an inspection of the abandoned coaling plant on the banks of the Thames River. This coaling plant had been in use from Civil War days down to shortly after the Spanish-American War and then had been abandoned in the interests of economy. Our instructions were to assess its potential value as a place where our submarine tenders could tie up and from which our submarines could operate in the deeper waters at the

Paul Foster was among the earliest U.S. submariners to get into combat. *Naval Historical Center: S-156-A 76-050-N*

eastern end of Long Island Sound and out into the waters of the Atlantic off Nantucket and Martha's Vineyard. We made a favorable report, and the next year this old abandoned base was re-activated and became what is now the submarine base at New London.

During that winter I was transferred as the executive officer on the submarine G-4, commanded by Lt. Ernest D. McWhorter. The G-4 was an experimental submarine in that it was built from an Italian design. The laws provided that all of our men-of-war at that time must be built in American shipyards and made from material fabricated in American factories. The drawings and specifications for the G-4, however, having been prepared in Italy, naturally were in the metric system, with the result that when the American steel mills rolled the plates which became the hull of the G-4, they used the nearest American-sized plate to the metric size specified. But where there was, as usually happened, a slight difference, they used the next larger or thicker size in the interests of safety.

The result of all this was that the G-4, on its first trials, after having been built at the William

Cramp shipyards in Philadelphia, was found to possess the absolutely unique characteristic, when submerged, of negative metacentric height, metacentric height being the difference between the center of buoyancy and the center of gravity. This, in turn, would mean that if the normal laws of physics prevailed and normal procedures of diving were followed, the submarine might turn upside down once it became submerged.

This deficiency was discovered before the G-4 ever was subjected to a full diving test, and the submarine was brought back into the shipyard, where seventy-five tons of concrete and steel were built into the keel so as to provide positive metacentric height. The postdesign improvisation resulted in the G-4 being unseaworthy because of its instability and its very, very rapid rolling from side to side in any kind of rough water. This, in turn, meant that the G-4 was assigned to operations in Long Island Sound and only occasionally was sent out into the Atlantic.

The ship was powered by four Fiat gasoline engines which were geared to two propellers. The fact that these were Fiat engines rather than the American-made diesel engines, which were then being installed in the K-boats, put us in the class of the very earliest type of American submarines, such as the B and C classes. The other striking feature was an arrangement by which the pitch of the propeller blades could be changed by pressing buttons on the bridge. We could steam at full power ahead, push a button without stopping the engines, and the pitch of the propeller blades would be changed so that we would back at full engine power.

The only bad feature of this arrangement was that we had to signal our engineers to throttle down the engines so that they would not race at a destructive speed during the brief interval when the propeller blades were at zero pitch and were not absorbing any of the power of the engines. This reversibility feature worked beautifully in the G-4, but it seemed to have escaped the notice of marine engineers and nautical engineers. Many years later, when almost the identical mechanism was employed in airplanes to reverse

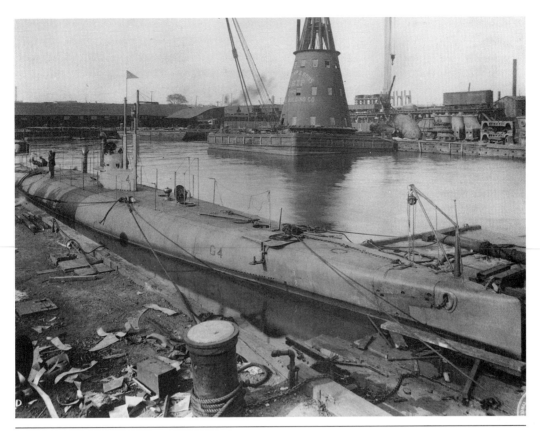

The low-slung G-4 is moored at her builder's yard in Philadelphia. The floating crane in the background bears the name of the shipyard, William Cramp and Sons. *Naval Institute Photo Archive*

the pitch of engines, it was hailed as a revolutionary discovery, whereas, in fact, we in the G-4 had used it for several years with great success, beginning as early as 1915. The G-4 didn't attract any attention in the Submarine Force, except as being a freak ship, and this particular feature didn't attract the attention of the high engineering authorities in the Navy Department or the engineering world.

In 1915 Lieutenant McWhorter was detached, and I became commanding officer. A classmate of mine became the executive officer. We operated with the other submarines of the Atlantic Fleet in maneuvers off Nantucket and Martha's Vineyard on two rather extensive war-game maneuvers, but mostly we operated out of New London, in and around Block Island, and around Fishers Island. The duty was not at all exciting.

Sometime in the autumn of 1915 the G-4 was selected by the Navy Department as a guinea pig in which Lawrence Sperry Sr. was to try out his gyroscopic ship stabilizer. Sperry and his engineers designed a huge gyroscope which, in effect, was a large steel flywheel which was to be rotated by an electric motor at an exceedingly high speed with a control mechanism such that its gyroscopic effect would be applied to abort the tendency of the ship to roll in rough weather.

When the ship stabilizer was finally pronounced ready for trial, we waited for a period of rough weather and then proceeded out into the Atlantic past Sandy Hook. We very quickly discovered that not only did the stabilizer fail completely to stop the rolling of the G-4 but also that the steel rivets attaching the gyroscopic mechanism to the special steel frames that had been built in and attached to the strength hull of the *G-4* were not heavy enough. Under the stress of interaction of the forces of the ship's stabilizer and the rolling effect induced by the waves of the ocean, these steel plates gradually began to move up and down slightly and to an increasing degree. The Sperry engineers became really terrified, because they realized that if this continued it was only a question of time before these rivets would be sheared off, and this five-ton flywheel rotating three thousand revolutions a minute or thereabouts would just fly off through the side of the ship. At their urging we turned around and went back to the navy yard and reported the dismal results to the Navy Department.

An investigation was held, and Sperry was indignant to learn that the Navy Department had not supplied him with complete and accurate data. The gyroscope was about 200 percent lighter than it should have been, and the whole installation would have to be redesigned and rebuilt. This was authorized by the Navy Department, which meant that the *G-4* was destined to a long period of inactivity in the Brooklyn Navy Yard with no prospect whatsoever of getting out to sea duty.

This carried through until our entry in World War I [in the spring of 1917]. After our declaration of war, the commandant of the Brooklyn Navy Yard, who had responsibility for the naval defense component of the defenses of New York City, telephoned the Navy Department and recommended that the Sperry experiment be liquidated immediately and that the *G-4*'s hull be filled up and restored to its original condition so that it could be made ready for war duty and loaded with torpedoes and made available to join the naval forces defending New York City.

The next day Sperry came down to the dock and was shocked beyond my powers to describe by the sight of the navy yard workmen lifting out all of the gyroscopic installations (*his* installations) and proceeding with the riveting into position of the old sections of the hull that had been removed. He was most indignant, and I feared that he might die of apoplexy right there on the

dock, because he felt that the Navy Department at least owed him the courtesy of advising him of this change in plans before he walked down and saw this great pet idea of his being summarily junked.

When the *G-4* was announced ready for sea duty, we were ordered to join the submarine flotilla then based at New London. I was assigned to be the guinea pig, or the vehicle, to be used by a group of Cornell professors in perfecting underwater listening devices for the use of submarines. It was clearly evident as these tests developed that the *G-4* was destined to remain in Long Island Sound and to continue its role of a vehicle for assisting scientists and college professors in developing various devices. I was intensely unhappy at the prospect of serving out a great war in such an innocuous capacity.

[Foster then went to Washington to ask that he be transferred to a ship operating in the war zone in Europe. The chief of naval operations was Adm. William Benson, who had been Foster's commanding officer in the *Utah*. Benson owed him a favor, but he declined to interfere in personnel matters. Benson had even turned down such a transfer request from his own son.]

My hopes really were at a very, very low ebb. I returned to New London and proceeded to carry out routine duties. A couple of weeks later the submarine tender *Bushnell* anchored in New London Harbor, and rumors spread in the submarine base that the *Bushnell* was going to take a division of submarines overseas. I knew, of course, that the *G-4* was physically incapable of undertaking any such mission, since our cruising radius would carry us only one-fifth of the way to the Azores, and we would be unfitted for patrol duty in European waters.

One day I went out on a routine trip into Long Island Sound with a couple of Cornell professors. We were somewhat delayed in our operations and were, therefore, about half an hour late in getting back to the submarine base. On this particular day I was in an utterly carefree frame of mind insofar as striking the dock or caving in the side of the submarine was concerned, so I

The officers and crew of the *G-4* are shown with their boat at the New London Submarine Base in 1917. Lieutenant (j.g.) Foster is fourth from the left; fifth from the left is the executive officer, Lt. (j.g.) William F. Callaway. *Naval Historical Center: NH 98036*

went upstream [in the Thames River], both engines on at full speed, turned around, headed back down the river toward an inboard docking space, and realized that the tide was running out, adding to the strength of the river current. As we came to the head of the dock, I pressed the button on the bridge and signaled the engine room, "Full speed astern." The reversible propellers, which I previously referred to, immediately came into play. Our headway was checked. We drifted gently alongside the dock. We couldn't have crushed an egg had it been between us and the dock stringer. It was an absolutely perfect landing.

The crew on deck threw out their lines and tied up the *G-4* immediately. I went ashore and strolled up the dock toward the submarine office, where I wanted to log in. I noticed a very erect, very military-looking captain on the dock watch-

ing our landing operation. I went by him with my cap at a cocky angle on my head and my chest puffed out, gave him a very snappy salute, and passed on and forgot about it.

Two days later, Lt. Cdr. Harold Bemis, my division commander, told me that Capt. [Thomas C.] Hart was the officer I had passed on the dock and that he had inquired about me. He was looking for an extra officer to carry on the *Bushnell* to serve as navigator or gunnery officer and as his aide, and more important, to serve as a spare commanding officer in the event that one of the commanding officers of the submarines that he was to take overseas became ill, or in case he decided to beach one of the commanding officers because he found his performance of duty unsatisfactory. I was further advised that Bemis had recommended to Captain Hart that I be selected

Capt. Thomas C. Hart, photographed in London during World War I. *Naval Historical Center: NH 95159*

for this post of spare commanding officer. The next day I had orders to call upon Captain Hart. I did so. He told me that if the idea appealed to me, he would have me transferred immediately to the *Bushnell*. This was done. I found myself then, I think almost by accident, transferred from a completely innocuous role to a very active role in submarines in World War I.

I should like to mention that Captain Hart at that time had the reputation of being the hardest taskmaster in the U.S. Navy. He was supposed to be absolutely ruthless, with no human kindness, and to be almost brutal in his dealings with both officers and enlisted men. There are all kinds of unsupported stories about him, but his efficiency was also recognized. I very soon found that he was exceedingly taciturn. I observed that in conferences of commanding officers he knew more about engines, he knew more about torpedoes, he knew more about navigation than any single officer who came under his command.

He treated me with a very cold courtesy. During the first two or three weeks of my duty with him, he summarily detached two commanding officers, because, so far as I could determine, he decided that they either didn't know their jobs or were temperamentally weak. When questioned, they would always back away, give ground; they never defended their own opinions, even when they felt that they were completely right. Captain Hart didn't want such a man as a commanding officer in any of the submarines that he was assembling to take overseas.

In the early autumn [of 1917] we sailed with a division of K-boats from Newport for the Azores. I was in the *Bushnell*. About two days out of Newport one of the worst storms or gales of the century hit us. The submarines were scattered. We lost contact with them by sight and even by radio. That night the seas were really mountainous. The *Bushnell* was rolling about forty-five degrees from side to side. I had the midwatch as officer of the deck. Captain Hart had gone below to his cabin. Cdr. W. L. Friedell, commanding officer of the *Bushnell*, remained on the bridge but became increasingly nervous and became seasick. This seemed to undermine his nervous stability. I repeatedly urged Commander Friedell to go to his cabin and take a rest. Ultimately, I virtually ordered him off the bridge on the grounds that he was sick and that he owed it to the ship to take a brief rest.

He left the bridge. My relief was so seasick that he couldn't get out of his bunk. I remained on the bridge until noon the next day. At daybreak Commander Friedell came back to the bridge. He felt better and was thinking clearly. We arrived in the Azores, and one submarine, I believe, got there ahead of us. Others drifted in one by one. One had turned back to Bermuda. One of them was, I think, some five days late in arriving.

We then turned around and returned to New London, where we picked up a division of L-boats under the command of Commander Bemis. We proceeded to the Azores, where we found the K-boats had established an improvised and very crude submarine base on shore and

These are American L-boats in Queenstown, Ireland, during World War I. A U.S. battleship can be seen beyond the conning tower of the *AL-1*. *Naval Institute Photo Archive; Burnell Poole collection, donated by Louis Davidson*

were conducting short patrols in the area. We refueled ourselves and the submarines and then proceeded to Queenstown, [Ireland], again encountering a full-scale gale en route, but we kept together. We arrived at Queenstown, remained there a few days, and were then ordered to Bantry Bay in the southwest corner of Ireland, where a division of British L-boats were based with a British tender. It was agreed that three American officers would go out on patrol in British submarines to learn the normal operations of the submarine patrol, and that while these officers were gone for an eight-day patrol, our submarines would get shipshape and ready for patrols and would make one-day cruises out of Bantry Bay to patrol off the west coast of Ireland. I was one of the three officers selected.

A month or so later Captain Hart and Commander Bemis became dissatisfied with the performance of duty of the commanding officer of the American submarine which had been designated *AL-2*, American L, so as to avoid confusion

with the British L-boats with whom we were operating. In consequence of this dissatisfaction, the skipper of the *AL-2* was summarily detached, and [in March 1918] I was ordered as commanding officer. I participated in several patrols, usually of eight or ten days' duration. Then we'd be in port at Bantry Bay for rest and overhaul for a similar period. Then we'd go out again.

On the first patrol that I undertook as commanding officer we were assigned to a line on a chart at a certain latitude ending near Bishop's Rock Light at Land's End, [England], and extending westward about forty miles. Our instructions were to remain submerged and use our listening devices during the daytime. If we picked up the noise of anything resembling that of a submarine propeller we were to try to make contact. If this were in fact a submarine running on the surface we were to torpedo it.

We would cruise very slowly underwater during daylight hours because of the limited capacity of our storage batteries. Then at dark we would come to the surface and recharge batteries. If the sky was clear we would get a good fix by the use of the sextant to determine our precise position. If we couldn't get a good sight by stars or in daytime by sun sight, and if the weather were hazy, we were to head in toward Bishop's Rock Light and get a fix from there so as to be sure that we remained in our assigned area. Any submarine whatsoever that Allied surface ships encountered outside of the specific areas assigned to British and U.S. submarines were automatically assumed to be German submarines. The standing orders were to shoot first and investigate later. During the course of the summer we were attacked or fired upon many times by U.S. and British surface craft.

In one case an attempted bombing attack by British seaplanes was carried on for a period of forty-five minutes by a plane overhead without our knowing it. The mechanism for releasing the bombs failed to function, and, therefore, we were not subjected to aerial bombardment. We were repeatedly fired upon when we were on the surface on the assumption that we were German craft. After exchanging recognition signals and establishing our identity, the firing would stop.

After each patrol there would be a short period of one week, sometimes two weeks, in Bantry Bay, during which the ship would be repaired, particularly the engines and batteries, the torpedoes rechecked, and the crew given an opportunity to recuperate their physical strength. The patrols in those days were quite exhausting to the officers and men because we remained submerged as much of the time as possible and the supply of fresh air in our submarines would become gradually vitiated during the day.

The oxygen would become lower and lower, so that near the end of an eighteen-hour submerged run, we would feel very perceptibly the lack of oxygen, and we would, of course, welcome the opportunity to come to the surface for a few hours to charge batteries and replenish the fresh air throughout the submarine. The air, of course, was circulated through chemical filters which removed most of the obnoxious odors from cooking and from other sources and which removed some of the other dele-

terious components in the air arising from the storage batteries or from the fumes of the hot diesel engines at the time of submergence after a period on the surface.

The most important episode of my submarine experience in World War I occurred on 10 July 1918, when, near the end of our allotted patrol in the Bay of Biscay north of Bordeaux, [France], we found one evening when we were charging batteries that one of our engine cylinders was cracked. This, of course, required us thereafter to operate on only one of our two diesel engines. I communicated this fact by radio to the tender *Bushnell* and was instructed to return forthwith to Bantry Bay so that a new engine cylinder block could be put on board the *AL-2* for installation. The reason given for our immediate return was that the *Bushnell* was scheduled to leave within two or three days for Queenstown for dry-docking.

This meant that the *AL-2* would be obliged to traverse waters south of Queenstown and along the south coast of Ireland and up the west coast of Ireland to Bantry Bay somewhat ahead of schedule—about three days ahead of schedule, as I now recall it. It also meant that because we had only one engine in operation, it would be imprudent to attempt to make very much of this distance on our storage batteries underwater. We would be obliged, therefore, to cruise on the surface.

On this particular day, 10 July, as we were heading in a generally northwesterly direction and were in a position about seventy-five miles south of Queenstown, we were sighted by a group of three American destroyers that were headed for Queenstown after having escorted a convoy of troopships into Bordeaux. The destroyers sighted us a short time after we sighted them and, in accordance with standard procedures, they opened fire immediately with their deck guns and increased speed. We were displaying our colors, which, of necessity, were of small size. Additionally, I called an additional signalman to the bridge, and we began to fire smoke signals in the air, which were of the color specified under our sailing instructions as recognition signals for that particular day. Apparently these smoke sig-

The *AL-2* is flooded down aft near the tender *Bushnell* so a crew of sailors in a boat can work on her port side torpedo tubes. The starboard tubes are visible out of the water in the foreground. She had no stern tubes.
Naval Institute Photo Archive

nals were not observed by our destroyers because they steamed toward us at full speed and continued firing as rapidly as possible under the belief that they had sighted a German U-boat on the surface. Of course, they were anxious to sink us.

Fortunately, none of their shells hit us, although we could hear them passing overhead and could observe the splashes of the shells on both sides of us. When the destroyers got within a range of about one mile, they did see our recognition signals and ceased fire. One of them circled us to verify our identification more thoroughly. After being well satisfied that we were in truth an American submarine and not a German submarine, the destroyer steamed past us close astern. The skipper megaphoned over his apologies and best wishes.

Somewhat later in the day, about noon, after we had passed to the west of Queenstown, we sighted to the north a group of small British patrol craft which were really converted fishing boats and small motorboats, all of which were lightly armed. They sighted us and gave pursuit, but we continued on our way for a while then submerged and came up a few miles farther west later in the afternoon. The British patrol craft were no longer in sight.

In the late afternoon we came near the southwest corner of Ireland and were somewhat uncertain as to our exact location because our sun sights during the day had not been very satisfactory. We were, therefore, obliged to steam in rather close to the coast in the hope of picking up Fastnet Light or some other landmark. The weather during the late afternoon was fairly clear, but there was a very brisk headwind which occasioned a quite choppy sea. We passed through an area in which evidently some Allied merchant ship had recently been sunk because the surface for several miles was dotted with debris ranging in size from that of a piece of driftwood to objects as large as a small rowboat. This made it difficult for our lookouts to identify these small black objects which would be sighted at the tops of waves a half mile or a mile ahead of us.

About 5:30 in the afternoon I got a satisfactory sun sight and went below to work out our position and plot it in our chart and from that determine the proper course for us to steer to hit the entrance to Bantry Bay in the early evening. While I was working out this navigational problem, Lt. Scott Ulmsted, the third officer on the *AL-2*, who had the duty as officer of the deck, called down through the voice tube that the lookout had sighted what appeared to be a spar buoy bearing approximately forty-five degrees on our starboard bow and distant a thousand or fifteen hundred yards. I ordered the officer of the deck to change course and head toward the sighted object. I took a careful look at the chart to ascertain if by chance there were any spar buoys along the south coast of Ireland in the area where we thought we were. I could find no such buoys on the map except very close inshore, and I quickly concluded that we could not possibly be that close to the coast without having sighted land itself.

In a period of about five or ten minutes, the officer of the deck reported that the sighted object could not be again seen, and he presumed that he and the lookout had seen some floating debris on the crest of a wave. He had no sooner made this report than there was a terrific explosion underwater which seemed to be very close aboard, near our starboard quarter—that is, abaft our beam and on the starboard side. I jumped up into the conning tower, and the officer of the deck reported that we had been torpedoed and that there was a huge geyser of water about 150 feet on our starboard quarter. I glanced through the small portholes in the conning tower and saw this column of water subsiding. As it subsided it created temporarily a smooth surface, or what we would call a slick, of maybe two hundred feet in diameter.

Near the edge of this slick I sighted about four feet of the periscope of a submarine which I realized, of course, must be that of a German submarine. I watched it for a few seconds and noted that as it moved through this slick it was building up "a bone in its teeth," indicating that the submarine was increasing speed. I instantly recognized from the position of the periscope that the center of the explosion must have been as close to the German submarine as to us, or even closer, and I realized that because the German submarine was submerged and we were on the surface, any damage suffered would have been more serious to the Germans than to us.

Also, from the appearance of the bone in the teeth I concluded that—contrary to usual tactics—the German submarine was attempting to get to the surface rather than to get into a position to fire another torpedo. This confirmed my snap judgment that the German submarine indeed had been damaged and that the damage was probably near the torpedo tubes in the bow of the submarine rather than at some other location in the hull. But, of course, this was sheer surmise, made very quickly.

I knew that if the German submarine reached the surface it would probably be able to outgun us, because our puny little three-inch gun on our forecastle was a very unreliable weapon and it took several minutes to bring the gun into firing position after the gun crew got on deck. In the kind of choppy sea then prevailing, the gun crew would have a very unstable and slippery deck on which to work. I concluded that I did not want any part of a gun duel with the German submarine. The thought occurred to me that since the submarine appeared to be damaged, the most effective tactic that I could employ would be to swing around and try to ram it or force it by the threat of ramming to submerge to a greater depth.

All of this took really only a matter of maybe thirty seconds to formulate in my mind. I gave the order for hard left rudder and the order to crash dive. I immediately started down the ladder into the control room. Pursuant to standard instructions, our ballast tanks were immediately flooded, and we went through the standard operations under which we would normally be completely submerged in a period of about forty seconds. As we swung around, our submarine began its dive, and the officer of the deck and the quartermaster on the bridge came down more precipitately than I had expected. This was due to the fact that the mess cook had gone up on the bridge to empty a bucket of garbage, so there were three men on the bridge instead of the usual two. This meant that these three men really had to scramble to get through the hatch into the conning tower and get the hatch closed and dogged down before we went completely underwater.

We went underwater smoothly and swung around on a course leading back to a position that I calculated would be some three to four hundred yards in advance of the position where I had last sighted the periscope of the German submarine. In the meantime, I was receiving from the man stationed on our underwater listening device reports that he could hear propeller noises, which he reported at frequent intervals. I thereupon swung the *AL-2* around to a generally northerly course and brought the sound of the propeller noises dead ahead and increased my own speed.

Some of the crew in the engine room and in the torpedo room aft of the engine room reported that they could hear the propeller noises of the German submarine as we apparently passed just over it. I asked the man on the listening device to give me a count of the propeller revolutions so that I could estimate the speed at which the German submarine was traveling. He gave me such a report, and from this I immediately concluded that the submarine was running at top speed. This, of course, was absolutely contrary to normal procedures in the case of a submarine encountering another submarine underwater. The objective in the standard procedure was to run ahead at dead-slow speed or remain stopped so that the other submarine could not use its listening devices to zero in on you. It was obvious, therefore, that the German submarine was endeavoring to get to the surface rather than to elude our position.

I increased speed and continued to hold the propeller noises dead ahead. Within a few minutes, our signalman on the K-tubes, which were the listening devices, reported that he heard a repeated underwater Morse code signal from the direction of our starboard quarter, and at the same time he was continuing to hear propeller noises dead ahead. He reported that this noise on our starboard quarter sounded like a whistle with dots and dashes. From this we concluded an attempt was being made by another German submarine to communicate with the submarine that we were pursuing.

Our signalman reported that this signal was repeated insistently but that no answer to it was audible. The signalman then reported that the propeller noises ahead had suddenly stopped. They had not slowed down; they simply came to a complete cessation. The underwater signal from the other German submarine continued insistently in diminished volume for a period of fifteen or twenty minutes, but it did not elicit any response.

I ordered the *AL-2* to the surface, and we made a careful visual search of the vicinity and could not see anything at all except some of the debris similar to that through which we had been steaming an hour or two earlier. There was no sign of any German submarine in any direction. We then submerged and remained as stationary as possible in order that our listening devices could operate at maximum efficiency. But after about an hour I concluded, in the absence of any sound whatsoever, that it was no longer useful to remain submerged. We came to the surface again and made another very careful search in all directions of the waters surrounding us. We could not find any trace of any submarine, nor did we observe any oil slick or anything of that kind. I gave orders to set course for Bantry Bay, and we proceeded on our voyage and arrived in Bantry Bay some four or five hours later.

I reported this incident to our division commander and gave it little further thought. There seemed to be a consensus of opinion on the submarine tender *Bushnell* that we had indeed made a distinct contact with a German submarine and that the chances were that the German submarine had sighted us on the surface and had fired a torpedo at us, which torpedo had either prematurely exploded or had struck our hull without being detonated and then had circled back and exploded near the German submarine. The consensus was that in view of the fact that the Germans had been utilizing at this period of the war a magnetic firing device on their torpedoes, which was designed to detonate the torpedoes in case the torpedo dived under its target instead of hitting the hull, the torpedo fired at us had been fitted with such a magnetic detonating device and fortunately for us had exploded the torpedo before it could strike the hull of the AL-2.

Some months later we learned from the British that they had tracked, by their radio-direction-finding systems, the entire voyage of the German submarine UB-65 from its German port out into the Atlantic north of Scotland and around Ireland and down into the Bay of Biscay, where it had been on patrol for over a week and then had apparently headed back home. At the same time, another German submarine had been tracked from its German port out around the north of Scotland and down the west coast of Ireland. At a time just prior to the torpedoing of the AL-2, these two German submarines were apparently on the surface communicating with each other by radio in the general vicinity in which our encounter subsequently occurred.

We then surmised that the two German submarines had kept a rendezvous and were exchanging information on the surface when they had sighted the AL-2 approaching on the surface from a southwesterly direction. We speculated that the homeward-bound submarine had asked that it be allowed to attack us so that the outward-bound submarine could conserve its supply of torpedoes, and that thereupon the German submarine UB-65 had submerged and had made an approach on us while the other submarine had submerged and proceeded toward its assigned patrol area to the southeast.

The British further reported that the homeward-bound submarine, which was positively identified as the UB-65, was never heard of again and that the outward-bound submarine, during the evenings of 10 and 11 July, had made a long radio report to Germany, evidently reporting the encounter between the UB-65 and the AL-2.

Shortly after the end of the war the British Admiralty published a list of German submarines sunk. In this list three German submarines were put in the category of "known sunk" by the United States Navy. One of these was sunk by the destroyer Fanning under Lt. Cdr. A. S. Carpender. A second submarine was credited to an American converted yacht and a British yacht, which were operating together on patrol in European waters. The third German submarine, the UB-65, was credited to the AL-2.

To conclude this account of the encounter, I think it might be of interest to include a statement made by Secretary of the Navy Josephus Daniels in a speech before the National Press Club in Washington in the early autumn of 1918. This speech was devoted to the activities of the U.S. Navy in European waters, and he described the encounter of the AL-2 with the German submarine in the following words:

> The AL-2 on the surface was torpedoed by the UB-65 submerged but turned and crash dived steeply in an attempt to ram the UB-65 and thereby forced the German submarine to a crushing depth on the bottom, from which it never arose. Had the AL-2 struck the enemy submarine, both boats would have been lost, but Lt. Paul F. Foster, the commanding officer, did not hesitate because of the risk and heroically offered himself, his crew, and his boat as a sacrifice in an endeavor to destroy the enemy. Lieutenant Foster's unusual daring as a submarine commander forms some of the most thrilling chapters of the war.

I might mention that it was largely for this incident that I was fortunate enough to be awarded the Distinguished Service Medal at the end of World War I.

4

Submarine School

ADM. STUART S. MURRAY,
USN (RET.)

In a naval career that included many highlights, perhaps the foremost for Admiral Murray came in 1945, when he commanded the battleship *Missouri* at the end of World War II and hosted the Japanese surrender ceremony in Tokyo Bay. That was thirty years after he had entered the United States Naval Academy in 1915 from landlocked Oklahoma. While a midshipman he acquired the nickname "Sunshine," partly because of his initials, S. S., and partly because of his sunny disposition. His class of 1919 graduated from the academy a year ahead of time because of the need to get more officers out into the fleet during World War I.

WHEN IT CAME time for us to put in our requests as to what we wanted to do after graduation, I'd been thinking about it quite a bit in my first class year. My brother Clive was in the Marine Corps and had been down at Quantico, Virginia. I'd seen him before he went over to Europe, about in August or September 1917, and I enjoyed it down there with the Marines. So when the academic year started in 1917 and the call came for volunteers for the Marine Corps, I submitted my application for it. In due course, it came back accepted. There were seven of us in the class that had requested the Corps, and all seven requests were granted.

In the spring, around the first of May 1918, we got our orders and had all of our Marine Corps uniforms ordered, to be finished and turned over to us just before graduation. I knew exactly where I was going upon graduation—in the Marine Corps. Then forty-eight hours before

Nestled on the Groton side of the Thames River, this is the submarine base at New London in 1918.
Courtesy of Rickart Connole

we graduated, all seven of us were called in about seven o'clock in the morning to the commandant of midshipmen's office to initial an order. That order was signed by the secretary of the navy, Josephus Daniels, and the gist of it was that we were not going into the Marine Corps. We were all going into the line of the Navy and would be commissioned as ensigns. For that reason, there were no members of the class of 1919 in the Marine Corps. At that time they thought they needed line officers a lot more than they needed Marine officers.

I might add that after signing the orders we were told, "All right, you can go down to breakfast now, and you've got permission to leave immediately after breakfast. You're excused from everything. Go out and get your uniforms as naval officers. Turn your Marine Corps uniforms in." I was disgusted. Oh, yes, someone said, "On the way out, sitting outside there, are your choices—first, second, third, and fourth choices—as to what type of duty you would like on graduation. Most of them are already full, but you can put on it anything you want to." Well, two of us

went out there together, Arthur S. "Beanie" Adams and I, and we both said, "Well, we can't go in the Marines; we'll fool them. We'll go in the submarines." Besides, there were a lot more vacancies in there. We didn't know a thing about submarines, but we thought we might as well try. The word's got "marine" in it anyway. So that's the way it wound up. We got telegraphic orders down there to go to the Submarine School and ten days' leave upon graduation before reporting in to the submarine base, New London, Connecticut, for instruction. That's the way I got in submarines.

Our first view of them was coming over to the submarine base from New London on the train. (The base itself is actually on the Groton side of the Thames River.) My first reaction was mostly curiosity—what were these things going to be like? As a matter of fact, if I recall correctly, they took us all down there the first day to let us look at them. They spent several days in taking us on familiarization visits to all the different types of submarines which were actually at the submarine base or at the New London Ship and Engine

The instructors at the first torpedo school at the New London base gather for a group portrait in 1918. *Courtesy of Rickart Connole*

Company, as it was then, and now the Electric Boat Company, part of General Dynamics. Some of the excess submarines had to tie up over there. There wasn't enough pier space at New London. They only had two piers up there then, but they were building others as they could.

When I reported, I found the Submarine School that we were to attend actually was not a formalized school as of that time. It had been going for one previous class. They were going to set up what they called an endless-chain system for turning out officers for submarines in the World War I building program. You just fit in with whatever was being taught when you got there and continued until you came back to where you started.

We were the first ten students to arrive for the endless-chain system. The plan was that the school would start in early July. In the meantime, we were to be given temporary duty around the

submarine base, as it was then. It had been an old Navy coaling station for about one hundred years, more or less, and was just being turned into a submarine base. The buildings were being built because they only had about four or five buildings in the whole thing, including a very small power plant. Everywhere you went there were excavations and buildings going up.

We were all assigned to barracks, buildings on what was called "upper base" to differentiate it from the waterfront section of the base. The buildings across the compound from us, about four of them, were filled with French sailors. The French were taking over several submarine chasers from the U.S. Navy at that time. They were tied up at some of the piers at the submarine base as well as going out on Long Island Sound to practice running them. The French were there until about the middle of July, when they left.

My first assignment there was as patrol officer in New London, Connecticut. Going to a waterfront seaport, as New London was at that time, and still is to a certain extent, is quite an education for a fresh-caught ensign, twenty years old.

However, after two weeks of that, I was assigned to periodic trips on a submarine going out on the day's operations. The rest of the ten of us were assigned to various jobs, such as communications officer, around the submarine base. At that time, D-boats (or "dog boats," as they were called) were the ones assigned to Submarine School. They were very small submarines, about 110 or 115 feet long and about 150 tons. They could back out from the dock and duck almost where they backed out, inasmuch as they only drew about twelve feet of water. They only needed about twenty feet of water to submerge. That's just about the depth of the water across to the other side of the river. They were very handy that way. In half a day they could go out and make several dives and come back in and still never be more than half a mile from the submarine base.

The others that were there were the G-boats. These were about 220 feet long and probably displaced about eight hundred or nine hundred tons. When I started going out on the submarines, I was one time out for about five or six days on the G-2. There were four of these G-boats at the submarine base to be used as school boats and also to go on patrol on Long Island Sound. This was the summer of 1918, and the German U-boats were quite busy around the East Coast of the United States. One of the very interesting things about the G-2 was the fact that she had great big wagon wheels on the bottom that were permanently down there. You could sink down to the bottom of the river, or the bay, and go right ahead on the wheels. We went up the Thames River several times from the bridge to the submarine base, running on the wheels. It was very easy on the helmsman, because the wheels kept the submarine right in the middle of the channel.

Also, the G-2 had what was called a drop keel, which was about a fifteen-ton hunk of pig lead on the bottom. There was a lever, just like your emergency brake, inside the submarine with which this could be released. It was a good idea, except periodically some sailor or officer or visitor stumbled over this lever, and off went the drop keel. When you dropped fifteen tons from a submarine submerged, it immediately shot to the surface. Not only that, but to put a new one in, they had to go in dry dock, which was an awful nuisance. They could compensate by adding additional water into their compensating tanks to take care of it, once they knew what had happened. But it took considerable time to take on thirty thousand pounds of water in one of those older submarines.

The Submarine School started finally, right after the Fourth of July 1918. As I said before, we were in this chain system, and each course was three weeks long. During those three weeks, you took that one subject and nothing else, as you did in some of the engine and battery experiments. Then you moved on to another subject, and another class would start in. By this time, a group of about fifty Naval Reserve officers had arrived and were put in various other types of work around the base and getting ready for the school. The group I was in consisted of ten of us right from the Naval Academy: Ens. James Fife from the fleet, a Naval Reserve lieutenant, and three Naval Reserve ensigns or jaygees. There were about fifteen in a class starting out. That was about the average size of the other classes that were starting three weeks behind us and so forth, right on through. In that way, every three weeks one group of about fifteen to twenty would graduate.

The total course was supposed to last about eighteen weeks, so our group was to graduate about 15 November 1918. We were the first one in this new system, although they had had a previous class that had graduated in early 1918. Other submariners had graduated in previous years, but it wasn't yet a formal school. They used them more there for a very short type of instruction where they could go out for training on some of the submarines right there as a group, rather than being assigned individually to submarines. Previous to that, all had been assigned individually to a submarine and picked up the training when they could.

This view shows O-class submarines moored in 1919 at the recently established submarine base at New London. The formal United States Naval Submarine School had started there not long before. *Naval Institute Photo Archive*

Beginning in 1917, they sent a group up there, I think about twelve or fifteen, for somewhere between four and six months. They took some formalized instruction in the various subjects, like diesel engineering, storage batteries, and electricity, but primarily they trained as a group, going out on the submarines. That was the group I mentioned graduated earlier in 1918, about March. Previous to that they had at times groups of a few who would be there for a little bit of training, but there wasn't any formalized instruction. Really, late 1917 was when they first started a Submarine School as such, and it really wasn't completely formalized until they started this endless-chain system in the summer of 1918.

The training we got there in the practical line in some of the courses, I think, was very good. For instance, one of the courses in engineering was a three-week course in diesel engines, in addition to about six weeks of the theoretical end of engineering. We had three weeks' practical work in which we would tear down completely and overhaul two diesel engines that had been pulled out of K-boats and set up at New London. That was part of the school's training, tearing these down and putting them together. I might add that the following class did the same thing—fixed up what we hadn't.

It was quite interesting, as well as very practical, in that you had to grind in the valves by hand. You had to actually get in there and do the thing with your own hands—absolutely everything. No assistance was given by any of the enlisted personnel, who were the experts and could tell you what the name of the thing was and how it worked—but they couldn't touch a thing. We had to do everything. It was regular training, which I think every one of us found later on was worth its weight in gold when we got out in submarines and had to do some of that ourselves.

The electrical engineering course was the same type of thing. You got down there and charged the submarine's storage battery. Not only that, you renewed the elements in it yourself. The book told you the theoretical way, but you did it the practical way of going down there and renewing the elements of a big storage battery. They were kind of small in those days. They only weighed about half a ton apiece, instead of the big ones now, weighing twice that or more.

The three-week course and actually going out on the submarines were, I think, the most interesting things. Because the time we were going out there in Long Island Sound and assigned to the submarine section of the course happened to be the same time the old cruiser *San Diego* was sunk off the Martha's Vineyard area, south of Newport, Rhode Island, in the late summer or early fall of 1918. The U.S. submarines were out there to look for the German submarine. It had been pretty well established that it had been a floating mine that the *San Diego* had hit. Nevertheless, the excitement was very high in that whole area. So we got to spend a couple of days out there on whatever submarine we happened to get piled into, looking around. Since the submarines were short of officers, by that time they figured we could at least stand a periscope watch, which was a primary thing.

We had a flu epidemic running rampant during the summer of 1918, and we were quarantined most of the time on the submarine base up there. Two of the members of my class decided that quarantine and having to stay on the base was a little too onerous for them. They jumped in the car and drove down into New York for the weekend. That was all right, but they got tagged by the Marines in going out the gate. The Marines didn't want to shoot them but got their license number and who they were. On the way back the next day, Sunday afternoon, they got them coming in. So they were promptly given general courts-martial, kicked out of Submarine School, and sent to general service. Our ten from the Naval Academy had shrunk to eight.

We were all there, just about four days before graduation, when the Armistice was signed in November to end World War I. They had a celebration and parade down in New London. It was interesting to see it and read about it in the papers. But I think the reaction of most of us was a little bit of disgust because we hadn't gotten out in the war with the submarines.

For my first fleet duty, I was ordered to the *R-20* and was told it was in San Pedro, California, or San Francisco—they were not sure which—but to head for San Pedro and report in there. That was kind of a routine thing in World War I, as well as World War II. They told you where they thought your ship was, and then it was up to you to find it. I was given ten days to cross the continent and report in on the day after Thanksgiving in 1918. Considering it would take four days' travel time, or about five days to be safe, I managed to get about five days' stopover in Oklahoma with my parents on my way out to San Pedro.

5

Beginning of the S-Boats

VICE ADM. GEORGE C. DYER,
USN (RET.)

Throughout much of the period between the world wars, the S class was a mainstay of the U.S. submarine fleet. Construction on the first of the S-boats began in 1917 and went on until the last was completed in 1924. All told, the Navy commissioned fifty-one boats of the class, though they were not identical. Two of the class, the *S-4* and *S-51*, were lost in well-publicized disasters in the 1920s. Some of the S-boats served on in fleet missions during the early part of World War II. Their principal contribution, however, was as training platforms in the 1920s and 1930s for many of the World War II submariners. As the account below demonstrates, going into submarines in the post–World War I era was not necessarily a permanent calling. Individuals moved in and out of the boats as part of their overall careers.

FOLLOWING WORLD WAR I, the United States brought four surrendered German submarines to this country. They were, of course, examined inch by inch. Among other superlatives of the German subs, they were able to dive much more quickly than ours. The Navy Department turned to the three submarine construction yards on the East Coast. They were each to design a submarine of 800 to 850 tons and build into it the highest submerged and surface speeds, the quickest diving time, the best depth control, the longest cruising radius, and a lot of other desirable submarine qualities. The Navy planned to run competitive tests between the finished submarines and, depending on the outcome, award contracts based on each boat's merit. The *S-1* was built at the Fore River Shipbuilding Company in Quincy, Massachusetts, the *S-2* at the Lake

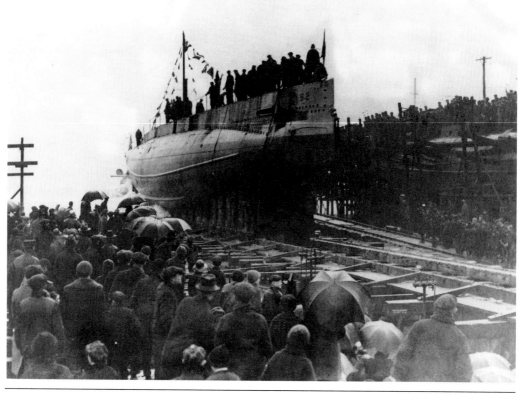

World War I had barely ended when the Lake Torpedo Boat Company launched the *S-2* on 15 February 1919. She was in active service until decommissioned in 1929. *Naval Institute Photo Archive*

Torpedo Boat Company in Bridgeport, Connecticut, and the *S-3* at the Portsmouth Navy Yard.

The prospective skipper of the *S-2* was Lt. Cdr. Lewis Hancock. He went to New London to get advice from other submarine commanders on the best choice as executive officer. Supposedly that's how I got the job. Lake Torpedo Boat Company always used Busch-Sulzer diesel engines in their submarines, and I had had quite a little luck with them. You had to have luck, because no amount of skill would make the darn things run well all the time.

I reported to the Lake shipyard in August 1919. The company was built around Simon Lake's idea of submarines based on his experiences as one of the very early submarine builders. He never had enough financial resources to really operate a proper company and, I believe, was not particularly blessed with business ability. Such a combination—an inventor and an absence of

business savvy—did not fit together for an easy financial life for the company.

Lewis Hancock was a very enterprising and capable officer. He and I lived at the University Club in Bridgeport; we were both bachelors. The other officers in the *S-2* were Lt. (j.g.) Albert J. Wheaton and Chief Gunner Biven M. Prewett. They were both excellent.

At that time, before a submarine could be accepted, it had to go through a test run of fifty-two hours. You ran forty-eight hours at normal cruising speed, and at the end of that you ran four hours at full speed. The Busch-Sulzer engine in the *S-2* had considerably more horsepower than the engines that were put in the *S-1* or the *S-3*, because Lake was anxious to develop a submarine that was faster than the ordinary twelve-and-a-half- to thirteen-knot submarine. The Busch-Sulzer engine was a two-cycle, high-speed engine. The *S-2* made sixteen and a half knots over the measured mile course, which was a real feather in Lake's cap.

When the Navy Department's Board of Inspection and Survey came up from Washington for this acceptance test, we ran the forty-eight hours with no great problem at all. We then got three hours and fifty minutes into the full-power test when a cylinder of one engine dropped a spray valve. The constant pounding of this spray valve at very high speed had fractured it. When it fell, it smashed everything inside the cylinder. That ended the first test, and the board returned to Washington.

We went back through all the steps that were necessary to get ready for another acceptance test. The second time we made it through, though I must say I prayed for the entire four hours the boat was at full speed. At 80 percent power the engine was wonderful; it ran like a sewing machine. But as soon as you got to full power, the engine labored terribly. Anyway, we got through the engine test.

We still had one more test to do, and that was our deep dive. We went out the next day and made, at two hundred feet, a very successful test dive. When we came back in, the Lake Torpedo Boat Company officials were down on the dock with the contract spread out on a table and fountain pens at the ready. The top man from Lake said, "Captain, how about signing for the boat?"

Lewis had pen in hand when I showed up, having followed him ashore. I said, "Captain, under the contract, the Lake Torpedo Boat Company is required to deliver this boat with the battery and the air banks fully charged. Since we've been out and have made the deep dive, the Lake banks need to recharge us. I recommend that you not sign until these things have been done." He laid down the pen and walked off, leaving the Lake Company officials madder than a hornet. The Navy Department had announced it would offer a bonus for the first submarine completed; the earlier the boat was finished, the bigger the bonus. Needless to say, they wanted to collect the money.

Lewis and I went back to the University Club. We had fully expected to shove off for the New York Navy Yard, where we would fit out for active service. The University Club had arranged to give us a going-away party that night. Lewis was quite a partygoer, I can tell you. At the end of this dinner, we retired to the card room to play poker.

At around 2300, I suddenly realized that someone was looking at us through the heavy curtains at the entrance to the room. It was Chief Gunner Prewett, who beckoned to me with his fingers. Biven whispered, "Both main motors are burned out." I said nothing to Commander Hancock but went rapidly to the S-2. There had been a fire in the motor room. The riser bars had worked loose, started scraping the brushes, gotten burning hot, and fired. The copper had melted and started spewing around the motor room, all over the bulkheads. The wreckage was widespread. I stayed at the boat for several hours. At about 0200 I went back to the club to make a report to the skipper. He was still there playing poker. He asked how long it would take to fix the damage, and I told him about four months. He said he wasn't going to hang around that long.

I went up to my room, took a bath—I was filthy from climbing all over the motors—and turned in. The next morning when I got to the boat, no skipper. I went in to see the senior naval officer at the Lake Torpedo Boat Company, Lt. Cdr. Raymond "Roaring Bull" Thomas, who was inspector of machinery. He, of course, had heard about the S-2 casualty. He kept asking me, "Where's Hancock? Where's Hancock?"

He was a very senior lieutenant commander, and I was a very junior lieutenant; he scared me. I kept saying, "Well, I haven't seen the skipper this morning."

And then Roaring Bull said, "When he comes in, I want to see him immediately."

After the mishap with the motors, I had drafted the necessary dispatches and notified the Bureau of Engineering, which controlled all the private building yards at that time. I also had contacted the commandant of the Third Naval District, the Board of Inspection and Survey, and the commander, Control Force (later called commander, Submarine Force).

At the end of the working day I got hold of Al Wheaton and asked him to go to the police station and look for Lewis. About a half hour

This photo of the *S-4*'s engine room was made on Christmas Day 1919, about the same time Ensign Dyer was struggling with problems on board the *S-2*, which was commissioned in May 1920. *Naval Institute Photo Archive*

later, Al called to say the police didn't know anything about him. I worried through the night and made up my mind the next morning I was going to have to report his absence.

I went to Commander Thomas's office and said, "I'm sorry to report, but Commander Hancock isn't present."

"Where was he yesterday?"

"I don't know, sir; he wasn't present yesterday."

"Have you made a report?"

"I have it here in my hand."

He took it, laid it on his desk, and said, "What have you done to locate him?"

"I had contact with the police in Bridgeport but haven't found him."

"Well, you'd better locate him and get him back on board, or I'll send this thing in. If he isn't here by the end of working hours today, it's going in."

I went back to the office. At around eleven the telephone rang. It was the chief of police at New Haven. He said, "Do you know an officer named Hancock?"

I said, "Yes, he's my captain."

"Have you got five hundred dollars?"

"No, I don't, but I think I can raise it."

"If you want to get him out of jail, it's five hundred dollars."

I collected all the money I could scrounge from Al Wheaton, Biven Prewett, several people at the University Club, and myself, and jumped on the next train to New Haven. At the police station I learned that Lewis had been drinking in a local watering hole. He wasn't happy when they closed the bar on him, so he backed his car up and drove right into the front of the building. By the time I got there, he was sobering up. I paid the five hundred dollars and got him out of jail.

On the train back—his car, of course, was a total wreck and had been hauled off to the junkyard—he said, "I've decided to go into lighter-than-air training. What do you want to do?"

I said, "I want to command a submarine."

"I'll go to the Navy Department and see what I can do for you." So that's how I got command of the *D-3*, which I joined in November 1919.

As for Lewis Hancock, he did go to lighter-than-air. The report on this absence never got into his record, since we found him in time. Six years later, on 3 September 1925, he died in the crash of the dirigible *Shenandoah* during a storm over Ohio.

Lewis Hancock was survived by his widow, Joy Bright Hancock, one of the pioneers among women in the Navy. Later, from 1946 to 1953, she was director of the WAVES (Women Accepted for Volunteer Emergency Service). As for the submarine S-2, she was finally commissioned on 25 May 1920 under a new skipper, Lt. Cdr. William Quigley. Of the first three S-boats, the S-2 had the shortest career, only nine years of active service.

6

Building the Submarine
Base at Pearl Harbor

ADM. STUART S. MURRAY,
USN (RET.)

At the outset of World War II, Pearl Harbor was a fully developed fleet base. Because the Battle Force was stationed there, the collection of ships became a magnet for the Japanese air attack that kicked off the U.S. entrance into the war. Even so, the base there was relatively young. It was only in the late 1930s that it became a home for more than just submarines. It got its start when Murray was an ensign, only a year out of the United States Naval Academy.

I N EARLY JUNE 1919, Submarine Division Fourteen and the tender *Beaver* sailed from San Francisco for Pearl Harbor. We were all thrilled to get going out to the Sandwich Islands, as we called them, and see the hula dancers. The trip out there on an R-boat was not what one would call a luxury-liner cruise on the *Lurline* or the *Mariposa* in more modern times. It took us eight days to get out there, and we thought that we were doing wonderfully well. I guess we were, by the times then.

Our division commander was Cdr. Felix Xerxes Gygax. When we arrived off Honolulu and rounded Diamond Head, the commodore ordered a baptismal dive in the "world-famous waters off Waikiki," as he phrased the message. We all submerged with varying degrees of success: it took about five or ten minutes to get under, since we had been using our number-three main ballast tank as a reserve fuel-oil tank. I'm afraid in more modern times we would have been prosecuted by the nonpollution people for letting oil slicks out of our vents when we flooded the after main ballast tanks, which had been full of fuel oil. But there wasn't nearly as much oil as one would think.

The new submarine base, with its prefabricated buildings, is seen here in July 1921, not long after Murray arrived to help with its construction. *Naval Institute Photo Archive*

We went into Pearl Harbor, and the channel still wasn't completely finished. They were still working on it, but we got in with a tug leading the way and a pilot on the tender *Beaver*. The submarines would do the best they could and stay off the bottom. We ran in on the batteries, not on the engines, because you could not reverse on those engines at that time. When we got around inside Pearl Harbor, after going through the cane fields on both sides of the Pearl Harbor channel, we saw what was to be our future happy home, the submarine base. I must add it was a sad-looking thing at that time.

There were two piers over there on the opposite side of the bay from the navy yard, and they were not completely finished. There were two buildings—tin-covered walls, one story, it looked like. But the only things you could really see were cactus and algaroba trees, full of thorns. The dredges were still working all around, and

they were still working on the docks to finish them up, but not that much work on cleaning up the base. The *Beaver* tied up to one side of one dock, and the six submarines tied up to the other side, so it wasn't too crowded with just the six of us there.

Commodore Gygax said the only way we were going to get the base built was to build it, and the first thing to do was to clean off the land. So each submarine was directed to get a permanent working party of fifteen men to clean off the land. Well, fifteen men out a crew of thirty-nine doesn't leave an awful lot to run the ship on and take care of it. But that was it, and we sent them up. They would stay on the tender, and we wouldn't see them except on paydays and to take them out for a dive.

Things were coming along pretty good there in July; then the month of August arrived and demobilization day. Practically all the enlisted personnel during World War I were on duration-of-war (DOW) enlistments, and the rest of them were reserves that were in. So all DOWs ended in August. It was sufficiently fast coming that we didn't have much opportunity to make any plans on it.

We could electioneer our crews to get them to ship over. I managed to talk nineteen of the crew of the *R-17* into shipping over to the regular Navy and continue on for two to four years—maybe only one to four years, but at any rate to stay on as regular members. The Naval Reserve officers were also being released at the same time, so we were not only short of men, we were going to be short of officers.

When the final chips were down and the transports hauled the men off to take them back to the coast for transfer for demobilization, the *R-17* had nineteen men aboard. The other submarines had all the way from three to ten; that was all. In order to even the thing up, Commodore Gygax directed that we all split up so we would have about the same number. Except he allowed us, since we had practically double anyone else, to keep ten of ours, which was a great concession since it wound up that the rest of them averaged about seven or eight when the final division was over. We couldn't even operate an R-boat with a crew like that.

All those working parties in the cactus fields stopped suddenly. We did have permission from the Navy Department to recruit on station and any other place. So we set up recruiting stations out at Schofield Barracks, where the Army was having their troubles, and also down at Fort Shafter and their Army posts on Oahu. Apparently our recruiting boys were persuasive, because we got in nothing flat about three hundred ex-Army people, a large percentage of them Filipinos. But we got choosy; we wouldn't take anyone less than a first sergeant.

We ended up by enlisting several hundred. So we got what you might call hands and feet. They didn't know anything about the Navy or anything about ships, so we had to set up a submarine base for recruit training. We set it up across from what is now Hickam Field, in the algaroba bushes over

there. We cut out a rifle range, using them, as well as giving boot training at the same time. We gave them about three- or four-week fast course over there and then sent them back to submarines in rotations of about fifty men at a time.

In the meantime, we would use the recruits who hadn't gone through boot training as cleaning squads on the submarines. Because they could shine brightwork, sweep, wipe off verdigris, and clean up in general, as well as furnishing the working parties for the cactus and algaroba. The regular crews of the submarines did the best they could in maintaining the submarines and going ahead and operating them. You took the crews of three submarines and combined them on one submarine in rotation and went out and operated for one day. Even at that you didn't have one full crew.

Finally, these boots got sufficient training from the old crews around there to really turn in good service. They later on became chiefs and everything else, and they were wonderful men. Apparently we picked some pretty good men from the Army. We finally got them squared away, so we got back to cruising. We were short of officers all the time. It was 1921 before we started getting officers in.

About the twentieth of December 1919, the USS *Chicago*, one of the cruisers from even before the time of the Great White Fleet, arrived in Pearl Harbor to be the submarine tender and station ship. Aboard the *Chicago* Cdr. Chester W. Nimitz had toured the East Coast of the United States and loaded it down with the so-called one-dollar houses. They were detachable, ready-made houses which could be put together by the numbers. He loaded it up with those to bring them out to the submarine base. The idea was that that was the building material for the submarine base, since you couldn't get permanent buildings built with the public works department. They arrived just before Christmas, and we started unloading them.

Commander Nimitz was not aboard the *Chicago* when the ship arrived; he was still on duty on the East Coast. He had orders to relieve Commander Gygax as commander of Submarine

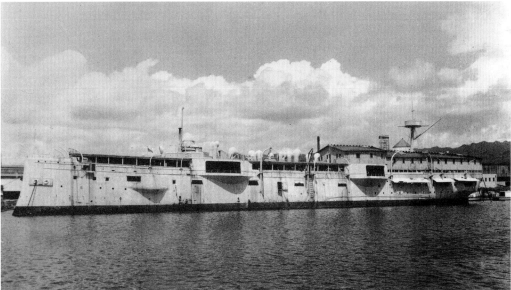

The old cruiser *Chicago*, which had been commissioned in 1889, served at Pearl Harbor from 1919 to 1935 as a submarine headquarters ship and barracks. She officially went out of commission in 1923 and in 1928 was renamed *Alton* so the name *Chicago* could be used for a new heavy cruiser. In this aerial view taken in 1920 at Pearl she looks essentially like the cruiser she once was. In the water level shot from the mid-1930s (*bottom*) her superstructure has been removed, and a wooden structure has been built on the stern to house submariners. With the construction of the new barracks ashore for submariners, the *Alton* was no longer needed. *Naval Institute Photo Archive*

Division Fourteen in Pearl Harbor, but he wasn't expected until around the first of April 1920. Nimitz had seen to it that these dollar houses were aboard. He knew that he was going to have to come out there and build a submarine base up from what it was, and he wanted as much material as possible out there to build it. So we had plenty of building materials to put together for the buildings and shops.

By this time there had been considerable cleaning off by the working parties of the algaroba and cactus. They smoothed the small hills around there, which were three or four feet high, filled up the ditches, and leveled the ground. Of course, during the cleaning-up period, as the cleaning would progress farther and farther from the waterfront, peculiar things were found in the cactus. These included such things as stills that had been set up by sailors to celebrate and a few things like that. On the whole, they did a very good job, so we could start making these portable houses into buildings.

In the meantime, we had drawn up our own plans, with assistance from the district civil engineers, for the type of buildings we hoped to have. Then it was up to the sailors to put the sectional houses together. After they would build a machine shop, or any other kind of shop, or temporary barracks for the men to live in, we would find doors and windows in the most unexpected parts. There were living rooms, kitchens, bedrooms—everything just went out in a line to fill in the walls. So a hundred-foot building was half a dozen houses all put together.

This process worked fine. We had lots of things left over, but by following the instructions, the sailors didn't have much of any trouble putting them together, because all the sections were numbered. Number 2 to stick into number 1, and so forth down the line with arrows as to what to stick to what. They really were surprisingly good. The only trouble we had was when we started hooking one house onto another one. Then we had to do a little improvising, but sailors are always good at improvising.

The only permanent building we had was starting in to be the crew barracks, which wasn't finished for two, three, or four years. It is still one of the present big barracks buildings for the crews. Then we had the two that had been built ahead of time as crews' barracks down closer to the waterfront. They were supposed to be temporary buildings. The last time I was out there was about four years ago, and they were still standing, so they were well-built temporary buildings.

In March 1920 I was ordered to relieve Lt. Cdr. Robert R. Thompson as commanding officer of the R-17. I took over from him early in the month. I was still twenty-one, and this was my first command. I might add I was what you might call a little tickled and vain about it, with my chest way out. We still were very short of officers, as I mentioned earlier. The only other officer I had on the R-17 with me was a warrant gunner. However, we managed to carry out all the operations with watch and watch as officer of the deck. The gunner was the executive officer, the gunnery officer, and the commissary officer, and I was all the rest. We managed to hang onto three of our chief petty officers on the R-17 after shipping over. We had trained them as junior diving officers and junior OODs and finally got them so they could stand daylight watches as officers of the deck. Finally, in the fall of 1920, we received a lieutenant (junior grade) who was an ex–chief quartermaster. He helped out a lot.

In April or May of 1920 Commander Nimitz relieved Commander Gygax as commander of Submarine Division Fourteen. We didn't know who this Commander Nimitz was, other than the fact that he had been on some of the earliest submarines, the A-boats and the B-boats. Also he, by the Navy Register, had received a course in training in diesel engines. But we didn't know much of anything about him, and we had been having considerable trouble with these diesel engines we had. They were called NELSECO engines; they were built by the Electric Boat Company.

Commander Thompson had been the commanding officer of the R-17 and then, when relieved, had become the base engineer and division engineer officer. After Commander Nimitz had been on the job about a week, he called Commander Thompson in for a meeting on the old *Chicago* and asked him what seemed to be the matter with the engines in the R-boats. Commander Thompson said, "Well, Commodore, they're just designed wrong. They're no good, and they won't run properly." He went on for about three or four minutes.

Commander Nimitz listened it out and said, "Yes, I hear you. You know, I was in on the design of those engines. I went through the building of them and supervised it. I went through the test and supervised that. We never heard anything at all, then, about what you're saying now. We didn't think anything like that could possibly be."

"Well," Thompson said, "okay, Commodore, I admit I don't know what it is all about, and I don't know how to fix it. We'd like to know how to fix it, but we don't know how."

Commander Nimitz said, "Well, that's fine. We'll see what we can find out." That was pretty much Commander Nimitz's method of operation. He let you hang yourself before telling you the truth about it.

The Holland-type submarines of that era had what were known as very vulnerable tails. When you came in alongside another submarine, the tail of the submarine could spin in toward it. The propeller blades would hit the propeller guards of the other submarine, and you got hit horribly. It was very easy to do. You could also come in at too much of an angle with the bow and hit the bow and bend it around. Well, I brought the *R-17* in alongside another submarine one day soon after Commander Nimitz had taken over, and my tail got in too close. I bent a couple of blades on the propeller. We had to admit that she had to either go in dry dock or the marine railway, or else pull them up high enough that you could change the blades—which you could sometimes—by the divers.

Naturally, I had to report it, because that meant I couldn't operate until I got that fixed up. So I went in and reported to the commodore what I'd done. I explained to him how long it would take to fix it. I couldn't carry out the oper-

Cdr. Chester Nimitz in the 1920s. *Naval Institute Photo Archive*

ations the next day, because they wouldn't have it done until the next afternoon. But they were working on it then, and it would take about two days to do it.

He made a statement: "Every submarine commander has a starting credit: one tail and one nose, or two tails, or two noses. When he's used up that credit, then he's going to be in trouble sometime. You're only half gone. You've only used one tail. Now, go on back and try not to take the rest of your credit." I might add that I've still got the credit for that other half.

7

Early Command

REAR ADM. GEORGE W.
BAUERNSCHMIDT, SUPPLY
CORPS, USN (RET.)

As Admiral Bauernschmidt explains in this memoir, his career took a decided turn when color blindness prevented him from serving any longer as a line officer. To continue to serve, he transferred to the Supply Corps, which proved to be a boon for the Navy. He brought to supply a practical knowledge of what the operating forces needed and was determined to provide it to them rather than citing various regulations as to why items might not be permissible for issue. Along with his knack for supply, Bauernschmidt was also a capable storyteller.

I N THE EARLY 1920s, while I was still an ensign, I was serving in the battleship *New Mexico* on the West Coast. At this time my wife Maude and I met Chester Nimitz and his family because we were the only two Navy families living in a development outside of San Pedro, California. I wanted to go into submarines, but Commander Nimitz suggested that I hold off until I made junior lieutenant. He explained that if I went to a submarine as an ensign, I would have a subordinate job without having a chance to command. I did as he suggested.

I left the *New Mexico* in Hawaii in June 1925 and went to the Submarine School. The Navy told me that I could go by destroyer through the Panama Canal, which would get me to New London Connecticut just in time for the school to start. Or I could get off the destroyer in San Diego and go overland, but I had to go at my own expense. Leave is something hard to come by, so I took the opportunity to go overland. I had just money enough for an upper berth and a ticket across the country, and enough left over to

The *R-2* provided an early command opportunity for Bauernschmidt, but color blindness knocked him out of the submarine service. *Naval Institute Photo Archive*

have a ham sandwich and a glass of milk three times a day.

Submarine School opened up a new type of work for me and was interesting. Two things worried me at the school. One was having to keep a notebook, which meant a tremendous amount of just brute effort to draw sketches and write down descriptions of various evolutions. It was necessary, but I remember it with displeasure. It was just a hell of a lot of work. The other was signaling. My mind just will not accept da-da-da, whether by ear or by eye, just as I have a blind spot with regard to languages. It was important for submariners to know blinker and buzzer. I worked hard at it while I was at the Submarine School, and I just got no place.

Well, I went from Submarine School to Submarine Division Nine out in Pearl Harbor and reported to the *R-5* as second officer. The full complement, I think, was three officers and thirty-two men, but they very seldom achieved

that. After a comparatively short time, I was transferred to the *R-3*, where I was not only the second but I was also the head of all the departments, there being no third. That was a bit onerous, but very instructive. You had your finger in every pie, and since all of them are interesting, there was plenty to do.

At that time there weren't many people who wanted to go into submarines, and there were never quite enough. At that time there was no extra pay for the officers. When the extra pay came in, then more officers were willing to go into the submarine business. You had to make so many dives a month in order for the enlisted men to get their submarine pay, and that was frequently a farce. If you were in port for repairs, or for any purpose, for any length of time, and it was apparent that your men weren't going to get in the dives necessary, you'd back off from the pier, trim down, sit on the bottom for a short time, surface, and then come back to the pier and chalk it up as a dive—just so the men could get their submarine pay. The commanding officer who missed getting in his necessary dives got some black looks from his crew.

In the spring of 1927, after I had been at Pearl Harbor a while, we got word that two officers were to be qualified to command submarines and ordered as commanding officers ahead of time because of vacancies. One of my classmates and I were the two selected, and instead of having to wait a year to qualify for command, we were qualified in about ten months. I took my examinations and passed them, and the examinations were very comprehensive. In order to qualify for command, among other things, you had to be able to operate every piece of equipment in the boat. So there was a great practical exam as well as a written and oral examination. In any event, I passed and became commanding officer of the *R-2*. That underscored the wisdom of Nimitz's advice to me.

The submarine base at Pearl was built of wooden buildings that were of a sort of nondescript character. The barracks were notable as being infested with bedbugs. Those bedbugs inevitably were brought to the boats, because the men used the same bedding in the barracks that they used in the boats. When we would go to sea, they'd bring their bedding down. Well, the *R-2* became infested, and I asked to have her fumigated. We went down to Honolulu to have it done, and they put a pickle barrel in the torpedo room with cyanide in it, dropped acid in it, then sealed up the boat with everybody off.

Well, after a couple of hours, after the gas had time to permeate the ship, we were supposed to open the hatches and leave them open for a short length of time, then start the main engines and pull air through the boat to ventilate it. Well, I, as all officers, would not send an enlisted man anyplace I wouldn't go. Since the engines had to be started, I started them. I put on a gas mask and went down in the boat and started the engines. I've never felt so lonesome in my life before or since.

During my time in the *R-3* and later in the *R-2*, I was detailed as air observer for section

attacks, when submarines would attack in formation—submerged. By flying over them, it was frequently possible to observe the manner in which they made their attacks. They aren't easy to spot from the air unless the light conditions are good. If you're going out cold and have no idea where they are, they're awfully hard to find.

I flew many times as observer for section attack until I made one flight and came in to find out that I had the overnight duty on board the old cruiser *Chicago*, which was used at Pearl Harbor as the submarine officers' quarters. I told a friend of mine to tell my wife that I wouldn't be home, and he forgot to do it. My wife, knowing that I was flying and I didn't come home, became very worried and eventually called up the *Chicago*. When I answered the phone and she recognized my voice, she hung up. She was satisfied I was in, but when I got home, she said, "Submarines or airplanes, but not both."

I had rather good luck in the *R-2* in that I was able to win an E. My scores for torpedo practices were rather high, but in most of them there was some lucky fluke—so much so that my division commander told me he'd rather have my luck than a license to steal. I once made a very faulty approach, made two or three mistakes in the approach. The enlisted man who was running the selector switch for me turned it too fast, washed out all of my errors, and I got a hit.

My first cruise in the *R-2* went to Hilo, on the Big Island of Hawaii. While I was there I found a Japanese practice squadron present with Vice Admiral Osami Nagano in command. Since I was the only American ship present, I made my official call on Vice Admiral Nagano, and then on to the commanding officer of his flagship and the two officers' messes. This was somewhat unfortunate, because the admiral gave me cocktails, and the commanding officer of the ship gave me Scotch and soda. In the two officers' messes, one gave me highballs and the next one gave me beer. I left the ship and got on a crack on the dock and followed it down to my boat and got into my bunk.

By the time the effects of the call had worn off, I was called and told that Admiral Nagano's aide was approaching, returning the admiral's call. So I went down and greeted him and, much to his surprise, took him below, into the tiny space that passed as a wardroom, and gave him coffee in exchange for the liquor that I'd had from his navy. He was surprised that I'd take him below, but there wasn't a damn thing he could see.

When I took him below he had to take off his sword and park it up against the fairwater. After he'd gone, the chief of the boat called me and said, "Captain, there's a job for you here. While you were down below, there was a discussion as to whether that sword of the Japanese was sharp enough, and one of the men drew it and wet his thumb and ran it down the blade. You've got to sew his thumb up." Well, a commanding officer of a submarine has to be everything. I sewed up the thumb.

The submarines of that era had limited endurance, so the time at sea was usually brief. Once we had a fleet exercise problem that was due to take a week or more. Recognizing the fact that the limited-capacity icebox then standard equipment in the R-boats would provide us with fresh provisions for only about three days, I had one torpedo tube emptied, cleaned, filled with fresh fruits and vegetables, and charged with nitrogen. When we were out of ice, we began opening this and found that our fresh produce kept very well. Other submariners were not impressed by the results. They didn't feel that I should immobilize a torpedo tube.

Well, this exercise took us halfway to San Francisco, and the R-2 was the farthest out of the submarines and had leaky fuel tanks. As the exercise was reaching its end, I came to the conclusion that we were about out of fuel. So I left the exercise without authority, since we had radio silence, and returned to Pearl Harbor. I actually ran out of fuel off of Honolulu Harbor and had to go to the fuel docks on my batteries.

Subsequent to this fleet exercise, there were other exercises with the Battle Fleet, during which the R-2 got in an attack on a capital ship and, upon surfacing, had a hard time avoiding the big ships with which it found itself surrounded. When the exercises were over, Rear Adm. Ridley

McLean began inspecting the submarines at Pearl Harbor. He was commander, Submarine Divisions, Battle Force at the time and, unfortunately, not a submariner himself.

The first boat that he inspected he criticized severely because in leaving Pearl Harbor and negotiating the channel on the way to the sea, he said the boat's commander operated his boat as though he were running a motorboat, doing the whole thing by seaman's eye and not using the plotting board, as was standard on capital ships, with which McLean was very familiar. When it came the R-2's turn to be inspected, my second officer and I went through the motions of plotting our way down the channel and satisfied Admiral McLean—who never realized that the boat was always at least one and sometimes two turns of the channel ahead of the plot.

The engineer officer on McLean's staff asked for the status of our battery. I replied that I had ten minutes at the one-hour rate, which meant that I had, when fully charged, one-sixth of a normal rated capacity, because the battery was a sick battery which I had tried to have replaced. He misunderstood me and thought I said ten minutes out at the one-hour rate. So when we were at sea, I was given a series of evolutions—man overboard, a buoy to pick up, collision drill, abandon ship, back emergency—and then ordered to make a crash dive. The sick battery died with the bow planes on hard dive and a big angle on the boat.

The rated depth of the boats was two hundred feet, and the pressure gauge in the control room registered two hundred feet at the time that forward motion was stopped, which meant that the forward end of the boat was well below two hundred feet. She was sort of standing on her nose. I executed standard doctrine for emergency. I backed, blew the ballast tanks, and prayed. There was enough juice left in the battery so that the motors turned over, thump, thump, thump, and checked our forward motion. Eventually the blown ballast tanks brought us up to the surface.

About this time, Admiral McLean, who'd been checking publications in the wardroom, stuck his head into the control room and asked, "Are we down yet?" Then he saw the hats on the hair ends of his staff. The staff engineer explained that he had misunderstood what I'd said about the battery. Admiral McLean called the inspection off. He was somewhat indignant and, upon his return to the *Holland*, which was his flagship, had his heart examined and then issued orders for me to go by myself to Lahaina Roads, off the island of Maui, for submerged training. If he had known anything about submarines, he certainly would have sent me with at least a tender, believing, as he did, that I and my crew were improperly trained. He never understood the sick battery proposition.

Sometime later, I submitted suggestions for structural changes in the doors to submarines to prevent the drawing of a vacuum in a boat, in the event that a door was suddenly slammed. Another suggestion was to mount the emergency lights on spring-loaded fixtures such as are in turrets, so that when the submarine was depth-charged, the light filaments would not break in the emergency lights, as they undoubtedly would in the fixed lights. Both of these suggestions were forwarded with adverse recommendations by Admiral McLean's staff. I was amused some ten years later, when I was at the Naval Research Laboratory, to find them working on a program to provide submarines with shock-resistant emergency lights.

After this cruise, which was in 1928, I took the crew to the Marine rifle range and qualified most of them in the use of small arms. My wife and children accompanied me to the range, where we lived in tents. It was very pleasant. Also, at long last, the *R-2* got a new battery. As the battery was being installed, I went on leave back to Maryland, and upon my return to Pearl I found that submariners were now granted submarine pay. It was a 25 percent increase in your base pay. However, at almost the same time I was found color-blind on an annual physical examination and relieved of command. So I drew the extra pay for about four months and never again served in submarines.

8

Loss of the *S-51* and *S-4*

ADM. ROBERT L. DENNISON,
USN (RET.)

Throughout its history, the U.S. Navy has lost several submarines in peacetime accidents. Each such loss has provided lessons that led to improvements in safety and rescue capabilities. Two submarines went down in the 1920s—the *S-51* in September 1925 and the *S-4* in December 1927. Each went to the bottom as the result of a collision with a surface ship. Almost all hands died when the submarines were lost: thirty-three of thirty-six in the *S-51* and all thirty-eight in the *S-4*. Six men in the *S-4* survived the sinking, but at that time the Navy did not have the capability to rescue crew members from boats trapped on the bottom. Out of these experiences came the McCann rescue chamber and the Momsen lung for breathing while ascending to the surface. Ens. Robert Dennison was a young naval officer at the time. Nearly forty years later he played a prominent role in naval history as commander in chief, Atlantic Fleet during the Cuban Missile Crisis.

WHEN I GRADUATED from the Naval Academy in 1923, I was assigned to the battleship *Arkansas* and soon discovered that one of the opportunities a young naval officer had for an early command was to go into the submarine service. In those days, all officers assigned to submarines had requested such duty, and in those days there was no increase in pay for hazardous duty, the equivalent of flight pay for an aviator. So it truly was a volunteer service.

When I found out that there was an opportunity for an early command in submarines, I consulted with a couple of officers whose views I respected. They advised me that if I really was sure I wanted to go into that kind of duty, it was quite

In the 1920s the submarines *S-50* and *S-51* operated together. Then, after a fatal collision sank the *S-51*, her sister stood vigil over her grave. *Naval Institute Photo Archive*

true that my chances for an early command were greatly enhanced, as compared with going to a destroyer or a cruiser or a battleship. I looked at it more as an opportunity to practice my profession, which I believe is command, rather than as specialization in submarines.

In any event, having made the decision, I applied for Submarine School and was accepted. I attended the school in New London Connecticut, and the boats that we used for training in those days were the old N and O classes. During my period of service at the school I was brought up short by recognition of the hazards of this duty when the *S-51* was sunk off Block Island.

Students were assigned to the *S-50* and *S-51* for the purpose of witnessing what was called an availability trial. These trials were made periodically by submarines in those days; they were both surfaced and submerged, and the trials lasted over a period, I believe, of about eighteen hours. In the *S-50* I was officer of the deck on the first watch, 8:00 PM to midnight, just before the *S-51* was in collision with the SS *City of Rome*. It was a beautiful night, completely clear. The sea was calm. We were in signal communication by blinking light until shortly before I went off watch.

The next morning, when we surfaced off New London to go up the river to the base, we were met by a large group of small craft, tugs, and one thing and another, going out to find the submarine that was sunk. They didn't know until they saw us whether it was the *S-50* or the *S-51*. As everybody knows, it turned into a salvage operation. The people were lost, although the water was really quite shallow.

Two years later, when I was assigned to the *S-8*, I experienced the sinking of the *S-4* after she was hit by the Coast Guard destroyer *Paulding* off Provincetown, Massachusetts. The *S-4* and the *S-8* were in the Portsmouth Navy Yard for certain modifications to their torpedo shutters. After this overhaul we were to go down south of Provincetown for certain trials, including submerged runs over a measured mile. I forget the number of days that were allotted for this. It was around Christmastime in 1927. The *S-8* finished her trials earlier than had been scheduled, so we turned the range over to the *S-4*. She started on her trials, and we started on around Cape Cod to go back to New London. The Navy in those days didn't have enough money to let us go through the ship canal, so we had to go all the way around in the rough and cold weather. Our radio transmitter went out, our receiver didn't, and after a few hours we heard a call for us on the radio and then a call for the

Capt. Ernest J. King (*center*) commanded the submarine base at New London from 1923 to 1926. He directed the salvage of the *S-51*, and that led to his later assignment in connection with the recovery of the *S-4*. He is shown here in early 1928 with individuals who had a prominent role in the *S-4* operation, Cdr. Harold E. Saunders (in the stocking cap) and Lt. Henry Hartley, commanding officer of the submarine rescue ship *Falcon*. *Naval Institute Photo Archive*

S-4. We couldn't reply, of course, and the *S-4* was on the bottom. So we turned around immediately, because we knew something had happened.

On the way back, we picked up more information, and we got back off Provincetown, as I recall, around midnight, perhaps a little before. We were the only ones there, and we were able to locate the *S-4* with our sonar and anchored quite close to her. We heard pounding from her hull. The water was relatively shallow, but the weather was terrible. It was so bad that the divers had an almost impossible job. So that, too, turned into a tragedy. We sent them down instructions, because we were going to have a lot of questions. They were to answer with one hammer rap on the hull for yes and two raps for no.

So we went all through the boat: "Is the engine room flooded? Is the control room flooded? Are there any survivors in the various compartments?" Well, it turned out there weren't any survivors except in the torpedo room. The rest of the boat was flooded, and, again, this had to be a salvage operation. In those days we didn't have the submarine rescue chamber that was later developed, along with the Momsen lung.

So that was very tragic and very sad, too. Two of my classmates were in the *S-4*. It was heartbreaking, because one of the very last messages we got in the prearranged code was, "Is there any hope?" We said, "Yes," everything possible was being done. But they couldn't be rescued, and all those men were lost.

After it became a salvage operation, Congressman Fiorello La Guardia, later the mayor of New York City and a very colorful character, came up to witness what was going on. He was sort of a fire-engine-chasing type. But he was quite a man,

The salvaged *S-4* is shown alongside the *Falcon* in December 1928 after the submarine had been recommissioned. She returned to active service until decommissioned in 1933. *Naval Institute Photo Archive*

and he came up to get in on this act and came aboard the *S-8*. We had no place for him, but I had to be up most of the time anyhow, so I gave him my bunk. And, believe me, it was wet and damp, and the whole boat was cold. The winter off Cape Cod is not too pleasant.

Then we were ordered back to New London to try out a fitting to be used on the *S-4*. We were a sister ship, obviously, so we were similar. Again, we went around the cape, and La Guardia almost got pneumonia. He was seasick and terribly uncomfortable and wet. As we were coming into New London, he talked to me about submarine duty and asked how we stood it. I told him it was because we enjoyed it, we volunteered for it, and the conditions were just part of the business. He

said, "Don't you get any money to take care of ruining your clothes and all the discomfort and hazardous duty?"

I said, "No, we don't." The enlisted men in those days got a dollar a dive, up to a certain number each month. The crewmen didn't have to pressure the skipper to make the dives, because we were interested in having these men get as much pay as they could, and the dives provided useful training experience. La Guardia was astounded at the idea that the officers in submarines didn't get any extra pay, so he said, "My God, when I get back to Congress I'm going to take care of it." And unlike many promises, this one was made good, and he did get a law through for us.

9

Far East Duty

REAR ADM. ERNEST M. ELLER,
USN (RET.)

In the course of a distinguished career that included service on Adm. Chester Nimitz's staff during World War II, Ernest Eller had a variety of duties. He also had a knack for expressing his thoughts that made him the winner of the Naval Institute's General Prize Essay Contest in 1932, 1942, and 1950. In the late 1940s he was the Navy's director of public information, and from 1956 to 1970 he was the director of naval history. The admiral had a gift for describing his experiences. Here are some of his observations about service in the submarine S-33. As an ensign he reported on board in December 1927 following battleship duty and instruction at the Submarine School.

N EAR THE END of a trip across the Pacific in the transport *Henderson*, my wife Agnes and I arrived in the Philippines. We went through San Bernardino Strait. Near it is a tall mountain, an extinct volcano that must be a mile and a half high. I remember seeing it far at sea, maybe fifty or sixty miles away. That was my first sight of the Philippines. Manila Bay was as fascinating as I thought it would be. It's really an inland sea, it's so large. We got settled in the Manila area, and then I reported to the *S-33*. This was in Submarine Division Sixteen, which was tended by the USS *Beaver*, a former merchant ship that had been taken over and converted to a tender in World War I. There was also another tender, the USS *Canopus*, with another division, so we had two divisions of submarines out there. We were based at the Cavite Navy Yard, which is close to Manila.

Mother ship *Beaver* looks after her flock of S-boats in the Far East. *Naval Institute Photo Archive*

We soon went up to Olongapo in Subic Bay, which is up the coast of Luzon, partway to Lingayen Gulf. We had a dry dock there, perhaps the old *Dewey* that was towed out there in the early 1900s. The submarine dry-docked, and we lived in government quarters. The government quarters for us young couples consisted of one building, which might have been a converted barracks. Each couple had one room, separated from the next by a partial bulkhead up to about two feet from the ceiling—not much privacy. We cooked some on the beach, and there may have been a common stove on the porch. I don't remember whether there were outside heads or not. For all this we sacrificed forty dollars a month, nearly a fourth of an ensign's pay.

My skipper in the *S-33* was Lt. Joseph "Nino" Gregory, and the exec was a jaygee, Jimmy Guillot. We had four officers and about thirty-five men. I had navigation, communications (radio and signals), supply, and legal. We didn't have much legal trouble, because the chief of the boat was pretty well allowed to run the discipline, much as the Marines do with their master sergeants—a very good system. In general, this worked perfectly. The chief of the boat was Hulse, a longtime submariner, a very clean-cut and admirable man, very efficient and capable. He knew exactly what to do in a crisis and always did it—a marvelous man to be associated with.

Each one of us had a small stateroom about ten feet long and five or six feet wide, with a bunk, a desk, and a very narrow locker. We kept our clothes and equipment in the tender. When you went on the submarine, you took only what you would have to have for that trip. We rarely were at sea longer than three or four days. Then you'd take a couple of changes of shirts, underwear, and socks. This was all you needed. Ens. Max Stormes and I occupied the same cubbyhole, and it was not much bigger than a double coffin. He slept in the upper bunk, because I was the navigator and stood all the four o'clock to eight o'clock watches. I did the star sights for celestial navigation in the morning and evening, so being in the lower bunk meant I could get out of the bunk and up on deck without bothering Max. The bunks were about two feet wide, and then you had about two feet more between you and the bare hull of the ship, because she was only 18 feet wide.

Of course, our main mission was training in an area where we might have to operate during war, so as to get acclimated to the conditions. Our submariners, of course, found that very useful when they were operating there in World War II. In fact, some of the ports that we went into during the war, the only naval officers who'd been there and knew anything about them were a few submariners and destroyermen.

The training year of any ship is a constantly busy period. We dived constantly, often several times a day. Much of our training was in the Manila Bay or at the edge of the bay. We sometimes operated to the north of the island of Corregidor, right at the tip of the Bataan Peninsula. The Philippines are in tropical waters, and this was one of the reasons that we went up to China in the springtime, because the climate was cooler. Manila had its rains, and it was always hot, even in the winter. There was some rain at any time, but it was hotter and very muggy in the summer. We got under way for China in late February or early March of 1928, not long after I joined the ship. Our division ran in column; I think we were the second sub astern of the *Beaver*. I've forgotten the interval between boats. It may have been two thousand yards in order to allow maneuvering and diving.

I was a poor celestial navigator to start with, because when we first sailed out of Manila and hit the northeast monsoon, I got seasick right away. I had a big bucket on the bridge, in order not to spray anybody, and I hoped I could navigate. On our first trip, we got out of sight of land fairly soon. Seasick, I didn't do too well on the sun sight. The captain left me alone, but we had to send our eight o'clock position at night to the flagship. Even though seasick, I could still handle dead reckoning and knew roughly where we were. The ship was rolling and pitching and yawing and heaving, the spray beating in my face, the horizon misty, and the sextant foggy. I had about as bad star sights as you could imagine. I got a fix with a triangle about ten miles wide, and it ended up being a hundred miles ashore on Luzon, so I reported the dead reckoning position. By the time we held war games off Shanghai later, I got pretty good. I'd wrap my leg around the stanchion, take decent sights with the sextant, and navigate with fair accuracy.

We went first to Hong Kong, which is one of a handful of the most beautiful views in the world. We approached it from the sea, through a difficult channel, with Mount Victoria as a backdrop. At night there's a gold tiara of light around it. In Hong Kong one little incident shows the character of the Chinese. Somebody told me about a tailor. I went to his shop, and he cut me out a suit from cloth that I liked very much. We were there only two or three days. I went in the last day to pick it up, but it didn't fit, so I said, "I'm sorry, I can't take it, and there isn't time to change it."

He said, "All right. Come back next time, I'll have it ready."

So we sailed, and in the autumn we stopped en route to Manila. About six months had passed. I walked into his shop and said, "Where's my suit?" He looked at me about a minute, then reached down behind the counter, pulled out a dusty package, and there was the suit. I tried it on, but it didn't fit, because I think I'd changed.

He said, "I fix, I fix." We were staying only overnight. The next morning it hadn't come, and we were about to cast off from the *Beaver*. Here came this sampan, paddling madly up to us. The tailor said, "Here's your suit."

I'd left everything in my little safe in the *Beaver*, so I said, "I don't have my money. I'm sorry."

He said, "All right, pay when you come back next time." So the next spring, when we came through, I went in and paid him, and it was all right. They had a custom of tearing up IOUs at

American bluejackets, armed with rifles, march down Kiukiang Road in Shanghai, China. The photo is reminiscent of a scene in the movie *Sand Pebbles* about a U.S. Navy gunboat in China during the interwar period. *Naval Institute Photo Archive; from Ewing Galloway*

New Year's, but I don't think it applied to foreigners. We could go anywhere and sign a chit. The Chinese would take it. They perhaps thought if you didn't come back, a friend of yours would come. I think they were treated honestly by most on account of that.

Among the various ports we visited were Swatow, Amoy, and Canton. I remember the run from Amoy to Shanghai was about two days or maybe three. We trained considerably en route: diving, making attack approaches, holding signal practice, and so on. One of the unique sights I've seen at sea was the sudden change from the blue-green of the East China Sea to a silt tan. There was a sharp dividing line—on one side green, and on the other a muddy yellow. Beyond the sight of land, the mighty Yangtze was reaching far out to sea. I suppose this was the ebb tide, but nevertheless we entered the mouth of the Yangtze and

still couldn't see land. It's just a part of the ocean as far as you can determine. At some distance inside the mouth, we turned left and went up the Whangpoo [now Huangpu] River to Shanghai.

During our voyage, most of our wives, if not all, arranged transportation on the P&O line, and we met them at Shanghai. I remember in Shanghai we moored alongside the *Beaver* in the Whangpoo. The tender would have movies at night. When I had the duty, Agnes would come on board for dinner and go to the movies with me. These were shown on the fantail, so people could see them from the shore, and the Chinese crowded the dock. These were silent movies, of course, so if you couldn't read the flashes of narration, you didn't know what was happening. A slapstick comedy evoked only silence on the dock. A dolorous love scene or a very sad and tragic moment brought forth a

In the months when relatively cool weather made the Philippines inviting, the U.S. Asiatic Fleet operated there. This scene shows the Jones Bridge over Manila's Pasig River. The sign on the building at right reads, Texaco: Champagne of Motor Oils. *Naval Institute Photo Archive; from Ewing Galloway*

great uproar of laughter. I don't know what they were thinking.

Agnes was staying at a very nice pension [hotel], Père Robert, not too far from the French Club, which was one of the delightful clubs of the world. On its dance floor you seemed to be dancing on springs. I think it must have been suspended. It had wonderful music, wonderful French food, Chinese food, Russian. We were there a couple of times, and it was just out of this world.

We were in Shanghai a short time, then sailed for Tsingtao [Qingdao], our summer operating area. Tsingtao had been built up by the Germans early in the century and had been captured by the Japanese in a very bitter siege during World War I. The Japanese were still in Tsingtao, which was a strategic port. It is far out on Shantung [Shandong] Peninsula, which marks the end of the Yellow Sea and the beginning of the Gulf of Chihli

[Zhili]. This was the submariners' operating area. Around the cape, at Wei-hai-wei [Weihai], south by east of Darien, was the British operating base. On beyond, maybe twenty-five or thirty miles, lay Chefoo [Zhifu Island], where our destroyers operated in the summer.

We had the best part, because the Germans had made a model city out of Tsingtao. They had built good solid buildings, widened the streets and lined them with trees, and built nice homes and hotels. We stayed at an inn four or five stories high, fairly close to the landing, as did lots of others in the Submarine Force. One interesting thing about China was the narrow margin of existence. I witnessed that everywhere but first appreciated it on an expedition out into the country from Tsingtao. I saw a very nice young man who had been educated enough in English to converse. He was catching grasshoppers to eat, but he was abashed and wouldn't tell me that. He said, oh, he was just catching them, but everyone knew why he was doing it.

In a port city the Chinese always fought for our garbage from the *Beaver*. We didn't have much in the submarines, because in port we all lived in the tender. A garbage sampan would come alongside. I remember one in Shanghai. The man had a couple of women in the boat, his wife and daughter, I suppose, and a little boy. He would catch the garbage in a big pot as it came down the garbage chute at the stern of the ship. He would pay for the privilege by providing a sampan with boatman for each submarine. I suppose he gave them part of the food from the garbage. He tried to get us to segregate the garbage, and sometimes the cook did, but this man took anything. Americans, as you know, are great wasters, while the Chinese were on a very narrow margin of existence.

In Tsingtao we went through our general gunnery, communications, battle efficiency competition, including engineering trials, high-speed runs, and so on. It was an excellent operating area, with few ships coming in and out, so we had clear operating grounds, except for the local junks and sampans. These were always around. Once, on a dive while we were coming up the coast, I was standing watch on the periscope. Our course converged on a big sampan or small junk with eyes painted on the bow to scare away the devil. Just as we got about twenty yards away—we were going to clear him because the bearing was opening all right—one of the fellows on the sampan saw this big eye, our periscope, coming at him. You've never seen such a wild thrashing of oars. The last time I saw him, the sampan was going over the horizon. I'm sure that to this day he tells about being chased by a sea serpent.

From Tsingtao we operated through the summer, conducting training exercises and war games. I can't remember having any problems with diving. Most troubles you have in diving come from a skipper who's indecisive and an exec who doesn't check. The exec is supposed to check every possible thing that could go wrong. Each person on a station reports ready, and a

group of lights comes on in the control room.

We were small, only a little over 150 feet long, and most of the controls were in the control room itself. The main problem you had to think about was the main induction valve, where the air came in for the engines. If you were cruising on the surface, half submerged, with just your conning tower exposed, you could still draw air in for the engine and the dive, first closing the main induction. The batteries would last for a while. They were huge batteries, about eighteen inches square, as I remember, and there were 120 of them. They covered the bilge of the boat from well forward to well aft. They would drive you at fairly good speed, maybe ten or eleven knots, for an hour or so. In a long dive at an economical speed of one or two knots, they could last at least twenty-four hours and I think longer.

We went through a typhoon once, and that was quite an experience. I've never seen rollers like them. They weren't waves but just great rolling tidal waves, with such large valleys between them that the boat would go down, completely out of sight of the horizon. With a big roller ahead and a roller astern, they must have been twenty or thirty feet high. We were battened down, everything closed except the bridge hatch, running low in the water so as to try to get as little trouble from the motion as possible, but you couldn't get away from it. We tried submerging once in those circumstances, but it was awful. The captain went down to periscope depth, and the sub was kicked around just as much. So he went down to nearly two hundred feet, and there was heavy motion even down there. It wasn't nearly the same, of course, but we were rolling, and with the foul air you'd rather go topside and take it.

The atmosphere on board the *S-33* got pretty thick at any time. This finally drove me out of submarines, because it ruined my stomach. The constant atmospheric changes, to which the body is not adjusted, affected some men's hearts, others' ears, and others' stomachs. Grease was in the air, and also a continuing buildup in carbon dioxide and a decrease in oxygen. We did purify with lime, to take out the carbon dioxide, and

This is the interior of the control room in the *S-45*, which was commissioned in March 1925, a little more than two years after Eller's *S-33* went into service. *National Archives: 19-9-9939-V; courtesy of Thomas Hone*

we had air bottles with oxygen to release as needed. Besides all this, the pressure changes are considerable when you go down to two hundred feet or even one hundred. The humidity got outrageous. The bulkheads dripped like Niagara Falls. And you had no room; you couldn't exercise. Even in good weather on deck, you had no deck room to amount to anything. It wasn't a healthy sort of life. On the other hand, we didn't stay at sea long, ordinarily only two, three, or four days. After a while, I loved navigation, and I loved submarines. I would have stayed in them if my stomach hadn't driven me out.

In the summer of 1929, we got word that Agnes's only sister had died; they were very close. That just broke her up, and it broke me up too. At the same time, my stomach was about to kill

me, and I got the idea that I ought to get out of the Navy. So I put in my resignation request and finished up the admiral's inspection, which we had just before we left. Then Agnes and I boarded the transport *Chaumont*. After quite a bit of sightseeing in various places we eventually got back to the United States and went to Washington. A medical examination showed there was something wrong with my stomach, so they put me in the hospital, then located at the old naval observatory, right downtown at Twenty-first and Virginia. They cut out an epigastric hernia, which I'd never heard of before. The doctor said, "You're still fit for active duty." Somebody from the Navy Department talked to me, and I withdrew the application to resign, but I never again served in submarines.

10

R-Boat Service

REAR ADM. EDWARD K. WALKER,
USN (RET.)

After graduating from the United States Naval Academy in 1925, Ed Walker served in coal-burning battleships on the East Coast. At that point he was designated as a "volunteer" to go to Submarine School, as were a number of his contemporaries. At the time going into submarines wasn't necessarily a permanent career commitment, but it did expose a number of junior officers to the boats. Some of them stayed and some didn't. Walker, for example, was skipper of the destroyer *Mayrant* during World War II and had Franklin D. Roosevelt Jr. as his executive officer. As a junior officer, he was assigned to Hawaii for duty in the tropical paradise that was home port mainly for submariners because the shipyard at Pearl Harbor was not yet nearly so well developed as it later became.

GOING TO MY FIRST duty from Submarine School, January 1928, I was assigned to the *R-8*. Going to Honolulu was like arriving in the land of milk and honey in those days. The Royal Hawaiian Hotel had just been built. The Moana was there, and the Halekulani, and that was it as far as Waikiki Beach. There was practically nothing on the far side of Kalakaua Avenue. The surfboard club was down there on the beach, down toward Diamond Head somewhere, and it was just a little wooden building. When we first got there, the skipper, Lt. E. I. McQuiston, took us in for two or three days. Then we found a little one-bedroom furnished house, very small, for fifty dollars a month. We lived in that for four or five months, and then moved into a new development on the Ala Wai Canal. It's about ten or twelve miles

These close-ups focus on the USS *R-1* and *R-4*, which were in Submarine Division Nine along with Walker's *R-8*. Each was armed with one 3-inch deck gun and four 21-inch torpedo tubes. R-1 *from National Archives: 19E-33-GG, Box 13, courtesy of Thomas Hone;* R-4 *from Naval Institute Photo Archive*

from Honolulu to Pearl Harbor, and the trains weren't much help, so the only way to get back and forth was by automobile. We lived in town the whole time. There were no quarters at all on the submarine base. Very few of the enlisted men were married; they couldn't afford it. A chief petty officer at that time got $99 a month, and if he was a permanent chief he got $125 a month.

I was assigned first to the *R-8*. My second commanding officer in that boat was Lt. George Dana. He had been assigned to the *S-51* and was detached just two or three days before it was sunk in 1925. In the R-boats we had one built-in bunk for the skipper and a couple of pipe-frame bunks just forward of his for the second and third officers. There were only three officers and a complement of twenty-five men. In this officer part was a little table like a card table with three chairs around it, and that's where we ate. Nobody had a separate room.

Our maximum speed was about thirteen knots, so we couldn't keep up with the fleet. Our mission was to act as shore defensive boats. The longest normally we ever went to sea was for fourteen days. These were simulated war patrol cruises; we had to do them once a year. These patrols went to Lahaina Roads off the island of Maui. We had twenty R-boats out there at that time. The *R-1* to *R-10* made up Submarine Division Nine, and the *R-11* to *R-20* were Division Fourteen. We had a squadron commander and two division commanders. We had a big office ashore, in the same place the submarine base was later. On one side there was a row of ten desks, room for two people at a desk and somebody else in chairs, enough for everybody. On the other side of this long room were the desks and so forth of the other division. We had the old cruiser *Chicago* then as a station ship for the submarines, and when we had to stay out there overnight on duty, we slept in the *Chicago*. When they built the new cruiser *Chicago*, the name of the old one was changed to *Alton*.

The R-boats seldom operated together; practically all operations were single. Most of the time we were like bankers. We were out at eight o'clock in the morning and back and tied up at four o'clock in the afternoon. And we'd run target practice on either destroyers or rescue vessels or something of that nature. Anything that was available was used as a target for firing torpedoes, and then we'd have to pick up the torpedoes and bring them in. In the R-boats we had no stern tubes and only four in the bow.

Of course, we had no torpedo control system. We had two things. We had what they called an "is-was," which was just a couple of circles with a compass on them. You could set one for your own course and also set for the angle on the bow of the target and from that figure out the target's course. And we had something called an angle solver. You set that up to find out what bearing to set your periscope on and to know when to fire the torpedo. You'd take just as few observations as you could so you wouldn't get sighted, because if you got sighted, you got penalized.

We would run against the tender *Seagull*. She would go only about twelve knots. But once in a while we'd get some destroyers assigned to us, and they would go up to twenty or twenty-five knots to train us in making high-speed approaches and zigzag approaches. Practically all the runs were zigzag runs, but at ten or twelve knots it wasn't too difficult. We had the so-called attack teacher that we all used to practice attack techniques on. It was on the beach and simulated an attack on a ship with various models put on the attack teacher to represent the type of ship you were going to attack.

When the boat was in port the enlisted men lived in barracks. They were screened, and the men all had bunks in this. There was also a mess hall for the men. When we'd go out for, say, fourteen days, we'd have to get as much food as we could. We didn't have any ice machines; we had literally an icebox. If there was enough ice in it for three days, you couldn't get any food in it. If there was food in it, you couldn't get any ice in it. So, in effect, we lived on canned food. It was somewhere around 1929 that they put in icemakers in each one of the R-boats. We thought we had died and gone to heaven. First of all, we could keep a lot more perishable food than we ever could before. And, of course, in a submarine the officers and the crew all ate the same chow. It all came out of the same frying pan. We had one mess boy to look after the officers. He was usually a Filipino boy, and he served our meals.

The smoke from frying the food was taken care of by the diesels, because you'd generally run with the main hatch in the conning tower open, and those diesels, of course, took an awful lot of air. That would pull the air right through the boat. But so many days of these fourteen-day patrols you had to be submerged all day long. Well, I tell you, with twenty-five or thirty people sweating in that boat and with 80-degree temperature, by the time you surfaced at night things were pretty raunchy.

Then as part of that cruise and training, we always had to fire a short-range battle practice with the deck gun. We'd submerge and make an attack on a target, then we'd come up and fire sixteen or eighteen rounds from the 3-inch gun. When you surfaced, you had to get off all the waterproof equipment, get the shells up through the hatch, load the gun and fire, then put all the waterproofing equipment on the gun, back down the hatch, back down to diving depth, and then fire water slugs out the torpedo tubes. It was really quite a thing, and you had only a very short time. You really had to train for it.

Even the skipper had to stand underway watches, because there were only three officers. You'd be pretty tired at the end of fourteen days of a three-section watch. We took one trip from Pearl Harbor to San Diego in the spring of 1930; it took us fifteen days. For the first three days we were in almost a typhoon, and every other wave was going right over the bridge, so you had to lash yourself to the bridge. And so much water was coming down the hatch that for part of the time we could run on only one engine, because we couldn't get enough air through the high induction to run on two. After two days we could still see the light on the north of Molokai. That was really something. That was quite a trip.

I was the engineer officer for about three and a half years in the *R-8*. The diesel engines could cause you lots of headaches. I remember one endurance run we were on when we couldn't get enough air pressure. We hooked up to the air compressors to put more into the air bottles, and the engine room was just black with smoke. You couldn't see where you were going. We finally had to give up the run. We just couldn't get air enough to run the diesels. Another time we made a trip over to Kauai, and on the way back one engine conked out and then another engine conked out. We were anchored just around the corner from Barbers Point on Oahu. We also had trouble with our radio, so we couldn't send any messages. First thing we knew, out came a boat looking for us to see what had happened.

With only about twenty-five men to do all the jobs, they had to be pretty versatile. We'd generally have about eight or ten in the engineering department, and then you'd generally have a chief petty officer and two or three electricians. And you had a quartermaster and a signalman and about eight or ten seamen second class. I know we had one enlisted man by the name of Howley. He was a first-class quartermaster. The kid could dive the boat all by himself. He could sound the diving alarm, go down the hatch, close the hatch, come down into the control room, grab the stern planes with his left hand and the bow planes with his right—they were electrically operated—and dive the boat.

Howley was a kid they picked off the New York waterfront just after World War I. I know the exec and I had to get out and get downtown one night to keep him from marrying a woman with leprosy. Oh, gee. These enlisted men were just like children in those days. And, of course, you lived right on top of them. You got a very liberal education about sex in a very short time. As somebody said, "If they weren't doing it, they were talking about doing it." Holy mackerel! Oh, they were something.

11

Oddball S-Boat

REAR ADM. WILLIAM D. IRVIN,
USN (RET.)

Much has been made, and properly so, about the enormous contributions that Adm. Hyman Rickover made in bringing the U.S. Navy into the nuclear age in the 1950s. The USS *Nautilus*, the world's first nuclear-powered submarine, was a monument to his vision and his methods. Subsequently, thousands of submariners got into his program only after undergoing his scrutiny and impressing him with their dedication. His work was his hobby, and he seemed to be doing it every waking hour. Rickover's own undersea experience was in two diesel submarines. After attending Submarine School in 1930 he served briefly in the *S-9* and then spent 1931 to 1933 in the *S-48*. One of his shipmates in the latter was Lt. (j.g.) Bill Irvin, who reported on board in 1932, fresh out of Submarine School.

WE HAD a very good tour up in the Submarine School, in the winter session, January to June. They posted the vacancies, and we students were to make application for different spots. Well, there was no vacancy for China. Nevertheless, I wanted to go to China, so I put in my request. The officer in charge of the school called me up and raised hell with me for being impertinent. There were no vacancies for China, and why did I put it down there?

I said, "Well, I want to clearly indicate that I want to go back to China again. I had some experience running around with the submarine people in China, and I thought it was really great, and I'd like to be there."

There were vacancies in Panama, one in particular in the *S-48*. Everybody really shunned that. The *S-48* had quite a reputation; she was one of

The calm waters of the harbor mirror the *S-48*, shown here at Coco Solo in the Canal Zone in the 1930s. *Naval Institute Photo Archive*

four S-boats that were really trouble prone. In 1925 she had run aground on a shoal up at Portsmouth and was badly damaged. The Navy was going to abandon her, but the shipyard workers brought so much pressure to bear that it forced the Navy to take action, bring her into the Portsmouth Navy Yard, and put her back into shape again. In 1927 and 1928 she was repaired, and the shipyard put a twenty-five-foot section in the middle, so she was that much longer than when she started.

The *S-48* had a faculty for getting into trouble every day of the week. Everything that could go wrong went wrong. Furthermore, she seemed to get the damnedest lineup of skippers. She went down to Panama in 1931, and she was an oddball. Nobody asked for her, and after my little go with the officer in charge at the school, I found myself assigned to the vacant billet in the *S-48*.

So my wife Carolyn and I went off to Panama, and the first year was pretty much of a nightmare. We had no place to live, so we had to live in vacation quarters. When a Canal Zone worker would go back to the States on leave, he would rent out his quarters while he was gone. In the first eleven months we moved thirteen times. Finally, at the end of eleven months, Carolyn said, "To hell with this," and she went back to the States. We moved into one place on a Friday afternoon and moved out Monday morning because the regular tenants came back unexpectedly.

The following year, the *S-48* came up to the States on a summer cruise, and in September we were back in Panama again. By that time I had a small set of quarters on the base at Coco Solo, and we moved in. They were pretty rugged. This was a ramshackle building with three apartments in it. The disbursing officer lived on one end, the torpedo officer of the base on the other end, and we had the one in the middle. The bathroom was on the front porch, then a bedroom, a boxed-in little sitting room affair, a dinette, and a kitchen on the back porch. The place was so flimsy thin that I recall sitting on the john on the porch one day, and Carolyn called me from the kitchen and asked what I'd like to have for breakfast. I said I'd like to have toast, scrambled eggs, and bacon, and the supply officer got the same breakfast. His wife had heard this, too, so she fixed them and served them to him.

Our mission there was to serve as part of the defense of the Panama Canal. The ridiculous thing about it was that the submarine base was on the Atlantic side at Coco Solo, but the Atlantic was so rough that there was really no protection at all. It's on the north side, and as a consequence it got all the turbulence of the winds. All the submarine operations were in the Pacific.

We would line up, starting at five-thirty or six o'clock on Monday morning and start the transit of the canal—all the submarines and the rescue vessel. It would take us all day to get through to the Pacific side. Then Tuesday morning we'd go down to the Perlas Islands. All the submarine operations were in the Pacific. We'd anchor out. Friday noon we'd plug back for Balboa, tie up at a pier there, and everybody who didn't have the duty would jump on the train and go back to Coco Solo Friday afternoon. Monday morning we'd get on the train going the other way. We did this for six weeks, and then we'd go back to the submarine base for two weeks. So you had a hell of a lot of separation during this time. A lot of the wives got to be confirmed alcoholics.

Lt. Cdr. Olton Bennehoff was the skipper of the *S-48*; Hyman Rickover, then a lieutenant, was the executive officer. The other officers we had were Fred Graf, Joe Danhoff, John Cross, and I. Red Metcalf, who had command of another submarine down there, used to call the *S-48* "the Prussian cruiser." You could count on the *S-48* to be in trouble, no matter what we did. If we all ran full speed from the Perlas operating area back to the base, the *S-48* would start out ahead of the pack—usually Friday at noon. Invariably, we'd have some damned thing break down,

and we'd be the last one in and, most frequently, miss the train. So we usually had to spend a lot of the weekend putting the thing back together again so that we could get under way on Monday.

Bennehoff was a wizard. He was one of the developers of the torpedo data computer, and he did all of it with hand-developed diagrams. He worked out these curves of all the different combinations of angle on the bow and course and speed of the target, and he put them on big Bakelite panels. Unfortunately, Bennehoff insisted they had to be such-and-such a size, and I kept saying they were too big. He said, "Stop arguing with me," so I went ahead with the work that I was directed to do. I got it all finished, pasted up, brought it down to the ship, and it wouldn't go through the hatch. The hatches were twenty-one inches in diameter, and this thing was twenty-five inches.

Bennehoff and Rickover would argue and argue and argue all day long when we'd get into a crisis. For example, there were times when it was imperative to surface immediately, and Benny and Rickover would stand there and argue about it. One occasion in particular, they were arguing, and the water was flooding into the engine room. I said, "To hell with it. Surface!"

Bennehoff turned to me and screamed, "I didn't tell you to surface."

I said, "We're at the stage you won't have to tell me much of anything. We'll be submerged—gone." It was only by getting up that we avoided greater damage, but this is the kind of stuff that went on all the time, and it was ridiculous. Both of them were brilliant men, but boy!

I thought Rickover was fine as a shipmate. He, of course, took my part repeatedly in battles with Bennehoff, so I thought he was great. I always found him most reasonable. He would listen when I had something to say. He didn't hesitate to counsel me—I was the chief engineer—because he was an old engineer who knew what he was talking about. If I stood up and argued with him, he'd say, "Now, look, Bill, I've heard what you have to say, but shut up and do what I said." I would, and it turned out invariably to be right. I used to get mad as hell at him, but, on the other

Lt. Hyman Rickover, the executive officer, appears in this group of officers on board the *S-48;* the photo was taken shortly before Irvin reported to the boat. *Left to right*: Howard W. Gilmore, Rickover, William R. Headden, Frederic A. Graf, and the skipper, Lt. Cdr. Olton Bennehoff. *Courtesy of Mrs. Eleonore Rickover*

hand, I had a lot of respect for him. I thought he was fine, and the men liked him too. He was much more reasonable than Bennehoff, and in a number of cases he took the part of the men, so of course they leaned to him.

We had a terrible situation one time on a dive. We had two machinist's mates, brothers named Davenport. They were Texas boys. One of them was a bow-planes operator on the diving station. In the S-boats the submarines were designed so that the diving station was just abreast of the periscope. The periscope and the diving station were in the same compartment. We didn't have a conning tower in the S-boats; we had a controller. Bennehoff insisted that we try this, that, and the other thing to speed up diving time and speed up surfacing time. Some of the things that he'd try were just plain foolhardy, because the *S-48* wasn't designed to do them. Furthermore, we had vents

and ballast tanks that just wouldn't take the kind of performance Bennehoff was trying to wring out of them.

I was standing at a diving station, which was just to the left of the periscope. The bow planesman was facing outboard on the port side of the station, the stern planesman the same, and Bennehoff, in one of his usual tirades, was screaming at me about the fact that I wasn't keeping the submarine level enough. I, in turn, would say to the bow planesman, "Put more dive on, take more dive off, take more plane off." Bennehoff, for some reason or other, was getting more and more irritated about this, and he turned and screamed to the bow planesman, "Do what he tells you to do."

Davenport turned to him and started to speak, and I reached over and put my hand on Davenport's shoulder and said, "Okay, don't say any-

Oddball S-Boat | 65

thing else, just turn around and do it." This seemed to infuriate Bennehoff even more. He said something else to the planesman, and Davenport started to turn around. With that, Bennehoff reached over and shoved him up against the bow-plane station. Davenport just continued around in the swing, and he came up with a punch and landed it on Bennehoff's jaw.

I swung my arms around Davenport, pushed him out of the way, and grabbed another man. I pushed him in on the place for the bow planesman and said, "Keep it on zero." Then I saw a chief who was standing there, and I said, "Take Davenport back to the engine room. Get him out of here."

Bennehoff by this time was going to do this, that, and the other, so I said to Rickover, "Don't you think we ought to surface?"

Rickover said, "Surface, surface."

Well, Bennehoff was livid, and he said, "Surface? Break up this run?"

So I said to Rickover, "You'd better say something to the captain, because we're going to have one hell of a fight here. He deliberately hit that man, and the man, in turn, very properly turned around and defended himself."

Bennehoff was screaming his head off, "What are we going to do to Davenport?"

Fortunately, Rickover managed to get Bennehoff calmed down. Not very long after that we had Davenport back on the bow-plane station, and everything was forgotten. These brannigans used to drive you crazy. You never knew what was going to happen next.

12

Developing the Fleet Boats

ADM. STUART S. MURRAY,
USN (RET.)

The early years of the U.S. submarine service included a good deal of experimentation as boats became larger and more capable. Diesel propulsion plants were often a difficulty, and so were questions of size and endurance. The submarines that served with great success in the Pacific in World War II were the fleet boats. They combined great range and endurance with reliable diesel engines. One who had a hand in the process was Murray, who reported for duty at the Portsmouth Navy Yard in mid-1933 as a lieutenant. He was not an engineering duty specialist, but he was an experienced submariner and put his seagoing experience to use.

T HE FIRST DUTIES assigned to me at the navy yard at Portsmouth were as an assistant shop superintendent and running the so-called inside shops. After about two or three months, I was changed to be assistant machinery superintendent, as they called it in those days, in charge of the work on the waterfront rather than in the shops. This was under Lt. Cdr. Merrill Comstock.

The USS *Dolphin*, which had been originally the *V-7* until they started naming the larger submarines after the S class, was just finishing up at the yard. The *Dolphin* was about fifteen hundred tons—a little bit smaller than the previous six V-boats but still much larger than S-boats by almost 100 percent. The *Dolphin* was finished and departed from the yard. My job there was to work on getting the final things finished. At the same time, the *Cachalot*, which was about eleven hundred tons, was being built. Lieutenant Commander Comstock was designated as prospective commanding officer of the *Cachalot*.

Lt. Cdr. Sunshine Murray was the first commanding officer when the *Porpoise* went into commission on 15 August 1935. *Naval Institute Photo Archive*

In those days the planning was not as detailed and efficient as it is now. Added to that was the fact that during 1933 there was a large reduction in force of the shipyard workmen due to the Depression. Approximately one-third of all navy yard workmen were laid off. This left only supervisors and rated civil service personnel to do the work. However, this made it very good working with the personnel, because you were working with well-trained and experienced men. No man on the yard had been there less than seven years, and the average was about fifteen years of employment in that yard. These were men whose families had worked in that shipyard for generations, so they were well grounded in the type of work they were doing.

The plans for the *Cachalot* were not as far ahead in the planning division as the actual production on the waterfront was—that is, the detailed plans of where the piping would go, where the wiring would go, where the small auxiliary machinery would go. So on the waterfront we had to fix, or point out, and draw chalk marks as to where the pipelines would go and where the wiring would go and where the small auxiliary machinery like pumps would go. We facetiously called it the "spit" planning method.

One of the leading men said that I would stand in the engine room and spit, and where the spit landed was where a pipe would go. It wasn't quite that rough, but it wasn't scientific, to say the least. The draftsmen would come down from the planning section when we had the pipe installed and draw their plans from where the pipes went rather than where they thought they were going. It was a very good method. There was no argument as to where a pipe went or anything like that, because it was already in. Now, of course, it's done much more scientifically, and it's all finished before they do anything like that.

We managed to get the work going very well and were working to finish the *Cachalot* consider-

The *Pike* goes down the building ways at Portsmouth Navy Yard on 12 September 1935. *Naval Institute Photo Archive*

ably ahead of time with the force that we had. I must admit that there was some feeling among the yard workmen, with no other construction in sight, that when they finished *Cachalot* and the overhaul work on the submarines in commission on the East Coast, they couldn't see much of a future in their job.

In June 1933, the National Industrial Recovery Act was passed. It was a national act to assist in the rehabilitation of all industry in an endeavor to overcome the Depression and get more work done, get more employees throughout the whole nation, and help the economy. The Navy was given a share of this, and as part of it, four submarines were to be built and paid for under the act. Portsmouth Navy Yard got two of these, and the Electric Boat Company in Groton, Connecticut, got the other two.

The submarines at Portsmouth were the *Porpoise* and *Pike*; the submarines at the Electric Boat Company were the *Shark* and *Tarpon*. These were

an entirely new type of submarine from the *Cachalot* or the former V-boats. They were slightly larger than the *Cachalot*, about 1,350 tons, and they were to have diesel-electric drive—that is, four diesel engines, each connected to a generator and motors driving the shafts. No more clutches between the engines and the propeller shafts. Of course, the motors driving the propellers didn't know or care where the electricity was originating, whether from the generator on the engines or from the storage battery for use submerged.

These were entirely new type things that were using, for the first time, high-speed light diesel engines. These ones that we had were the Winton diesel engines, built in Cleveland, Ohio, by the General Motors Corporation. They were V-8s, as we called them. In other words, sixteen cylinders, 1,500-horsepower engines, so the total horsepower in all the engines was about 6,000, which was higher than most of the other small engines had been before and were absolutely identical with the ones used on the Boston and Maine Railroad, except they used a straight eight and not the V-8 that we had. When we were short of spare parts, due to nonarrival or anything like that, the Boston and Maine was very helpful in that they would trade spare parts with us. We could get them right off of their diesel engines or from their diesel shops. I might add it worked the other way at times also. They borrowed from us.

The *Porpoise* was designated as the first one of the class. The keel was laid in the fall of 1933. They did a very nice thing, I think, by designating four boys, ten to twelve years old, all Navy juniors whose fathers were attached to the shipyard, as the keel layers; they did all the work in actually laying the keel. My son Stuart was a rivet holder, which was very interesting since in 1918 his mother had a similar job in the keel laying of a destroyer at Mare Island while she was a makee-learn draftsman in Mare Island Navy Yard in California.

Some of the interesting things that we ran into which were anything but too interesting at that time—but to show in a small way how things have improved in the years since that time—we tried to align propeller shafts. In fact, we had to align them to some extent on the building ways, before the ship was launched, in order to get the engines installed at the same time. During the sunlight of late summer and early fall, in Kittery, Maine, with the sun on the stern of the ship, the stern would move way over. During the night, when it cooled off, it would come back. This movement wouldn't seem to be much, but it was a matter of between ten and twelve inches. We decided that the only way to align those shafts was to work at night, after 2:00 AM. So we made marks as to where it was in the daytime and where it would come back to around 2:30 or 3:00 AM, then start to work at 2:00 AM and work until 4:00. After 4:00 it would start moving again. That was due to the heat making the metal of the hull contract and expand; so it moved it because it was the strain on the long line of a hull. It moved quite a bit in the 250 feet that the hull was from bow to stern.

Also, there was another innovation on the *Porpoise*. We made a complete mock-up, as it was called. That is, we built a wooden model of the submarine compartments, each individually, to exact scale. The shops could take their piping and all their machinery down there, and wooden models of it in the actual piping if they wanted to, to get the bends and actual locations in there, so that when it was taken down to the ship it fitted in the right place. There was no more of the so-called spit alignment that there had been on the *Cachalot*.

Everything proceeded along fine in 1934 with the *Porpoise*. After Lieutenant Commander Comstock was detached in the spring of 1934, Lt. Cdr. Isaiah Parker relieved him as machinery superintendent, and I continued on as the one and only assistant to handle everything on the waterfront. Parker handled everything inside and in the offices, and I handled everything outside and gave him all the dope on what was going on. That's the way things worked very well.

In the summer of 1934, I was detailed as additional duty to be the administrative aide to the commandant, who at that time was Rear Adm. Pluvy Kempff. My job had always been the one which would supply the emergency relief aide—why, I don't know. But for three months I had to be his aide from 9:00 AM until 4:00 PM, when the admiral would leave the office. Before and after those times, I would have to do my work on the waterfront, which kept me quite busy—probably out of trouble.

Then progress on the *Porpoise* continued, according to schedule—in fact, ahead of schedule. It was due to be completed in late 1935. I began to wonder where I was going for my next sea duty, which was due in the spring of 1935. Since I had been in submarines practically all the time except a short exposure of the year in battleships in 1921 and 1922, the detail officer said I should go to surface ships. First he said I would go to destroyers. That was changed. Then he said I would go as the navigator of the USS *Milwaukee*, which was a light cruiser based in San Diego. That pleased me very much, but then my orders didn't come up, and I got a telephone call from him, and he said I was going in command of the *Bass*, which was the V-2. My orders were finally issued, and I got them the first part of April. Then I got a telegram about ten days later canceling them, so I didn't know where I was going. I managed to get on an Easter special train trip down to Washington to see the detail officer. The result of it was that I was ordered to command of the *Porpoise*, and my orders were issued very shortly thereafter.

The *Porpoise* was launched in June, and I rode her down the building ways, as was customary. I had two hats on—both as prospective commanding officer and as assistant machinery superintendent in charge of the waterfront for all machinery work and responsible for getting that ship tied up again with the assistance of the yard pilot.

This assignment pleased me very much. It was a brand-new type submarine and it was going to the West Coast, where I wanted to go. Being there, where I was doing an awful lot of things, those minor things you can always do, and knowing the people doing it, I got a lot of innovations in just the way I wanted them, where there were no detailed plans that required it had to be that way. Lt. Heber McLean, the prospective commanding officer of the *Pike*, the sister ship to the *Porpoise*, had already reported in by that time. He said the only thing he wanted was that anything that was done on the *Porpoise*, do it on the *Pike*. He figured he'd come out ahead on that.

One of the rather amusing things on that was that since I'm six feet four in my bare feet—bunks being normally six feet two to six feet four in the Navy—I've always been cramped in a bunk aboard a ship. That was particularly true on a submarine, unless I was lucky enough to get a locker on which I could place my feet for a few inches' extra room. On the *Porpoise* I got a seven-foot bunk installed for the commanding officer. The commanding officer of the *Pike* was only about six feet flat. He didn't realize for about a month after it had been installed that his bunk, which the yard workmen installed on the *Pike* as well, was also seven feet. I might add I enjoyed that bunk very much indeed. When I last saw the *Porpoise* in 1944, she still had that seven-foot bunk.

13

Submarine Tender

REAR ADM.
GEORGE W. BAUERNSCHMIDT,
SUPPLY CORPS, USN (RET.)

In a previous chapter, Admiral Bauernschmidt recalled switching from submarine command to the Supply Corps. In 1935 he reported aboard the USS *Beaver*. She had been launched in 1909, had served as a merchant ship until World War I, and then was taken over by the Navy and converted to a submarine tender. In 1932 she moved to Pearl Harbor to augment what was then a modest navy yard. She serviced Submarine Squadron Four, which comprised twenty-three S-boats and the large submarine *Argonaut*. As this story demonstrates, her crew did more than just tend submarines.

M Y FIRST SUPPLY CORPS duty was as disbursing officer of the *Beaver*. I took to logistics right away. Disbursing and accounting were somewhat of a chore, but the field of logistics—of supply—I liked. I took to that like a duck to water. I loved it.

I had additional duty on the *Beaver* as the submarine division intelligence officer. I was assigned duties, as the *Beaver* moved around the Hawaiian Islands, to inquire into the activities and proclivities of the Japanese portion of the population. I came to the conclusion then that most of the native-born Japanese and all of the American-born Japanese were loyal Americans. I so stated in my report, an opinion which the blitz at Pearl Harbor proved to be correct. Later on, I knew the colonel who commanded the Nisei outfit in Italy, and the stories of his boys are fantastic—the most decorated unit in the Army.

As the division intelligence officer, I was permitted to take my automobile aboard the *Beaver*. Whenever we stopped at an island, my car was

For many years Tai Sing Loo chronicled the Pearl Harbor Navy Yard in his artistic photographs. In this 1933 shot the *Beaver* tends her brood of boats. *Naval Institute Photo Archive*

off-loaded, and I went about my duties of inquiring. In this I met members of the big families of the islands and engaged in conversations. From them I got their opinions and a great deal of history, the early history of Hawaii, some of it fascinating.

I also was to interview a man on the Parker Ranch, and I caught him as he was about to take off on a hunting trip. He said he'd be glad to talk with me, but I'd have to come along with him. He handed me a Savage Imp rifle and a shotgun, and we jumped in the car and went off. It was the only time I've ever been gunning. I'll never go again, because I'm not at home with a shotgun, although I am with a rifle. I shot the shotgun ten times and got four quail and two pheasants, and I'm sure I could never match that again.

The rifle was even more fun, because there were a large number of wild sheep on the ranch that the ranch owners tried to exterminate. They always asked people who asked for permission to gun on the ranch to take a rifle and shoot sheep,

just shoot them and leave them. It was quite sporting, because you could get as close as 250 yards and then get one shot standing and one shot running, and the sheep were gone. The young sheep that I shot I took back to the ship with me, four carcasses, which I skinned out and had the butcher dress. It was very fortunate that I did so, because about this time there was a Matson Navigation shipping strike. We lived on pheasant, quail, and sheep while other people were doing without meat.

I had been told at the Supply Corps School that an examining officer always looked at the disbursing officer's safe. If it was neat and tidy, it created a good impression. Well, the safe that I found on the *Beaver* was in deplorable condition. So we took it apart. In the back recesses of the thing, I found some blank bills of exchange that were unnumbered. Now, they were antiques. Bills of exchange are very negotiable pieces of paper and to the best of my knowledge had been numbered and accounted for by number for at least thirty years. So far as I was concerned, they were hot potatoes, so I sent them on to the Bureau of Supplies and Accounts for disposition. I don't know what they ever did with them, but they probably burned them very promptly. They could have been taken ashore in a foreign country with forged signatures, and almost any sum of money could have been obtained on them. They were, in effect, lost. We had to take the safe apart to find them.

As part of this whole process, we took all the nickel parts of the safe and sent them over to the submarine base and had them nickel-plated. My storekeepers and I chipped and red-leaded the safe and then gave it a coat of black enamel and began putting it back together again. When the nickel-plated parts came back to us, they came back in a bucket. We began reassembling the safe, and when it was all done there was a bolt left over. So we took it apart again and started from scratch and still had a bolt left over. When it was left over the third time, I said, "To hell with it. The safe works, and we'll just stick with it."

A little while later, the repair officer at the base, an ex-submarine friend of mine, asked me how I made out with my safe. Did I have any trouble? And I said, "Yes, a little."

He said, "I thought you would. I threw in an extra bolt and had it nickel-plated."

14

Submarine Detailing

REAR ADM. JOHN F. DAVIDSON,
USN (RET.)

In this era of computers the capabilities and desires of naval officers are stored electronically. But even with part of the process automated, the human element is still needed. There is an art to matching the right submariners to the right billets on board submarines. Lt. John Davidson became familiar with that art in the period before World War II.

I N 1936 I was just winding up a tour in the *Cachalot*, having learned a hell of a lot from the skipper, Merrill Comstock. I was about to put in for postgraduate school in ordnance, because it seemed in those days that people who were ordnance PGs always went to the top. All of a sudden, a letter came from the detail office in Washington to our skipper, saying, "What would you say to John Davidson as the assistant to the detail officer in the Bureau of Navigation?"

Merrill blew me up to the sky and then convinced me that that's what I ought to do. I said, "What about PG school?"

He said, "The best PG you can get is the Bureau of Navigation. If you get it in personnel, that's the best postgraduate work you can do." So I ended up going as the assistant submarine detail officer with additional duty as the detail officer for all ensigns and jaygees. That was perhaps as fascinating a job as I ever had, because in those days we were on Constitution Avenue in Washington, in the old Main Navy Building, along with the other bureaus. I had an opportunity to observe how the Navy was run.

Capt. Chester Nimitz was the assistant bureau chief, and my boss turned out to be, if anything, even more influential than Comstock had been.

That was Cdr. Swede Hazlett. He turned out to be someone from whom I could learn something every day; he was just a fantastic person. Then I had enough contact with Captain Nimitz to learn a lot from him, too.

Of interest, perhaps, to people nowadays would be how we handled the personnel situation in those days. We had no computers. We had no way of keeping lists. It was plain, everyday pen-and-ink drudgery—really pencil, because you had to erase a lot. We had a slate book, and in that slate book I had to print each year the first name, middle initial, last name, rank, and serial number of every ensign and every junior lieutenant in the Navy. That was one column. Duty assignment was the next column. I don't remember all the columns, but there were columns all the way across in a big ledger. After you had made up that whole thing, then you had a column marked "To be ordered to"—the next duty assignment. Also we had what we called a data card and put all of the various items in there: marital status, three requests for next duty, and all such things.

At that time all ensigns were either in battleships or cruisers, and some of the jaygees by that time had gotten into destroyers and so on. Whenever we had in mind transferring anybody, each year I would write a letter to the captain of the *Arizona* and the captain of the *Oklahoma* and so forth and say, "It is planned to send Ensign So-and-So to Submarine School." And you gave them a slate of what you planned to do. It was all in a personal letter. At first I used to write them out longhand and let the secretary copy them, but I found out that was too time-consuming, so I learned to dictate those letters. I also corresponded with the individual junior officers a great many times. I soon felt that I knew and recognized the name of every young officer in the Navy, because I'd printed his name so many times.

We also heard from those outside the Navy. A letter came in from a senator—I think he was from Pennsylvania—saying that the parents of a young ensign were very, very disturbed because he was on a destroyer on the West Coast, and he very much wanted to be on the East Coast. I looked up in my book and found the boy had requested to continue duty on the West Coast. He was very happy. So Swede Hazlett said, "Why don't you write him a letter and get a personal opinion?"

I wrote a letter to the young man. He wrote back. By that time I think he had made lieutenant. He said, "Dear Lieutenant Davidson, The last thing in the world I want is to come east. I'm engaged to marry a girl out here in Long Beach, and my parents don't want me to marry her, because they've got a girl back there in Johnstown, Pennsylvania, they think I should marry. So they asked the senator to intervene and get me ordered east." So we informed the senator very politely that we had a letter from the boy himself that gave us his reason that he was very much in love, intended to get married out there, and that he would not like to be sent back. The senator understood.

Captain Nimitz once had a letter from a senator requesting something, and he sent it down to me to prepare a reply for his signature. I was pretty much green in the job, and the day after it went up for signature, he appeared in the office and sat on the corner of the boss's desk. He said to me, "John, I have this letter you prepared for my signature. Before I sign it, I wonder if you've ever heard the story about the difference between a lady and a diplomat?"

I said, "No, sir."

"Well, if a lady says no, she means maybe. When she says maybe, she means yes. If she says yes, she ain't no lady. With a diplomat, if he says yes, he means maybe. If he says maybe, he means no. If he says no, he ain't no diplomat."

15

Developing the Torpedo Data Computer

REAR ADM. EDWARD K. WALKER,
USN (RET.)

One of the truly effective tools used by U.S. submariners in World War II was the torpedo data computer (TDC), which took in data on a target ship's course and speed and then transmitted orders that were cranked into torpedo guidance mechanisms shortly before the torpedoes were launched. The TDC was an analog computer but still a step up from previous aiming methods, so it took some getting used to. A figure in bringing about the new system was Lt. Cdr. Ed Walker, who served in the Bureau of Ordnance from 1938 to 1940. His predecessor was Lt. Cdr. Olton Bennehoff, whom we have met earlier as commanding officer of the *S-38* in Panama.

W
HEN I GOT to the bureau, I was assigned to torpedo fire control in the fire control division. At that time nobody was handling it because Lieutenant Commander Bennehoff had left. We had worked a few years earlier on the Mark 1 fire control system. In the fall of 1938 they sent me to Panama in the USS *Snapper*, which was one of the first submarines to get the Mark 1 system. I was down there for a couple of months observing firing, and then I came back and wrote a report and made several suggestions that I thought should be made. Then I was given the job of writing the specifications and overseeing the design and procurement of the new system, which was then known as the torpedo fire control system Mark 2.

One thing I observed was that communication between the officer in the conning tower and the officer operating the TDC was very difficult. I decided that what we needed was a torpedo data computer in the control room. I recommended

that, and so they assigned to the project a civilian engineer named Enright, who was in the design section of the Bureau of Ordnance. He was the one who conceived the idea of a TDC in the control room that fit the contour of the hull in the conning tower. We got that approved with no problem. I don't think the bureau chief or assistant chief gave a damn how it worked, but the head of the fire control section thought it was a good idea. He didn't know anything about submarines anyway.

In addition to that, there was another change. The original Mark 1 TDC had a follow-the-pointer system for keeping the gyros set in the right direction. One pointer hooked to the torpedo gyros, and the other one to the computer. You just matched the pointers. In gun fire control, this was done automatically by elevation indicator-regulators and azimuth indicator. So I said, "Let's put an indicator-regulator in the torpedo

fire control system," because it could do a much better job than any man could do.

The whole weakness of the system was range. We didn't have a very satisfactory range finder for the periscope. We had a gadget that clipped onto the periscope, but it wasn't too accurate. So the commanding officer would get the range, and he'd say, "Fifty-two hundred yards." The data computer officer was standing practically beside him, and he'd crank the fifty-two hundred yards right into the computer. The only other input concerning the target was bearing. With the help of Mr. Enright, we designed a periscope bearing transmitter by which we could send target bearings directly from the periscope to the torpedo data computer. The periscope was raised from time to time to check the target's bearing. When the skipper wanted to transmit the bearing, he'd just press a button on the handle of the periscope, and that would send it to the TDC.

The submarine's course and speed were entered into the TDC automatically. With all this information, the TDC continuously generated target range and bearing and also torpedo gyro angle for both the bow and stern tubes. The range and bearing of the target were checked visually or by sonar from time to time, and corrections were made on the target's estimated course and speed to bring them into line with the latest observations. Later, as World War II progressed, it became evident that night attacks by surfaced submarines using torpedoes against convoys were very efficient. Therefore, a target bearing transmitter was mounted on the bridge to aid in making these night attacks.

The first TDCs were not very well received at first by my fellow submariners. Most of them said, "I can fly better by the seat of my pants. I can do it better by bow and arrow." Well, they were just too damn lazy to go learn how to use it. Well, the war finally convinced them of its value, because with things moving so fast, the minds of the skipper and TDC operator can't work together fast enough to counteract all the moves of enemy ships, especially when there's a lot of movement going on around you. When there's more than one target, you've got to shift from one to the other. You just can't work that fast unless you have some kind of computer help. And so the skippers found that out.

16

The *Squalus* Rescue

CHIEF MACHINIST'S MATE
WILLIAM BADDERS, USN (RET.)

In the 1920s, as recounted in the chapter from Admiral Dennison, two U.S. submarines were lost without possibility of recovering crewmen trapped below. Those losses led to the development of the McCann rescue chamber, which proved to be a lifesaver in 1939. On 1 March of that year the *Squalus* had been commissioned with Lt. Oliver Naquin as her first skipper. The boat successfully completed some test dives off Portsmouth, New Hampshire, on 12 May. On the morning of 23 May she went out again, this time for more tests off the Isle of Shoals. She experienced flooding aft, and twenty-six men drowned there. Another thirty-three men were still alive in the forward part of the boat. The nation's attention soon focused on the attempt to bring the men out alive.

IN THE SPRING of 1939 I was part of a unit that was doing experimental dives in the open ocean. We were working down a few feet each day. We had just got to 375 feet, I guess, and we had bad weather—fog, and no place else in the world has it like Portsmouth, New Hampshire. We just couldn't get out and operate. We had a limited number of days to use the *Falcon*, a submarine rescue ship. The day before our last day with the *Falcon* it cleared enough to let us get out to sea. I made a dive from the *Falcon* to the bottom in 420 feet of water. That was the deepest dive that had ever been made at that time in the open sea.

Then we had to get out of there, get our gear and stuff off the *Falcon*, drop them at New London, and we went back to Washington, D.C., where the Experimental Diving Unit was based.

These two photos show the McCann bell on the stern of the submarine rescue ship *Falcon* at the time of her work in delivering *Squalus* survivors to the surface. *Naval Institute Photo Archive*

We were still doing more work with helium and oxygen, perfecting the equipment, and working on recompression tables. On the twenty-third day of May 1939, about ten o'clock in the morning, we got word that a submarine was down just outside of Portsmouth, New Hampshire; we were to stand by with our personnel and equipment.

Some of the men rushed home, got a change of clothes, and packed a small bag. Sure enough, about eleven o'clock it was determined that the Squalus was down and that some of the men on board were alive. The experimental unit, equipment and personnel, were to get to the scene of operations as soon as possible. Three other men and I took a bit of the equipment over to the Anacostia Naval Air Station, and we caught a Marine Reserve amphibious plane from there and flew into Portsmouth. We got in that evening. Lt. Cdr. Swede Momsen, two doctors, and some other divers had taken another plane and got in a little ahead of us.

By the time we arrived at the Portsmouth Navy Yard that evening, it was determined that there were thirty-three men alive in the forward part of the submarine, but they hadn't been able to make any communication with anyone in the after part. They weren't sure whether there was anyone alive back there or not. The submarine was down in 242 feet of water.

We got our equipment in operating condition and were transported by fast boat out to the Sculpin, which was a sister ship of the Squalus. We were waiting for the Falcon. She was in New London, Connecticut, and she was speeding to the scene of operations as fast as she could with men and equipment and the McCann rescue chamber. She arrived sometime early in the morning and got in position for diving operations. All of us who had come from Washington went on board the Falcon.

Of course, the first order of business was to see what could be done about the men who were trapped in the submarine. The Squalus had released a buoy with a telephone cable, but it broke after the commanding officer, Lt. Oliver Naquin, had reported that the men in the forward torpedo room were in good shape. After that the only

communication was through oscillators and people hammering on the hull.

The buoy cable being broken loose from the Sculpin left us with no means of knowing just exactly where the Squalus was. The Coast Guard was out, and one of their boats was dragging grapnels around. After the grapnel hit into her, the line to it plumbed straight up and down, which indicated where the ship was. When the Falcon planted her moorings, they were planted around this area, of course, and then that line was used as the down line for the first dive that was made. The first business was for a diver to go down and hook up the downhaul wire for the rescue chamber. That was the wire that pulled the chamber down to the escape hatch to rescue survivors.

Boatswain's Mate Martin Sibitsky, one of the divers on the Falcon, made the first dive. He went down this line, and just a second or two after he hit the bottom, he said on the underwater telephone, "You're not going to believe this, but this grapnel hook is caught in the railing not more than three or four feet from the forward hatch of the Squalus, where we have to take the men out." It couldn't have been placed any better if a diver had gone down and put it there himself.

So the downhaul wire was shackled on with this grapnel line and lowered to Sibitsky. He hooked on the downhaul wire on the same dive and came up. The rescue chamber was put in the water ready for operations. The crew went on board to operate it; a diver by the name of Harman and my later partner, Torpedoman John Mihalowski, were the two operators for the first trip. The chamber went down, and everything worked fine, and they brought seven men to the surface. That was the capacity of the chamber—seven passengers and two operators.

During the first trip down, fresh air from the rescue chamber was circulated through the submarine's forward compartment. Clothing, blankets, food, and things of that kind were given to the men. The only danger that we thought about was that there was always the possibility of a bulkhead giving away so there would be flooding in the area or gas getting in. Fortunately, in this operation we had good weather, because there was always the possibility of one of these crazy squalls coming up so that we'd have to run to get away with men alive on the bottom.

I was put in the chamber with Harman for the second trip. On the way down I got to thinking that I had operated this chamber probably more than anyone else in the Navy, and I knew that it could handle more than seven men. As we went down to the hatch, I decided that I was going to bring more than seven men out on my trip, for the simple reason that if we brought out only seven at a time, it was going to require five trips. If we brought out an extra man or two each time, they could be brought out in four trips. So on my first trip I brought nine men up. I hadn't said a word to anybody on topside about it, but I came up with nine men with no difficulty at all and unloaded them out of the chamber and onto the deck of the *Falcon*. There a doctor examined them quickly, and then they loaded them up and took them to the hospital in Portsmouth.

Well, I was also going to make the third trip in the chamber, and I knew that when I made the second trip. I got the men out of there as soon as I could, dogged the hatch down, and got started down again. I think it was Momsen who said to me, "You brought out too many men on that trip, but do it again and bring up nine the next time." So I brought eighteen men out of there, and I've got their autographs on the wall, on that list of survivors.

On the fourth trip, the operators went down to bring the last survivors out. On the way up the chamber got fouled on the downhaul wire. It couldn't go up or down, so we had quite a time getting that load of men to the surface. We had to send a diver down to cut the downhaul wire loose at the submarine, and the chamber had to be pulled up very carefully. If it came up too fast, it could displace water out of the ballast tank and cause some damage. It took three or four hours to get the last men up. Lieutenant Naquin, the skipper, was in that last group.

On my first trip down in the rescue chamber, I opened the hatch and the first couple of men came out of the *Squalus*. When that happened,

the first thing that entered my mind was, Boy, why couldn't we have had this when we had those six men alive in the *S-4*? That was in December 1927, and they had to finally die down there because we had no way of getting them out. If we'd just had that rescue chamber then, we could have saved those six men just as easily as we saved the thirty-three on the *Squalus*. In fact, it would have been much easier, because she was down in only 102 feet of water.

Rear Adm. Cyrus Cole was commandant of the Portsmouth Navy Yard and in charge of the operations. The next day, after all the *Squalus* survivors were off, he said, "We've got to determine if there's any life left aft in the submarine. It will require a trip of the rescue chamber, open the hatch aft, and determine for sure if the after part of the submarine is flooded or dry."

Well, some overhaul work had to be done on the chamber to replace this downhaul wire and everything. They did this work during the night, and the next morning Mihalowski and I were selected to make the fifth trip with the rescue chamber, this time to the after hatch. After the downhaul wire was hooked up, Mike and I got in the chamber, and down we went. For this trip the chamber had to be secured over the hatch and then pressure built up inside the chamber equivalent to the bottom pressure. Otherwise, if you unscrewed the hatch with the rescue chamber at atmospheric pressure, and the after part of the submarine was flooded in a depth of 240 feet, the water would have come right up out of the submarine and into the rescue chamber.

So we had to sit the chamber down in place over the hatch, dog it with hold-down bolts, and then build up the pressure. If we had become incapacitated or passed out from compressed air, we'd have been hooked up down there just like the men in the submarine with no way of getting us out. Fortunately, nothing happened.

Sure enough, when I first partially undogged the hatch, a gush of air came out of the submarine. I was down in the lower compartment of the rescue chamber handling the hatch. Mihalowski was handling the valves, pressure gauges, and all in the top compartment. He hadn't built

Chief Badders sports his newly presented Medal of Honor on 19 January 1940. He is also wearing the Navy Cross awarded for his role in the salvage of the *S-51*. *Naval Historical Center: NH 57891*

up quite enough pressure; otherwise, the air wouldn't have come out. As soon as he built up a little more pressure in the rescue chamber, the air stopped coming in. I opened the hatch the rest of the way, and it was flooded right up to the neck of the hatch, which indicated there couldn't possibly be any life down there.

We made the report to topside, dogged the hatch down, released the rescue chamber, and came on to the surface. That indicated that rescue operations were finished, and it was now strictly a salvage operation in bringing the submarine up. We went to work on it with pontoons, drying as many compartments as practical with ballast tanks and whatnot, and raised her.

It turned out that there was a lot of work to do to get the submarine ready to go into dry dock at the Portsmouth Navy Yard. We had to get the pontoons off of her and get her on an even keel and in proper position for going in on the keel blocks. We had to work real late that evening to be sure to get her in on the next day, the fifteenth of September, which was my birthday. So being done with that job was my birthday present from Admiral Cole.

On 19 January 1940, Secretary of the Navy Charles Edison presented Medals of Honor to four men who were involved in the rescue of men from the *Squalus:* Chief Metalsmith James H. McDonald, Torpedoman 1st Class John Mihalowski, Chief Boatswain's Mate Orson L. Crandall, and Chief Badders.

17

Encounters with Corpses

REAR ADM. CHARLES A. CURTZE,
USN (RET.)

Once the living men had been recovered from the *Squalus*, it was time to bring the boat herself back to the Portsmouth Navy Yard and remove the bodies of those who had drowned in the after section. Later she would be cleaned out, repaired, and restored to service. Her new name was *Sailfish*, and she went on to serve in combat during World War II with a new crew. Admiral Curtze, a junior officer in 1939, was an engineering duty specialist. In this account he several times mentions Bob Evans, the author of the chapter that follows.

A T THE Portsmouth Navy Yard, I was shipbuilding superintendent for the *Searaven* and the *Seawolf*. Lt. Bob Evans had the *Sculpin* and the *Squalus*. They were already in commission before I even launched my two. It used to be traditional for the shipbuilding superintendents to go on the trial trips of the submarines that they had built. One reason was it gave the crew of the ship confidence; if the guy who built the boat's going to go out in it, he must think it's okay. And we, of course, ran classes after work every day for the crew of the submarine.

I knew Bob Evans then from Naval Academy days and MIT days, when we did graduate work. He was a year ahead of me, but we were very, very good friends. I held him in the highest possible regard. He was a low-key guy, wouldn't take much guff from anybody, but he believed in what he was doing. In any event, we talked about the prospects of the crew and training of the crew of the *Squalus*.

The bow of the *Squalus* breaks the surface during her salvage. This view of the boat inspired President Franklin D. Roosevelt to suggest that she be renamed *Sailfish* after being repaired, and she was. *Naval Institute Photo Archive*

I was perfectly happy with the *Searaven*, because my group was attentive, they asked intelligent questions, and they closed up the boat every day after work for dry dives and all this sort of thing. So by the time they were really ready to go to sea I thought they were ready. Bob, however, felt that the crew of the *Squalus* was beyond everything just plain arrogant. They knew all about everything, and you couldn't tell them a damn thing.

He said to me, "Charlie, I'm not going out in the boat on the trials, and I don't recommend you do it. Don't feel sorry for them. Don't go. You don't have to go. No one's going to force you to go, because you're not a qualified submarine officer anyway. Just don't go, because I just have a queer feeling about the fact that they're not ready. I don't know what will happen, but they're not ready." So when I was asked to substitute for Bob I said, "No, I'll go on my own when the time comes." Bob didn't go either, and the submarine was lost.

The salvage of the *Squalus* is well written up in other publications, and there are books written about it. I don't need to go into it, because I wasn't really involved in the salvage of the boat from the Isle of Shoals into Portsmouth. I was involved in it after it got into Portsmouth and trying to get squeezed into the dry dock with pontoons and everything else on it. And I'm pretty sure Bob even did the docking on it. Before we got into dry dock we had shifts. I worked one shift of ten hours a day, and Bob worked the other shift of ten hours a day. I just happened to be on the shift where lots of things were happening.

My boss was Lt. Cdr. Floyd Tusler, who was a very difficult man in my opinion but technically a pretty smart one. He was standing on the beach, not going aboard the boat to see what it was like.

I volunteered to go on board when the ship was still sunk. In other words, the bow was just barely out of water and the boat was submerged back to the forward crew's space access hatch. Then came the conning tower beyond that. Then there was the forward torpedo room escape hatch forward of that. It was out of water something like 20 percent of the length, and the after end of the thing was actually on the bottom. However, there were pontoons that could be blown, and it could be lifted off the bottom. That's actually how he got her into the dry dock finally. But Tusler said to me, "Charlie, you go on board, and I'm going to blow all the tanks starting with one."

So I climbed on board the ship, and I knew that the forward escape trunk was touch and go. You couldn't safely open the damn thing the way the boat was. But I figured if we could get some of the water out of the after end of the boat, the boat would come up enough so that it would be dry at least high tide. The tidal range is about ten feet there. So I went down below, and everything went swimmingly. I closed the flood valves by hand. The vent valves could be closed on deck; the divers could have done that. But a lot of flood valves jammed halfway because the sand had gotten up in the flooding valve.

When we found out that we couldn't get any more tanks blown because the tanks' bottoms wouldn't close and the flood valves wouldn't close, I started worrying about getting water out of the after crew's space, which we hadn't been in yet. That's where the valve was. And the bodies of the dead crew members were still in there. So I decided that we could get in there if I could jack the watertight door open. That watertight door happened to open aft against the pressure. I could jack the thing open with a hydraulic jack with steel strongbacks in between the frames of the door and control the influx of water from the after compartment. Then we'd dump the water into the refrigerating spaces, which were just forward of that watertight door at the after side of the control room. So we pumped away and pumped away, and I finally got the water level down so I could open the door and go into the aft compartment.

There was nobody with me. Tusler was on the boat screaming, "Go back and check the bulkhead ventilation stop valve. Close that because that's where the water's probably coming from." Well, I agreed with him on that one, but getting back there was pretty difficult because the water was over my head back there. I had to go down the whole length of the compartment by hanging on the wires and pipes in the overhead, and otherwise in water practically up to my shoulders. It was colder than hell. I couldn't stand on deck, so I was hanging down from the overhead.

Then I had go to into the crew's head on the port after side of that compartment and take a deep breath because I knew there would be an air pocket over that. I dumped in underneath that thing and got a hold of the lever to close that valve, but it was jammed tight. I didn't have a light or anything else, but I could feel with my hand that the valve had been surrounded. This I knew had been surrounded with one-eighth-inch plating just to guard against that so if there was any sudden flooding that valve could be closed and prevent intercompartmental connection and flooding. But that valve was completely jammed in the open position because of the collapse of the entire surrounding structure.

As I made ready to get out of that thing, I moved my hand over, and I hit one of the dead crew members in the face. At first I couldn't figure out what the hell I was feeling. Then I panicked for a few seconds, grabbed my breath, and ducked underneath. I got out into the other compartment, where I could swing open and finally be in control. I did have a light hanging from the overhead of the compartment way up where it was still dry. I was pretty much calmed down by the time I came out. So I walked up over the side and on the beach and said to Mr. Tusler, "The valve's jammed."

"It can't be."

I said, "Mr. Tusler, the valve is jammed." And I described it, not as detailed as I just did here, but I said, "It's just jammed."

"I don't believe a goddamn word of it. Go down and look again."

I was just about to say, "I'm not going to do

it," which was what I wanted to say, when Tusler's assistant, Lt. Al Zollars, saw that things were brewing between Tusler and myself. Tusler had a very short fuse, and Zollars could see that I would probably get court-martialed for disobedience of orders if I did what I was wont to do. So he jumped right in and talked to Tusler; they were on a first-name basis because they were only a couple of classes apart. He said, "Floyd, I'll go in, and Charlie can come along with me and hold my hand while I'm going in through the hard spots." So I thanked my lucky stars, because I had an excuse then to go in with somebody. And I wasn't about to go in there again alone. I couldn't do any good anyway.

Zollars and I went inside the submarine, where no one could hear us. I told him exactly what I'd done and what I'd found and to look out because he'd find a corpse floating on the surface back there. As I remember, there were three of them in that compartment. I don't know of any more, but I remember one sprawled over a mess table and one in the head, all bloated and floating. There was a third one, I think, but I'm not sure of that. So, of course, Al Zollars found out the same thing I'd found out. Then we came up topside, and Tusler was mollified apparently, and he left.

In the meantime Lt. Oliver Naquin, the commanding officer, came on board, and he said to me, "Curtze, I'd like to go down below with you."

I said, "Well, sure." I was all wet anyway, and I was pretty sure he didn't want to get back into the compartment where the corpses were. I still had the door open, and water was pouring in through the ventilation duct, but we were keeping ahead of it. So we got to his cabin, and he went in. He opened his officer's safe there and pulled out a napkin ring. All naval officers in those days used to carry around a sterling silver napkin ring, and they always had engraved on there their commands or their duties and one thing and another. He picked up this thing, wiped it on his pants, and said, "Oh, sterling silver. Just like my crew." Then he put the damned thing in his pocket.

We went up topside, and on the way up he said to me, "Charlie, I'm going to lunch now. Don't you go into the compartment where the

questionable valves are located because I don't want anybody from the shipyard tampering with the situation and changing it before there's official witnesses to what was being done."

My first reaction, which I didn't say out loud, was, You son-of-a-bitch. I've been down here all morning long in that compartment, and I know better than to touch anything down there. Because any submarine particularly that's been salvaged has a thin coating of oil—the oil just covers everything—and you couldn't possibly touch anything in there without leaving a telltale smear or something. But he didn't say anything about it. It was about 12:30 when that happened. He shoved off and never came back on board for the rest of the day. He went on board the *Falcon* to have lunch with the skipper. Left me down there until finally I decided that I would just go topside and forget it. So that's what I did.

In the meantime, I saw that he was climbing up on the conning tower shears and rehoisting the American flag over the sunken ship. Admiral Cole was recommissioning the ship and saying, "This ship will live to fight again. Witness we're recommissioning it now." This was Naquin up there with all the photographers taking pictures and one thing and another. That's the last I ever saw of him. Maybe he hung around the dock a little bit, but he never went on board the submarine. Never.

After we got the *Squalus* in dry dock, Bob Evans and I then went shift on shift ripping out all of the machinery. In those days you could pretty much salvage any of that stuff if you got it washed down with steaming hot water and then dried by air and lubricate sprayed. And even diesel engines, I found during World War II, I could get started again if I used the proper treatment, even though they had been submerged or covered with firefighting water. As I passed by the induction valve, of course, I looked at it and put my flashlight up against it, but I wouldn't have touched it for a million bucks.

Everything was just exactly the way it should be. And I knew that the indictor board had shown green lights, all things "go" at the time the boat sank. They didn't have any formal court of inquiry,

This is the after battery room of the *Squalus* on 15 September 1939, after the water had been pumped out. *Naval Institute Photo Archive*

as I remember, but they had perhaps a board of investigation. I didn't know very much about the legal differences between these two at that time, but no testimony was taken. People just investigated it and looked and wrote up something. I never saw the report.

The newspaper people by that time had plenty of time to come down on board one of my boats and look at the valve and see how it worked, and they knew more about it than they needed to know. There was a tremendous amount of pressure being built up in the local press to exonerate the crew and blame the shipyard for faulty valve operation. I knew that wasn't true, and I don't know what Bob Evans said, but I knew Bob Evans knew it wasn't true. He wasn't down there with me at that time, but he was there shortly thereafter.

So they sent this board of investigation there, under a commander named "Crow" Dunbar. His nickname was Crow because he had a very hoarse, low voice. He was a nice enough guy, and he said to me, "The only way we can find this thing out before anybody touches the valve is to test it. Can you rig it for testing?"

I said, "Yes, sir. I sure can." I had been dying to do it. We rigged a tank-testing pump, which is a small hand pump with about an inch in diameter and maybe a five-inch stroke, and you could pump up tremendous pressure with the thing. We dumped the suction end into a bucket of hydraulic oil and pumped the oil into that hydraulic manifold, and of course there weren't any openings anywhere in the system except the one that I put the connection on. We pumped the thing up, and the valve closed at thirty pounds. Well, it was designed to close at five hundred or something like that. And the valve was also not only a valve that ran the latch but the first motion of the piston in there unlatched the thing, and the last inch or so of travel passed oil into the hydraulic chamber that operated the valve closing gear.

There was a latch that kept the valve open when you didn't want it to close accidentally. But when you wanted it to close, you put pressure to it. That lifted the latch and permitted it to close. At the same time it permitted the valve to close, it just opened the port through which hydraulic oil could then flow into the cylinder that operated the main part of the system. And it operated at thirty pounds.

Then I got thinking about the thing in trying to reestablish the scenario of how the darn accident happened. It was my opinion—and I don't know how Bob felt—that the valve was reopened. All the valves were, in fact, closed. The boat had built up air pressure enough, which is part of the doctrine, a couple of inches of air pressure to make sure the boat is tight. That's why it showed the green board, and everything was okay.

By that time all the vents were still open. The floods were open to vent the tanks and remove any remaining air so the boat could be controlled in a neutral position. The vent manifold closed in one direction. There were valves for the negative tank, the safety tank, and the engine air induction, and then there was the hull ventilation induction valve nearby. And those valves unfortunately reopened in the same direction that all the rest closed, which was a design oversight to be sure. But with good training of the crew, no other submarines were having a problem with it.

The skipper, Lieutenant Naquin, was out to break the record for submerging, which was, I believe, forty-five seconds for a crash high-speed submergence. The man who was keeping time on this thing told me that the boat leveled off long before forty-five seconds. He thought they had broken the record, but, of course, the boat filled with water on the stern because these two valves were open; the boat's stern went down and didn't stop. It leveled off at fifty feet. It just went down at an angle and then sank. So I believe that they accidentally reopened those two valves when they were trying to vent tanks.

Bob Evans and I were talking about it, that the skipper was trying to establish a three-section watch bill even before he really had the ship well shaken down. He was trying to get ahead of the game all along, I suppose. And I understand that the particular section that was on the induction manifold at that time was on it for the first time. So I can't prove or disprove it, but that's my opinion of what happened.

18

Another View on the *Squalus*

CAPT. ROBERT L. EVANS,
USN (RET.)

In the spring of 1939 Lt. (j.g.) Bob Evans was stationed at the Portsmouth Navy Yard. On the morning of 23 May, the day the *Squalus* was trapped below, Evans had decided to stay ashore. His decision demonstrated—as is often the case—that fate and circumstances can play major roles in how lives turn out. He also provided his own thoughts on what led to the submarine's problems that day.

I SAW THE CREW of the *Squalus* depart that morning for trials. One of my concerns at that time was that we had some promotion exams to take. The submarine was now about finished, so I had gotten some leave, and I was going home to study. Oliver Naquin asked me if I didn't want to come along that morning. They were hollering at me from the boat, "Come on, come on." I was somewhat tempted to go, but I didn't. I'm kind of glad I didn't.

I went home, and the phone rang about noon. It was the production officer, Cdr. John Hale. He called me up and said, "Come on over here. I've got something to show you." He showed me this dispatch from the *Sculpin*, saying the *Squalus* was flooded from the control room aft. I thought, That can't be. There's no reason why that should happen. It turned out that the main engine air induction valve hadn't shut. Then I began to wonder what I did wrong to make that thing not shut. Well, I couldn't figure out what that could be unless it was rigged wrong when they decided to rig it for dive.

We had an all-night watch. We had people on watch from then on for about three days, until things got straightened out. It was quite a relief

The effects of her prolonged submergence are apparent in this dry-dock view of the *Squalus* made on 15 September 1939. *Naval Institute Photo Archive*

to see all those people that were in the forward part of the submarine come back out again still alive.

I think Oliver Naquin was a competent individual. I think he was good. There's no question in my mind that he and Lt. Bill Doyle, the exec, both thought they had a pressure in the boat when they didn't. But if you've ever seen a manometer wiggle when you put a pressure in the boat, it's pretty hard to tell whether that thing is above its initial point or at the initial point after its wiggle.

There were two valves on top of the ship. One was a ventilation valve with an air-conditioning coil inside it, and the other was this great big engine air induction valve. They were both big valves, but the engine air induction valve was bigger. There were two pipes from those that went back to the engine room and the after battery room in all submarines of that type. At the end of

those pipes there were hull valves which could be operated by hand. They could be operated by hand if you didn't have any obstruction or any interference. If you didn't close them before water started coming through that main engine air induction valve, you couldn't have closed them. No one could have stood near where that hand wheel was; the water was just coming through there too fast.

Cdr. Andy McKee was there at Portsmouth then, and he had an explanation for why the main air induction valve didn't close. It's the only plausible one I know of. Lt. Cdr. W. D. Wilkin was the skipper of the *Sculpin*. One of the specification requirements was to go from diving trim on the surface to periscope depth in sixty seconds. Wilkin couldn't do it. And one of the reasons that was adduced for why he couldn't do it was that the free-flooding openings in the bottom of the superstructure on the top of the submarine were not big enough to let water come in fast enough to have that happen. You could look through the periscope and see the water coming over the top, into that superstructure area. So the idea was to cut those holes bigger and make them big enough so that they would flood fast enough to have the water come in the way they were supposed to.

Oliver Naquin's boat hadn't been modified; neither had the *Sculpin* when Oliver was out to dive. I think he was trying to dive fast. What I think he did was open the flood vents and then pull the handles that were supposed to close the air induction and ventilation valves. The hydraulic system has an accumulator in it that has a finite number of cubic inches associated with it. My recollection is that the pressure on that thing was seven hundred pounds per square inch. When you opened the vents and opened the floods, Andy said, that depleted the accumulator's oil to the point where now the pump had to start and fill the pressure up again. Apparently the pump never got the pressure filled up enough so that the big valve would close.

When the *Squalus* was brought in after it was salvaged, they tied it up at what we called a coal shed. The stern of the boat was on the bottom—although I don't think we knew that—and the bow was up. We had a great big trim on the boat. Finally we decided someone ought to go in the boat. Charlie Curtze, myself, Al Zollars, and Bill Doyle went in with a little hand hydraulic pump. And we had an electric submersible pump. The forward torpedo room was fine. There was a little bit of water in it but not much. The forward battery had some water back near the door to the control room. Maybe we pumped it out enough to get the water down below the coaming. There was quite a bit of water in the control room. So we went in there and started pumping on it, and the water kept going down. We thought we were doing fine. Actually, what was really happening—but we didn't know it—was the tide was going out. The water in the boat was going out with the tide.

Anyway, we got to the after battery room and pumped some water out of it, then got back to that valve and disconnected the hydraulic piping from the hydraulic system. We put our little pump onto it. It was rigged in the proper sequence so that it should work. At sixty pounds pressure the valve opened and closed very nicely. No trouble at all after three months' submergence. So it was not the valve's mechanism that was at fault. I think that Andy's hypothesis on this thing was correct—that the pump just hadn't been able to build the pressure back up high enough in the hydraulic system to make that valve close. So it didn't.

After the *Squalus* was salvaged, the inside was a mess. After a while at the pier, she went in the dry dock. They removed the bodies at that time. The hospital did that. There were twenty-five instead of twenty-six. Somebody got out of the after battery room. He was in the after battery room and got into the skirt around the hatch. There was an air bubble in it, and I think he opened the hatch and was trying to use a bucket. The submarine sailors used to tell me about using a bucket—hold it over their head, and it's full of air. It's buoyant as hell. If you can get out of the submarine, you'll go up pretty fast. You have to keep remembering to breathe out as you do this, too, and I'm not sure people know that much about it. You have to be an expert to do it. Most submariners never get the opportunity to do it that way. I think this guy tried that. He never was found.

When the *Squalus* was salvaged, her bow came soaring up out of the water, inspiring the new name *Sailfish* that was applied to her in February 1940. She was dewatered, cleaned out, repaired, and then recommissioned with her new name on 15 May 1940. During World War II she sank seven ships. In an interesting quirk of fate, one of the ships she sank—as described in a later chapter in this book—carried prisoners from the *Sailfish*'s sister *Sculpin*. Carl LaVO has well described the intertwined fates of the two submarines in his 1994 book *Back from the Deep*.

19

Grandstand Seat at Pearl Harbor

VICE ADM. LAWSON P. RAMAGE,
USN (RET.)

During World War II Red Ramage was one of the top American submarine skippers. That experience was still ahead of him when war began for the United States on 7 December 1941. At the time he was a lieutenant and had recently reported to the staff of Rear Adm. Thomas Withers Jr., commander, Submarines Scouting Force, Pacific Fleet. Ramage's job was as the force communication and sound officer. Until the middle of 1941 the admiral and his staff had been based on board the light cruiser *Richmond*. They moved ashore to offices in the Pearl Harbor submarine base and after a time were joined by Adm. Husband E. Kimmel, commander in chief, Pacific Fleet, and his staff.

I HAD THE DUTY that Sunday morning, so I fully intended to go out to Pearl Harbor early. But my friend, Lt. Cdr. Ed Swinburne, who was our flag secretary, said that he would take the duty until ten o'clock, because he was a bachelor and in no rush to go home. Promptly at eight o'clock, our telephone rang, and I answered it. Ed said, "Get out here right away. The Japs are attacking Pearl Harbor."

Actually, I thought he was pulling my leg. So I said, "Oh yes, Ed, I know you can handle that situation. You can take care of it until I get there."

"No, no," he said. "No fooling, this is the real thing."

"I know, Ed," I answered. "I don't know what's bothering you, but don't lose your balance."

And Ed just kept insisting it was the real thing. About that time, there was an explosion right in the neighborhood. All of a sudden, some hysterical woman cut in on our telephone

This is an aerial view of the Pearl Harbor submarine base in October 1941. The U-shaped building near the piers is the headquarters for the Pacific Fleet commander in chief and for commander, Submarines, Scouting Force, Pacific Fleet. The U-shaped building farther inland is the submariners' barracks. *National Archives: 80-G-411198*

line and said, "Oh, something terrible has happened. What should I do? Who should I call? Who am I talking to?"

At that point, I told Ed I'd be down to the base to see him shortly. I walked to the front part of the house and looked out over Pearl Harbor. I could see that there was some smoke and could see some action out there. Then I turned the radio on, and there was a nice piece of church music wafting through the room. Someone interrupted the program to say that the Japanese were attacking Pearl Harbor. That was about the extent of the announcement, and the station went right back to playing its beautiful hymns and so on.

I immediately got dressed and took off for Pearl Harbor. The first wave of planes had passed over by the time I got to the naval base. But on the way out there, every conceivable vehicle was loaded with sailors—buses, taxis, and everything else—rushing to get out there. When I got up to our office on the second deck of the supply building, I looked out the windows and discovered that I had a grandstand seat for the whole performance. It was absolutely fantastic to see these planes just sliding right down to not more than two hundred yards in front of me. It was just incredible to see the whole line of battleships engulfed in fire and thick black smoke.

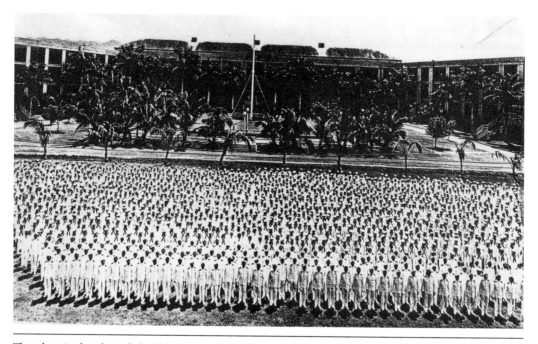

The submarine base barracks building at Pearl Harbor has housed thousands of undersea warriors over the years. Tai Sing Loo captured this image on film shortly before World War II. *Naval Institute Photo Archive*

It wasn't too long before most of the Pacific Fleet staff had arrived. I remember Admiral Kimmel pacing back and forth there in front of us, his jaw stuck out. We were all just dumbfounded that this could happen. But there it was—not only in Technicolor but with sound effects and all. In the midst of it, the thing that I think was most apparent was that none of us was at all concerned about his own safety. This is a funny thing, but it's typical of many combat operations. When you're in a dangerous situation, you figure something could happen to somebody else, but it's not going to happen to you. There might be terror if the danger is coming pretty close to you, but the Pearl Harbor attack was not being directed at those of us in the headquarters building.

The transformation that morning from peacetime—calm, everyday routine—to complete alert was really striking. I have never seen anything comparable happen so quickly in my life. When I wasn't watching our ships being attacked, I was busy trying to contact our submarines en route to Pearl Harbor. There were three P-boats, the *Pompano*, *Plunger*, and *Pollack*. They were about two

hundred miles east of Hawaii, just returning from overhaul on the West Coast. We had the *Gudgeon*, with Joe Grenfell in command, down at Lahaina Roads. Bill Anderson in the *Thresher* was coming in from Midway and was just about off Barbers Point on the island of Oahu.

I had all the communications to myself there in the submarine base, but all of a sudden we found all our circuits, receivers, transmitters, and everything else preempted by the commander in chief, Pacific Fleet. Cdr. Germany Curts was the fleet communication officer, and Lt. Cdr. Donald Beard was his radio officer. Don really rose to the occasion. They both did a magnificent job. Everybody did. Don managed to get reels of wire from all over; I don't know how he did it. I saw him running down the corridor with reels of wire from positions up in the office on the second deck, down the stairs, out onto the docks, and into the submarines so he could use their transmitters and receivers. I've never seen so many things come on the line so fast.

Our submarines in the Hawaiian area weren't brought in. We told them to go south and lie low until the attack was over. We told everybody to stay clear. That was the primary thing at that point, not to make the situation any more complicated than it was already. As soon as we could find out what had happened, we would bring them in. It was primarily for their own good to stay clear of that debacle.

During the next two or three weeks, I saw Admiral Kimmel frequently, because our offices weren't more than thirty feet apart. I didn't have any personal conversations with him, but I could see that he was tremendously shocked and upset. Naturally, he would be. Nobody had had the slightest inkling that the Japanese would be brassy enough to attack Pearl Harbor and our whole fleet there.

One of the things we did after the attack was begin to censor all the mail. I was absolutely amazed at the attitudes of the mothers telling their sons to get out there and kick you-know-what out of the Japanese. They were really belligerent, and they hadn't even seen the thing up close the way we had. I've never seen such language and such virulent hate, and these were letters from mothers to their sons. I never expected that something could stir up such emotion across the country. And I don't think the Japanese ever realized that they could touch off such a reaction either.

20

Disaster at Cavite

REAR ADM. NORVELL G. WARD,
USN (RET.)

Shortly before the beginning of World War II a number of new fleet submarines went to the Asiatic Fleet in the western Pacific to beef up U.S. capability. The fleet commander in chief, Adm. Thomas Hart, evacuated most of them as war approached, but the *Sealion* and *Seadragon* were immobilized at the Cavite Navy Yard in the Philippines while undergoing repair work. Ward was executive officer of the *Seadragon*.

W E STILL HAD approximately a month to go on our overhaul when the war started. As a consequence, a great deal of equipment was torn down. Our decking was all torn up. Sections of it were being replaced when the Japanese bombed Cavite around noon the tenth of December. We manned our .50-caliber machine guns up on the bridge. I think we even had men on our 3-inch gun, as did the *Sealion*, which was tied up alongside of us outboard.

We watched the Japanese bomber formation go over at about twenty-two to twenty-five thousand feet, watched them make a practice run from west to east, then turn around and come back and make their first bombing run from east to west. We saw the bombs drop on the pier and other buildings up in the shipyard. We saw them release, we saw them coming down, but we knew on that run that they were going to miss us, just a little bit over that way. And they did. That's when Dick Voge, captain of the *Sealion*, turned to Pete Ferrall, skipper of our boat, and said, "You know, I think we're damn fools staying up here on the bridge."

Pete said, "I agree with you." So Dick cleared his people off the topside, and we cleared ours off

The incomplete *Seadragon* slides down the building ways at Electric Boat in Groton, Connecticut, on 21 April 1939. In the war that followed a few years later, the submarine would be hit by a Japanese attack in the Philippines and serve as the scene of a widely publicized appendectomy performed by enlisted Pharmacist's Mate Wheeler Lipes. *Courtesy of Elizabeth Ann Schafer*

the topside. Dick Voge had all of his go down below into the control room, whereas on the *Seadragon*, some of us stayed up in the conning tower. I stayed up in the conning tower, along with Lt. (j.g.) Sam Hunter, our chief pharmacist's mate Diaz, and two or three others. Pete Ferrall went down to the control room.

It was on the next run the Japanese formation made that the *Sealion* received two bomb hits, one right on the conning tower, and the other in the after engine room. Of course, if anyone had been in the conning tower in *Sealion*, every one of them would have been wiped out. The *Sealion* lost four men who were back in the after engine room and the maneuvering room when the bomb hit.

Shrapnel from the *Sealion*'s conning tower went through ours. It took off the back of Sam Hunter's head and shattered Diaz's arm. I was standing there with my hand on Sam's shoulder, and I was fortunate in that I only got scraped across the belly by some of the shrapnel. So Sam was killed right away and, of course, the conning tower was filled with smoke from the blast on the *Sealion*. I pulled Sam out of the conning tower and with the help of someone else, we laid him over on the pier. So Sam was killed, Diaz was injured, and I had a superficial wound.

The blasts that hit over the after engine room of the *Sealion* stove in our pressure hull back abreast of our maneuvering room, right at the bulkhead at the forward end of the maneuvering room. We had a seepage of water. Not much. Our office space and living barracks where the men had all their gear were wiped out or set on fire. But we started working like

This was the scene of devastation following the Japanese bombing attack on the Cavite Navy Yard on 10 December 1941. The bow of a submarine can be seen at the extreme right side of the photo. *Naval Institute Photo Archive*

the devil to get clear of the *Sealion* and get clear of the pier.

In the two previous days, once the war started, we had been working like the devil to get ready for sea. And when it becomes urgent, you can suddenly get power on in a relatively short time. And it was urgent then. There in the yard was a submarine rescue ship called the *Pigeon*, under Cdr. Dick Hawes, who was a legendary submariner and diver. "Spittin' Dick" did a tremendous job helping all the ships in the yard on that day. He finally came over, put a line on us, and pulled us out into the stream where we dropped anchor, and we figured that about five o'clock that afternoon we'd be able to get power to our screws from the battery.

At approximately five o'clock, we had power on our screws. Under our own power, we went over to Manila's inner harbor, where the tender *Canopus* was, and tied up alongside her. Then the repair crew from the *Canopus* worked for several days to improve our mobility, to put down some sort of planking on the deck and the other things that had to be done. Also, they formed a plate that conformed to the curvature of the hull and welded it over the part where a seam had been made by the bomb blast that hit the *Sealion*. When I left roughly ten or eleven months later, that plate was still there. The only additional thing that had been done was to add two or three more beads of welding around it, and the *Seadragon* survived the entire war.

21

Escape from the Japanese

CHIEF SHIP'S CLERK, CWO-2,
CECIL S. KING, USN (RET.)

In the waning years of the U.S. Asiatic Fleet in the Far East, Yeoman 1st Class Cecil King was assigned to the flag allowance of the fleet commander in chief, Adm. Thomas C. Hart. The old China Station had a good deal of allure attached to it, but that faded as war approached. In the summer of 1941 the admiral and his staff left their flagship, the heavy cruiser *Houston*, and moved ashore to head-quarters in Manila in the Philippine Islands. When the Japanese attacked the island of Luzon, King managed to escape on board the old four-stack destroyer *Peary*. It was a perilous voyage to the Dutch East Indies island of Java, still in Allied hands in January 1942 but facing imminent danger.

THE JAPS WERE MOVING our way awfully fast. The *Houston* was sunk in the Battle of Sunda Strait. The light cruiser *Marble-head* was damaged extensively and headed on back to the States. It became obvious pretty soon that things were going downhill fast, and we'd have to leave. One morning we were told we would be ground troops, part of the multina-tional ABDA [American-British-Dutch-Australian] Command. The plan was that we would stay there, which didn't suit me too well. But then it was a very quickly shifting situation.

The next word we got was that the submarine *Sturgeon* was over at Tjilatjap, on the other side of the island. Some injured burn patients off the *Houston* were going to be put on the *Sturgeon*. I was given a sack of classified items and instructed to go to Tjilatjap. At Tjilatjap, at least one night, a bunch of us Navy guys were billeted aboard a Dutch ship named the *Zandam* out in the harbor. I remember that we hadn't been paid in a long

Cecil King had reason to smile as a chief petty officer during the World War II because of his narrow escapes from the Japanese. *Naval Institute Photo Archive; courtesy of William King*

time and all of a sudden we got paid. We got paid in guilders—we called them "gliders." We had no idea what they were worth. We had a poker game on the *Zandam* that ran all night long—playing for guilders—and at one time I had the most enormous stack of money in front of me. I broke even before the game was over, but I was rich beyond my wildest dreams at one point there.

I'm not sure now exactly how I got ashore from the *Zandam* and to the *Sturgeon*. There was some difficult logistics in getting from point A to point B, whether you walked or bummed a ride. I damn near missed the *Sturgeon*, because I was late getting to the dock where she was. In fact, she was about to pull out. But, anyway, I remember getting on the submarine and checking in.

We got out of Tjilatjap on the twentieth of February, and we were on the *Sturgeon* several

days, going to Fremantle, Australia. We were not under any kind of a direct attack that I was aware of. We apparently had some problems. It's not always great being a passenger. There were reports of Japanese submarines in that area, and I found out that what really worried a submariner more than anything else was another submarine. At least that's the impression I got. They didn't worry so much about the destroyers. I don't know why.

Once we got to the Australia area we couldn't surface for about two days because of where we were and the Jap forces around us. We were submerged for quite some period of time. Anyway, when we did surface, the fresh air was like champagne. I remember that was so beautiful. But then we made an uneventful trip to Perth. That really was the effective end of any Philippine or

Asiatic Fleet adventures that I had. Because in Perth it was just 100 percent the opposite. We were just there, and all the Australian men had gone overseas. There were a hundred beautiful Australian girls to each American sailor. Just all of a sudden it went from night to day. Instead of being shot at and picked on by the Japs and everything, people were asking for our autographs, if you can imagine that—just overnight.

Because Yeoman King was still carried on the crew list for the *Houston* when she was sunk on 1 February 1941, the Navy Department reported to his parents in Texas that he was missing and presumed dead. They had already put up a gold star in the front window of their home to honor him and were quite shocked when he called from Java to pass on the news that he was alive and well. Some while later he visited his hometown of Aransas Pass, where he had the pleasure of reading his own obituary and learning that he had been the subject of a nice memorial service.

22

Reservists at Submarine School

VICE ADM.
EUGENE P. WILKINSON,
USN (RET.)

In the 1920s and 1930s the Naval Academy was about the only source for college-educated officers in the U.S. Navy. As war approached, however, the Navy faced a considerable challenge in training sufficient numbers of officers for its rapidly expanding fleet. Some Reservists came from Naval Reserve Officer Training Corps (NROTC) units at various universities, and the service set up a number of other programs as well. Eugene "Dennis" Wilkinson, a graduate of San Diego State, was commissioned in 1940 after undergoing officer training through the Naval Reserve's V-7 program. He was a junior officer in the heavy cruiser *Louisville* and then volunteered for Submarine School. At the time he expected to serve his wartime duty and then return to civilian life. As it happened, however, the Navy kept offering him jobs he liked, and he didn't retire from active duty until 1974. In the meantime, he went to Submarine School in 1942 and demonstrated himself to be a master psychologist in talking to the officer in charge.

I VOLUNTEERED FOR submarines when it was obvious that we weren't going to get out of the military service when our year was up. I chose submarines because a small ship would provide responsibility quicker. Also, it was a chance to get three months back in the States and see my girl. It got me back home. That was part of the reason, probably a big part. Our Sub School class had sixty students; we had thirty Reservists and thirty regular Navy. I observed some different problems there.

Every Saturday morning we'd have a special exam, and that exam was supposed to count one-quarter of your aptitude mark plus the evalua-

Cdr. Karl G. Hensel was officer in charge of the Submarine School from August 1941 to December 1942. *Naval Institute Photo Archive*

To the Submarine School with my great admiration and affection —

Karl G. Hensel

tions of the teachers. The aptitude mark was important because it counted one-quarter of your overall class standing. And you got your duty assignments according to your class standing. So that first aptitude mark came out, and all the Reservists were the last half of the class. There wasn't one overlap, which was a little odd. Well, as it happened, this exam they gave every week for several weeks in a row, by some good fortune I had cracked it. Just by chance one week they threw in a surprise exam on buoyage. I had got interested in that, and the week before I happened to have read about it and got interested and studied it thoroughly. There wasn't anybody knew all these things about buoyage except me, and so I had a 4.0 and everybody else was down there further and further.

Then they had an exam on Rules of the Road, and the same thing happened to me. It

happened that several weeks in a row I had a 4.0 on that surprise any-subject quiz. And I'm telling you, the average of those quizzes was probably 2.5 or something. So, as it happened, if I took my marks and counted them, I was in the top third, but I was graded as probably about fortieth in the school. So my aptitude from all my senior instructors had to have been under 2.5. In other words, they had never done what they said, got aptitude marks and averaged them. So nobody was less than 2.5 in aptitude, except I had to have been on account of these quizzes I had cracked. So—tongue in cheek because I'm a humorist—I went around and asked for an appointment with the CO of the school, who was a crackerjack guy.

This was Karl Hensel, a good man, smart. He was really good at fire control and approaches and whatnot, and he ran the teachers' training

Hensel (*front row, center*) poses with this prospective commanding officers' course at New London in February 1943. The other two officers in khaki were both lost with their boats. Lt. Cdr. Howard Gilmore, at left in the top row, put the *Growler* in commission on 20 March 1942 and was killed 8 November 1943. Mannert L. Abele (*front row, left*) commissioned the *Grunion* on 11 April 1942. She was lost in the Aleutians in the summer of 1942. *National Archives: 80-G-88577*

thing for that. And I was good at that. So I went in and told him how much I liked submarines and how bad I felt that I didn't measure up. "What are you talking about?" he said, because I was doing pretty well scholastically in that school.

I said, "Well, here's what I had on the quizzes. And here was my aptitude. It's obvious mathematically, see, that I'm rated as unsatisfactory in aptitude by these people that I admire as leaders." Butter wouldn't melt in my mouth. Absolute poker face. I was really putting it to him, making it seem that I just didn't measure up, and asked when I could expect other duty. I said that if I didn't have the aptitude for submarines, I felt really bad. He looked at me for a long time. He told me, "I'll square it away. Get the hell out of here."

I said, "Aye, aye, sir." The next month all the aptitude marks were read. I don't know whether the new marks were fair but they certainly weren't like they had been, and I was marked number one in tactics.

After that—I've forgotten the exact figure now—but I think when I finally retired I had probably sat on nine selection boards. In the beginning it really made a difference whether someone was a Reservist or from the trade school, as we called the Naval Academy. Hey, now it doesn't make a damn bit of difference at all. All they care about now is the quality and performance of the guy. I saw that change during my time in the Navy. And I was on the inside where I really knew. I saw that totally change, and it was good that it did.

23

Drum at War

REAR ADM.
MAURICE H. RINDSKOPF,
USN (RET.)

After graduating from the United States Naval Academy in 1938, Ensign Rindskopf had the obligatory early duty in a surface ship, the battleship *Colorado*, attended the Submarine School, and then began his submarine service in the antique *R-4*, based in Key West, Florida. After that brief tour of duty, he reported to the Portsmouth Navy Yard, which was then building the *Drum*, first of the new *Gato*-class boats turned out by that yard. His first day in the new assignment was 11 November 1941, then still known as Armistice Day in honor of the end of World War I. When he reported to the recently commissioned *Drum*, World War II was already in progress in Europe and about to engulf the United States.

W E WERE THE LEAD SHIP in the group in the yard and working toward sea trials within a couple of months. Lo and behold, on 7 December, when my wife Sylvia and I went to dispose of trash at the local town dump, we heard on the car radio that Pearl Harbor had been attacked. One of my new shipmates in *Drum* was Lt. Manning M. Kimmel, the chief engineer. His father, Adm. Husband Kimmel, was commander in chief of the Pacific Fleet during the attack on Pearl Harbor.

I rushed back to the ship and learned that *Drum* was supposed to provide the sole antiaircraft protection for the shipyard. We quickly had a 3-inch gun installed on the after deck. The administration building had a captain's walk on the tower. It was manned around the clock because of the expectation that German bombers would be along at any moment. So panic set in, I

guess you would say, at the Portsmouth Navy Yard. They quickly got us completed, and by the end of December we were already out to sea, maybe a month and a half early, to start our trials. Anybody who's been to sea in New England in the winter knows it's not particularly pleasant, but we got through our trials, including the deep dive.

One of our tests involved measuring the ship's acoustic signature, and that was done in Gardiners Bay, off Long Island. This required the ship to anchor and trim down to put all the machinery deeper in the water. As the technicians measured unit after unit, they requested that the ship flood down a bit more. This resulted in *Drum* settling to the bottom in about twenty-five feet of water—cold water. The skipper, Lt. Cdr. Bob Rice, was on the bridge, and the water came up to his waist; he did not appreciate this caper. In spite of this we completed the test. On 17 February we bade a tearful farewell to wives and girlfriends and got under way for Panama.

After a trip through the canal, we arrived in Pearl Harbor in mid-March 1942. We had been traveling with *Gato*, the first ship of the class, but she had some material problems that required her to stop in San Francisco. As a result, we were the first new-construction submarine to get to Pearl after the attack. It was an extremely sobering experience to see the *Oklahoma*, *Arizona*, and all the other ships that had been destroyed or damaged during the attack. However, the submarine base and the submarines that were alongside were untouched. That was one of the biggest mistakes the Japanese made—that and not attacking exposed fuel tanks.

We spent a week or two training off Pearl, and by that point the situation in the Philippines was becoming desperate. We were loaded with concentrated foods, medical supplies, and awful-smelling vitamins. Our mission was to take the items to the island of Corregidor. We went to Midway and there joined forces with a small merchant ship that was full of antiaircraft ammunition and also directed to go to Corregidor. That skipper was delighted that he would have a warship as escort. I know he would never have made it, and whether we would or not was problematical. Before we could sail from Midway we learned that Corregidor was about to fall, and we were ordered back to Pearl Harbor. We unloaded all of the medicines and vitamins, which were not very pleasant to live with, and took on a full load of torpedoes. These were the Mark 14s, which had problems. We lost innumerable targets because of them. We sortied for our first war patrol on 17 April 1942.

As the gunnery officer of the *Drum*, I became the torpedo data computer operator. The TDC at that time was a basic analog computer in the conning tower of the submarine, but it was a significant step forward over what we had previously. I made eleven war patrols and operated the TDC even when I was the executive officer. We sank fifteen ships and damaged eleven more. In terms of tonnage sunk, this put us eighth on the list of successful submarines, but maybe fifteen or more of the first sixty torpedoes I was involved in firing failed to function properly, either exploding early or not exploding at all. Some exploded as soon as they were armed, and that's a major jolt—to have six hundred pounds of torpex go off about three hundred yards from the submarine.

One of the curious events of my submarine career happened on the first patrol. We were in an area from Tokyo well down the southern coast of Honshu. Because there were so few submarines out there, we had all that lucrative territory open to us. Our skipper, Bob Rice, was a very sophisticated officer whom I consider one of my mentors. The night we approached the coast he decided to sleep on the bridge, because that would put him close to the action in case something happened. The crew rigged up a bunk spring and mattress for him. About midnight an airplane went overhead, we dove the submarine, and the mattress floated off. It had the boat's name on it and was recovered by the Japanese. In no time at all, the U.S. forces intercepted a radio report from Tokyo Rose, a turncoat who made propaganda broadcasts designed to lower American morale. She reported that *Drum* had been

Rindskopf uses a sextant as navigator of the *Drum*.
Courtesy of Rear Adm. Maurice H. Rindskopf

sunk, because the Japanese had recovered this mattress. Fortunately, it wasn't true, but that was the last time the CO tried to sleep near the action.

In early May 1942 we made our first attack, without radar. It was a night surface attack, something that had really never been done before the war. We fired two torpedoes, got two explosions, and sank what turned out to be a seaplane tender. It was *Mizuho*, the largest ship, at nine thousand tons, that a submarine had sunk up to that time. We also fired that night on a destroyer. We now know that the torpedo ran deep, under the target. It failed to explode, but it did make the enemy angry enough that he and his buddies dropped depth charges on us—maybe one hundred of them—in the next twenty hours. Bob Rice visited with all the officers, explaining how to conduct ourselves if we were forced to surface and wound up being captured. In retrospect, many of the depth charges were distant, though we didn't yet have enough experience to judge that; we probably could have cleared the area safely sooner. Nonetheless, it was an exciting start to the war, and afterward we had a great meal of ham and eggs.

At the time of the attack on *Mizuho*, Captain Rice was certain that we had a sinking. When we returned to Pearl Harbor about six weeks later, the Submarine Force staff was on hand to congratulate us, because they had intercepted distress calls from the ship and knew she had sunk. That was the first experience I had with communications intelligence in action. I knew nothing about Ultra messages at the time. That came later, when I was executive officer.

I recall wondering, as we readied *Drum* for departure on its second patrol, if there was some reluctance to venture forth again. Indeed, there were risks, but at that point few boats had been lost in action. Later, of course, the Submarine Force would suffer the highest percentage of casualties in the Navy. The second patrol was the antithesis of the first—no action against the enemy. And we were unsuccessful in another respect as well. Eunice Rice, the skipper's wife, worked in the code-breaking section of the Navy Department. She agreed to send *Drum* a message when Sylvia had our first baby. The message came while we were under attack off Truk Atoll. Since it was sent only once, rather than six times as an official message would have been, we failed to receive it. It was when we returned to Midway in September that I learned our son Peter had been born on 25 July and that all was well.

There is another story about Eunice Rice worth relating. She was, in her position, privy to *Drum*'s comings and goings. She sent the wives a round-robin note as we returned from each patrol, something that was less than legal. It also nearly got me in trouble, because on one of the periodic phone calls I made to Sylvia I mentioned something about Eunice's messages. That alerted the censor, who listened in and could cut off the call. This apparently filtered back to Bob Rice, who took me aside to provide some fatherly advice on security.

More patrols passed, we got a new skipper, Lt. Cdr. Barney McMahon, and eventually I fleeted up to become executive officer after Manning Kimmel had held the job for a while. The way we ran the ship, the captain had the command watch assignment until midnight. Then I took it from midnight until dawn when we made our daily dive. After leaving the bridge at 4:00 AM I would pick up a cup of hot soup or other goodie from the galley and then head for the decoding room. I would toil away for an hour or more decoding messages that had arrived during the night, while we were on the surface. It was a manual coding system, not like the machines we used later. Only the captain and I were permitted to decode an Ultra message, which reported to us intelligence that had come from decrypting intercepted Japanese messages.

I recall a time when we learned that we would probably encounter a Japanese ship before the day was over. I said nothing to anyone except the skipper about the message, but I did don a garish yellow Aloha shirt I had purchased in Honolulu. Sure enough, the ship came in sight, we fired, and sank it. We went back to Pearl Harbor, had our refit, and did some training. We came back out again, and once again an Ultra opportunity came along. I put my yellow shirt back on. This time almost every crew member had on a yellow shirt. I've used that as a case of leadership by example, and it's a pretty good story.

There are a couple of other interesting tales worth relating. McMahon was an inveterate cigar smoker, and one of his favorites was a Cuban cigar, when available. He would go through a regular routine after an attack: "Take her down, rig for depth charge, and bring me my cigar." In a short time, the air in the conning tower, without ventilation, became blue. It was then that I would wander below, through the ship, to assure the crew in the galley, engine rooms, and after torpedo room that all was in good hands. In reality, it was to evade cigar smoke.

I should also tell the story of *Drum*'s Jesus. He was Signalman 1st Class Al Galas, who sported a full blond beard, and he would spend literally hours in front of a mirror, combing his beard incessantly. He even got written up for it in the ship's paper, which was published periodically.

Between war patrols, Rindskopf relaxes on a beach in Australia in October 1943. *Courtesy of Rear Adm. Maurice H. Rindskopf*

In the 1990s Al appeared at several of the ship's reunions in Mobile, Alabama, where *Drum* is now as a memorial. By then he no longer had the beard.

Before leaving the McMahon era, I should report that the first Naval Academy graduate to come aboard after *Drum*'s commissioning was Lt. (j.g.) Charles M. Young, class of 1942. His father, Capt. Cassin Young, had been killed on the bridge while in command of the heavy cruiser *San Francisco* at the Battle of Savo Island, off Guadalcanal, in November 1942. He came aboard *Drum* with great determination to avenge his father's death and was a dedicated, effective officer who became my exec when I fleeted up to command.

In the summer of 1944, only six years out of the Naval Academy, I was fortunate to become skipper of *Drum*. Cdr. Delbert Williamson, who had made two patrols as commanding officer after relieving McMahon, developed gallstones. We were then in Majuro Atoll in the Marshall Islands. Williamson went back to Pearl Harbor,

had his operation, and never came back to the ship. I was offered the opportunity to train another skipper or to take command. That decision was easy to make. I became the youngest fleet boat CO at that time and the first in my Naval Academy class. I was not yet twenty-seven.

My first patrol in command was from June to September of 1944 around the Palau Islands. We had a poor area with no targets, so we didn't sink any ships. We did pick up a couple of prisoners from a sampan we sank by gunfire. One became an excellent assistant in the galley. The second patrol I made was in the Taiwan area in October 1944. We were then ordered to the east side of Leyte Island in the Philippines, just before Gen. Douglas MacArthur made his famous "I have returned" landing. All we saw were a couple of aircraft but no surface ships, so two days before the landing we were ordered north into the Luzon Strait. Lo and behold, shortly after that MacArthur and his people went ashore, and shortly thereafter came the major ship battles.

While we were up north we did run across some significant targets; we sank three ships and damaged another between the twenty-fourth and twenty-sixth of October. I was honored to be awarded the Navy Cross for those.

At the end of my second patrol in command I heard from my first skipper in that boat, Cdr. Bob Rice. He was then in the Bureau of Naval Personnel as the submarine detail officer. We had exchanged some correspondence, because it was inevitable that one day I would leave the ship. I suggested that maybe it was time I should get Sylvia out of New London, where she and our little son Peter had been living with her folks. I thought that we ought to get off on our own and see if we could run the family show by ourselves. In his wisdom, Bob Rice said, "No, you're going to the Submarine School staff." So I left *Drum* in November 1944, exactly three years after I had arrived, and went back to New London. There I joined thirty-two other former skippers, all of them Navy Cross recipients. I was assigned to the tactics department under Cdr. Chester W. Nimitz Jr., along with Lt. Dennis Wilkinson, who later commanded the nuclear submarine *Nautilus*, and Lt. Jim Calvert, who later commanded the *Skate*.

24

Breakers Ahead!

CAPT. EDWARD L. BEACH,
USN (RET.)

Among the best-known American submariners of World War II was Capt. Ned Beach, a degree of fame that came to him retroactively. In the 1950s he wrote the highly successful novel *Run Silent, Run Deep*, which gave the public, through fiction, a realistic picture of what the war at sea had been like. Beach wrote other novels about submarines, and he wrote a nonfiction account of his life and career, *Salt and Steel*. The following excerpt is from that book. In the descriptive prose for which he was famous, Beach told of an incident from his first submarine, the USS *Trigger*, which had gone into commission in January 1942 with Lt. Cdr. Jack H. Lewis as commanding officer. After her training concluded, the submarine's first operational mission was to patrol off Midway in June.

THE STORY of the Battle of Midway is well known. Less well known is the part the *Trigger* played in the battle, far from distinguished, except in the negative sense. It was the night of 3 June 1942. We were patrolling our sector on the surface some twenty miles east of Midway when, at about 0330, according to Lt. (j.g.) Steve Mann, whom I came to relieve at the prescribed time, 0345, as officer of the deck, the stars began to move strangely above him, the heavens changed in ways they never had before, everything became disoriented. Shouting down the hatch, he discovered that the captain had come into the conning tower and, without notifying anyone, had ordered the helm put over and the course changed. Then he went below again, without any further word. Steve was incensed and upset; but since it was the captain who had

taken this liberty, there was nothing he could do except pass on to me what he did know, and promise to tell me what was going on as soon as he found out.

Shortly after I had pronounced the formal words, "I relieve you, sir!"—even though Steve had not been able to tell me what direction I, as his relief, was supposed to "drive"—Steve sent word from the wardroom that we had received orders to close Midway to a distance of two miles in anticipation of a Japanese landing effort at dawn.

The *Trigger* bored on toward Midway at full speed. Having no knowledge of the navigational situation, or what the captain's intentions were, I was much concerned and kept a vigilant watch, particularly ahead, where I presumed Midway must be. At no time during this period did our skipper come on the bridge, nor into the conning tower immediately below. I thought he must be doing some important work over charts in the wardroom, and when I sent down word that I

was beginning to see things in the distance ahead I was startled to discover no one knew where he was. My staring eyes, fully accommodated to the darkness (I discovered later that I had been blessed with excellent night vision), had begun to make out some sort of low-lying disturbance on the horizon. I called this down to the captain, thinking he must be in the control room. Learning he had possibly gone forward to his stateroom, I asked for the navigator to be called. Penrod Schneider, executive officer and navigator, came on the bridge, admitted he did not know what was going on, had not been briefed, and was not night-adapted. Recognizing my concern, he went below to check the charts, promising to give me more information as soon as he could.

We drove on relentlessly at eighteen knots, and I became aware of something glittering on the horizon. Perhaps it was my imagination; perhaps it was ships—if so, no doubt Japanese; but my strongest impression was as though lights were reflecting from the windows of a small building upon a distant shoreline. I reported this to Schneider in the conning tower.

Shortly thereafter, the captain came on the bridge and, after a long look through his binoculars, went below, once again without saying a word. I made several reports that I could see land and distant buildings several miles ahead. Finally, from the conning tower I was told to desist, that there should be no land in sight, that I must be "seeing things." It was understandable that we should all be pretty tense, with a Japanese landing attempt expected within hours. Finally, however, with the sight of tumultuous white water just ahead I shouted down to the conning tower that, if it was not land, I was looking at the wakes of several big ships that had just crossed our bow. Our rudimentary radar gave no indication of anything, but at this moment our quartermaster of the watch, an experienced sailor who had heard everything and was diligently searching ahead, as on the bridge we all were, shouted out in a voice full of fright, "Breakers! Breakers ahead!"

And suddenly it was all very obvious. There were great black rocks ahead, waves splashing violently upon them! The captain and navigator dashed up on the bridge beside me. "All back full!" roared the captain. I heard the click of the engine-order telegraphs and could sense the propellers stopping and taking a bite in reverse direction.

"Sound the collision alarm!" our captain shouted; I heard all the ship's alarms sound, without pause, one after the other. The effect was as if they had all sounded at once: collision alarm, general alarm, and a single blast on the diving alarm. (We discovered later that the chief of the watch in the control room, startled, had rung all the alarms in sight.)

Disaster was on us. The rocks were huge, and so were the waves splashing over them. No one thought to order the rudder hard over, which might have helped the situation. Maybe I might have done it, but by giving direct orders the skipper had taken over the conn. Nothing was done with the rudder. More important, however, when the diving alarm sounded, the electricians took the main engines off the line, shifted to battery propulsion, and, following the boat's standard orders for diving, reversed the direction of the propellers a second time, putting them ahead full. As the result, never even slowing our headlong pace, in accordance with dive procedures we continued to drive ahead full speed on the batteries.

Helpless, having totally lost control, we on the bridge saw our boat drive full speed onto the rocks. We struck with a horrendous clang. I was looking dead ahead right over the bow, and saw it rise irresistibly out of the water, reaching heavenward in a desperate, agonized leap. I actually thought that, somewhere behind me, we must have broken in half. I saw our bow slammed sideways to starboard, and then several more diminishing bumps as we slid forward. Finally, and very quickly, all forward motion stopped. The ship lay half out of the water at an improbable angle. That we were seriously damaged we had no doubt. Our stern was partially submerged, our bow jutted out over grey sand and big coral rocks. We had driven our ship aground at full power, and she was stuck fair.

We had been informed the Japs were due to try to land on Midway that very morning. There was nothing we could do to help ourselves, let alone fight them. If their aircraft, or their battleships in for shore bombardment, which operation orders had mentioned as a possibility, were to see us helpless on the reef, that would be the end of us.

However, the *Trigger* had not broken in half, as I had first thought. Internally there was indescribable confusion, but our super-strong submarine hull had received no damage that we could detect. Our engines were not injured, all systems functioned normally. Our stern was still in deep water; we restarted the engines and backed with full power, but finally gave up. There was no budging from our impaled position on the rocks.

A signal searchlight was brought up, and in the growing dawn we could see, now clearly outlined in the morning twilight on the far side of the Midway lagoon, exactly the buildings and shoreline I had been describing before we struck. Whatever it was that had glittered faintly now glittered strongly; and finally the insistent blink-

The *Trigger* exits Midway to go on wartime patrol after Lt. Cdr. Roy Benson became skipper. In the foreground are the island's famous goony birds. *Naval Historical Center: NH 94736-KN*

ing of our signal light evoked a response. To our message that we were aground came the answer, "Are you inside the reef?" This hadn't occurred to us, but a later look at the chart showed it was not a foolish question.

"Outside the reef!" we said. "Send tug!" We hoped for a regular Navy tug, a big seagoing ship with powerful engines. Instead, a tiny tug appeared, so small it resembled a toy. In the meantime, mindful of the Japanese attack expected at dawn, we had manned our antiaircraft battery: two thirty-caliber machine guns on the bridge, and our three-inch antiaircraft gun on the main deck. If the Japanese planes appeared, we would at least shoot back, although, looking at our tiny armament, it was evident these guns were only symbolic.

The tug tossed us a heaving line, put a hawser on our stern, and began to pull. The water boiled up behind her in a very respectable effort for so small a vessel. We backed emergency at the same time with all the power our engines could give us. Nothing happened, and then the hawser broke. At this point, I felt sure our brand-new *Trigger* was doomed to spend the rest of her days on the reef; but maybe the tug had done some good, maybe a small tide had raised the water level a little, perhaps we had indeed increased our draft forward just before striking. Before the tug came we had blown our ballast tanks absolutely dry, pumped overboard much of our fuel, and all our extra water. We were preparing to jettison torpedoes through our bow tubes when someone noticed our ship had unaccountably come alive. There was a definite motion as she lay among the rocks. "She's moving!" he shouted.

All hands not otherwise engaged were ordered on deck to sally ship, cause her to roll by running from one side to the other. I stood on the after part of the bridge and tried to coordinate the ship's movements with hand motions. They ran back and forth across with a will, but there seemed to be no corresponding movement of the ship, and just as I was giving up that effort as a bad job, again I heard the cry, "She's moving!" and to our delight, with her engines under maximum load, clouds of black smoke pouring out of her four main engine exhaust ports and her two auxiliaries too, our good ship slid backward off the rocks and into deep water!

It was a time for cheering, despite apprehensive glances at the sky where Japanese aircraft might suddenly appear. Having gotten rid of everything disposable with the exception of torpedoes, we were far out of diving trim. There was no way our boat could submerge until we reballasted (got water back into our trimming tanks to equal the weight we had pumped or blown out), and this was not a rapid process. We therefore cruised about aimlessly on the surface, our pitiful antiaircraft battery manned and ready, the ship so high out of the water that her forward torpedo tubes were exposed. Below decks everyone was frantically checking everything we could think of checking in case of some unnoticed damage—who knew what air or hydraulic line might have ruptured under the sudden stress of colliding with Midway's coral sea wall?—when suddenly two other U.S. submarines surfaced nearby.

We had been ordered to close Midway to a distance of two miles, each submarine in its own pie-shaped sector. The boats to either side of us, we later discovered, seeing us on the surface thought we might know something they didn't know, or were more daring than they, so they surfaced also. The three submarines maneuvered about aimlessly in their sectors, warily watching for the enemy—none came—listened intently for news or instructions on our radios—nothing there either—and somewhere during this period the *Trigger* finally got enough water in her tanks to compensate for what we had discharged in

lightening her. Without any fanfare, we submerged. Once at periscope depth, we raised the periscope to check on our friends, but they were nowhere to be seen. They had concluded that indeed we knew something they didn't, and when we dived they did too.

We remained on patrol a few days, stopped briefly at Midway, where those of us able to get ashore had a quick look at some of the damage wrought by the Japanese attackers, and then we went on our way back to Pearl Harbor for drydocking and repairs.

Looking over the damage on the island, consisting of a couple of hangars destroyed and some burned-out aircraft, I could hardly visualize that this represented most of the visible cost of a great victory at sea. It was dramatic, but the damage encompassed only a small area, and was not at all impressive in terms of what had been at stake. The battle had taken place hundreds of miles away; and none of the warships that fought and destroyed each other, except for a few submarines, ever saw even one of the other side. It was to this that we undoubtedly owed our lives, for had any Japanese aircraft appeared in force over Midway while we were on the reef, or afterward before we were able to dive, we would have been a most inviting target, and they could not have resisted an all-out attack.

Repairs to the *Trigger*'s bottom took about a week. I was amazed at the speed and flair with which the welders and shipfitters in the dry dock waved an enormous piece of curved steel plate, suspended on wire cables from a huge crane, down to the dry dock floor near her bow, deposited it gently, and then maneuvered it with other simple but heavy tools into exactly the place they wanted it. Within a week we were back at the submarine base, preparing this time for the training we should have had before being sent to Midway.

25

Battle of Midway

REAR ADM. ROY S. BENSON,
USN (RET.)

In 1942, Benson was serving as executive officer of the *Nautilus*, which was then one of the largest submarines in the world with a submerged displacement of four thousand tons. Early that year Benson was promoted to lieutenant commander; his skipper was Lt. Cdr. Bill Brockman. For the most part U.S. submarines were not a factor in the tide-turning June 1942 Battle of Midway. The *Nautilus* was certainly an exception, not only for her successful torpedo attack but also because her earlier attacks drew the Japanese destroyer *Arashi* to investigate and hold her down. When the destroyer then hustled to rejoin her task force, her course led U.S. dive-bomber pilots to the Japanese carriers, which they attacked with great effect.

TOWARD THE END of May of 1942 we were ready to go out to Japan and to sink targets if we could find some. But we didn't go there directly. We knew when we left Hawaii that we were supposed to go by Midway, but we did not really know what was going on. We had about twenty submarines leaving Pearl at about the same time, and that certainly was unusual. These were placed in a circle around Midway, at a radius of about fifty miles. The idea obviously was to give early warning. I didn't know that the intelligence people suspected a Japanese force was coming along, but I suppose we were simply told that we should report anything that we saw.

On the fourth of June we in the *Nautilus* were located to the northwest of Midway. Before dawn we had submerged, because it was getting light enough to be detected on the surface, but it still wasn't light enough that when we dove we'd be able to see through the periscope. Very soon after we submerged, the sonar operator heard sounds of the propellers of ships. We couldn't see anything, but the sound was coming from a northwesterly direction.

As soon as it got light enough that we could see, we stuck the periscope up, and, my goodness, we were in the midst of a great number of ships. We assumed that they were the enemy until we could get a better look. We got all six of the forward torpedo tubes ready to shoot. We came up, and the skipper took a look, and he determined that they were indeed enemy, and he started shooting torpedoes but didn't hit anything. That was the first time that anyone on board had been involved in firing a torpedo war shot—that is, one with an explosive head.

Immediately we heard Japanese destroyers making a lot of noise, and so we went deep. We had a baptism in depth charges. We hadn't heard these before, so we had a chance to listen and find out what they sounded like. We were down about 250 feet, I guess. The limiting depth of a submarine at that time was 300 feet. The Japanese could have been lucky enough to put a depth charge right next to us, and that would have been curtains. But there were no results from that first encounter—either way—and then they proceeded elsewhere.

When we came back up, all the ships had disappeared, but we soon saw an aircraft carrier in the distance. Our dive-bombers had hit her while the *Nautilus* was being depth-charged. The carrier had stopped, and she was burning. Some kind of a ship was near her bow, and we presumed an effort was being made to take her in tow. We proceeded over in that direction. I'm not sure why we didn't fire first at the ship that was trying to take her in tow. However, the stopped, burning ship was an enemy aircraft carrier, a choice tar-

Roy Benson in 1942, soon after his promotion to lieutenant commander. *Courtesy of Rickart Connole*

get. We got over there to maybe a little under two thousand yards and fired. I think we fired all the bow tubes and turned around and fired all the stern tubes. We got three explosions, and there was increased smoke and fire. Then aircraft flew over and dropped bombs. We sneaked away.

Now, later on in the war we wouldn't have done everything exactly the way we did. We would have stuck around, but you have to learn. As we were sneaking away, there was one tremendous explosion, and we came up to periscope depth and took a look in that same direction; there wasn't anything there, not even smoke or fire. We got credit for sinking the *Soryu*.

26

Peril at Fifty Fathoms

BILLY A. GRIEVES

In all, the U.S. Navy lost fifty-two submarines during World War II. When the odds were calculated, each submarine had about four chances in five of surviving. But that still meant one in five did not make it back. In addition, there were quite a few narrow escapes. Grieves was a torpedoman who served on active duty from 1939 until he left the service as a petty officer first class in 1945. He reported to the USS *Thresher* before the war started and was part of her early patrols, one of which included making clandestine weather reports from the Tokyo area leading up to the famous Doolittle raid of 18 April 1942. After that she headed back to Pearl Harbor for a shipyard period.

A T THE CLOSE of the overhaul period, Cdr. William Anderson was relieved of command. Our new skipper, Lt. Cdr. William J. Millican, was a stocky Irishman from Brooklyn. He had commanded the *S-18*, a World War I–type submarine, on war patrols in the Aleutians. His first official announcement as the *Thresher* headed out on her fourth war patrol was that our final destination would be Fremantle, Western Australia. Exuberant plans flew throughout the boat. We were not sorry to leave this area of the Pacific. Every boat entering these waters had, at some time, been attacked by our own air or surface forces, and some were seriously damaged. Submarine crews had learned to have little confidence in any force that did not wear dolphins. But had we known what was coming, our excitement would have been more constrained.

Passing the International Dateline, we neared the island of Maloelap in the Marshalls. On 6

July we entered Enijun Pass submerged. Later in the morning, as a Japanese convoy zigzagged toward the pass, a three-thousand-ton tanker with escorts came into periscope view. The crew was at battle stations with the boat submerged. As the convoy closed to our shooting range, we fired two torpedoes in measured sequence. They streaked for the tanker and then produced one loud explosion in the starboard quarter. The tanker staggered momentarily, then began to settle by the stern.

Following the torpedo wakes, the escorts stung us like hornets. The sea around us boiled with depth charge explosions as the *Thresher* sought deep water. The attack continued for three hours, and it was after dark before we could surface, still hotly pursued by the escorts. Sometime after midnight the chase was abandoned. The *Thresher* had taken nineteen depth charges and sustained no damage.

With such an early success, the crew was in high spirits as we headed for our next destination, Kwajalein Atoll. We learned that an advanced Japanese navy base was located there; the prospect of sinking a man-of-war excited the crew. As daylight dawned on a peaceful sea, we entered Gea Pass submerged. Several ships came through the pass during the day, including three submarines, but none came within shooting range. As darkness settled over the islands, we surfaced to charge batteries but remained in the pass.

Lt. Larry Julihn was on the bridge on 8 July as the first faint light of dawn began to break over the horizon. It would soon be time to dive. The batteries were charged and the galley ovens were cooling down after the night's baking. This reverie was shattered by the sonar operator's cry, "Fast screws on the starboard bow!" as out of the mist loomed a large Japanese patrol craft on a collision course with us.

"Left full rudder! Clear the bridge!" shouted Lieutenant Julihn, as two blasts of the diving alarm rang out. While the lookouts dropped through the hatch, we could hear the shouts of Japanese seamen across the fifty yards that separated us. But as the conning tower dipped under, a heavy stream of salt water poured down from beneath the hatch gasket. In the race to get under, the lieutenant had lost his sandal, and it had become lodged between the gasket and the hatch. We had no choice but to surface again.

We broke the surface with the Japanese ship close aboard and were seen immediately. Although we cleared the hatch in seconds, the patrol craft was directly over us as we headed under. Depth charges straddled us as we reversed course and headed out of the pass. All day and into the night the patrol craft pressed the attack until, finally, about 0200, we eluded it and surfaced to begin a much-needed battery charge. Then, at sunrise, we headed back into Gea Pass.

The sun was just breaking when the captain sighted a Japanese ship. The first thing he noticed about her as he peered through the periscope was the snow-white brilliance of her sides. She appeared brand new. She was steering a straight course as she came through the pass with no escort. The sky above her, however, was dotted with aircraft providing coverage from above. By 0815 the captain could plainly see her decks lined with Japanese, all in clean, white uniforms. She was a 4,836-ton motor torpedo boat tender, the *Shinso Maru*. Commander Millican ordered battle stations.

As the target neared, her course, range, and speed were systematically programmed into the torpedo data computer. We waited quietly off her track until she closed to shooting range. Then we fired two torpedoes at five-second intervals. The first passed beneath her stack, the second beneath her quarter. Two great explosions blasted her hull into three sections. Commander Millican looked through the periscope and reported as all three sections disappeared from the surface in a huge cloud of steam. Breaking-up noises were clearly audible for some time, as the *Shinso Maru*'s watertight compartments ruptured. Where the ship had been, the water came alive with survivors, and Commander Millican decided to remain close by to watch for anybody who might come out to rescue them.

Suddenly, a thunderous, earthshaking blast hit directly off our starboard bow. Light bulbs exploded with a shower of glass and dust, pieces

In this vivid drawing by Mark Freeman, the *Thresher*'s propellers spin furiously as she attempts to free herself from a grappling hook dropped by the Japanese. *Naval Institute Photo Archive*

of cork insulation fell from the overhead, men were lifted clear of their bunks, and two heavy wrenches used to open torpedo tube doors were blasted off their spindles and crashed to the steel deck, contributing to the bedlam. It was a dramatic reminder to us that aircraft carry depth charges too.

"Check for damage!" came the order from control. But we had already begun. A close check revealed no serious damage—or so we thought then.

Now the attack began in earnest, and we headed for deeper water out of visual range of the aircraft. But as we inched downward, depth charges continued to fall all around. At three hundred feet, sound reported destroyers' screws bearing dead astern. They approached at high speed and unerringly homed in on our wake.

Then, mysteriously, all depth charging ceased. Why should they cut off the attack when they seemed to have an accurate fix on our position? Wherever we turned, the screws above followed. What we did not know was that the *Thresher* was leaving a brilliant, revealing trail on the surface.

What had happened was this: The 3,421-pound Mark 14 torpedo, which left the tube at its maximum speed, forty-seven knots, received its impulse from four hundred pounds of air stored in an impulse bottle located in the superstructure above the torpedo room. The very first depth charge had cracked a silver-soldered connection to the impulse bottle for the number 1 tube. So the *Thresher* was releasing a stream of air bubbles to the surface.

Then a strange disaster struck. Since the attack began we had been rigged to run silently;

hull ventilation and all unessential motors were shut down, communication was in whispers, and all movement through the boat was restricted. So we were startled when a loud, clanking noise, emanating from the starboard bow, began moving along the side. Then it reached the after torpedo room and was gone. What now? The stern planes operator was the first man to know that trouble had not left us. Suddenly, he could no longer control the angle of the boat. Then realization dawned: A large grapnel had hooked into the stern plane guard. We were being brought to the surface—stern first.

The *Thresher* displaced fifteen hundred tons on the surface, but submerged our buoyancy was neutral, neither heavy nor light. A small ship, therefore, could bring a three hundred-foot submarine to the surface. All eyes in the control room were on the depth gauges as our stern began to rise and the needle began to creep upward. The captain's face showed no emotion, but his orders were clipped. "Hard dive on the planes! All ahead emergency!" Full amperage poured from the batteries to the motors, and the *Thresher* shuddered violently as the screws bit the water with a thrust of power. Seconds passed as revolutions per minute increased in mammoth confrontation, giving new meaning to the term "tug of war." But the grapnel held fast.

The energy in the batteries could not last for long with such extravagant expenditure of power, so the captain ordered, "All stop." He decided that more weight might slow the ascent. In a series of orders that followed, we first flooded the after trim tank, followed by the water 'round torpedo tank (a tank located in each torpedo room that supplied water to fill the tube before outer doors were opened), then the four stern tubes, and, finally, the torpedo room bilges were flooded to the deck plates. But there was no perceptible slowing in the rise. A second full-power thrust was poured to the screws, but the *Thresher* continued to rise steadily, inexorably.

We made further attempts, but as we passed two hundred feet, reluctantly resigned ourselves to the possibility of capture. But Commander Millican was not about to turn his ship over to a

hated enemy. He ordered us to destroy all confidential material, to demolish the radio decoding equipment, and to place demolition charges for scuttling. There was no need for silence now. Radiomen went to work with sledgehammers. Gunners' mates headed for the torpedo rooms.

Each torpedo room carried one fifty-five-pound charge of TNT. When these were placed between the warheads of the reload torpedoes and detonated, the *Thresher* would be blown out of the water and, hopefully, so would the enemy. But as we placed the charges we were sobered by the thought that for men swimming in the water, there would be little chance.

By now, the *Thresher* was rising above 150 feet with a severe down angle. With stubborn determination, the captain tried another approach: "Flood forward trim," he commanded. This further increased the precipitous down angle and our weight all-over. Then he ordered, "Left full rudder! All ahead emergency!" Again, the *Thresher* shuddered and the bow began to drop, turning slowly to port. Then, magically, the grapnel was off! Did the cable break? Did the maneuver cause the stern to lift, slipping off the grapnel? Nobody knew the answer, but with tons of extra weight, we plummeted toward the bottom. "Put a bubble in bow buoyancy!" came the order, followed closely by "Blow bow buoyancy!" As the high-pressure air hit the tank, the bow heaved upward with a jolt, checking the descent. The *Thresher* was free.

In the minutes that followed, all concern for silence was abandoned as we frantically discharged water ballast overboard to regain our lost trim. Now that we were off the hook, the destroyers began depth charging with a fury. Sensing a kill, other patrol craft had joined the attack and the sea echoed with explosions. There was no relief. But gradually, the darkness that settled over the area obscured our trail of bubbles.

Finally, we lost our pursuers in the darkness and gratefully came to the surface. We had received forty-one depth charges and two bombs in the previous twelve hours. We set course for Truk Atoll in the Carolines.

27

Sub Sailors' Liberty

JAMES B. O'MEARA

During World War II Jim O'Meara served as an electrician's mate in the submarine *Seahorse*. The story here, however, goes far beyond the recollections of one individual. He is not speaking for every submarine veteran, but he is speaking for thousands of them—and for hundreds of thousands of sailors, soldiers, airmen, Marines, and Coast Guardsmen. In most cases they were young men uprooted from their families and sent to serve in combat. Even in a boat crowded with shipmates, submariners often felt a sense of loneliness because of the infrequency of feminine companionship. The sense of urgency for these men was heightened while on shore because the potential for early death created a desire to make the liberty candle burn brightly.

LOOKING BACK after all this time, it's hard to believe submariners accomplished so much with so many of them so very young. Some of them trained in Sub School and were somewhat ready for sea, but many of them, myself included, went from a relief crew on a sub base to a war patrol, and it was a matter of learning from the "old salts," the twenty year olds, or finding some other line of work.

There does not seem to be enough said about the sailors who came back from patrol and spent their time in a Quonset hut at Midway or Guam before shipping out again. If they were really lucky, they spent a few weeks at the Royal Hawaiian Hotel in Honolulu.

No matter where they were, they were thinking of women, getting home, and booze—not necessarily in that order. Believe me, after a few

A smiling Jim O'Meara poses for a studio portrait while ashore during World War II. Because he borrowed the jumper from a friend, his sleeve bears a rating badge that is not his own. *Courtesy of James B. O'Meara*

months at sea with seventy or eighty guys who were allowed one freshwater, three-minute shower a week, thoughts of a pretty woman occupied much of their time. The guy who said he did not dream of a woman all his off-watch time is the same one who said he was not afraid during a depth-charge attack.

The rotation system on the boats was such that after five patrols you could get back to the States or get reassigned to another submarine. This worked out pretty well, because it could be a goal, and after each patrol you could figure roughly when you would be seeing your wife or girlfriend—or any woman—again.

The problem with this setup was that after the fifth patrol, the odds started working against you, as supposedly the life of a submariner was good for only five. Every time you returned to the dock at Pearl, or wherever, you would get the word of the boats that were missing. Sometimes your buddy was gone; other times it might be a boat you just got off of.

Your buddy on the lost boat had made his last liberty with you, and you thought now about the lousy experience it had been. The two of you had scrounged around to find a clean uniform and splashed a lot of shaving lotion on your face, then boarded the bus for the great adventure to take place on Hotel Street in downtown Honolulu. This consisted of an hour or two drinking the terrible stuff they called whiskey, getting your uniform all messed up, avoiding the shore patrol, and getting in line to get laid.

Looking back, it was a degrading and certainly humiliating thing to do, but it needed to be done, and for some of them it was their last tender moment. The sub sailor would now have something to freshen up his dreams. I don't know what you would call it, but it certainly couldn't be described as a romantic love scene, and to think of it as a great sexual experience would be reaching a bit.

It was actually a release of energy stored up for months or perhaps for years. It happened in a matter of a few minutes with a prostitute who lay

O'Meara (*second from left*) relaxes with his shipmates at a wartime liberty hangout. *Courtesy of James B. O'Meara*

with maybe fifty or a hundred servicemen daily. The young sailor, probably in his teens, possibly not too long from the farm and usually inexperienced about sex, had just returned from a two-month patrol. He had been depth-charged, shot at, and had to crash dive every day—scaring the hell out of him.

He now found himself in line with hundreds of assorted soldiers, Marines, and fellow sailors, most of whom were half drunk. Many of them went through many of the same things the sub sailor did and endured the terrible things that happened to the land fighters. They must have thought their approaching five-minute interlude with a naked woman would he the most wonderful experience in their lives, and in some cases it probably was. For the sailor this might have been the greatest thing that had happened to him. This was what he thought about, dreamed about, during those long days at sea. He had a woman in his arms who was treating him like a lover, even though he wasn't.

There were some on the *Seahorse* who didn't go in for this rough type of entertainment. They were married or true to their girls back home. Some didn't even drink. Indeed, many of the enlisted men weren't old enough to drink, although I can't remember ever being asked for an ID card. I do remember them giving out chits for beer when we docked at Midway or Saipan, and some of the nondrinkers gave away their chits. They preferred playing softball to drinking. I guess we all were trying to cram in a few hours of excitement after those long months at sea.

If you weren't involved in some enemy action, that watch routine of four hours on and eight hours off could be pretty boring, and thinking about your girl in the States could be mighty frustrating. A liberty or leave in the United States was another story entirely. The married men would get to see their wives and families, and the single guys—if time and distance allowed—could get together with their sweethearts. This brief meeting with loved ones would leave all the bad, lonely times at sea behind and in many cases turned out to be the most precious time in a young sailor's life.

The number of days at home depended on whether you came back for overhaul of your boat or assignment to a new one under construction. Either way, the time was gone too soon, and you started counting the hours until you went back. Then, after a week or so of trial runs, it was back to your patrol area and dream time again with sweet thoughts of the girl at home. But after a month or so on patrol, that scene on Hotel Street with the ladies who didn't even know your name started to seem exciting again.

28

Surface Action

CAPT. PAUL R. SCHRATZ,
USN (RET.)

Early in World War II Paul Schratz served in the heavy cruiser *Wichita* in the Atlantic before volunteering to go into submarines. Two factors led to his decision: the undesirability of duty around Iceland and a hankering to be in a smaller ship. In early 1942 he started Submarine School, and after completing that he was assigned to the school boat *Mackerel*. Lt. Cdr. Bill Wylie, with whom Schratz had earlier served in the *Wichita*, was a friend. Wylie became the first commanding officer of the new boat *Scorpion*, which was being built at the Portsmouth Navy Yard. Lt. (j.g.) Schratz reported for duty in the summer of 1942, probably at the behest of the first skipper.

THE *Scorpion*'s exec was Lt. Cdr. Reggie Raymond. The first time I met him was at a party in Portsmouth on the evening my wife Henrietta and I arrived in town. I walked into the room, looked casually around, and fastened my eyes on Reggie. Almost from first meeting, I believed him to be the greatest naval officer I'd ever met, and absolutely brilliant. He and I became very close. He was an inspirational leader; the crew worshipped his footprints. He and I were totally simpatico and frequently got Bill Wylie, a fine skipper, into all kinds of trouble. From the earliest Portsmouth days, Reggie and I became a very effective team. He was exec and navigator. I, as fourth officer, handled torpedoes and gunnery, and I was the boat's first lieutenant. Reggie and I talked the CO into doing things he might not have done otherwise, but he had great faith in us, and it was a very harmonious wardroom.

For our first war patrol, March of 1943, we had a good patrol area off the Japanese home

Through World War II, U.S. submarines were equipped with deck guns for surface actions. Combat artist George Schreiber depicted this scene of a gun crew during an exercise on board the *Dorado* in 1943. The *Scorpion*'s crew operated a similar gun, though the atmosphere was undoubtedly a good deal less casual than in the practice run shown here. *Navy Art Collection, Washington Navy Yard*

islands, but the force was short of torpedoes, so the *Scorpion* went out with a half load of mines. Operating south of Honshu on the approaches to Tokyo Bay, we were ordered to lay a minefield. We laid two fields of ten Mark 10s in one, twelve Mark 12s in the other. We later got credit for sinking three ships, sank three others by torpedo, and had an all-around good patrol. But more was to come. On the way to the area from Pearl a few weeks prior, we had met a Japanese patrol vessel off Marcus Island. Facing the first real enemy with a green untested crew leaves a tense lump in the pit of the stomach. The pucker factor makes the palms sweat and creates a nervous urge to urinate. We had to avoid

detection until completing the mining mission, but there was a lot of talk—false bravado, perhaps: "Wait till we come back. We'll catch you, you bastard."

Reggie had made earlier patrols with the British in the Mediterranean with Tony Miers, who earned the Victoria Cross for his patrols, many of his sinkings by gunfire. Reggie's sea stories about life with Tony Miers were enough to turn anybody's hair. On our return, with torpedoes and mines expended, we were looking for trouble—a gun target. One remaining torpedo in the tube had been taken down to two or three hundred feet and exposed to sea pressure. Despite careful routing and our special

This was the result when the *Scorpion* fired a torpedo at a Japanese patrol vessel in April 1943, a few days before enemy gunfire killed Reggie Raymond. In the foreground is a 20-mm gun barrel. *Naval Institute Photo Archive*

treatment on the exploder impeller, there was strong doubt it would work. On 30 April, we met the Japanese patrol vessel again and decided to take him on with our 3-inch popgun, our two 20-millimeters, .30-caliber machine guns, and automatic rifles. We put the enemy's 5-pounder out of commission, but he returned heavy small-arms fire.

A few minutes later, Reggie, firing a Browning automatic from the bridge, was instantly killed by a machine-gun bullet. I was on deck alongside the gun, and about the same time, I got hit with a ricochet, bouncing off the conning tower and catching me in the center of my jacket, tearing the zipper loose and fusing into it. I got only a small scratch in the center of my chest. Two of our 20-mm crewmen were also hit and slightly wounded. Well, the shock of Reggie being killed—it's just impossible to

describe. The skipper ordered the last torpedo made ready, we backed off to five hundred yards, and fired. The torpedo ran perfectly and in a spectacular explosion, sent the patrol vessel to the bottom in a matter of moments. Our troubles were not over. Simultaneously, a lookout reported an aircraft coming in out of the sun to attack.

We dived as soon as we could get people below, but we were forced to leave Reggie's body behind. The crew was in a state of shock, me above all. We were both expecting orders after the patrol to be CO and XO of the submarine *Runner*, which Mike Fenno was giving up. We surfaced after dark, and, while lying to, Bill Wylie and I conducted a burial service. Many of the crew broke into uncontrollable sobs, the only time I've ever known of it happening. When we got back to Pearl, the division com-

Capt. Paul Schratz (*left*) was detached from the diesel boat *Scorpion* shortly before her fourth and final patrol in World War II. Here he presents the original commissioning pennant from that *Scorpion* on the occasion of the commissioning of her nuclear-powered namesake on 29 July 1960. Receiving the pennant is Cdr. Norman B. Bessac, first skipper of the new submarine. Alas, the nuclear-powered *Scorpion* was lost with all hands while making a transit of the Atlantic in 1968. *General Dynamics Corporation*

mander, Capt. Leo L. Pace, said he would dedicate one torpedo nest by each ship in his division to Reggie's memory.

Our first daughter, Regina, born a month later, commemorates Reggie's memory for me. I've often wondered, had he and I taken over *Run-* *ner*, what sort of record we would have made. Surmises are free, but this is history. Of one thing I'm sure: He was the greatest loss the submarine service suffered throughout the war. And because of him and Bill Wylie, *Scorpion* became the sentimental favorite of all the ships I served on.

29

Stern Skipper

REAR ADM. JULIAN T. BURKE JR.,
USN (RET.)

As demonstrated by Slade Cutter earlier, serving under the toughest taskmaster can sometimes be the best way to learn one's craft. In the middle of World War II Lieutenant (j.g.) Burke was new to submarines after combat operations in the battleship *North Carolina* and a tour at the Submarine School. A chance encounter on the way to the war zone led to his receiving excellent training at sea—and it probably saved his life.

A
S I WAS finishing up at Submarine School at New London in the spring of 1943, I went up to ship's service. A distinguished-looking, nattily dressed lieutenant commander with three Navy Crosses on his chest came in. He had a mustache and was very rigid, stern looking. Another officer was there and said to an enlisted man, "Did you see Captain Donaho over there? Boy, he's been doing a great job." That was my first awareness of Glynn "Donc" Donaho.

My wife Betty and I went from there to Washington and then by train to Chicago and the West Coast. It turned out we were on the same train with Captain Donaho. He had made five war patrols as commanding officer of the *Flying Fish*, and they had sent him back for a rest. He was back and was apparently putting on a public speaking tour to promote and sell war bonds. After later getting to know him, I'd say he was the last guy in the world that should have been on a public relations trip. I didn't meet him at the time, but he was on that train, and then later on the same train that went from Chicago to San Francisco. He and his wife had a Chinese amah [combination maid and nanny] with them. They would get out at every stop, pace up and down, and then get back on the train.

Betty and I stayed in the Claremont Hotel across the bay in Berkeley and hoped that we were going to be delayed. But about two days later I got word to report in for transportation, and I was put on a Pan American flying boat. I took my seat and found that the gentleman right across from me was Lieutenant Commander Donaho. He was just as stern all the way to Pearl Harbor, hardly opened his mouth. Donaho was the senior passenger aboard, and the pilot came in and sat down and tried to be personable, but not much happened.

When we got to Pearl Harbor the next morning, we were going ashore in the boat to the landing, and all of a sudden he said to me, "Where are you going?"

I said, "ComSubPac [commander, Submarine Force, Pacific Fleet] for duty, sir."

"Come with me," he said.

I went with him to one of the carryalls, and he told the driver to go to SubPac. On the way in he said, "Naval Academy?"

"Yes, sir."

"Class? What ship?"

I answered all these questions, and when we got to SubPac he took me up and introduced me to the flag secretary, who at the time was the personnel officer. *Flying Fish* was still on war patrol, and he said, "When's the *Flying Fish* getting in?"

The flag secretary said, "Two weeks."

"Who's being transferred?"

"Styer and Gurnee." The two had made maybe three or four war patrols.

"Who's replacing them?" Donaho asked.

So the flag secretary named a couple of people who were ensigns out of my sub school class in New London.

Donaho said, "I want Burke here."

The guy said, "You can't have him. He's going to the *Wahoo*."

"I don't like that," Donaho said. "You're transferring two academy people, and I need at least one replacement."

"You can't have him. We don't have them."

So Donaho said, "Well, I'll go down and see Sunshine. Where is he?" Capt. Sunshine Murray

Wearing his cap at an angle was a career-long trademark for Glynn Donaho, who eventually became a vice admiral. The unsmiling expression was apparently a trademark as well. *Naval Historical Center: NHF 168-B/P-15*

was the ComSubPac chief of staff. So Donaho went down to Murray's office, and he came back and said, "Sunshine says I can have him."

I had an academy classmate and Submarine School classmate named Willie Burgan. "Oh," said the personnel officer, "Burgan is going to the *Wahoo*." So Burgan was put on the *Wahoo* to replace me.

When I was told that I was going to the *Flying Fish* and Donaho walked off, satisfied, the assistant flag secretary came over and said, "You poor bastard. That's the biggest SOB in the Submarine Force."

The *Wahoo* came into Pearl within the next ten days. Burgan showed up some time after that and reported in. I had a very good friend and classmate already on that boat, Richie Henderson. The *Wahoo* went out on the next patrol, then was in for three weeks, and I saw Richie several times. Then the sub went out on the next patrol and was lost with all hands. So I have had very generous feelings about Captain Donaho. Just the chance of being on the same airplane with him probably saved my life.

After a time, the *Flying Fish* came in off of war patrol and immediately went in the shipyard at Pearl for overhaul. I became the torpedo officer and started working with the other officers on board. I discovered that Lt. Walt Small, apparently, was the first exec on our boat who had been able to please Captain Donaho. I could see why he was able to deal with Donaho because Walt's as sharp as anybody I've ever seen. A very demanding person, and he was good. He had the answers. He was the TDC operator the first patrol that I made. Although the assistant approach officer was somebody else, Walt was the guy that was discussing the problems with the captain. I just was standing there as the assistant, learning how to do it and setting the dials to give the train order to the torpedo tubes.

We finally got out of the shipyard, and we went over to the sub base. The ship's crew was on leave in the States while we were in the shipyard. Captain Donaho had come back, and he had already had his leave, so he was there all the time. A very unfortunate thing happened concerning the crew. The crew that was on leave were men who had been on a lot of war patrols, and they came back and blew their stacks. They reported in to the submarine command at Mare Island, and eventually they were sent over as a group to the Twelfth Naval District headquarters in San Francisco for transportation. I would say there probably were at least thirty-five or forty of these people.

While they were waiting around, some of these guys went around the corner to the nearest bar, and before long some of them got drunk and began to play too cozy with some of the girls in the naval district headquarters. Well, this got up to Com Twelve, and he sent for the submarine administration captain in Mare Island Navy Yard and personally chewed him out for the misbehavior of the *Flying Fish* crew.

Captain Donaho didn't know anything about this. About two or three weeks later Donaho was at a party up on Makalapa, near Pearl Harbor. There were several commanding officers and so forth there, and he was up there talking with Adm. Chester Nimitz and Adm. Charles Lockwood, who was ComSubPac. The submariner who had been chewed out in San Francisco had arrived in Pearl Harbor. He came up and saw Donaho there and, notwithstanding the fact that Nimitz and Lockwood were with him, personally dressed him down and gave him hell for the behavior of the *Flying Fish* crew. This had a profound effect on Captain Donaho. He came back and told us about it, and then he called the crew together. He didn't chew them out, but he said he wanted to let them know what happened. My own perception of this was that it made him a lot more human than he had been before.

Our division commander was Cdr. Karl Hensel, who had been officer in charge of the Submarine School before I got there and was a very bright guy. Donaho and Hensel didn't like each other, and I remember hearing one of our ship's officers say he heard them up on the forecastle one day talking to each other. He said you could tell how they felt just by the way they were circling each other like a couple of dogs. The problem was that when the war started, we had these older people who were in command of the boats, and very quickly they were replaced by the next generation of people. All of a sudden, the officers in this next generation were sinking ships. They had done it; the men who were their division and squadron commanders hadn't done it. So the younger men resented being told how to do it by somebody who hadn't been there.

I liked the way Captain Donaho operated. During the exercises that we had, we had intensive training. When I first went up on the bridge to be an officer of the deck, I was standing top watch, and he personally instructed me. He must have talked continuously for about two full watches, and finally he said, "I've told you everything I need to tell you. I'm not going to talk to you unless you do something wrong." Then he took his position whenever we were on the surface on the after end of the bridge—the cigarette deck, we called it. The routines that you had there were very rigid. For example, the people up on the bridge, including the officer of the deck, had their binoculars at their eyes continuously for four hours. Except for when you needed to get permission to wipe them off, you were expected to keep those binoculars up there. You can argue about whether that was a sensible thing or not, but we came back, and not all submarines did. I never saw another submarine in my experience that had the firmness in detail of operation and supervision.

So we went out on patrol via Midway, and then we headed for the Marianas. On the way we got word through a nightly intelligence message that there was a carrier headed for Japan. Before long we had a rendezvous with this Japanese aircraft carrier. It was around midnight, full moon, one destroyer escort ahead. We were pretty far out. We got in to about two thousand yards, which for an electric torpedo was not close enough, and we fired six torpedoes. The first torpedo came back on a circular run over the ship before the second one got out. It went by like a truck, and you could hear the damn thing circling. Finally, after about seven minutes, there was an end-of-run explosion that lifted us off the deck; it was a thoroughly frightening experience.

From there we heard two explosions, and the carrier went on to Japan. I think we claimed damage, but that's all we could claim. Then we headed on for Palau. After we'd been patrolling there for a few days, a convoy came out and headed toward Japan. We tried to get in, but we were too far out. They had lots of aircraft. This was daytime. We couldn't attack on the surface at that time, but watching Donaho go through his motions as the attack officer for me was an experience.

I was just overwhelmed to see how he operated. He was like a finely tuned machine. He never kept that periscope up more than ten seconds. He could spin, and he could look around and he could drop the scope, and then he would try to remember what he saw, and he would spit it out for the attack party. Finally it was evident we weren't going to get in, so we secured from battle stations, and he turned the conn over to Walt Small, the exec. I was standing next to Walt, who said, "What do you think?"

I had my back to the hatch, and I said, "That bastard is really good." Walt looked over my shoulder, and he looked kind of funny. I turned around, and that bastard was right behind me. He smirked, turned around, and went down the hatch. I never had a problem with him the rest of his time on there.

30

Special Missions

REAR ADM. NORVELL G. WARD,
USN (RET.)

In 1943–44 Ward commanded the *Guardfish*. His early experiences as skipper were marked by frustration and missed opportunities. Once a Japanese destroyer zigged away just in time. Another time a lookout mistakenly reported a bird as a Japanese aircraft, so the *Guardfish* dived instead of making an attack. Such are the fortunes of war, but they also had an effect on assignments. Ward later achieved success when his luck improved, but in the meantime his submarine served for a time as a clandestine troop transport and lifeguard. Murphy's Law was evidently at work, because one thing after another went wrong. On 20 September 1943 his boat landed a reconnaissance party on the island of Bougainville in the Solomons.

I BELIEVE THIS OPERATION and the next ones were the cause of many patrol problems associated with my shortage of success. And they contributed greatly to many of my decisions. I think the recon party was landed over in the vicinity of Empress Augusta Bay on the western side of Bougainville. That was near the beginning of our second patrol. The landing had a great negative impact on the results of the second patrol, because we had to off-load torpedoes in Tulagi—except the ones we had in the tubes—in order to carry the recon party and their gear in the torpedo rooms.

They had inflatable boats, and they had something in sacks. I'm not sure what. It was a Marine recon group with either a major or lieutenant colonel in charge. They had native scouts with them. We took them into the Empress Augusta Bay area at a particular point on Bougainville and dropped them. My men manned the boats both

The crew of the *Guardfish* musters on deck in August 1944 for the ceremony in which their boat received the Presidential Unit Citation for her wartime exploits. In the foreground, rising from the submarine's teakwood deck, is the pedestal for mounting a deck gun. *Courtesy of Elizabeth Ann Schafer*

times, in and out. We waited around for seven days to pick them up while they made their reconnaissance, then returned them to Tulagi.

I got familiar with Guadalcanal during that period, also, because when we went into Tulagi, they carried me over to the Marine headquarters in Guadalcanal to brief me on what I should be doing. Things were pretty tame at Guadalcanal by that point. Occasionally they would have something come down and try to run in reinforcements or pick some Japanese up off of Cape Esperance at the northeastern tip.

During the seven days that the recon party was ashore, I was available to go out and look for ships as long as I could meet the date and time to recover the recon party. But the area I could look at didn't have much in the way of targets. After I had checked the accuracy of an aerial survey map, I tried to get down to the Shetland Island area and see if I could find anything, but there wasn't enough time to do anything. I do believe I spotted a Japanese submarine making a run to the southeast, but I wasn't able to make an attack on it. We weren't in position when we spotted it. They were going southeast, which told me he was headed for Guadalcanal, probably to pick up some people. That was the only thing I recall seeing during the period they were ashore.

Then I picked the recon party up and carried them back to Tulagi. There I picked up my torpedoes, not suspecting their condition, and headed out on patrol. On the eighth of October, we sank the *Kashu Maru*, which was about seven thousand tons, as I remember it. I had to stretch my time in the area to the very maximum in order to make that attack. I had received orders to return to Tulagi on a certain date for another special mission, and I gave the special mission higher priority than sinking ships. This might be considered poor judgment and a "lack of aggressiveness" on my part.

I had to leave the area early that night in order to arrive in Tulagi and make my rendezvous at a specified time. We picked up a convoy shortly after dark and *after* I had started for Tulagi. This followed a period of not having seen any other targets the entire time we were in the area. The *Guardfish* made a night surface approach. I said, "I'm going to get one ship out of this convoy." I fired six torpedoes at the largest target we could spot. One torpedo exploded prematurely, which gave the escorts my location. As soon as the torpedoes were fired, the escorts turned toward me. So I headed clear of the convoy and took the course that would take me to Tulagi. I bent on all four engines, because I figured I had to make an average speed of about seventeen knots to make my rendezvous.

When I built up to full power, or close to full power, I discovered that I'd nicked one of my props. One of the blades had hit some debris in the water. At least this was our belief. After the patrol we found it was a bent shaft. We hadn't discovered it during our slow-speed surface operation or submerged operation. But as soon as we got up to speed, the tail started vibrating, really bouncing up and down. That led to another problem. I guess about nine or ten o'clock that morning, I received a message from the commander that my special mission was delayed: "Remain in the area."

At that time, I spotted a ship headed up to the north. In analysis later I determined it must have been a decoy because he was steaming around singly, a small freighter making all kinds of smoke and without any apparent destination. Anyway, I fired three torpedoes at it from my stern tubes, and every one of them was a surface run. This meant that the vibration had upset the depth mechanism. I forget the particular part that was affected by it in the torpedoes, but every one of them ran on the surface and at slow speed. I think what happened, as a result of excessive vibration, was that the overspeed trip function—as sometimes happens—didn't cut the engines. In any event, they malfunctioned.

So this meant I had two grave problems. On the one hand, the prop problem would make it easy for me to be picked up on sonars listening for it. On the other hand, I had to do something on the torpedoes in the after room. Well, the torpedomen got to work and determined to fix the torpedoes in the after room. But another thing that we found out in making that attack was that in off-loading our fish in Tulagi, we hadn't drained them of all lube oil, so when they started running, they were smokers, which left a trail of smoke on the surface of the water, which wasn't desirable either. Not only would the target be alerted, but our location and firing position would be disclosed.

All these things sort of compounded. Since my rendezvous for this special mission was canceled, I was then ordered down to lifeguard off of Rabaul. The Army Air Forces was going to fly some B-17s up for a photoreconnaissance mission over Rabaul from New Guinea or northern Australia. I was ordered to a lifeguard station at a particular point off the entrance. While I was on lifeguard station, they told me what time the planes were coming over. Near that time I had two targets appear. One was a submarine headed into Rabaul, and I had every intention of making an attack on that but didn't get the attack solution to it. In other words, from the time I picked it up until it was out of torpedo range, we never did have a good solution. So I refrained from firing a large spread at the submarine. If it had been under any other conditions, I'd probably have fired smoking torpedoes at it, anyway. Whether I would have hit him or not, one will never know.

Then, shortly after that, a tanker with an escort headed out of Rabaul and came within range. My primary mission was lifeguard, so—with the torpedo condition I had—I made the decision not to make an attack on that and thereby render myself ineffective as a lifeguard because the Japanese would have known I was there. I would have disclosed my presence. The tanker was escorted. The fact that I would have

A beaming Commander Ward sports the ribbon for the newly awarded Presidential Unit Citation just to the left of his dolphin insignia. *Courtesy of Elizabeth Ann Schafer*

received depth-charge attacks was just one of those things. But they'd have known I was there, and it was a question of judgment: Which should be primary, being the lifeguard for the B-17s coming over, which I was sent there for, or disclosing my presence and aborting the lifeguard mission? My torpedo situation entered into the decision process. In the endorsement on the patrol report, the submarine commander said I should have attacked the tanker. I didn't. That was my judgment at the time.

The next day, as I was leaving the area, I ran into another escorted convoy, fired a spread of torpedoes at it, every one of them a smoker, and one prematured. Every ship avoided the torpedoes, and the escort investigated me. That was the result of going into Tulagi at the beginning of the patrol. When that was over, I proceeded back to Tulagi and picked up the Marines for insertion on Bougainville on 25 October. This was just before the Marine landing at Empress Augusta Bay. I picked up the same group I had taken in for

recon earlier, landed them, but I wasn't going to pick them up. They were going to join their buddies when they came ashore. So I had three days in the area before clearing out.

The Marine passengers were just as friendly as could be. They knew what they were going to do. I don't think they liked the close confinement, but they appreciated comfortable berths and good food and a lot of fresh water. When the time came to put them ashore, they knew where they wanted to land. Certainly we had to navigate precisely, and we would come in submerged and fix our position. After surfacing, I would take them in as close to the shoreline as it was feasible to navigate, which was usually within one thousand yards of the beach. So that they had a very short row to get ashore.

These landings were all made under cover of darkness. After off-loading that group, I took three days, on my own initiative, to reconnoiter Empress Augusta Bay, because the chart the Marines were going to use wasn't completely accurate. It was one made from photoreconnaissance. They'd come up with three different charts. I found the first one I had used, in taking the first recon party in, was fairly accurate. Then they came up with a revised edition of it, based on further photoreconnaissance from the air. They gave me this one to use. When I took this recon party in, I found that there was a discrepancy of more than a mile in positioning between the first chart I had and the subsequent ones. So I reported this right away, and I told them I was going to stay in the area and make further observations to determine accuracy or inaccuracy of either one of them, which I did.

In making these observations, I also discovered three pinnacle reefs in the landing area. I kept my depth finder going while I was in there, and all of a sudden, things began to shoal. I estimated that there were two pinnacles within ten feet of the surface. I did this at night, after I'd discovered them during submerged operations, by just running depth tracers on them and getting as close to the pinnacle as I could. It was useful, but apparently some destroyers disregarded them, because one or two destroyers ran aground on a pinnacle during an operation. That pinnacle had been plotted by me. I'm not sure whether the word was disseminated or not. In the heat of battle, they may just have got a little closer to it than they expected. I can't render any judgment on that. But the pinnacle had been plotted and reported.

After I completed my survey, I headed for Brisbane to wrap up that patrol. It was an interesting patrol but long—seventy-one days from port to port with fifty-six in the combat area. It had a lot of variety to it, too. I derived a great deal of personal satisfaction from doing what I did, but I didn't sink many ships, and that is the frustrating part of it.

31

Scouting the Gilbert Islands

REAR ADM. WILLIAM D. IRVIN,
USN (RET.)

In the years between the World Wars, the U.S. Navy experimented with some monster submarines, the *Nautilus*, *Narwhal*, and *Argonaut*. The *Nautilus*, which was originally named *V-6* in the old letter-number system, was 371 feet long and displaced 3,960 tons submerged. By comparison, the standard fleet boat of World War II was 312 feet long and had a submerged displacement of 2,424 tons. In August 1942, because her size permitted carrying passengers, the *Nautilus* transported the 2nd Marine Raider Battalion, commanded by Lt. Col. Evans Carlson, to a daring mission ashore on Makin in the Gilbert Islands. After a conventional patrol against Japanese shipping, she landed Army scouts in the Aleutians and then underwent overhaul. In September 1943 she was back in the Gilberts to gather information for a planned amphibious assault by Marines two months hence, the beginning of the Central Pacific campaign. Her skipper was Lt. Cdr. Bill Irvin, newly in command, and her exec was Lt. Richard B. Lynch.

O N MY FIRST patrol I got a very odd assignment. The *Nautilus* was ordered to do a job at Tarawa, Abemama, Makin, Nauru, and Ocean islands, making a photographic reconnaissance preparatory to their invasion. The idea was that these pictures could be developed into panoramic views of the beaches to be used. It was pretty much a new idea. There had been a little of it done, but very little. There was a submarine camera, but it wasn't worth a damn.

Fortunately, Ozzie Lynch, my executive, was a real camera nut. He was a photographer of the first order, and he devised a scheme whereby he

The behemoth *Nautilus* is shown in August 1943, shortly before her successful mission to gather intelligence about the Gilbert Islands. She sports two 6-inch guns, one forward of the conning tower and one aft on a raised gun deck. In October 1943 the *Nautilus* brought her pictures of the Gilberts back to Pearl Harbor, where they were used for planning the upcoming invasion. *Naval Institute Photo Archive*

used a reflex camera of his own on the periscope with a little tube that he had fabricated so that we could put the periscope up, slap this camera on the end of this tube, take a picture, and then rotate the periscope a few degrees at a time until we had gotten a panorama from one position that swept something on the order of thirty degrees. Then, of course, we'd get the periscope down and move off to another location.

We photographed the coasts of Abemama, Tarawa, and Makin, and then our mission was changed while we were out on patrol, cutting out Ocean and Nauru islands. We found that the first island, Tarawa, was occupied. There was no question at all, in my opinion, that it was heavily fortified. You could see that from close approach to the beaches. We didn't know how energetic the

Japanese were. The amphibious force had briefed us that we were not to disclose ourselves, because this would jeopardize the whole operation.

Incidentally, Lynch was also the navigator, and he was forced to use 1845 charts that were developed by a British sailing vessel called the *Essex*. It didn't take us long to find that our positions didn't jibe at all. Every one of the charts was wrong, and they stayed that way as we moved from one island to another. Lynch studied away on this thing and then finally came up with the idea that our position was correct but the map was incorrect. So by fixing our position and rotating the chart onto the position, we found that the charting vessel had almost a constant six-and-three-quarter-degree error, counterclockwise. By rotating our position each time six and three-quarters degrees, we found that we jibed. That was Lynch's discovery. He was the real expert and deserves sole credit.

We had to take these pictures and satisfy ourselves that they were good, because if we took them and went back to Pearl with the negatives and then found they were no good, the whole thing was for naught. Consequently, we had to develop the pictures on board, and the darkroom had to be such that it had no vibration, because the pictures would be very grainy to begin with, and if we had vibrations they would be impossible.

Still another thing. Before we sailed, the Marines were going to take Tarawa and Abemama, and the Army was going to take Makin, Nauru, and Ocean islands. The scheme, then, was such that they put on board the *Nautilus* a Marine captain and an Army captain. The Marine captain would observe a beach after I observed it and describe in his terms what he could see, and that description would accompany the pictures.

After the exercise was over, the commander of the amphibious force said that what we did proved to be absolutely invaluable, because the rotation was something that had really thrown them into serious trouble taking courses from the ships to the beach. It would have thrown them off into areas other than where they were destined, and there would have been pandemonium if the courses hadn't been corrected—together with the descriptions.

Well, during the course of our patrol and the subsequent time period, the amphibious force's plans were changed, and they took the Army out of the picture. But these two officers put on quite a performance while they were on board. The Marine was a very fine Reserve officer. I subsequently kept in close touch with him.

The Army captain was belligerent. He had a hell of a time getting along with the people in the ship, and he went out of his way to cause trouble, time after time. I had to admonish him any number of times about the fact that his conduct was just out of order. He was trouble from the word go. He had come aboard and had emphasized to me in his first interview that he was aboard for

two purposes: first, to get these descriptions of the beaches, and second, to make damned certain that he got a combat decoration. He'd read all the data about the fact that if the patrol was successful, everybody aboard got a combat insignia. He wanted to make certain that he got his, and it was necessary for me to do my part in seeing that the ship got to its destination.

He also had trouble with the pharmacist's mate. When we sailed, one of the first stops we made on the way was at Johnston Island to take on additional fuel. By the time we got there, my pharmacist's mate, whose name was Potts, came to see me and said that he was having an awful lot of trouble with that Army captain. He thought maybe it would be wise to drop him off at Johnston Island.

I said, "We can't. He has to do this Army job."

Potts said, "He's been constipated since the day he walked aboard, and he gets worse every day."

"Well, go see the doctor at Johnston Island and see what you can do for him. If the doctor has some dosage that can be used, double it. Take care of it that way."

He went to see the doctor, and the doctor gave him a dosage. We sailed from Johnston Island, and Potts kept saying to me, "I don't know what we're going to do about him, Captain, he's so constipated. Just nothing works."

Well, we made this patrol, with the Army captain settling down after a time, but he was still obnoxious when he had an opportunity to be. The Marine was doing a fine job. When we surfaced at night, we would copy the SubPac radio messages, and then somebody had to sit as the messages arrived and decipher them. Normally, the officers who were off watch would do this, and I said to the exec, "Since these two haven't anything else to do, I'm going to assign them to the job of deciphering all these messages."

I talked to the Marine about it, and he said it was a great thing. He didn't have anything to do, and he'd like to. The soldier complained about it, and I said, "Your complaint notwithstanding, you're going to have to do it." Well, night after night, they would have to wait until the messages came in, and then they would start deciphering them. I used to come down from the bridge after we surfaced at night, also waiting for the messages to be completed. Each night I'd come down in the wardroom and play Concentration, that card game where you overturn a card and match one that's turned over. I used to play one of these men one night and another night the other. They weren't doing anything otherwise, just waiting for the messages.

I came down one night, and I heard the two officers arguing as I was about to step into the wardroom. The Army man said to the Marine, "I don't give a damn if you are tired, and I don't give a damn if you do feel you have to get some sleep. It's your turn to play with the old bastard, and I'm not going to take your place." So I found out that this was not a volunteer occupation on their part at all. It was a chore.

The last night we had on patrol we were at Makin, up in a bight—an area of water partially enclosed by land. All we had to do was finish a group of pictures up in this bight, which we did about noon, but we had to stay submerged. Makin was occupied by the Japanese, so we couldn't disclose our presence. So we turned to go and were heading back out of the bight. I left the engineer officer on watch in the conning tower, and I said, "Just keep heading out of the bight. We should be out about four or five o'clock. Then we can turn around the coast, up along the shore. If the situation is satisfactory, we'll surface, bombard the place, and then turn and run for home." We had two 6-inch guns.

I was down in the wardroom with some of the other officers. All was quiet, and all of a sudden the battle alarm sounded. I thought, "My God, we're jumped. What could have happened?" I went racing for the conning tower. Just as I got there, I got a report from forward torpedo: "All tubes are ready." As I stuck my body through the hatch, I heard the engineer officer say, "Fire one, fire two, fire three."

When he said, "Fire three," I screamed at him, "What happened?"

He said, "I'm firing at a tanker."

I jumped to the periscope, took it away from

him, and said, "Let me see it." I swung it around in the direction he indicated, and I could see on the surface of the water the wakes of three torpedoes headed right over to this tanker. I said, "My God, if I can see them, what must that ship be seeing?"

I got an answer in a hurry. There were two heavy explosions. I swung around, and I saw a plane diving in. It had just let two big bombs go. Here we were in this bight. We didn't have much room to go either to the right or left, no place to go but out. We went deep, and while I was looking around at this plane, I swung the periscope back at the tanker. It was changing its course, and an escort vessel on the other side of the tanker was swinging around and coming back to it. We were in for it; the plane could just sit up there and spot us for the escort to go to work on us.

Well, for the next three or four hours, we just ran deep, as silently as we could, and stayed on a course out of the bight. We didn't have any cushion on the sides. I thought if there was any current at all, we were not going to be able to take any cuts to right or left, and we'd just have to pray to God that we'd get out of this hole. It was nightmarish in the conning tower. The Japs had a fine case of rats caught in a big trap and just had to squeeze it down to get us all. With this atmosphere prevailing, our pharmacist, Potts, who had been so busy treating our Army captain for constipation, stuck his head up through the hatch and said, "Captain, you'll never believe it, but my prize patient is now loose as a goose, and I'm having a hell of a time treating him."

After about four hours, late in the afternoon, I ventured up to the surface. I couldn't see anything of the escort vessel, but there were about four planes combing back and forth. We not only had to get out of that slot, but we had to get far enough out so that we could get on the surface and run, because the battery was almost flat. When we exercised at battle stations, we pulled a lot of power. We managed to pull out into deep water, and it was beginning to get dark. But those damned planes were combing back and forth over our path. At first, I could see their blue exhaust, but then the blue exhaust seemed to change to

Cdr. Bill Irvin beams after receiving the Legion of Merit in a ceremony at Pearl Harbor in April 1944.
National Archives: 80-G-222500

red. I thought I saw these reddish lights going back and forth across our track.

So I said to Lynch, "You stay below in the conning tower and keep plotting, and I'll stay up here alone. Keep everything on the que vive down below, and if I dive through the hatch and say, 'Dive,' take her down as fast as you can, because that means that plane's coming in on us."

Finally, after a period of time, Lynch climbed up the hatch, and I said, "Get down. I'll stay up here alone."

He said, "No, relax. That plane you're running away from is not a plane; it's Mars." Mars had come up over the horizon, and we were running

away from it. So we got out and, having fussed in the slot, instead of bombarding the place, we thought we'd just run for home, which we did.

While we were happy to get back safely to Pearl Harbor, I was saddened by a final incident. Our patrol had been declared a successful one, and we were awarded the combat insignia. But at the same time the Navy Department came out with a new regulation that restricted the award of the insignia to members of the Navy and Marine Corps only. Our poor Army captain lost out. I made a plea for him to ComSubPac, but it got nowhere.

32

Saga of a *Sculpin* Survivor

CHIEF MOTOR MACHINIST'S
MATE GEORGE ROCEK,
USN (RET.)

The submarines *Squalus* and *Sculpin* were built in the late 1930s at the Portsmouth Navy Yard as sister ships. As we have seen, the *Squalus* sank in 1939, was refloated, and later returned to service as the *Sailfish*. The *Sculpin*, which had been nearby on the surface when the *Squalus* was raised, subsequently went to war also. On 18 November 1943, while tracking a Japanese convoy, the *Sculpin* endured a depth-charge attack. The explosions damaged the boat's depth gauge, and she broached on the surface as the diving officer tried to bring her to periscope depth. That alerted the Japanese, who again pounded her with depth charges. The U.S. submarine resurfaced to engage in a gun battle, during which she was further damaged. The diving officer decided to scuttle her to keep her from being captured. Twelve of the men chose to remain on board to avoid being captured. One of those who opted for death was Capt. John Cromwell, on board as a prospective wolf-pack commander. He did not want to run the risk of giving up classified information, particularly his knowledge of Ultra. Cromwell was awarded a posthumous Medal of Honor for his sacrifice. More than forty of the men of the *Sculpin* went into the sea and were captured by the Japanese. They were able to reveal the fate of their submarine only after the war, when they were released. One of those men was George Rocek, who was in the after engine room during the battle against the Japanese. He recalled going into the water and being picked up by the crew of a destroyer, where the prisoners were bound, blindfolded, and beaten. The destroyer delivered them to Truk Atoll, site of a large Japanese naval base in the Caroline Islands.

The *Sculpin* was photographed here on 1 May 1943, shortly after completing an overhaul period at the Mare Island Navy Yard. Before the year was over, she was lost in action. *Naval Institute Photo Archive*

WE ARRIVED IN TRUK and were taken to their outdoor prisoners' compound, an area of about thirty square feet with three cells on one side. Each cell had a hole in the floor for a toilet. Our food rations consisted of one rice ball a day and a few ounces of water. Water was a scarcity on Truk; they relied on rainwater for their supply. We had three wounded men in our cell, so we all took turns standing to allow more room for them. Lt. George E. Brown Jr. tried repeatedly to get medical attention for the wounded men, to no avail. After the fifth or sixth day, their wounds were beginning to smell and finally they were taken to the hospital.

We were let out of our cells twice a day for about ten minutes, an event which we gratefully looked forward to. Repeatedly, we were taken out of the compound for questioning, always blindfolded. If you hesitated in answering a question, you received a whack across the rear with a piece of wood larger than a bat. I learned to bide for time by saying I didn't understand the question. The Japs had their own interpreter, and

he couldn't speak English too well, so I was able to get away with it sometimes.

About the tenth day, they shaved all our hair off and issued us Japanese Navy undress blues to wear and a square, flat, wooden block with Japanese writing on it to wear around our necks. Then the three wounded men returned from the hospital. One man had his hand amputated and the other, his arm. They told us the amputations were done without any anesthetic and they were questioned at the same time.

We were then taken to the shoreline in trucks, blindfolded. Here we were divided into two groups—there were twenty-one prisoners in my group and twenty in the other—and put aboard two Japanese aircraft carriers. Our group went aboard the *Chuyo*, where we were taken below decks to a small, locked compartment. This group of prisoners included the wounded men.

On board the carrier *Chuyo* conditions were bad. Food was available, but very little water; we only received a few ounces a day per man. The compartment was crowded and the ventilation was practically nonexistent.

Motor Machinist's Mate George Rocek stands in front of his father's tailor shop during a leave period while the *Sculpin* was in overhaul. *Courtesy of George Rocek*

But this torture was to end in the death of the Jap carrier. At midnight on 31 December 1943, the ship was rocked with a terrific explosion as it was hit with a torpedo from the USS *Sailfish* (formerly the *Squalus*), whose crew had no way of divining that their own countrymen were on board. Submariners themselves, the prisoners cheered the blast even though they knew if the carrier went down they would probably not survive.

A few of us were sitting on deck, and when the torpedo hit, we flew straight up about two or three feet in the air. We could sense the carrier had lost power, and smoke filtered into our compartment. We heard various alarms sound off and damage-control men running and yelling. On deck below we could hear the frantic Jap crew attempting to shore up the bulkheads with timber, but a heavy sea was running and nullifying the efforts of the damage control party. Soon we heard the bulkhead collapse and water pouring into the compartment below us.

As the water rose to our compartment, we yelled and pounded on the locked hatch. We undogged the hatch, but it was locked on the outside, and we couldn't break it open. We then removed the metal pump handle from the head (about three feet long) and used it as a pry bar, then we all pushed and pulled, and on the second try the hatch broke open. I don't think you could have done this on an American ship.

We held hands and let one man try to find the way to topside. It was dark and the air was full of smoke. Through smoking compartments we tried to reach the main deck. Frenzied Jap damage-control men ignored us, and we finally reached topside, which by now was covered with smoke. A small compartment yielded life jackets, which were quickly donned. Further along we found the galley, which was hastily looted of food, particularly bottled soft drinks. This is where we finally filled up on liquids to quench our parched throats.

Beyond the galley we found a ladder leading to the flight deck, and here frantic Japs were passing timber for life rafts by means of a human chain. On the flight deck they were lashing the poles together to make rafts. I saw only one twelve-foot boat in the water with three high-ranking officers in it. A Jap officer pulled us out of the line and escorted us to the flight deck where we were stripped of our life jackets, and they started to tie us. In the confusion, however, only eight men were tied and the others quickly freed them. There were many life jackets in the compartment below; why they didn't use them, I'll never know. Only about a third of the Japs had life jackets on.

An internal explosion rocked the ship, and the Japs began passing out stores of beer, candy, canned goods, and rice, with even the prisoners coming in for a share. Despite the explosions, the carrier remained afloat. But high winds, mist, and huge swells made good submarine weather and the prisoners waited for the submarine to close in for the kill. *Sailfish* made its second strike despite the protective Jap destroyer. A violent explosion shattered the carrier, a column of smoke billowed up on the port side, and within minutes the ship started down with a heavy port list.

Japanese crewmen and American prisoners together crowded to the starboard side, including Jap officers with their long swords stuck between their life jackets and overcoats. In the melee, the prisoners were separated. Dinty Moore (chief signalman) and myself were holding on to a collapsible searchlight on the flight deck, about thirty feet off the starboard side. As the carrier was going down, about a hundred feet from the water, I yelled to Dinty, "Let's go," and I slid down the flight deck into the sea. The suction was so great that I could not break surface after going under. I then believe an air pocket pushed me closer to the surface, for I could see light and I made one more attempt and broke surface near a raft. I swam over to it and hung on for dear life. I never did see Dinty Moore again. Already on the raft were an officer and a messboy from the *Sculpin*.

Fearful of stopping because of the lurking submarine, the Japanese destroyer *Urakaze* circled the rafts for about five hours before they finally made a run to pick up the survivors. She came by with one Jacob's ladder and a number of lines trailing over the side. When you grabbed the lines and the ship rolled, you slid right back into the sea. Your best chance was one Jacob's ladder. One time, I grabbed the ladder while the other two men grabbed the lines. A Jap officer stepped and crawled over me, forcing me under. I was very weak by now, but luckily a huge swell pushed me onto the Jacob's ladder again. I threw my arm through the ladder and latched onto my wrist with the other hand. They pulled the ladder and me both topside. The other *Sculpin* men were not able to pull themselves up, and the Japs jabbed at them with poles trying to knock them off the lines. That was the last time I ever saw any of my shipmates from the carrier *Chuyo*.

Apparently, being dressed in their undress blues, the Japs must have thought at first I was one of their sailors. They hauled me and the ladder up and left me lying on deck. I was just too weak to move. Then four sailors picked me up and carried me to the fantail. I was sure they were going to throw me overboard, but then they must have been ordered to return me amidships, and I was put in their laundry compartment. They did not tie me up or even close the hatch. Later that afternoon, I felt the turbines wind up and the ship picked up speed. I was left alone in the compartment and as night came on, I began to get very cold and started shaking badly. There was a metal tub or tank that was filled with water in the compartment, the water felt warm, so I climbed in the tub and sat down, with only my head above water. I stayed there for the rest of the night.

The next day I received numerous visits by a Jap chief who did a lot of talking and then slugged the hell out of me and left. Every hour or two later he would return and do the same thing over again. He also mentioned Tokyo, Doolittle, and gave me the cutthroat sign. One young Japanese sailor came, and he managed to motion that he worked in the engine room. I managed to convey to him that I did the same kind of work. About a half an hour later he came back and gave me a hard cracker and motioned me not to say anything. It took me a long time to eat the cracker because I couldn't work up any saliva. The next morning we arrived in Yokohama. I was never given any food or water on that ship except the one cracker.

As we entered the port, I saw many of their merchant and naval ships that were heavily damaged. After tying up, along came that same chief again with three men and about fifty feet of rope. They tied and blindfolded me so I couldn't even move. A few hours later another chief, larger than the average Jap, came in and untied me and loosened my blindfold so I could see downward. He then tied my wrists together and led me with the loose end to the gangway, where I had to put on a pair of "go-aheads" [flimsy rubber sandals]. I was put in a small craft and rode for about fifteen

During the latter part of World War II, this prisoner-of-war camp at Ashio, Japan, housed survivors from a number of U.S. submarines. *Courtesy of George Rocek*

minutes. I now began to realize I was the only *Sculpin* crewmember from the carrier *Chuyo* to survive.

After reaching shore, I was led through a part of the city. I could see the women's shoes and bottoms of their kimonos. I felt a little funny at first, because the seat of my uniform was torn out from sliding down the carrier flight deck. We arrived at a railroad station and sat down on a bench. I heard the chief talking to a woman, and after a few moments, he removed my blindfold—apparently she wanted to see my face. She was a doll—and dressed stateside with a short skirt and high heel shoes. He replaced my blindfold and a short time later we boarded a train. The train was very crowded, so we had to stand for about an hour or two. After getting off the train, he insisted I run. I could see the road, which was narrow and stony. I pointed to his shoes, the rocks, and my "go-aheads," which kept falling off.

He understood but then motioned he wanted to get me to Camp Ofuna in time for eating, which we did.

On arriving at Ofuna, I was turned over to a stateside-dressed Jap who spoke perfect English. Most of their intelligence interrogators spoke good English and were educated in the States. He asked where the rest of the men were, and when I told him about the carrier being sunk he became very irritated. They had moved most of the *Grenadier* crew out to make room for us. The commander of Ofuna could not speak English and refused to believe a Jap carrier got sunk, but he could never understand what happened to the other men.

It was at this camp that I was reunited with the remainder of the *Sculpin* crew, who had sailed on the other carrier. We believed we would become registered prisoners of war but were sadly mistaken. . . . Ofuna was a secret questioning and intimidation camp run by the Japanese navy for nothing else but to pump or beat military information out of the prisoners. It was mainly comprised of aviation and submarine POWs, except for a few civilians.

One man was designated to a cell and no talking was allowed. Every week or two, you were questioned by a different interrogator. They then would compare notes to see if you lied on certain questions. We all had made up fake stories on Truk and memorized them. I believe most of us said it was our first patrol. My story was that I spent a year each at New London, San Diego, and Pearl, and the sinking was my first patrol.

If you were sitting outside on the bench and had your eyes closed, periodically the guard would silently stand in front of you and put his bayonet close to your eyes. Since no talking was allowed, we used leg-pressure warnings to make each other aware of the s.o.b. This was not a work camp. Every Saturday was bath day and shave. We were shaved by their barber, or butcher.

Most of the wounds I received in my lower legs were not healing. The Japs had no medication to speak of; you had to wash your own bandages. The medication I received looked and smelled like fish oil. I remembered my father's advice—to urinate on wounds. So I had Ricketts, MM1c [machinist's mate first class], urinate on my legs. After a period of time, all wounds healed except one, which was near my left leg shinbone.

The *Sculpin*'s only surviving officer, Brown, was kept in solitary confinement when not being interrogated, put on reduced rations, given frequent beatings, and threatened with death if he refused to answer questions. He divulged only information, which was contained in *Jane's Fighting Ships*, to which he was allowed free access. He was able to convince his tormentors that, being the engineering officer, he knew nothing concerning matters of policy, fleet organization, plans, or logistics.

[In early 1944 the Japanese transferred a group of American prisoners from the submarines *Sculpin*, *Grenadier*, and *S-44* to Ashio, a copper-mining camp near Tokyo. There they did heavy

manual labor. Rocek also recalled seeing submariners from the *Tang* and *Perch* at the camp. His leg wound eventually healed when a U.S. Army medic, who had been captured in the Philippines, ground up sulfa tablets and sprinkled the powder on Rocek's shin. Months and months passed by in a routine of work and starvation. Then came the summer of 1945.]

Our first indication of the war ending was observed when the day shift was brought back to camp and no one left camp thereafter. A few days later, we fell in for quarters and the Japs began to abide by the Geneva Convention rules concerning POWs. They painted the rooftops with large POW letters and doled out their supplies of clothing, shoes, and so on, which we so desperately wanted and needed. The supplies and some food packages were donated by the Canadian Red Cross.

About a week later, some of our carrier planes buzzed the camp in the process of locating all POW camps, as we learned later. A few days after that, one of our four-engine bombers made a food parachute drop about one hundred yards in front of the camp. We really feasted then—day and night. We then made up a list of the Korean and Japanese mineworkers who had treated us decently. They were brought to camp and we gave them all the supplies of clothing, food, and so on that would be left behind. They all left with tears in their eyes.

A week later, we were escorted to town and boarded a train for Tokyo. The secret police, or Kampia, were posted throughout the town and we saw no civilians outside. On arriving at the station, the first person to greet us was a U.S. Army nurse with cigarettes and candy bars. What a beautiful sight! We were put in a large waiting room and waited for trucks and busses to take us to the wharf, where they had a decontamination station set up and hospital ships alongside. We were told if we ate too much we could get ill, but I can't recall anyone doing so.

Some POWs were flown back to the States. I was sent to the USS *Ozark*. They had more than enough volunteers for mess cooks. You could go through the mess line as often as you wanted

Rocek (*left*) poses with *Squalus* survivor Jud Bland during a visit following a joint reunion of crew members from the sister submarines *Sculpin* and *Squalus/Sailfish. Courtesy of George Rocek*

until the food ran out. I went through three times, but I know some men went through five or six times. It was like putting food in an acid vat. We were still hungry during the night, and the commanding officer gave orders to break out the C-rations.

We stopped in Guam for a few weeks for thorough physicals before heading for the States. En route to the States, a few men lost their senses and had to be taken to sickbay. During the first year, I believe we all had to fight down the sensation of going over the deep end. We arrived in Frisco and all submarine men were the first to depart. The Submarine Force had individual cars, with an officer assigned, for each man, and they took us to a hotel for a large welcome dinner. We were all impressed and proud to be submariners, and we knew that we had not been forgotten.

33

Aide to Admiral King

CAPT. ROBERT E. DORNIN,
USN (RET.)

One of the real characters in the submarine service in World War II was Dusty Dornin. His Naval Academy classmate Slade Cutter, skipper of the *Seahorse* during the war, recalled Dornin as both competitive and aggressive. There was a friendly rivalry between their boats—and sometimes not always friendly. As a result of his success commanding the *Trigger* at sea, Dornin in 1944 found himself being considered for a shore billet rather than more time in submarines.

THE QUESTION has been put to me many times how I was selected to be Adm. Ernest King's aide, Admiral King being the head of the largest navy the world has probably ever seen, one of the sternest, most correct type of admirals.

I have given this much thought and have decided the following. I was a commanding officer of the submarine USS *Trigger* and had made three very successful war patrols. Prior to that, I had been executive officer of the USS *Gudgeon*. I made nine war patrols in a row, which is more than par for the course. I was due to be relieved on completing my ninth patrol, which was fairly successful. We had sunk a submarine tender with valuable torpedoes and personnel and the admiral of all the Japanese submarines aboard, plus a destroyer and so forth.

So coming into Pearl, I felt pretty good, and there was everybody down there to welcome me, including Admiral Nimitz. I thought, "What the hell is this?" Well, to make a long story short, Admiral Nimitz invited me up to his house for lunch, which was rather unusual. He proceeded to make me two strong martinis and tell me I had

Lt. Cdr. Dusty Dornin, commanding officer of the *Trigger*, is shown at a Pearl Harbor awards ceremony prior to receiving a medal from Adm. Chester Nimitz.
National Archives: 80-G-218069

been selected to be Admiral King's aide. Vice Adm. Charles A. Lockwood was there also. I figured out that they wanted me back there in Washington sitting at the right hand of King, hoping I'd feed the proper information to them about the submarine warfare in the Pacific. So I let them know I wouldn't go. "What? Are you crazy?" one of them asked. So Admiral Nimitz and Admiral Lockwood asked me to go back to the ship, think it over for twenty-four hours, and then come back and tell them.

I didn't go back to ship; instead, I went to the submarine skippers' lounge in the bachelor officers' quarters and proceeded to have a few beers and give the boys the dope on what had happened. They all said to me, "My God, Dusty, you don't say no to a couple of admirals, much less the commander in chief of the Pacific Fleet, Admiral Nimitz. And besides that, we understand that there are seven hundred women to every able-bodied man back in Washington." I proceeded to give that some thought and

decided that maybe the boys had something.

So I accepted the job and then had to wait around for three months before going to Washington. I was not due to relieve until 1 June of 1944. Then I got wondering what in hell Admiral King would want with me. I was only a little over nine years out of the academy, I was only thirty-one years old, a lieutenant commander, and had no staff experience. Later on, I found out that Admiral King wanted a bachelor aide around the class of 1935, and one who was a successful submarine skipper. The old man was quite proud of submariners. One time he was the commanding officer of the submarine base in New London. Also, he had five daughters, four of whom were married, and the unmarried one, Florie King, was about my age, about thirty years old.

I spent most of the next three months in the San Francisco Bay area, Mill Valley, California, which was my home. I got married while I was there, but I didn't bother to notify anybody in the Navy. So I arrived in Washington and reported on

Dornin (*right*) relieves Cdr. Charles C. Kirkpatrick as Adm. Ernest J. King's flag secretary in 1944. *National Archives: 80-G-47156*

1 June to relieve Cdr. Charles Kirkpatrick, a submariner and later the superintendent of the Naval Academy. When he started briefing me, I said, "Well, the first thing, Kirk, I'd sure like to know where I could live."

He said, "Hell, you can live on the *Dauntless,* the flagship of the commander in chief of the U.S. Fleet." It seemed the old man lived aboard, and there were only four of his personal staff who stood duty on the yacht. He further went on about how much the old man needed some company and also talked about how Admiral King had a daughter who wasn't married and maybe I could see fit to escort her.

I said, "But Kirk, I'm married."

He turned white and he said, "What?"

I said, "I'm married. It's all right with me if my wife can live with us."

And he said, "Oh, shit."

I got the job anyway.

34

Crossing the Equator

REAR ADM. JULIAN T. BURKE JR.,
USN (RET.)

One of the time-honored traditions of the Navy is the King Neptune ceremony, which takes place when a ship crosses the equator. In some ways it is similar to a college fraternity initiation in which the new men go through an experience of hazing before they are accepted into the brotherhood. Those who crossed the equator previously are known as shellbacks, and it is their job to inflict mayhem on the pollywogs who are joining their ranks.

IN JULY 1944 the *Flying Fish* went into Brisbane, Australia, after a really difficult patrol. We had a horrible experience on being depth-charged on that patrol. We got pushed down to about five hundred feet, and we were lucky to get out. The Japanese had us, but I think they must have run out of depth charges.

When we got to port, everybody else went to Sydney on leave, but I just was too pooped out to do anything. I was the ship's navigator, chief engineer, and first lieutenant. After a month of that, I collapsed, and I went to bed for about two days just to get sleep. I figured out after it was all over that the longest I'd been in bed was about an hour and forty minutes, and I was really drained. I'm sure we sank some ships on that patrol. In May and June we sank four ships. I just don't remember what we sank and what we didn't, because it was just all a nightmare.

On the way to Australia, we went across the equator. When I'd crossed the line my first time on the battleship *West Virginia*, we had a big court. The chiefs and first class were all on the court and beat the hell out of all of us. And there were a lot of shellbacks there. They seriously outnumbered the pollywogs. Well, this time it was the other way around. There were only about seven or eight of us that had crossed the line, and they had to use me to make up a court. I didn't want to do it, but they insisted, and so they made me the Royal Barber. Well, half the ship had beards, and so I had some electric shears and shaved off half the beards and half the hair and so forth. In fact, one of the guys was so furious when I cut his beautiful beard half off that he spit in my face.

Well, after you've been submerged and been through a lot, you accepted it and laughed, but not everybody did. A few years ago, one of our crew members did a marvelous job of finding where the crew members were living. He began to get enough people to put a reunion together for the *Flying Fish*. I missed the first two reunions. The first one was out west, and the second one, I guess, was going to be in New London. Unfortunately, the date conflicted with the graduation of my oldest grandchild in college, so I couldn't do it, but I did help the crew members. I got on the horn and got some doors opened in New London, which they much appreciated.

Well, this guy and I talked on the phone from time to time, and he was someone whose hair I'd cut. He said that it ruined liberty for several men in Brisbane, because the girls thought they were diseased and wouldn't date them. But after we'd been working on this reunion together, finally one day he called up and said, "I just want to tell you, I owe you an apology."

I said, "No, you don't."

"Oh, yes, I do."

"Go ahead and apologize."

"I hated your guts for fifty years," he said. "But you're not so bad after all."

"Were you married then?" I said.

"Yeah."

"Your wife owes me."

35

Black Submariner

CHIEF INTERIOR
COMMUNICATIONS ELECTRICIAN
HOSEY MAYS, USN (RET.)

In World War II nearly all submariners were white. The exceptions were black men who were cooks and stewards to serve the officers. They were segregated by berthing assignments and by occupation, but the togetherness, close quarters, and shared danger in submarines led to the forging of links with their white shipmates. They were literally all in the same boat. Hosey Mays entered the Navy from Denver, Colorado, in early 1943.

WHEN I WENT to boot camp, they told me I was a mess attendant. I said, "What is that?" I had no idea what a mess attendant was, but I soon found out. In our class they asked for volunteers, and I was one of the few chosen to go into submarines at that time. We had taken aptitude tests, and I remember out of about twenty or thirty guys, there were only five of us that were sent up to New London, Connecticut. I spent one day in the Submarine School. Then they told me I was to go to the bachelor officers' quarters and take my training as a mess attendant. That included preparing and serving the food for the officers.

When I went on board my first submarine, I was a steward's mate first class, equivalent to a seaman first class at that time. The *Crevalle* had been built at Portsmouth Navy Yard and was commissioned in June 1943. I reported on board soon after that, when she came to New London for training prior to going overseas and to the war zone.

There were only two blacks on board the *Crevalle*. The other man was a fellow by the name of Timothy Pennyman, who was out of Cleveland, Ohio. We became friends the same day I got on board. We served the officers together and went on liberty together. In the forward torpedo room there were two bunks, right beneath the overhead, and this was where the stewards slept. It was our own little space, which they called the "bridal suite" because there were only two racks and they were side by side instead of stacked vertically. You didn't last if you had claustrophobia, but it still took a little while to get used to the tight quarters.

The crew of the *Crevalle* accepted us. Our officers and captains didn't put up with any bull-jive. And there wasn't any place for animosities or anything like that. I've heard a lot of stories, but in my career I've never come across that in any ships that I've ever been on. You were one of the crew, and you did your job. But then, of course, when we went over the gangway on liberty, we went our separate ways because of the times and segregation. We had our own liberty places where we went; we didn't associate normally with the crew or with the white elements on the beach.

When we got under way from New London, the submarine went to Panama, the Galapagos, Pitcairn Island, and Brisbane, Australia. We had a ceremony for crossing the equator, and that was a ritual I'll never forget. We went underneath the line, not over it. As soon as we dropped the hook at the Galapagos, we had our initiation. King Neptune came aboard and so forth. There was some hazing, including walking the plank. There was a man up on the periscope shears with a rifle to ward off sharks. As soon as I hit the water, he let off a couple of rounds. If a guy didn't swim, he learned how right then. The whole thing was fun.

When we first started in the training for combat, they tried to acclimate you to a depth-charge attack by using practice depth charges during drills. In the real thing, you heard the noise but never really got accustomed to the Japanese depth charges. They told you that the ones that sank you were the ones you couldn't hear. If you heard them go off, you knew you were okay. The whole crew had jobs on battle stations. You just sat there and waited and watched and prayed with the rest of them. The most fear I remember was when we

When the *Crevalle* was in Australia in 1943, Mays interrupted liberty long enough to pose for this portrait. *Courtesy Hosey Mays*

got our first contact with the enemy. After that you sort of got used to those situations.

The first problems we ran into because of race came in Australia. After our first patrol out of Brisbane, the *Crevalle* operated out of Fremantle, near Perth. It was segregated almost worse than the States. Australia has a black population, the aborigines. We, the black sailors, were not allowed to associate with the black Australian women. When we reached that country, its motto was "Keep Australia white." Our executive officer talked to Pennyman and me and told us what we could and couldn't do as far as fraternization was concerned. If the white American military police or shore patrol caught us associating with Australian black people, they would send us back to the ship or read us the riot act. The white Australians called us "black Yanks" and wanted to feel our hair and feel our skin. They had never seen black Americans before. You hear about the Australian war brides. The white boys could marry the Australians, but you never heard of a black one marrying any Australian.

After a while, as far as liberty went, you began to find out that after dark things could happen. We went to what I would now call "safe houses." This was sort of an underground setup where you could go and be discreet. They were not nightclubs or anything like that, but we would play cards, listen to music, dance, eat some chow from the base, and have a drink. It was a good way to relax between war patrols. There was a chain of information that told you about these places. We heard about them when we got there, and then when other new fellows would come, I could tell them places where they could go and have a nice time. We didn't have to frequent the hotels and other places where the majority of the sailors hung out. Normally, black Australians ran these safe houses. If whites came to those places, they just didn't get in.

One of the things that gave me satisfaction was qualifying for my dolphins as a submariner. The stewards went through the process just like everyone else. You had to go through the training, and you had plenty of time to study and make out your notebooks while the boat was under way. You definitely had to know a lot more than just the steward rating. You had to know the whole ship—electrical systems, air systems, fuel systems, and how they worked. I didn't stand watches per se, but I liked to do it sometimes to change the routine. I'd take the helm, for instance, for relief purposes or serve as a lookout. Sometimes I'd go in the maneuvering room and engine room and learn what was happening there. When we came in from a war patrol, I got my dolphins, and for initiation my shipmates threw me over the side there in Fremantle when the boat was alongside the tender.

We did have plenty of action in those patrols. There was a custom that the black guys were always in the gun crew for the deck gun we used on the surface. I remember on the *Crevalle* I was the first loader on the 4-inch deck gun, and Pennyman was a fuze setter. We had a number of gun actions in which we shot at other ships.

Tankers and cargo ships were the main targets. Sometimes we fired at patrol craft, and they would shoot back. The gun crew had no shelter at all when we were out there. After it was over, we'd go down there and get our little shot of brandy, which they called "medicinal." When we shot torpedoes, Pennyman and I were always in the reload crew. Those torpedoes were heavy, and they needed a lot of manpower on those things.

After making the first two patrols in the *Crevalle*, I moved over to the *Bowfin* when the relief crew was rotated. I had made petty officer second class by then, and I made two runs, number five and six, on the *Bowfin* out of Fremantle. Both of those submarines had excellent war records. I remember one action on the *Bowfin* when Cdr. John Corbus was the skipper. This was in August of 1944, and we went into the harbor at the Japanese island of Minami Daito. We sank a couple of small freighters that were tied up to the wharf and knocked out a traveling crane that was on the wharf.

Corbus said to us, "I want to get you boys home," and that's what he meant. Some people criticized him and called him "Jittery John," but I liked him. He was my style, because I wanted to get home too. He did his job, but he wasn't one of those hard chargers. I remember that when we were under depth-charge attack, he would be in the forward torpedo room smoking cigarettes. He would just walk back and forth, lighting cigarettes, putting them out, and lighting up again.

Since the stewards were in the wardroom, serving the food, and making up bunks, we heard a lot of what the officers were saying. They trusted us and spoke openly, so we had to be discreet. They didn't have to tell us not to spread rumors and so forth. The officers did a good job of keeping the crew informed. After the submarine got under way, they told us where we were going. They would put a chart on the bulletin board and draw the ship's course. But you couldn't say anything when you were in port and were writing home, because the officers censored all the mail. You'd pretty well censor yourself, but if somebody said something he shouldn't, the officers would clip it out with scissors. The officers

Combat artist Griffith Bailey Coale recorded this scene of the tender *Pelias* and a group of between-patrols boats at Fremantle, Western Australia. A movie screen on the fantail provides a clue as to evening recreation. A garbage chute descends from the ship's port quarter. *Navy Art Collection, Washington Navy Yard*

were even reading their love letters, but the guys didn't care.

We did various things for recreation when the boat was under way. We had records that would come out with various radio shows on them. We always played cards of some type—five-card stud, maybe, or draw poker. We played acey-deucy and did a lot of reading. A guy always had a paperback book of some kind sticking out of his back pocket. I enjoyed the western stories. One novel that went all over the boat was *God's Little Acre*. It was about a poor white family in Georgia and was pretty sensational for its time. I'll always remember that one.

We got a great break in the routine when the *Bowfin* got into Hawaii. The armed forces had taken over the Royal Hawaiian Hotel as a rest camp for submariners and pilots. We got the best treatment that was allowed at that time. I was wondering, for instance, where I would take a shower, because our bathtubs were always full of beer and ice cubes. You could go out into town,

go to the nightclubs. You didn't have to leave the hotel if you didn't want to for the two weeks the boat was there. Everything was given to you; you were waited on. They had boxing matches that they called "smokers." They had movies. They had outstanding chow. They had everything but the ladies of the night.

One time in the summer of 1944 the *Bowfin* was there in Pearl Harbor, preparing to come back to the States for an overhaul, and the *S-28*, an old submarine, was on the other side of the pier. She was in Hawaii to serve as a training boat, a target for other ships. Destroyers would look for her to get sonar checks and so forth. They went out one morning, and they left part of their crew in port. That evening the crew came back in preparation for the ship to come in, but she never showed up again. The *S-28* was lost with all hands on 4 July 1944.

After the sixth run of the *Bowfin* I was transferred to Submarine Squadron Thirty, a new squadron with new boats and everything. We were sent back to Fremantle on the tender *Howard W. Gilmore*. I stayed there the rest of the war, from April 1945 until September. Then I came home on the submarine tender *Clytie*. We cleaned out all the men and all the supplies and so forth and proceeded back. Of course, all the boats went back on their own.

During that trip, which went all the way from Australia to New London, Connecticut, I worked for Capt. C. O. Triebel, who was a division commander at that time. He introduced me to a lot of things about working personally for an officer. That was a new adventure for me as a steward. Each morning I would knock on his door and go into his cabin with coffee in my hand. I would stand by his bed, and when 7:30 came he would just reach up, without opening his eyes, and take this cup of coffee. He was something else. Once we got back to New London, the division was disbanded, and people went here and there.

After that, I had a lot more submarine duty over the years. I was on the USS *Bluegill*, USS *Besugo*, USS *Sterlet*, USS *Grenadier*, and USS *Atule*. In the late 1950s I left the steward rating. A high percentage of the black stewards stayed in the Navy after the war. They didn't go back home to Alabama, Mississippi, and places they had come from. The Navy life was good for them. They got out of the cotton fields, and they got out of the segregation down South. They found a new life in the military. It wasn't all that bad. But then, after a while, the rating became so top-heavy that they didn't have a chance to advance any higher. So a directive came out saying the Navy wanted hundreds of us to change our ratings to electrical specialties. I was then a steward first class.

I tried to switch over, but at first nothing came of it. Later, when I was on shore duty at Great Lakes, Illinois, I put in another chit, and it was okayed. The schools were there, so I was just in the right place at the right time. I was sent to school to become an interior communications electrician, and I was also sent to gyroscope school. After that training, in 1959, I was able to change my rating over to IC electrician. But it didn't happen right away. I went to sea in the *Grenadier* to get some experience as an apprentice electrician and then later took the test. I was a steward first class striking for IC electrician. I had an old chief there, L. V. Miller, a white guy out of Jacksonville, Florida. He took me under his wing and saw that I made it. You have to have a mentor, and he was it. I stayed on that boat for almost four years until I made chief petty officer.

Later I was transferred to IC school and went there as an instructor—quite a difference from what I did when I first came into the Navy. It didn't start that way, because it just wasn't practical at the time. But it all turned out really well. It was a way of life that suited me, and I have a lot of good memories of shipmates.

In the 1960s the nuclear submarines were becoming more and more prominent, and they were appealing to the younger guys. They didn't need us older guys by then. I stayed in the diesel boats until I got ready to come out, and that's what I did. I retired in 1968 from the *Atule*, out of Key West, Florida. Then I stayed in the fleet reserve until I finished five more years to complete my thirty. It was a good career. I definitely felt a lot of pride.

36

Wolf Pack Operations

VICE ADM. LAWSON P. RAMAGE,
USN (RET.)

Cdr. Red Ramage was brave, aggressive, innovative—and seemingly oblivious to danger. He took command of the USS *Parche* when she was commissioned on 20 November 1943 and then was part of one of the early submarine wolf packs. In the boat's first patrol, she started out from Pearl Harbor in January 1944. The first successes for the wolf pack came on 4 May. During a subsequent patrol, in the early morning hours of 31 July 1944, Ramage and his pack mates got themselves amid a Japanese convoy that offered targets aplenty. Some of the lessons learned earlier paid off that night.

I THINK THE MOST significant thing that greeted us in Pearl Harbor was the fact that, first, we were going to join up as a member of one of the first wolf packs that were going out. Second, and this upset me, I learned that they were going to paint us a lighter color. I wanted to be the blackest cat out there, but they had gotten some of these experts working on the camouflage problem, and they decided that maybe complete, total black was not the best color. So they proceeded to paint us up and send us out on a convoy exercise off Oahu. It didn't take any time to convince me that they were right. I was amazed by the effect of these different shades of gray on the hull—that they just painted you completely into oblivion. You just couldn't see this submarine at any distance at all. That relieved all my anxieties in that regard.

We were adopting the German procedure in using the wolf pack. The boats were the *Parche*, the *Bang*, and the *Tinosa*. The skipper of the *Bang*, Tony Gallaher, had not made any war patrols.

That was the reason why the division commander, George Peterson, decided to ride the *Parche*. After a few preliminaries and discussions of how we would put this thing together, we departed. While we were en route to Midway, the division commander and I put together our first wolf pack instructions and passed them to the others when we arrived in Midway for fueling.

The difference from lone-wolf operations was primarily the positioning of the submarines. Two submarines would try to get themselves in position ahead on either bow of the target. The third submarine would be the trailer, and she would take station astern in case the target was damaged, and then she could pick off the cripple. Or, if the target turned or reversed course or eluded either of the two advance submarines, she would be in a position to attack.

The other aspect of this was that we didn't want to be patrolling right together all the time. We didn't want to be continually on the alert for one of the others in the immediate vicinity. So we divided our patrol area up into sixty-mile squares, and each submarine was assigned to a twenty-mile lane, sixty miles long. This broadened our front for detecting the target in the first place. Then, as soon as somebody made contact, he would relay the word to the other two subs, and they would close in.

In early May the *Tinosa* and the *Parche* tangled with a convoy. We made our plans and actually exchanged them on the surface by voice radio. We decided to dive if the Japanese ships headed our way. Sure enough, the convoy obliged and started coming toward us. We both dove simultaneously and spread out. Just as we got in position where I going to attack, this outfit zigged again, so I was lucky to get in one attack and fired my spread of torpedoes. I got one ship. The *Tinosa*, being over in the direction in which they turned, was able to get in, and I think she got two or three ships.

Finally, we got word of another convoy coming up from the south, and we exchanged plans, which we did in the night. The next morning the convoy showed up, and we started trying to trail them on the surface. But it wasn't long before air-craft came out of Formosa and forced us down. It wasn't until after four o'clock when the aircraft departed and we were able to get up and start closing in. As we got up to within ten miles of them, this one surface escort picked up the *Parche* and started coming out in our direction. We noted that the convoy had changed course, so we turned parallel and just kept going full speed on the surface. This escort was gradually closing, but we hung on, knowing that soon we would have a chance to throw him off, which is exactly what happened.

About one o'clock the next morning, the convoy headed for the China coast. I knew that it couldn't go in that direction very long and would certainly have to snap back shortly and head to the northeast. I decided to close in and take my chances on getting in position for a submerged radar attack. We started in, and by the time we got in to about four thousand yards, the whole formation had changed course back to where I anticipated, to the northeast. We were right in there close, so I decided I might as well go ahead and pick off the first two ships. So I fired four torpedoes at the first one, which was a big transport, and got her, and then immediately shifted to the second one with the other torpedoes and got her.

I think the *Tinosa* had hit the convoy earlier in the evening, from the other side. There were still about four or five ships left. I had no torpedoes left in the bow tubes, so I had to maneuver into position to get a stern shot off into this third big ship that I wanted to hit. I drove in and swung around to bring the stern tubes to bear, and every time I did this fellow would open up with machine-gun fire. By the time I would get lined up, I was out about a thousand yards, and these were electric torpedoes, which I didn't have too much faith in to begin with—and furthermore they were much slower than the steam torpedoes. The torpedo run would have been too long. I made my second pass around with no more success.

Then my torpedo officer came up and asked permission to reload the bow tubes with the steam torpedoes. This was something that was absolutely unheard of. No one had ever considered reloading the torpedoes with the submarine

An intense Red Ramage faces the camera during World War II. *Naval Institute Photo Archive*

on the surface, charging around at twenty knots in contact with the enemy and subject to dive without notice. Because once you got those torpedoes out of the racks, they were like greased pigs. You could lose control of them, and they could really mash people down there.

I questioned him on it, and he assured me that he was ready to do it. He had cleared all the bunks out of the torpedo room, and he guaranteed that he could keep that torpedo from getting loose, so I said, "All right, go ahead." While we were in the course of going around again, he reloaded two torpedoes forward. Then we drove straight in and let them have it. That took care of the third ship. It was a great big ship staring me in the face, and I wanted so badly to sink it that I was willing to go to any length to get some steam torpedoes reloaded forward. Maybe that was a rather foolhardy decision, but like everything else, if it works out, it's fine.

About that time we saw the *Bang* sitting there on the surface, so we said, "Okay, you take

charge." He got two ships with his last two torpedoes. He and the *Tinosa* were then all out of torpedoes, and I still had ten, one for each of my tubes. So they immediately departed for home and left me to sit around there for another ten days to take the consequences. They were not too pleasant, for the Japanese kept that place under complete and total surveillance the whole period. In any case, we finally ran out of time and headed home. That was one of the first really good, successful wolf packs, I think.

We went into Midway for refit. Then I was informed that my division commander, Lew Parks, was going to take the next wolf pack out and he was going to ride the *Parche*. We went through quite a ritual with him, because he was pretty much of a stickler for detail and everything else. He had many ideas how to fire torpedoes, because he had, of course, made three war patrols himself in command of the *Pompano*. So it was a different sort of a ball game with him than it was with George Peterson, who went along with anything and took any suggestions. He left the individual operations of the boats to the skippers. Nevertheless, things worked out very well.

In early June, we were getting ready to depart for the second patrol of the *Parche*. At that point I don't think the real impact of our surface reload had become general knowledge, but it certainly was a very significant first as far as our submarines were concerned. Skippers like Gene Fluckey and Dick O'Kane and others adopted that system. That's how they got their big bag of ships too.

The whole trick was to keep the torpedo from getting away and sliding into the tube. If the submarine took a down angle, there was nothing to prevent that torpedo from going straight and hitting the bow doors. Of course, it would take up against the stop bolt, but that could be easily sheared off and then go right out through the doors, and you could flood the submarine. The main thing was to control the movement of that torpedo into the tube. We did a little more work on it, and I was convinced that this was the answer to reloading on the surface, as long as you were willing to take the chance. This, of course, was the basis of our success subsequently.

The new wolf pack left Midway on 17 June. They called the wolf pack Parks's Pirates. I was more or less inclined to call it the Head Hunters, because we had the *Hammerhead*, the *Steelhead*, and me, the redhead. Our first contact with the enemy was just south of the Bonin Islands. Later we got out on our patrol station, which was what they called the "Convoy College" area, south of Formosa and north of the Philippines, out to about the Pratas Reef. Convoy College was an operational area. It was right across a convoy route, and usually they had three wolf packs in this area, which was divided into three sections.

Each day we would move sixty miles, either to the east or west or to the north or south. This procedure continued for the first week or ten days, and we didn't sight anything. It was pretty discouraging. We were all ready and waiting, because this was pretty much the same area where we had gotten our convoy on the first patrol. Finally, one evening shortly after dinner,

we got a call from the conning tower that they had targets on the radar at about twenty miles. I went up to take a look at the radar and saw these three pips, so we changed course to head for them and went ahead on four engines. We went to general quarters and got ready for a night surface action. Parks, the wolf pack commander, came up to see what was going on, and all of a sudden there were flashes on the horizon. So Parks asked, "What was that?"

I said, "Well, they're shooting at us." Soon there was ka-boom, ka-boom, ka-boom, and the water splashed all over us. So at that range the Japanese obviously had us on radar, and their gunnery was damned good—far better than I would have ever believed possible on an opening salvo. Apparently there were two cruisers and a destroyer. They were fast, and obviously the targets were pretty good size. I'd say the range at which they opened up was about fifteen thousand yards, which is about seven and a half miles. This was the first indication that they had a pretty good radar on those ships.

Parks headed for the hatch and I said, "Where are you going?"

He said, "I'm going below. You can do whatever you want."

After considering that for a moment, I decided that maybe that was the better part of valor if they were going to continue that sort of gunfire. And certainly the convoy wasn't going to come anywhere near us if they knew we were there. So there wasn't any point of pursuing this convoy any farther unless we could do it submerged. So we dove, and the Japanese sent one destroyer over in that area to do some pinging, but the convoy continued on.

That was about the only thing that happened there for a while. We had been getting a lot of intelligence reports about convoys coming north and coming south and usually outside our particular area. Parks decided we'd better get over and get on their track in each case. As a result, we were running back and forth on the surface practically all the time out there, and we were getting exasperated as time went on. Obviously, the Japs must have had planes up there spotting and saw us. We got word all the way from Pearl Harbor: "For God's sake, stop charging around on the surface out there; they're spotting you." The Japanese saw where we were and told the convoys to divert, so we were just giving away the whole show.

Finally, our patrol time had run out. It came time for the *Hammerhead* to leave, because she had to continue on down to Perth; so she departed. The wolf pack commander asked for an extension and got it for another five or ten days. We certainly didn't want to go home empty-handed after all this. I had vowed before we ever left that if we got into a convoy, I was going to get my swag, regardless of the others, and get out. I wasn't going to be left behind like I had been before.

We surfaced one night about the third day of this extension and got a message from the *Steelhead* that they had contacted a convoy, which they were trailing. They gave us the course and speed of the convoy and position. We immediately went on four engines and proceeded on a course to intercept. We started on this chase about eight o'clock in the evening. Time was going on, and we weren't getting any more information from the *Steelhead*, and we weren't getting any contact with the enemy. I got greatly agitated and insisted that we better contact the *Steelhead* and ask him what was going on. Parks was reluctant to open up and query the *Steelhead*. I kept insisting. Finally, he said, "If we haven't heard anything from them by 12:30, we'll go ahead and ask." So 12:30 came and no message. So we called and asked the *Steelhead* where he was and where the convoy was. Sure enough, as I had suspected, the convoy had changed course shortly after the initial message and was heading southeast. We were way off in right field—about thirty or forty miles away from the convoy, which we had to make up.

We swung around and headed in, and it wasn't until about three o'clock in the morning that we finally made contact with the convoy. The Japanese ships were all darkened, and we were coming in from almost due west on an easterly course. We approached on their starboard quarter. We saw that they had one escort on the starboard beam and another farther forward on the starboard bow. We had no idea where the *Steelhead* was, but we presumed that she was over on the port hand, which was where she should have been according to the regular patrol doctrine.

As we came in we noticed that there was another escort moving out in our direction from the head of the convoy. I decided there was no point trying to go in around these escorts, so I made a reverse spinner and turned outboard and came around and under all of them to get inside the escorts. But no sooner had we made this turn and come in on a course heading into the convoy than we found out that they had changed course ninety degrees, to the southwest. Now we were dead ahead of them and closing fast, so fast, in fact, that we didn't really have time to get a setup on them. One in particular was right on us, and before we could do anything we were alongside, and the Japanese ship was going by at twenty knots at about a hundred yards.

So I said, "Okay, we'll swing around and get him." We came around and let fly a couple of torpedoes at him, but he was still turning, and we were turning, so that wasn't a very well organized shot, and apparently both those torpedoes missed. About that time we saw two big ships, so we headed over that way. As we had made our turn, one of the ships was on our stern, and the torpedo officer said he had a good setup on the stern tube. So I said, "Okay, let him have one torpedo out of the stern." He did, and we know we got a hit. We don't know really whether that ship sank or not, but that was our first hit.

Then I took aim on the other one and let go four torpedoes from the bow. Every one of those hit—one, two, three, four—right down the side of the ship. We were firing now to kill with every shot; we weren't firing spreads. This happened to be a tanker, and she went straight down. So now we had cleared all the torpedoes out of the forward tubes—six gone there. We swung around and brought the stern to bear on another ship, which happened to be a tanker also. We let three go at that, and all three of those hit, but the ship only went down by the bow and got a small fire going; she continued on. And that took care of all the torpedo tubes. We had fired ten torpedoes, and all the tubes were empty. Then we saw a transport about dead ahead of us. So they called up from below and said they had two torpedoes ready, loaded forward. So we fired those two at the transport. We caught her well on the bow and the beam and she went on down.

Next we decided we'd better go back and get that tanker. Of course, now we had no torpedoes forward again, and they were busy reloading aft. As we came up under the stern of this tanker, we cut as close as we could in order to keep out of the way of his deck gun. The ship was well down by the bow, and the gun was practically pointing in the air. We came tight under there and crossed his stern, and we were heading out to what we saw was another ship, a good-sized ship, on the other side of this group. All of a sudden, he began shooting. Of course, now he could see. The whole place was alight with gunfire; everybody was shooting at everybody and anything. But nobody, I felt, could see us, except for this rooster tail of a wake that we were laying out there, going through at twenty knots.

The light came mostly from rockets and stuff, and the searchlights, I guess, were flying around there, but I didn't pay too much attention to that. I was watching more particularly where I was going, and I could see the silhouettes of the ships. The light was sufficient for me to see where everybody was. But when they began shooting right down our wake, it began to get a little bit hot. In this case we decided we had best put the tanker out of her misery. As soon as we got enough distance, got out seven hundred yards or so, we let go with three torpedoes out of the stern and put that tanker down. So now we had two tankers and a transport and a hit in the first ship.

Just as we got to this point, we saw an escort trying to ram us, so I said, "Let's hang on here for more speed from the engine room." As soon as we got across his bow, I turned hard right to come parallel with him and threw our stern out away from him. We slid down and passed each other about fifty or a hundred feet or so, enough where we could shout at each other. Everybody was screaming.

Then there was another escort just beyond and closing fast. I didn't want to run into him. As soon as we cleared this fellow, we saw a big transport dead ahead. My men said they had torpedoes loaded again, two forward. So I said to fire one right down the throat. We were lined up directly at him and let two torpedoes go. I could see that one of them wasn't going right, but I think the other one hit, which put him down by the bow. Then we continued down and swung out to the left to bring our stern to bear on his starboard side. We let one more go, and that hit him directly amidships and put him down.

Now we had four ships sunk and one damaged, and it was beginning to get a little bit light—a little too light. And we couldn't see any other ships that were of any consequence. Mostly there were just escorts now, just charging around and shooting whatever small weapons they had. So we decided to pull clear and get ready to dive for the day, to get some distance between them and where we were going to dive. As we did, we saw the Japanese signaling to each other, trying to take a reading of what had happened. One of our quartermasters said, "I guess they have a lot of reports to fill out too."

I think the Japanese had about nine ships in this convoy. We picked out the five ships of any size. Of course, the *Steelhead* had been working on them all night. He had them fully alerted. He got credit for a couple, but I think they gave him credit for two of the ones we got. I don't know, but at least, according to the book, they gave us both credit for the same ships. Whether he hit anybody or not, I don't know. He had been firing at them from pretty well out. He was about three thousand yards when he was firing.

When we got to Pearl, of course, Admiral Lockwood came down, and he was very pleased with our patrol. He congratulated us very early. But in due time they reviewed our patrol report. The chief of staff, Commodore Comstock, wrote a note to me. He was talking about our shifting of the torpedoes while under way and said, "This was foolhardy, very dangerous, and an undue risk" or whatever. Anyway, he said that as long as it came out all right, we got away with it, but we shouldn't do it again.

A frail President Franklin D. Roosevelt presents the Medal of Honor to Commander Ramage at the White House in January 1945. The president died three months later. *National Archives: 80-G-47645*

The night of the incident was 31 July in 1944, and I received the award of the Medal of Honor in Washington on 12 January 1945—six months later. It was awarded by President Franklin Roosevelt. In fact, he was a pretty sick man at the time, and I think he went off to his meeting at Yalta right after that. It was only three months before he died. As a matter of fact, when I went into his office and came face to face with him, I didn't recognize the man. His face looked like it was about two inches wide. His profile was still good, but he was just wasted away, and it didn't look as if he had any legs in his pants. He looked like he was just kind of set up in the chair, which he probably was. A very sick man—amazing that he stood for reelection and was looking forward to another four years under those conditions.

For the convoy attack on 31 July 1944 the *Parche* was credited with sinking the 10,238-ton tanker *Koei Maru* and the 4,471-ton passenger-cargo ship *Manko Maru*. The *Steelhead* was officially credited with sinking the 7,169-ton cargo ship *Dakar Maru* and the 8,195-ton transport *Fuso Maru*.

37

Rescuing POWs

REAR ADM. ROBERT W. MCNITT,
USN (RET.)

Along with Red Ramage, one of the handful of World War II submarine skippers who lived to receive the Medal of Honor was Cdr. Gene Fluckey of the USS *Barb*. He has told his own story in the popular book *Thunder Below*, published in 1992 by the University of Illinois Press. His first executive officer in the *Barb* was Lt. Bob McNitt. In addition to supporting Fluckey in the boat's combat operations, McNitt used his navigational skills to help rescue Allied prisoners of war in September 1944. At the time the *Barb* was part of a wolf pack that also included the *Queenfish* and the *Tunny*. They were operating in the South China Sea.

T HERE WAS ANOTHER wolf pack south of us. *Sealion*, *Growler*, and *Pampanito* got onto a convoy that had a couple of ships in it that had prisoners of war on board. They didn't know that. These ships were not marked. As far as they could tell, these were freighters.

Sealion hit the *Rakuyo Maru*, which had 1,350 prisoners of war aboard—Australian, New Zealander, and British—who had been up on the Burma railroad. They had been hauled down to Singapore and were now being taken back up to the Japanese islands as labor. After the attack they cleared the area, and *Pampanito* sank two ships, one of which was the *Kachidoko Maru*, which had 750 prisoners of war on board. I think they lost probably all of those. But here was a major tragedy, and we in the *Barb* were unaware of it.

Since this wolf pack, Ben's Busters, did not give us a contact report, we didn't know they were into the attack. After a couple of days and no action, we had pulled off and gone back east to the Bashi Channel between the Philippines and

In the *Barb*'s wardroom are the wolf pack commander, Capt. Edwin Swinburne (*left*), and the submarine's skipper, Cdr. Eugene Fluckey. *Courtesy Rear Adm. Robert W. McNitt*

Formosa. I remember clearly around midnight or so a couple days later we got the message from ComSubPac saying that there were Allies in the water. *Sealion* had gone back through the area and just by luck happened to find a couple of the Allies and realized what had happened. Then they called in *Pampanito*, and they rescued a hundred or so. They got them on board as best they could and sounded the alarm. So our job now, with *Queenfish*, was to go find them.

The attack on the *Rakuyo Maru* was on 12 September, and this was four days after the sinking. We had about 450 miles to go. We weren't sure where the survivors would be, and our problem was how do you figure where a drifting object would be on the water after four days of drifting? Actually, two more—it would take us another two days to get there, so six days. Fortunately, I had in my navigator's notebook a clipping I'd taken from the *Naval Institute Proceedings*

written by a Coast Guardsman. Never knowing when this would be handy, I'd cut it out and stuck it in my book. It gave a very good description in a few paragraphs on how to combine wave, current, coriolis effects, and wind and calculate what the drift would be. We laid these vectors down on a chart, ran it out to where we thought the men would likely be, set a course for it, and took off on the surface at maximum four-engine speed, about eighteen and a half to nineteen knots.

We were delayed en route by a contact report from *Queenfish*, which had a long-distance radar contact on a convoy at thirty-six thousand yards. So *Barb* and *Queenfish* positioned themselves for a night attack. *Queenfish* got in first, fired, got one hit on a ship. Then *Barb* got her shot. We came in on the starboard bow of this group, which was alerted now but still hadn't dispersed. As we made our approach on the surface and were just about to fire, Gene on the

Barb shipmates (*from left*): a bearded Bob McNitt, Ed Swinburne, Max Duncan, and Gene Fluckey. *Courtesy Rear Adm. Robert W. McNitt*

bridge realized along with the lookouts that there was a big, big ship in there that was overlapping with one we already had our target bearing on, and it looked like a carrier.

Since the two were overlapped, we fired a spread of six torpedoes, which covered both of them, and hit and sank both. One was the *Unyo*, which was a carrier, and one was the tanker *Azusa*, which was probably full of gasoline because it blew up with a huge, huge explosion. While this was going on, a frigate, which was an escort probably only about fifteen hundred yards from us, saw us on the surface and turned toward us. We watched. I was in the fire control party down below, so I could see the picture developing from the reports. But Gene was on the bridge, and he could see this frigate coming at him. He could see the bow wave, and yet he wanted to get all his torpedoes off, and we continued to fire even after we dove. It was an extraordinary attack, and we got out just in time.

The frigate went right over us, but they were so alarmed by this explosion over there that they either forgot or didn't realize they had us, and so

we were not depth-charged as she went over. We were submerged for about an hour as the depth-charging was going on all around us but not close, and within an hour we surfaced and continued. It was another call that Gene had to make, because he still had a couple of torpedoes left: Should we stay on the surface and pursue and get one more ship or carry on?

We had a bit of a conference on this, because we knew already that the weather was turning bad. It looked to us as though it was typhoon weather, and we knew we'd arrive shortly after daylight on our original track. There was no way we could increase speed. We'd already been delayed an hour submerged, and Gene, with the concurrence of Ed Swinburne, our wolf-pack commander, said, "We'll go. Let them go." So we continued to make our run for the survivors. At about, I guess, 9:30 in the morning we were right there and amazingly right in the middle of the wreckage. The prediction by this Coast Guard officer was just right. Amazing after all this.

It was an awful sight. There were bodies all over the place, grossly inflated—all blown up and floating. The crew came up on the bridge, because we'd let them come up on the surface and take a look. It was such an awful sight that nobody wanted to stay there and watch it. So we went through this mass of wreckage and bodies until we found a raft where men seemed alive. We made the approach and tried to pass them a rope with a bowline in the end of it right close aboard and handed—almost threw it—across the raft, and these men just sat there and looked at it.

They were beyond comprehending what was happening to them. They were so far gone. You'd tell them to put the rope over their shoulders, and they'd pick it up and look at it. They were just too weak and too uncomprehending. So the only thing to do was to go get them. So three or four of us just took these lines, put them around our shoulders, took another line, swam out, and got them. We brought them back with a cross-chest carry and helped drag them up over the side of the submarine. In an open sea, with big swells and the rounded shape of a submarine, it was not easy to get them on board. All of them fainted when they got on board. None of them could even stand up. When we got them up on the deck, they crumpled. I think we got fourteen of them.

Of course, they had been terribly treated as prisoners of war on the Burma railroad. They'd been cooped up inside the hold in almost the way the slave ships were. They were undernourished, without enough water, and scared to death when the ship was torpedoed. They'd just managed to escape. They told us that there was a dinghy towed astern of the ship as it sank or as it was about to sink—it took quite a while to sink—and the Japanese officers were back aft in the dinghy towing astern, figuring if the ship didn't sink they might come back on board. Some of the prisoners went back aft, dumped the dinghy, and drowned the officers. There were no Japanese anywhere alive. These guys were ruthless, weak as they were. So out of 1,350 survivors we got just a few. *Queenfish* got 18 and we got 14. Only 32 were left. By midafternoon a typhoon was upon us.

Late in the war, a smiling Bob McNitt sports dolphins and the submarine war patrol pin. *Courtesy Rear Adm. Robert W. McNitt*

As these men were hoisted up on deck, they were stripped of their clothes and then wiped down a little bit. They were all covered with oil, covered with sores, weak, emaciated, and half dead. They were handed in a chain down the hatch, down the ladder, and into the crew's mess. A table was laid out as a kind of a receiving station, and they'd be laid out on top of the table. Then some of the crew who were designated as nurses would wipe the oil off and clean them up a bit. All their eyes were in bad shape, and most of them were unconscious while this was going on.

There was the story about one of them, Jack Flynn, an Australian, waking up and looking up and seeing these big American sailors and saying, "I'll write home and tell the old lady, 'Kick the Yanks out. I'm coming home.'" This endeared him to the crew instantly. I have a little club flag in my house that Jack Flynn sent me forty years later, saying, "I don't know how to thank somebody that saved my life forty years ago."

38

Enemy Rescue

JAMES B. O'MEARA

Much has been made of the stark choice for Japanese servicemen between surrender and death. Time after time, events made clear to Americans that the Japanese considered surrender to be the height of dishonor. The kamikaze attacks by airmen and the "Banzai" charges by soldiers ashore were manifestations of the ethic that called for one to die fighting. For Japanese navy personnel whose ships had been lost, the option of a fighting death was largely taken away because they no longer had weapons with them. Thus the honorable exit was drowning, and few were taken prisoner from the sea, especially because of the mutual hatred that often existed between enemies. Jim O'Meara, an electrician's mate who served in the submarine *Seahorse*, recounts an incident from mid-September 1944 that was an exception to the norm.

T HEY HAD BEEN in the sea for five days, and the lookout reported them as objects in the water. They were naked except for life jackets, and when he was pressed for a more detailed report, the lookout said they looked like coconuts. After several minutes of maneuvering the boat toward the mysterious objects, which the other lookouts and the officer of the deck couldn't see, I was the one who finally determined the identity of the objects. These were men in the water, and their closely cropped heads were blackened by the sun, so they did indeed look like coconuts.

There were five of them, and one was in bad shape. His arm was broken, and he was cut up and in obvious distress. Our skipper, Cdr. Charles "Weary" Wilkins, decided to take this man on board for questioning.

The crew of the *Seahorse* musters on deck after return to port. She is shown here moored alongside the tender *Holland*.
Courtesy of James B. O'Meara

Of the other four, two seemed anxious to come on board, and the other two were hanging onto each other, face to face, with one seeming to keep the other from looking at us or trying to swim toward the boat. They all knew we were an enemy submarine, and one of them preferred to stay in the water to die rather than come on board. As it turned out, four were left bobbing in the sea, and Japanese shipping in the area was very scarce, so their chance of being spotted again was slim. They were in our patrol area, so no other American sub would be taking a big chance to surface and stop for four men in the water.

Anyway, we got under way while our wounded man was lying on the deck in the crew's mess. Doc Keeler, our pharmacist's mate, was taking care of him. The little guy was probably doomed

from the start, but then a torpedoman came through the open hatch. He was the biggest man on the boat, wore a full beard, and was armed with a machete. I suppose he intended to have some fun with our prisoner. He stood over the prisoner and looked menacing, but he was just fooling around. I don't think he had any idea that the prisoner was going to die, but I saw him die soon afterward. He may have been scared to death. The burial ceremony, such as it was, consisted of getting him into a mattress cover, weighted down by a 5-inch shell, and somehow getting him up the hatch and over the side.

Captain Wilkins wanted a prisoner for intelligence purposes, so he went back to find the remaining men. It was getting dark, and it was going to take some good eyes and keen navigation to find the four heads in the open sea at dusk. We did locate them, and one wonders what those desperate men thought when they saw us slowly approaching in the same manner as before and preparing again to take one of them aboard. You would think they would all have been ready to come on board rather than spend another night in the water. However, only one got lucky, and Seiza Mitsuma was dragged up the side and helped down the hatch. After we had Mitsuma aboard, the *Seahorse* again turned toward her patrol area. The after lookout kept his glasses on the remaining three men until the mounting waves and darkening skies slowly made the three coconuts disappear from view.

This new prisoner was in desperate shape. The sun had burned and blackened his head. His face was swollen, and his lips were burned and split. He couldn't tolerate our food, and our cook wasn't too anxious to prepare special dishes for him. We made a nest for him on the deck in one of the torpedo rooms. The torpedomen weren't too happy about him being there.

The little guy slowly and reluctantly came around, and so did the torpedo gang. In fact, before the patrol was over our prisoner had become something of a pet. He picked up a little English and became our unofficial mess cook. He seemed happy with his cleaning rag and broom in the crew's mess, fussing and shining the quarters. To the men who rescued him he explained that he was the radioman on a bomber that had been shot down. He said it was his captain who seemed so belligerent, and it was the captain who held the navigator, facing him away from our boat when the rescue was made.

He completed most of the patrol on the *Seahorse*, and I suppose he was entitled to a combat pin for his part in sinking a Japanese destroyer. Actually, the only part he took was being handcuffed to a bunk in the crew's quarters. A chief, armed with a .45-caliber pistol, and another enlisted man were next to him, ready to do him in if he became noisy or disruptive. There really wasn't much the guy could do, but we couldn't give him free rein on that crowded little boat during the approach and the attack. Strangely, he seemed just as anxious and excited during the attack as we were, and though it might have been an act, he seemed relieved and happy with the sinking.

Some of our more experienced and war-weary crew members, who could only think of this man as an enemy—which he was—couldn't forget the thousands of Americans who had been lost. Some perhaps had been victims of the actions of this bomber crewman. It fell their lot to prepare this man for his reception at Pearl. They said the Marines would perform unspeakable things upon his body and end up beheading him.

Mitsuma left the boat at Pearl Harbor when the *Seahorse*'s patrol ended. Two big burly Marines came up the gangplank to get him. He couldn't see them because he was blindfolded and handcuffed. He probably figured, as he was being led down the gangplank, that he would have been better off had we left him in the water. Of course, we didn't treat prisoners that way. As it turned out, he survived the war and was returned to Japan, eventually to become a successful businessman.

Upon his return to his homeland, he was looked down on, as death was preferable to capture. He has since been contacted and visited by one of the lookouts who first spotted him. The *Seahorse* crew has even invited him to our reunions at the SubVets conventions. It has been many years since the crew of the *Seahorse* has seen Seiza Mitsuma. If he is still around, we wish him well and want him to know—we ain't mad anymore.

39

New Bride, New Boat

CDR. JOHN D. ALDEN, USN (RET.)

World War II had profound effects on the social lives of young men and women—and in many cases boys and girls—in the United States. The usual courting period was often foreshortened because of the frantic need to get men into action overseas. The "girl he left behind" was a common theme, as was a sense of urgency brought on by a future that was uncertain at best and nonexistent at worst. Ens. John Alden was one of those young men. He had met Ann Buchholz at Cornell University in 1942. By early 1944 they were engaged and making plans for marriage at the same time he was making plans for service in submarines.

A T THE New London Submarine Base my classmates from diesel school and I were told that our class at the Submarine School would not start until 1 April, and we would be assigned to one of the training boats until then. My roommate, Ens. Ed Carey, and I were ordered to the USS *Pike*, an older boat that had been retired from patrols in the Pacific but was one of the most modern of the subs used for training. Because we would be extra officers on board and there were no bunks for us, we would normally stay ashore at night and were given rooms at the bachelor officers' quarters. Ed and I were delighted to be assigned to such a good boat, and I knew I could count on remaining stateside for a good three months. I called Ann immediately, not even recognizing that it was Valentine's Day. We wanted to be married in two weeks, but Ann's mother said that more time was needed to prepare for the big event, so we set 11 March, three weeks later, as the date for our wedding.

In 1944 newlyweds John and Ann Alden faced an uncertain future as they began their married life together but prepared for imminent wartime separation. *Courtesy of John D. Alden*

The captain of the *Pike* was Cdr. R. C. Lawver, who was of the old-fashioned type to whom ensigns did not speak unless spoken to. The other officers were congenial, and most had already made war patrols on other subs. On 16 February, two days after the call to Ann, I made my first dive. From then on, I learned a great deal about running a modern submarine.

After some searching, because living quarters were scarce in wartime, I found a basement apartment in a house on Church Street in Groton, Connecticut. The location was ideal, with easy access by bus to the base, and on 23 February I signed up for the apartment. It consisted of an eat-in kitchen, bedroom, and a bathroom; furniture was basic. For heat the apartment had a coal stove that Ann would later struggle to master. In

the kitchen was a small electric cooking stove with two burners and a box-type oven. The "refrigerator" was a wooden box in the window, which was all right in the winter. With food rationing in effect, we didn't need much storage room. I tried to buy other things we would need and get the place fixed up for Ann's arrival. I asked her brother Art, who was undergoing Army training in New York City, to make reservations for our honeymoon there.

During my spare time on the base, I made a point of visiting the different types of submarines there, including a British boat and an Italian one; I found all of them very interesting. A French sub was there as well, but I was not able to get on it. Her crew cooked and ate on deck, and one of the *Pike*'s officers who was assigned to it had all kinds of stories to tell. He said the boat actually had a wine tank, and he told how loose coal from the topside stove had gotten caught under the deck hatch and caused the sub to start flooding. He thought it was quite hilarious.

In due course, the captain granted me six days' leave, and I left for Ann's small hometown of Claverack, New York, south of Albany in the Hudson Valley. The next morning we rushed to the county seat to get our marriage license from a town official. We were married that afternoon in Claverack's old Dutch Reformed Church, which was closed to save fuel but was opened specially for the occasion. Ann's brother, who was to be the best man, arrived from his Army post at the last minute. Her Cornell roommate, my two sisters, and two of her sisters were the bridesmaids. My parents were unable to make the trip from Nebraska. We had a reception at Ann's home after the service and left by train that evening for the city.

In New York we stayed at the Prince George Hotel on Thirty-Fourth Street, and for the next three days we had a wonderful time. We went to the play *Arsenic and Old Lace*, the opera *Pelleas et Melisande* at the old Met, a concert by the New York City Symphony under Leopold Stokowski, and Shakespeare's play *Othello* with Paul Robeson in the leading role. We did some shopping, ate in Chinatown, and just enjoyed the time together. On the fifteenth we took the train to New London and moved into our first home together before I caught the bus and reported back to the boat the next morning.

The *Pike* usually went out each day with a load of enlisted men from the Submarine School. They would rotate through the various duties expected of them. We student officers did the same, and in addition we were required to start a qualification notebook and trace out the important operating systems of the boat. The *Pike* even had an early model of the torpedo data computer, or TDC, on which the officers practiced making attacks. I left the *Pike* on 30 March, had one day's leave, and reported to Sub School on 1 April as scheduled.

The school was a letdown after serving on a real submarine. Many of the instructors struck us as pedantic, and the courses were cut and dried, based around the antiquated O-class boats that made up most of the training squadron. Instead of learning about the latest torpedo data computer, we were taught to make attacks using old manual devices. I had to make a new notebook, learn the archaic diving routine, and trace out the primitive systems of an O-boat of 1914 vintage. Probably the best part of the program, at least in our minds, was having occasional lectures by officers fresh from the fleet. I remember being especially impressed by Cdr. Roy Benson. What we concluded from these experienced skippers, as I wrote in a letter home, was that much of what we were being taught was "cursed and reversed in the fleet." I had a bit of a scare when making the one-hundred-foot practice escape in the escape tower. I couldn't seem to get air into my Momsen lung. I signaled to the safety divers, who pulled me in and found that the air valve hadn't been opened. Sent back to try again, I made the escape successfully and passed the test.

As the four-month course drew to an end, we all anxiously awaited orders. I had requested a new-construction boat and stood high enough in the class to get my choice. I was greatly gratified when Lt. (j.g.) Charles Biesecker and I received orders to the *Lamprey*. It was being built at Manitowoc, Wisconsin, on Lake Michigan, and was scheduled to be commissioned in November. For the time being, however, we were to be assigned to one of the fleet-type boats at Groton for further instruction. Graduation was on 1 July, and I reported directly to the USS *Cachalot* right there at the school.

The *Cachalot* was a bit smaller and a few years older than the *Pike*, but it had many of the characteristics of the new boats. It was engaged in training prospective commanding officers (PCOs), most of whom were fresh from the Pacific and preparing to command their own boats. In order to give all the PCOs their turns to make approaches and attacks, we were often out quite late, and I might not get home until after midnight. I also stood regular watches every third day. So as a newlywed I didn't have

The *Lamprey* was built quickly because of the urgency of the war effort. Her keel was laid on 22 February 1944, she was launched 18 June, and she was commissioned 17 November the same year. The sideways launching was necessitated by the limited water near the inland shipbuilding site. *Naval Institute Photo Archive*

as much time at home as we would have liked. Ann volunteered to help at Naval Aid, mostly driving enlisted men's wives to and from appointments in the official car.

In mid-July Ann went back to Claverack to see her brother off to war. On the day she got back we moved next door to share a house with a woman who had been kind to us. Our first landlady had gotten difficult to live with, snooped around the apartment when we weren't there, and was always criticizing the way Ann did things, so it was a relief to move. Some of the neighbors told us that we had put up with this lady longer than any previous tenants had.

As the *Lamprey* came closer to completion, her prospective skipper, Cdr. William T. Nelson, asked me to take special courses in communications and photography in preparation for my new duties. The photography course was fun. Basically, someone handed me a camera and told me to go around and shoot up a roll of film. Ann and I took photos around town and finished up at Ocean Beach, and that was about the extent of the course. I took leave in the middle of September, and we made final preparations to move to Manitowoc. Because of gasoline rationing, we had to get a special allotment of coupons to cover the planned mileage. I had bought a 1938 Ford coupe from a departing classmate and had the engine rebuilt. Unfortunately, it didn't do too well on fuel economy, and we ran out of gas in Illinois. Fortunately, we finally found a gas station that accepted some coupons that had already expired, so we were able to drive on and arrived at our destination on 27 September.

The *Lamprey* people who were already there had lined up an apartment for us. The people of Manitowoc were very kind and supportive of the submarine crews. The city itself reflected its German heritage with a neighborhood bar on practically every corner and a church on every other one. I checked in with the Submarine Training Activity for temporary duty and immediately began learning my new boat and getting acquainted with the officers and crew. We found that the shipyard workers took special pride in turning out well-built submarines. They made a particular effort to keep the boat clean on a daily basis, which was in contrast to other building yards, which left litter to accumulate and be cleaned up at the last minute.

On 14 November our crew had the traditional commissioning party, followed on the seventeenth by the commissioning ceremony itself. Captain Nelson had previously commanded the *Peto*, the first submarine built at Manitowoc, and had made four war patrols. The fact that three of our officers had served on earlier Manitowoc boats and asked to come back was a reflection of both their affection for the city and its people, and the excellence of the shipyard's product. I was the seventh officer, and my assignment was communications, radio and signal officer, and ship's secretary.

We spent the next three weeks running tests alongside the pier, then trials on the surface, and finally diving trials. With all the tests satisfactorily completed, we prepared the boat for its trip to the ocean. This involved taking off the periscope shears and putting the submarine into a barge-like floating dry dock that would be towed through the Chicago Sanitary Canal, Illinois River, and Mississippi River down to New Orleans. Removal of the periscope shears was necessary because of some low bridges along the way. A few of the crew were selected to ride the boat down, but the majority went by train.

On 7 December Ann and I packed up, sold our car, and caught the train for Chicago. There we boarded our sleeper car and arrived at New Orleans the next day. We registered at the Roosevelt Hotel at a rate of five dollars per day and had several days' leave to enjoy the city before the boat arrived on the thirteenth. We heard the Don

Cossack Chorus, took a river trip, ate at La Louisiane restaurant in the French Quarter (ignoring cockroaches on the wall), and visited a newspaper plant.

Soon it was time to report to the repair base at Algiers, across the river from New Orleans. There the boat was put back together, and we made final preparations for departure. On 17 December I said farewell to Ann, who had train reservations to Norfolk. She would visit her sister and brother-in-law there before returning to Cornell for her final term and a half. After we said good-bye, I rejoined my shipmates, and the *Lamprey* shoved off for the Panama Canal. We were on our way.

The *Lamprey*'s war patrols in the Pacific included a variety of duties and took her as far as Australia. At times she was a lifeguard submarine for American aircraft, and at other times she sought out enemy shipping. In May 1945, when targets for submarines were increasingly scarce, the *Lamprey* and *Blueback* engaged in a surface gunnery duel with a Japanese submarine chaser. In July, one of Alden's shipmates, an experienced submarine officer, began seeing Japanese ships that weren't actually there and otherwise acted erratically. He had been through a severe depth-charging in a previous boat and was finally overcome by combat fatigue and was left at a British hospital ship at Subic Bay in the Philippines. In mid-August the Japanese surrendered, and the war was over.

In the aftermath the *Lamprey* returned to the West Coast and went through overhaul at the Hunters Point Naval Dry Docks in San Francisco and mothballing at nearby Mare Island Navy Yard. John and Ann were together as the shipyard figuratively drained the life from the submarine. On 3 June 1946 the skeleton crew hauled down the submarine's flag for the last time and decommissioned their boat. Alden was one of seven plank owners who had been in the *Lamprey*'s crew from beginning to end.

After his submarine service Alden became a Navy engineering duty specialist and a distinguished author. His book *American Steel Navy* is a classic that celebrates the fleet the United States

In 2004, on the occasion of their sixtieth wedding anniversary, the Aldens gathered to celebrate with their extended family. *Courtesy of John D. Alden*

created at the end of the nineteenth century and beginning of the twentieth. He has written widely on submarines, and his meticulously researched *U.S. Submarine Attacks during World War II* is consid-ered the most complete source on the subject.

In 2004 Ann and John Alden celebrated their sixtieth wedding anniversary. They have six children, eight grandchildren, and one great-grandson.

40

Abandoning the *Darter*

VICE ADM. EUGENE P.
WILKINSON, USN (RET.)

During the Battle of Leyte Gulf, the submarine *Darter* torpedoed and damaged the Japanese cruiser *Takao*. The *Darter* and her sister ship *Dace* pursued the crippled cruiser through the channels of Palawan Passage in the Philippines. Just after midnight on 24 October 1944, the *Darter* grounded on Bombay Shoal. Efforts to free her were unsuccessful, so the crew evacuated to the *Dace* and rode safely to Australia. At the time the *Darter*'s engineer officer was Lt. Dennis Wilkinson, who later became the commissioning skipper of the first nuclear-powered submarine, the *Nautilus*. Wilkinson was chosen for that job despite the fact that he was not a Naval Academy graduate; he was, however, brainy, brash, operationally competent, and a hell of a poker player.

T HE *DARTER* RAN aground on Bombay Shoal after our attack on the Japanese fleet. It must have been about midnight. We called for help. The *Dace* was operating in our vicinity, in company with us. She found what course we'd come in on, and she got us on that bearing and came in up our stern and stopped just before she reached us so she wasn't aground. We went aground with four engines running at 75 to 90 percent. We really ran up on that thing, so that we lost suction in the engine rooms all the way back to the maneuvering room. I went over the side and swam around the ship and dived down under it. I came back and told the captain, Dave McClintock, "We'll never get off." We probably only had seven or eight feet of water under us instead of our usual seventeen-foot draft. We were up high and dry.

The *Darter* looks incongruously high and dry as she sits on Bombay Shoal after running aground during the Battle of Leyte Gulf. *Naval Institute Photo Archive*

So we sallied the ship and did all those things, but nothing worked. I was the first person to leave. The captain said, "Who will take a line to the *Dace?*"

I had been overboard and swum around that ship and under it. I was younger and could swim better then, and I thought, "My God, we might all not get off, so I better go first." So I said, "Captain, I will." I had a chance to be a hero. I could have put a knife in my belt and swum over that line, but instead I popped the rubber boat and paddled over. Then we used all the rubber boats

and went back and forth, back and forth, down that line. We got everybody off and everybody on the *Dace*. The *Dace* got there at 4:00 AM and we got off just before light. We were all over in less than an hour to the *Dace*. At 7:00 there was a Japanese destroyer alongside, and the *Dace* had no torpedoes left.

As part of abandoning the *Darter* we were destroying the communications and setting the explosive devices. When we finally left the ship, we started a fire in it, which was a mistake in a way. We'd set the devices forward, aft, and amid-

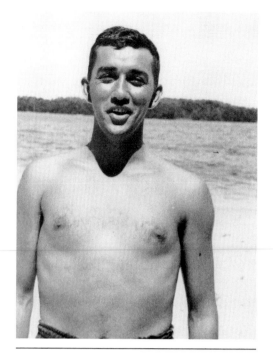

Lt. Dennis Wilkinson sported swimming trunks and a grin when the *Darter* was in rest camp between patrols in 1944. His swimming skill came in handy later in the year when the *Darter* ran hard aground. *Courtesy of Vice Adm. E. P. Wilkinson*

Janice Wilkinson's photo remained on board when the *Darter* was abandoned, but her husband did salvage the record of his poker winnings. *Courtesy of Vice Adm. E. P. Wilkinson*

ships, but they didn't go off. In my opinion the connections to the devices had been burned by the fire. By the time we realized the problem, all of us were over on the *Dace*. We had lots of men who volunteered to go back and set the explosives again, but that was too risky.

During our patrol in the *Darter* I had a picture of my wife Janice mounted in my stateroom. As we were about to leave the ship, I ran back down, but I didn't get my wife's picture. I got the poker record book—in which I was the one most ahead. My wife's never forgiven me, even though I got the picture duplicated. As we got on the *Dace*, the captain said, "Well, at least one thing. We start a fresh book."

"Oh, no," I said. "Here's the poker book right here."

The *Dace* had been extended on patrol, which had run them low on fuel. She was free to go back to Perth in Australia, but they didn't have enough fuel to run down on two engines. We had to go at a more economical, one-engine speed to Australia. So with two crews on board we were making seven or eight knots down to Australia. And they ran very low on food. We were down to mushroom soup and peanut butter sandwiches. And with two crews on board there was no place to sleep. We flaked out on deck, and one thing we did do: We spent a lot of time in the wardroom, and we played poker. I'm ashamed to say that on the way down to Australia we cleaned out all the *Dace*'s officers; we won their money playing poker.

41

Dodging Mines and Praying

REAR ADM. JULIAN T. BURKE JR., USN (RET.)

By 1945, the final year of World War II, the Pacific Fleet Submarine Force had inflicted a great deal of damage on the Japanese merchant fleet. The strategy of crippling the Japanese supply lines was so successful that the targets available for the ever-growing number of U.S. submarines had severely diminished. Vice Adm. Charles Lockwood, the force commander, promoted the mission of going into previously unavailable waters. The Sea of Japan, which lies between the Japanese home islands and the Asian mainland, was cordoned off by mines. Finding a way through those minefields was a further test of courage for submariners who had been through a great deal already.

IN THE SPRING OF 1945 the *Flying Fish* went to the San Diego destroyer base and had installed what was called an FM sonar. Its purpose was mine detection. After it was installed, we went over to the sound lab, and the technicians from Cal Tech [California Institute of Technology] came and got the FM sonar connected. Then over a period of time we got into a training program on detecting submerged mines so we could get into the Sea of Japan.

We trained and began to have exercises, and, theoretically, the sonar was supposed to pick mines up at fifteen hundred yards. Well, more practically, depending on the water, the gradients, the temperature changes, and so forth, you might pick them up at three hundred and up to seven hundred yards. If you were lucky, in some isothermal waters you could pick them up at a thousand yards. Then the word came out that Vice Adm. Lockwood, ComSubPac, was going to visit our ship. He arrived with staff members

Officers of the *Flying Fish* relax at a rest camp between patrols. In the center is Cdr. Bob Risser, captain of the boat and wolf pack commander for the foray into the Sea of Japan. Lieutenant Burke is in the second row, wearing a baseball cap. The nickname "Stinky" written across his shirt is a comment on the atmosphere on board the submarine. *Courtesy of Rear Adm. Julian Burke*

who were involved. Cdr. Barney Sieglaff was the project officer, so it was called Operation Barney. I think we as a group had nine submarines that had been equipped at this point in time to go into the Sea of Japan. To the best of my knowledge, Admiral Lockwood and his key staff members rode every single submarine to observe how we were doing.

We went through dummy minefields, and we did this with Admiral Lockwood more than one day. I was amazed to see him on board. Of course, I didn't know what the stakes were, and I didn't have his responsibility. The exercises were not confidence building, because the sonar ranges were not long enough, and your ability to maneuver submerged was very limited. You damn well knew that if you got something directly ahead of you, you might not be able to get out of its way. On the last run with Admiral Lockwood on board, we had a mine sitting up on the forecastle when we surfaced. We had entangled the cable in our bow planes.

Finally we left San Diego, and I'd say of all the departures I have ever made—knowing what I was facing—that hit me harder than anything. I didn't know whether I was ever going to see my wife Betty or daughter Tina again. Betty had no idea what I was up to, except I just broke down when I told her good-bye. It was tough on the whole crew. They knew what we were up to, but they didn't know the details.

After a stop in Pearl Harbor, we went on to Guam. By that time, ComSubPac had moved to Guam, and we tied up to the *Holland*, which was his flagship. Barney Sieglaff was there and provided detailed intelligence. They gave us the best intelligence that I ever saw about where we were going. We had intelligence that had been developed probably by OSS or some group back in Washington. They had the depths of the water and all the charts that had been made of the Sea of Japan. We knew what the currents were. We knew what the percentages of chance of getting through. We were going through Tsushima

In early June 1945 the *Flying Fish* moored next to the tender *Holland* at Guam, which by then was the headquarters for commander, Submarine Force, Pacific Fleet. Submariner Burke is at left; at right is his older brother Andy, a B-24 pilot for the Army Air Forces. *Courtesy of Rear Adm. Julian Burke*

Straits, and there were nine submarines. Commander Earl Hydeman of the *Sea Dog* was the senior commanding officer. I guess we were in Guam about a week and then we left and we were divided into three wolf packs of three each. Ours was Risser's Bob Cats, because Bob Risser was skipper of the *Flying Fish*.

In June our particular team was sent up not too far from Vladivostok, but it was still on the Korean side. We were probably the second team that went in. The water was cold; it was down in the thirties. When we went in, I think my maximum degree of terror was operating. It was worse than being depth-charged. We knew that the currents through there were strong—at least four knots in some places. We had all of these statistical projections and so forth, but you knew if you hit one of these mines you were a goner. So we dived, as I recall, around four o'clock in the morning, maybe five at the latest.

We had to go through a field of moored mines on cables. Our people didn't know where they were. All they knew was that mines had been laid. We knew that we were going to be submerged for a long time, something like twelve to sixteen hours, and we knew that the conning crew couldn't stay at battle stations all that time. So the captain and I divided it. We had two teams, and so he took the conn at the start. We took two-hour stints because of the pressure.

We went through four lines of mines during the day, and I had the conn at least twice. I remember the pure terror of being able to see a mine for the first time at about seven hundred yards. We picked up one, and all of a sudden this sonar gear was swinging back and forth so slowly. When it detected the mine, you had a visual picture on a scope, and it would make a ping. On the first line of mines I went through, we had about ten mines on the screen, and it was going ping, ping, ping, ping, ping, ping. Every damn one of those pings was hitting me in the gut and creating terror back there in my mind, I can tell you honestly that I spent much of that day on my knees praying that I wasn't going to buckle, because I knew how important it was to keep my courage and be an example to the officers and crew.

I made a point of getting through the ship a lot during the day to pat the crew on the back and try to let them know how we were doing. I don't know how often I did, but I know that I went through the ship on that day a lot. I was just scared to death, and finally we got through. We were riding along at periscope depth, and I had a disagreement with Bob Risser, the captain, because I thought he had exposed the periscope too much. There was a fishing boat in periscope sight. I thought we were too close, and I let him know. I told him, "What we've been through, to stick your scope up that high is wrong." I was wrung out. It's the only time he and I ever had a rift. I felt badly about it, and afterward he called me in his cabin and he said, "Look, we've been friends. I want to stay that way." So we were.

Once we got through the minefield, we got into the Sea of Japan, and we had fog and cold weather. It was stinking weather, and we didn't see much in the way of ships. As I best recall, we sank two separate ships. I don't think they could have displaced more than two thousand tons apiece. They were coastal inland-sea type ships, and we sank both.

Also, we got into a fishing fleet one day and tried to get these guys to give up and transfer; then we were going to blow up their boats. They wouldn't get out, and I don't know how many fishing boats we sank, but we sank a lot of them with our deck gun. That was not good psychologically with the crew and the officers. I didn't like it. I didn't protest the captain's decision, but it happened.

I don't know how many we sank, but I would say ten or fifteen at least; it was terrible. The first ship we sank, we got him at night with radar, and we hit him. He sank, and we were trying to pick up a prisoner. They were all over the place, and

they wouldn't come on board. They'd swim away when you would approach. Finally, by daybreak, we were out of sight of land. We found a survivor who agreed to come on board. We brought him on board and kept him up in the forward torpedo room shackled to a torpedo rack.

This man had been in the deck gun crew of his ship, which was a merchant ship, and he had pictures of himself in the traditional Japanese attire. He sort of looked like the actor Charles Boyer, and so he was called Charlie. Before long the crew began to spoil him, and the captain had been warned about it. We, the officers, had to police it, but we couldn't sit on it twenty-four hours a day. He was on board for at least two weeks, I think, and the captain was very careful to let the crew know that it was important not to spoil prisoners because we needed to get intelligence out of them, and the crew just didn't go along with it.

Charlie couldn't speak English, but constantly he and the crew were up there doing sign language with each other. He knew we were coming into port, and he asked for a pen and paper. He wrote something out in Japanese kanji [characters of the written language], and it was addressed to the captain, which the captain had translated after we got back to Pearl. He said that because of the fact that he had been captured alive, as far as his family and his community, he was dead and would be of no use in the future. But he wanted the captain to know that he expected to be tortured, and he was treated with humanity and kindness, and he would give his life to the cause of peace forevermore. I wish I had a copy of that letter, but I wasn't thinking that way at the time. He had a big impact on us, I think. It was the first time that I had ever been that close to a Japanese. Years later I ended up in Japan on duty and was surprised to find out that they weren't such bad people after all, after I got to know them, but they're like the Germans. They had this thing in their past that you have to always remember.

After a while, time had run out on us. We had an operation order that specified that we would go in there on a certain day and come out on a certain day. So we headed for the rendezvous point. We had all gone in one at a time, and the idea was that we were going to come out the same way. Captain Hydeman, in the *Sea Dog* was the senior officer. He was responsible for getting us out, and we rendezvoused up in the Sea of Japan, probably as much as fifty or sixty miles west of La Perouse Strait.

We on board *Flying Fish* were debating how we were coming out and looking at the depth of the water and the channels and so forth. I think all of us just didn't want to go through the agony and terror of running the minefields submerged and were willing to risk it on the surface. When we had the rendezvous, *Bonefish* didn't show up. I don't recall whether we waited twenty-four hours or not, but in any case we did wait a while.

Then the decision was made to come on out, and the decision was also made to come out on the surface.

We came out at maximum speed, and we headed for the straits. Before long we saw some shipping. I'm sure they were Russian, because they were lighted. How many I don't recall, but I just remember that there were at least two lighted ships. One of our submarines was lighted up by a searchlight from one of these ships, but we kept on going and we got through. It seemed like an all eternity, but it wasn't nearly as bad psychologically to us as the submerged approach when we went in.

42

Not Enough Fish

CAPT. WILLIAM F. CALKINS, U.S.
NAVAL RESERVE (RET.)

When the Navy's Submarine Force got under way at the beginning of the twentieth century, the boats sported the names of fish and other marine life. In 1911 the Navy adopted a letter-number system for designating the boats and applied it retroactively. Thus the *Plunger* became the USS *A-1*, the *Adder* became *A-2*, and so forth. By the early 1930s the alphabetic designations had reached the letter V, and more submarines were in the offing. In 1931 the V-boats were given fish names, and the alphanumeric setup was abandoned. By World War II even fish names were in short supply. William Calkins was a citizen-sailor of that era and a gifted writer with a nice touch of whimsy, as he displays here.

WHEN THE NAVY launches a new vessel, many people have had a hand in the event: designers, engineers, shipfitters, draftsmen, stenographers, welders, bookkeepers, and accountants. Literally thousands of civilian and naval personnel have made their contributions to each new ship of the Navy. And at some point along the line, somebody has to give her a name. This is the traditional, official responsibility of the chief of naval personnel.

For more than two years during World War II, this was my job—dreaming up names for naval vessels so that the chief could recommend them to the secretary of the navy for assignment to an endless stream of new construction.

Now, compared with destroyer or advance base duty, naming ships in Washington can be regarded as on the plush side. There's nothing to it, I thought. So the Navy has another ship, so all

Plaice

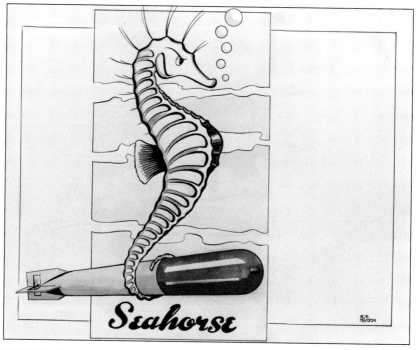

Seahorse

While Calkins was sometimes sending out fishy pictures to the crews of submarines he named, the Disney Studio artists were creating cartoon images. In the case of these two, the *Plaice* and the *Seahorse*, the cartoons really do look like the sea creatures that bear their names. *Navy Art Collection, Washington Navy Yard*

I have to do is think of a word, and that's that. Hah! Little did I know.

Although I was a sedentary sailor, not to be confused with the forces afloat, I came to live amid peril of a most peculiar sort. I almost gave a general stores–issue ship the name of a star which had been named by the astronomer who discovered it after his mistress's pet poodle. I did name a submarine after a sea slug with a most unmentionable seagoing nickname. What it occasionally cost the Navy to burnish the names off all the equipment on some ship when I had goofed and had to rename her hurriedly, I'll never know (and would rather not).

Before the Navy entrusted me with one of its Reserve commissions as a lieutenant (j.g.), it made certain I was a college graduate. Then, by assigning me to the ship-naming detail, it gave me the opportunity to acquire another liberal education.

Like everyone else in the Navy, I knew vaguely that each category of naval vessels is assigned a general source from which the names of all ships of that type are drawn: states for battleships, cities for cruisers, and so on. But this is only an easy beginning. There are many classes of ships, I learned. I soon found out that the Navy usually had more ships than I had names.

Submarines are named for fish or "denizens of the deep." At the peak of the shipbuilding program, the Navy had around five hundred submarines afloat, a-building, or a-planning. And that's a lot of fish, I can testify. There are nowhere nearly as many fish as you may think there are. More particularly, since ichthyologists seem to prefer Latin names for fish, there are even fewer fish names that the average citizen-sailor can (a) pronounce, (b) spell, or (c) even recognize as belonging to a fish.

The reasonable names like *Trout, Bass, Salmon,* and *Shark* were used up long before I appeared. I was reduced to scrabbling around for names like *Spinax, Irex, Mero,* and *Sirago.* You never met any of these on a shoreside menu.

It takes some long stretching to hook other than the most common fish names to submarines and have everyone know you are naming them

after fish. Even the so-called common names can be rough. Here are four: tenpounder, red squirrelfish, shiner, big-eyed scad. Nobody could possibly name a U.S. naval vessel the USS *Big-Eyed Scad.* Nor can you use their real names—the ones on their birth certificates, so to speak—which go something like this: *Elops machnata* (Forsskål) or *Holocentrus diameda* (Lacepede).

We fudged a little and came around twice. There is a USS *Shark*; there is also a USS *Tiburon,* which is shark in Spanish. There was the gallant USS *Wahoo* and the USS *Ono*—same fish. There were the *Jack,* the *Amberjack,* the *Ulua*—same fish. There were the *Pompano* and the *Pampanito,* the *Devilfish* and the *Diablo,* the *Chub* and the *Hardhead* (both minnows, but we couldn't name a fighting ship the USS *Minnow*), the *Tuna, Tunny,* and *Bonita* (all kissing cousins if not the same), and the *Eel, Moray,* and *Conger* (which look remarkably alike). We never figured that we could put *Sardine* on the Navy list, but we named the USS *Sarda*—same fish.

Naming a sub for the sea slug, as already mentioned, was a somewhat unsuccessful action. The name *Trepang* sounded pretty good to me. Maybe not as good as *Salmon,* but the choice then wasn't extensive. The book said it was "any of the holoturians, mostly species of *Stichopus* and *Holothuria,* esp. *H. edulus.*" I didn't know what all that meant, but what the heck. It lived in water, so it was a denizen of the deep. Somebody should have told me it was a sea slug (with an ever ruder nickname)—and he did, but not until she was afloat. Once a ship was afloat, it was even harder to rename, so, as far as I know, somewhere at sea or in mothballs, there is the USS *Trepang,* probably affectionately known to the undersea Navy as the USS *Sea Slug,* if not something worse.

One of my fondest memories of Washington is when I went over to the National Museum to bid goodbye to Dr. Alexander Wetmore, the director. He and his corps of scientists had contributed to the war effort above and beyond the call of duty. As we parted, Dr. Wetmore said, "Calkins, you have been an amusing fellow to work with. You know, in the early part of the war, you were naming your submarines after our fish, but I learn lately that *we have been naming our fish after your submarines.*"

And that is exactly what happened. When the going got really tough, I tried a new tack. I would read the dictionary until I came across a name that sounded sort of fishy. Then I would ask one of Dr. Wetmore's ichthyologists if he had a fish by that name, knowing darned well that he didn't.

When he had checked his card file without finding the name, I would ask him if he could find me a blank card. The taxonomists are constantly identifying new subspecies, differentiating them by minor features from their near relatives. The scientific name is fairly automatic—genus, species, and subspecies, which may be the name of the discoverer. But often no one gets around to giving them popular names.

So the ichthyologist and I would thumb through the cards until we found a likely blank one, add the name I had devised, and there was the Navy's newest sub, named after a perfectly bona fide fish, with its name properly listed with the U.S. National Museum. Supply and demand, that's all it was.

It wasn't long before the sub skippers started asking for pictures of the fish for which their new boats were named. I do not recall which fish

started it, but by then we were at the bottom of the ocean, grabbing anything. When the National Museum fellow showed me the picture, a horrible nightmare haunted me. It was a sub skipper about six feet tall, a former tackle at the Naval Academy. He had red hair and he wore the Navy Cross and a flock of battle stars. He came stomping into Arlington Annex and draped that picture, frame and all, around my neck—from the top.

In short, this particular fish from the bottom of the depths didn't look impressive or gallant or remotely like a submarine. It was mostly all head and had stupid-looking popeyes and a skimpy tail. Furthermore, it didn't look as if it would be attractive to the female of the same species. You couldn't even have used it for bait.

What would happen to the happy-ship spirit of the USS *What-Ever-It-Was* when that monstrosity arrived aboard? Quickly I reached a command decision: In the highest tradition of the naval service, I sent him a picture of a trout.

Thereafter I kept a handy file of pictures of trout, salmon, barracuda, and similar fish for such inquiries. The pictures on the wardroom bulkheads may have occasionally confused visitors who really knew fish, but I couldn't help it. The war had to go on.

43

SubPac Operations

REAR ADM. NORVELL G. WARD,
USN (RET.)

The success of U.S. submarines in the Pacific during the last two years of the war owed a great deal to two officers in particular. Vice Adm. Charles Lockwood was the Pacific Fleet Submarine Force commander, and Capt. Dick Voge was his operations officer. Commander Ward was Voge's assistant. From his vantage point he observed the strengths of his leaders and made contributions of his own.

COMSUBPAC SHIFTED his operational headquarters to Guam in February of 1945. I moved from Saipan down to Guam, and we ran all of our operations from there. ComSubPac had a very small staff in Guam. They were in the submarine tender *Holland*, which had been converted to be Admiral Lockwood's flagship with a good operations center and good communications center. The officers SubPac had in Guam were his flag lieutenant; Dick Voge, the operations officer; Bill Irvin, the communications officer; me, the assistant operations officer; and a chief warrant officer, who was the operations writer. We also had a few enlisted men, quartermasters, and so forth, to help us in the operations room, and the required communications staff of watch officers and radiomen. We received and transmitted our own messages from the *Holland*.

We had the ideal operational organization in Guam—small. I wrote all the messages that we sent out every night, and Dick Voge would review them all, change the wording, and things like that. Then we had to take them up to the admiral to get them released. I maintained a synopsis of all the operations. I'd go through all the patrol

At left is Vice Adm. Charles Lockwood, known as "Uncle Charlie" throughout the Pacific Fleet Submarine Force. With him is his assistant operations officer, Commander Ward. *Courtesy of Elizabeth Ann Schafer*

reports when they came in and make excerpts from them that we needed for our immediate attention. Adm. Chester Nimitz as Pacific Fleet commander in chief was there in Guam as well, and Dick Voge and the Admiral Lockwood usually attended Admiral Nimitz's morning conferences.

I found that my day usually started about six o'clock in the evening and would go until two o'clock in the morning. Messages from submarines at sea would start coming in at sunset. Then we would have to compose replies to them or issue additional orders before we turned in at night. In other words, we were getting back right away to the submarines at sea. So it would be two o'clock or so before either Dick or I would turn in. Then we were in the office again about eight o'clock. We would be busy until one or two o'clock in the afternoon. Then we'd take naps because of the very slack period during the afternoon. Around four or five o'clock we'd go up on deck and get exercise and get ready for dinner. After dinner we went to work again. Being on a small staff, being busy all the time was a very satisfactory working situation.

Admiral Lockwood went over to Camp Dealey, which was the submarine recreation camp on Guam, every Saturday. He would go over and get his exercise. He'd play volleyball or some activity. Then he would have two or three drinks, have a picnic supper, and play poker until eleven o'clock Saturday night. After he finished, he would pack up and come back to the tender and go to bed. He took Dick Voge over on one Saturday. The following Saturday I would go over with him. He made sure that one or the other went over with him each Saturday. That was virtually our only recreation, every other Saturday.

There couldn't be a better man to work for than Admiral Lockwood. He was a perfect gentleman—smart, meticulous. If he found something wrong, he would confront you with it in a very pleasant manner. He never said anything that was harsh, to my knowledge. That's why everyone in the Submarine Force loved him. He listened to what people had to say—all the skippers he talked to. He could talk to any man or officer. He always was trying to get information, trying to make a point whenever he was with someone. He treated subordinates with respect. He respected the experience and the judgment of his subordinates. And he was very thorough in his approach to submarines. He had good, sound policies. If anything needed to be done, he made sure it was done. He was the one who was instrumental before he went to SubPac in verifying that our torpedoes were running too deep. He was that kind of an individual. Someone would point out something, so he would seek a solution to it. I think, actually, he overworked himself. From the time he went to SubPac staff until the war was over, he was going sixteen to eighteen hours a day and longer if necessary.

Captain Voge had a great mental grasp to keep the picture of the entire Pacific theater in mind. I did pretty well myself. I can't recall names and some of these events now, but when I was on SubPac staff, I was a walking encyclopedia of things that had occurred. I could go through a patrol report, read it, and the essential factors just stuck in my memory: dates, skippers, the action, what happened, and all of that. So that pretty soon Dick Voge would say, "How about so and so; what's doing?" I was sitting at the other end of the op center, and without referring to any written matter I could give him the essential facts, and 95 percent of the time or greater, I was correct.

We used the information to order operations. I knew where the productive areas were. I knew, in my judgment, who the better skippers were, the ones who would do a better job in particular areas. And I was able to cite case after case. If Dick Voge questioned why I was assigning a particular submarine to a particular spot or a particular area, I was very frank in telling him why I had made that selection. There were some skippers who wouldn't do a very good job if they were sent to such-and-such a spot. It was a subjective judgment, or call it whatever you want. Since Dick had assigned me that part of the operations, I was exercising my judgment. As long as I satisfied him and the admiral, it wouldn't be questioned.

Dick knew many of these things himself, but I had information he didn't have readily available. He was thinking of so many other things. He was being drawn more and more into the plans for future operations. He was the one who was going up to Pacific Fleet headquarters on operations that were going to occur off Okinawa and then eventually strikes on Japan. He was the one who was flying down to where a commander who was going to conduct the operations happened to be at that particular time. He would go down and conduct the discussions with him. So much more of the detail work on current operations that he had been doing back in Pearl Harbor earlier devolved onto me as he became more involved in future operations.

Our experience was helpful in doing the jobs. Both Dick Voge and I had been through the war

The SubPac staff gathers late in the war for a group shot. Vice Admiral Lockwood is in the front row, directly below his three-star flag. All the officers on one side of him have their legs crossed right over left, and the opposite is true on the other side. *Courtesy of Elizabeth Ann Schafer*

as skippers. We were reading patrol reports that the skippers submitted, correlating their patrol reports with what we knew was probably available in the area from intelligence reports, and then just making a judgment on how aggressive they were in pursuing contacts and developing attacks. It was something that I find it difficult to put my finger on. It was almost intuitive, when reading a report, to know that more could have been done or more couldn't have been done. A pattern would be developed by each individual commanding officer, so that we made judgments as to which ones would be the most productive in a given area. It was not infallible, but it was pretty darn reliable.

There was a willingness to give a second chance to some people who hadn't done so well the first time. This was one of the policies of Admiral Lockwood. Everyone had a second chance, unless there was something flagrant that indicated that you were liable to lose a submarine if that skipper carried it out again. I don't know of any of those cases. Admiral Lockwood leaned over backward to give every skipper at least two chances.

When skippers came to Guam from patrols, Admiral Lockwood, Dick Voge, and I debriefed them thoroughly. Dick and I went over each skipper's patrol in detail with him. By that part of the war, I knew most of the skippers personally, so it wasn't like you were working with someone whom you had not known. And I don't believe many were surprised by those who were extremely successful or surprised by those who were unsuccessful. I was not alone in that.

We had a deliberate program to pull somebody out of a boat after a certain number of patrols so he wouldn't get reckless and careless. ComSubPac had a policy that was generally followed of no more than five successive patrols. If the schedule of a boat was such that there was not a rather long break between one or another of the patrols, then it was four successive patrols. The reason for it was well recognized: to prevent someone from getting stale or from just getting worn out.

In addition to trying to sink ships, we continued to provide lifeguard services for Army bombers going to Japan. After Iwo Jima was captured in the spring of 1945, we had more submarines available then for lifeguard work. But then we had to move them in closer to the main islands to perform lifeguard duty closer to Honshu. Before Iwo Jima we maintained lifeguards essentially from about 150 miles from Saipan at intervals to about 300 or 400 miles from Honshu. When Iwo Jima had been taken and the airfield completed there, then there was the place the B-29 bombers could drop into if needed.

There were fewer and fewer targets as the war drew to a close. That meant we had more and more lifeguard submarines. And this is why it was so desirable to select the men we considered to be the best skippers for those areas where there were remaining targets. We relegated the ones whom we considered would be less productive to lifeguard duty. Some of the skippers came up and questioned why they were spending so much time on lifeguard assignment. I won't say that I was outright frank and direct in telling them why. I told them, "This is an area where we think you can do the best job. The timing is such that you'll be getting out there." You couldn't come out and tell them that you had a low opinion of them. It was a relative thing. And whether our choices were good or not, we'll never know. But we tried to do it that way.

As 1945 wore on, we knew the war was coming to a close. It was just a question of time. The last month of the war we practically had nothing to work against. We were trying to make up targets. I think they found very few during the last two or three weeks of the war. We had a large majority of our submarines up around the empire doing lifeguard duty for naval and Army Air Forces strikes. That was about all we could find.

In August the Army was getting ready to drop the first atomic bomb. I knew something was up when they were laying on the first strike against Hiroshima, because the Twenty-first Bomber Command asked us to remove submarines from the track the strike was going on. I asked the liaison man at the bomber command, "Tell me what you're doing, that you don't want any submarines on this mission."

He said, "I can't tell you a thing." So I knew there was something going on, but what it was, I didn't have the foggiest idea. We soon found out.

Army bombers dropped the first atomic bomb on Hiroshima on 6 August 1945 and the second on Nagasaki three days later. The Japanese soon capitulated, and hostilities ceased on 15 August. On 2 September the battleship *Missouri* was the site of the official surrender ceremony. Vice Admiral Lockwood, on behalf of the Submarine Force, stood nearby on the veranda deck of the *Missouri* as the Japanese emissaries signed the surrender documents.

44

The Postwar Naval Reserve

CAPT. RICHARD B. LANING,
USN (RET.)

During the course of his naval career, Dick Laning was forward looking, an innovator. He brought to his billets both imagination and energy, as well as a seabag full of experience in submarines. In World War II he was executive officer of the *Salmon* when she survived a horrific depth-charge attack and limped back to port. Later in his career he was the first commanding officer of the Navy's second nuclear submarine, *Seawolf*, and skipper of the *Proteus*, the first tender to service deployed Polaris submarines at Holy Loch, Scotland. Here he recounts his experiences just after World War II.

I N EARLY 1946, following a wartime period in which I served largely in submarines, I took command of the *Pilotfish*. That was an interesting tour of duty, particularly in preparing the boat to be a target in the Bikini atomic bomb tests. After the bombs were dropped, though, the *Pilotfish* no longer needed a skipper, and that meant I needed a new job.

I wanted to go to the Northeast, because my wife's folks lived near Boston. I also wanted to check in on Harvard's business course in case I decided to get out of the Navy. The assignment that the Bureau of Naval Personnel (BuPers) sent me to was ideally suited to my needs at that point, because I needed to figure out what I wanted to do, and I needed to do something good for the Navy. My new duty gave me a chance to do both.

My boss was Capt. W. S. G. Davis, who was in charge of surface and submarine components of the Naval Reserve in the First Naval District. At the time I reported, he was sitting behind an

enormous desk with papers piled high and not much getting done. He told me that my objective was to build up the submarine Reserve—the highest priority in the Navy, according to Secretary James Forrestal. I asked Captain Davis what my budget was, and he said, "Zero." Then he explained why, and I agreed with him. He said, "Secretary Forrestal feels that it is not proper for the Navy to spend taxpayers' money to convince the taxpayers that they should join the tax-supported Naval Reserve. He feels it's up to the citizens to do that."

"Okay. What assets do I have? Do I get a car or a truck or anything like that?"

"You get the use of trucks, and you have a secretary, Miss Codescetti," Davis said. "You're pretty much free to do whatever you can."

They proved to be all I needed. I soon found out that a Naval Reserve hold had been put on all the war surplus warehouses, and the warehouses were all over the port of Boston. So I got a Jeep, a guy from the War Surplus Administra-

tion, and a couple of assistants. We drove to those warehouses and tagged anything I thought we might want for the Naval Reserve program. Only after each warehouse had been tagged were they free to open it up and sell the rest. Holy smoke, I lined up fifty major machine tools, all kinds of building materials, equipment, complete galleys, complete sickbays—stuff of all kinds, in huge quantities. Instead of just taking care of the submarine Reserve armories, we were going to have nineteen armories in the First Naval District. So I got about twenty or twenty-five of everything and had them all red-tagged. That took about a week. I thought, "Boy, I'm starting to see this outfit build. These are assets."

Now we had to find a way to man the new Reserve units. In addition to submarine Reservists, we were looking for surface sailors as well. Early in the game, I asked myself, "Why would somebody who just finished with the war want to join up with the Naval Reserve?"

You could hear people saying, "Well, the last thing I want is to have anything to do with that damn brass again." But it seemed to me, in fact, that what these people were going to miss was the camaraderie that they'd enjoyed in the service. You could see that in the enthusiasm of people who belonged to the Veterans of Foreign Wars and the American Legion. That's what they went to those things for. So if we could take advantage of that feeling in setting up the Naval Reserve, we would be ahead.

Well, one way that we did it was to try to make the social side of the Reserve part of the procedure—getting everybody to meet everybody in the Reserve activity in a given area. We tried to set it up so that we had a local bar that could form a social focal point. By hook or crook, I happened to come into possession of many pieces of naval artwork. Much of it was piled up as war surplus because it had been in buildings that had been demobilized, and all this stuff was sent to a central point. So we took these pictures and dealt them out to some of the bars. Once the bartenders heard that there was going to be a new source of customers, they were delighted and went out of their way to make the Reserve meeting night a big night at the bar.

All this helped. I talked to a good many Reservists who regularly drove as many as 150 miles to come to meetings. A couple of ex-Seabees, for example, used to drive a long way into Boston for their meetings, because there weren't Seabee centers all over the district. It paid off, especially in the submarine Reserve. The old submariners got together, and they were able to pass their enthusiasm on to the new people. It worked very well. The First Naval District was the first in the country to fill up its divisions within the first year.

While all this was going on, I realized that poor Captain Davis couldn't seem to get a decision on anything. He would just put things in the mail and thought that was going to get something done. Since there was a local Reserve naval air station in the First District, and it had a lot of airplanes available, I figured, "What the hell? Once a week down to Washington—that's no problem." So about half the Thursdays we'd fly

down there, have about two or three hours of business, and come back again. We'd make phone calls first and have everything ready to walk through. Consequently, very few of my pending items were pending more than a week; I could just get them done.

OP-21 was the sponsor for the submarine Reserve in Washington at that point. The folks on the submarine desk had always been responsive in that way, and they took it on here too. BuPers also had an office to support the Naval Reserve, but I never went there. I did go over their heads a few times, and I can give you an example. The congressman from Salem, Massachusetts, was George Bates—a very sharp guy, very pro-Navy. His son was a Naval Reserve officer on active duty in the Supply Corps. The son later resigned his commission to run for Congress when the old man was killed in a plane crash. The nuclear submarine *William H. Bates* was named for his son.

Congressman Bates was present at my first submarine Reserve meeting at one of the big restaurants in his district. I was trying to get people stirred up about the program. I got a bunch of newspaper publicity for the meeting, and many people attended. I made my presentation during this meeting, and when I got all through, somebody said, "You know, there's something that really puzzles me. How can you have a submarine Reserve without a submarine?" I saw Bates taking all this in.

The next morning I went to a staff meeting at district headquarters. The chief of staff used to ask for comments. When he got to me, I said, "I am sorry, but I've gotten us in a lot of trouble. I practically promised these people a submarine, and we don't have one to give them." I had been thinking about this all night—how the hell to get a submarine. Finally it occurred to me that outfitting the national Reserve program required a total of thirty-five submarines, and that it would be an easier task getting that number than getting just one. If I got the idea sold, it would be the right thing to do. And so the chief of staff asked me, "Do you have any solution?"

I said, "Yes, I think I can get thirty-five submarines."

To promote the submarine reserve, Laning arranged to have a seal photographed on board the USS *Seal*. *Naval Institute Photo Archive*

Rear Adm. Morton Deyo was the commandant of the naval district, and he was sitting there. He didn't mind. It turned out that nobody would mind; all I had to do was go do it. So I wrote to the best people I could, and the following Thursday I went down to Washington again. I went to see Congressman Bates, and I told him I was there to get some submarines, that I would keep him informed if he was interested. I also thought to myself, "Anytime I need to now, I can call up his staff people and tell them, 'Somebody is giving me trouble getting the damn submarines.'"

It turned out that I didn't have to. I went over to the submarine desk people in OpNav [Office of the Chief of Naval Operations] and told them my plan, and they thought it was a good idea. The thing they had in mind was that this would keep some submarines alive that might otherwise die. So I had agreement from OP-311. The people

there suggested I go further. I ended up talking to the chief of naval operations, Adm. Chester Nimitz, about the situation. He said, "It's perfectly logical to me." The chief of naval personnel bought it right away also, which was important, because he was chief of the Naval Reserve.

They both called the secretary, and Mr. Forrestal said, "Fine. Do it."

So I went back to see Congressman Bates, and I told him, "It's done. They all agreed."

"Wonderful," Bates said.

So now my credibility in Salem and the other Reserve locations was way up. The Navy did a marvelous planning job during some of the conferences in deciding what condition to put these submarines in before turning them over to the Reserve. Its idea was to fill up the plugs and do other things so that a boat wouldn't sink and wouldn't catch fire, but so that most of the equipment would operate. Each submarine would be tied up by a pier. She would be unable to dive but still available to teach most of what a Reservist needed to know. While converting the submarines to Reserve use, all of the lead ballast was taken out of the bottom. Things had to be changed very carefully. That was agreed upon, because we didn't want to make any of the changes irreversible in case the submarines would have to be reactivated.

The Portsmouth Naval Shipyard was told to start off with some of these boats. We got estimated dates and this sort of thing. We arranged for some of the Naval Reserve people on active duty to take care of the thing, so that was all set-

tled. I went back to Salem again and told the Reservists there of our progress; they were just full of cheers.

Shortly after that, one of the first submarines to be delivered was the *Seal*. The *Seal* was brought down to Boston, and for the event I wanted some pictures in the newspapers. So I called the editors and told them what was going to happen. The tie-in for the *Seal* was just beautiful. I went to the zoo and borrowed a seal, and the seal sat on the bow of the *Seal* as the submarine approached the pier with a band playing and photographers present. We got all the photographs you ever wanted.

45

Submarines and Ice

DR. WALDO K. LYON

When Waldo Lyon retired in 1996, after fifty-five years of government service, he was unquestionably the nation's expert on under-ice operations. His pioneering work began shortly after World War II. In 1947 he became head of the Submarine Studies Branch in the newly formed Navy Electronics Laboratory (NEL). His interest and drive pushed the Navy forward into this area of research, and his expertise continued to grow as he made mission after mission. He was the founder of the Arctic Submarine Laboratory, based in San Diego. He was on board the nuclear submarine *Nautilus* to provide guidance when she made the first under-ice transit of the North Pole in 1958, and he was along when submarines developed the ability to surface through the polar icecap. Lyon died in 1998 at the age of eighty-four. In tribute to his pioneering efforts, the submarine *Hawkbill* scattered his ashes at the North Pole the following year.

Long before the nuclear-powered submarines were able to make it to the pole, other explorers and scientists sought to get there in diesel boats. British explorer Hubert Wilkins made the first attempt during a private venture. He purchased the Navy's surplus *O-12* for one dollar, had her converted for ice work, and renamed her *Nautilus* at the Brooklyn Navy Yard on 24 March 1931. That summer she was the first submarine to travel under the Arctic icecap, but she didn't make it far before falling victim to a host of mechanical problems. She broke down, and the USS *Wyoming* had to divert from a midshipman-training cruise to tow the *Nautilus* to port. The *Nautilus* was scuttled in a Norwegian fjord on 20 November 1931. Lyon talked with Wilkins and had data from the 1931 efforts when he began his own.

A tugboat tows the *Nautilus*, formerly the USS *O-12*, from the Philadelphia Navy Yard to a shipyard in New Jersey during her conversion for under-ice work. The old superstructure has already been removed. *Naval Institute Photo Archive, International News*

WHEN WILKINS did his work under the ice it was really before sonar was developed at all, or at the period when it was just beginning. So he had to make his attempts with no help. He and his crew made the attempt to go under the ice in the North Atlantic, north of Spitzbergen, Norway. The chief scientist on board was Harald Sverdrup, a Norwegian who was one of the founders of modern oceanography. In the late 1930s he came to San Diego to become the director of the Scripps Institute and was in that job after World War II. On the military side, Allan McCann, a submariner, had been at the Philadelphia Navy Yard as a junior officer when the *O-12*, which had been slated to be scrapped, was sold to Wilkins. He was interested in Wilkins's efforts, but he was disturbed by the method that Wilkins was attempting, which was to use the submarine as an

upside-down sled. Wilkins's idea with the *Nautilus* was to go under the ice, then become positively buoyant and slide around under the ice.

Shortly after World War II, McCann, as a rear admiral, was commander of the Pacific Fleet Submarine Force and in position to do something about his interest in ice operations. But now that sonar was available, McCann knew that it was no longer necessary to ride directly under the icecap. In the summer of 1946 he took submarines north into the Bering Sea, but they didn't do too much other than find out it was cold and miserable on a submarine because they didn't come prepared for the problem. And there was no connection with the science side.

Later that year the Navy was planning an operation called High Jump to Antarctica for early 1947. We figured it was worth including a submarine, so we wrote a letter from the Navy

After the *Northwind* cleared the *Sennet* out of the ice, a heaving line flies through the air toward the icebreaker to set up a tow.

Electronics Laboratory to the chief of naval operations to make that suggestion, and back came the word—granted. Keep in mind that at that time there were lots of submarines, lots of ships, and people were looking for things to do. So there was no reason not to, and no one knew just exactly what would happen either. The *Sennet* was then assigned from the Atlantic Fleet to join the operation. I joined the *Sennet* late in 1946, somewhere down off the tip of South America.

The *Sennet* was a regular fleet submarine from the war. It was well equipped with the sonar of the period. The primary interest was the searchlight sonar system, which is a long-range pulsing sonar that sends out a pulse and gets an echo back. It also had the QLA [FM sonar] scanning system that was used during the war for transiting minefields. It presented targets on a screen like a radar screen and permitted the crew to see a number of targets and avoid them.

At that point I had no feel for what we were going to run into with the ice cover. I knew nothing about it. I'd never seen a piece of ice on the sea. I had no concept of what the problems might be, and that was the real reason for taking the submarine down to Antarctica. The *Sennet* was part of a task group to go into Little America in January 1947. The group included the *Mount Olympus* as flagship, two attack-cargo ships, the *Yancey* and *Merrick*, and we were all escorted by the Coast Guard icebreaker *Northwind*.

Normally in the Ross Sea at that time of year the ice would be fairly open, but in that particular year the ice did not break up, and it was very difficult going for an icebreaker followed by two big ships and a submarine. As the last ship in the column the *Sennet* had a lot of difficulty trying to work her way through the ice on the surface.

The *Northwind* tows the *Sennett* through the Antarctic ice pack. *Naval Institute Photo Archive*

Many a time we suddenly got closed in with ice all around.

We didn't dare submerge because we were not visualizing the problem, but I did realize that we were not equipped to know the clearances and know what the story of the ice cover was once we got underneath. I had sonar systems looking ahead of me, but I had nothing to tell me what was going to stop us if we were trying to surface while under the ice. There was ice for hundreds of miles in all directions. So these were enormous obstacles and having no experience and no background, one doesn't start an experiment in such a situation.

After maybe a week of trying to get through the ice with all these ships, Rear Adm. Richard Cruzen, who was in command of the task group, decided to take the *Sennett* out of the column so the cargo carriers could go to Little America and set up a camp. So the *Northwind* proceeded to lead the cargo ships wherever they could see an opening in the ice and just take the submarine separately back out of the ice and into an open

part of the Antarctic Ocean. To get out and do it quickly we tried following the icebreaker, but that became difficult in heavy ice. The *Sennet* got hung up on pieces of ice kicked out from the sides of the *Northwind*.

Then we tried towing, which worked very well—after they broke a few cables before getting one that was heavy enough. The icebreaker towed the *Sennet* by bringing her right up near the stern of the *Northwind*, where there was a towing notch. I guess this was one of the most harrowing experiences that one has on a submarine, just because of the noise rather than the danger. When we were being dragged through the ice at the end of a cable, the ice scraped along the sides of the hull and made a shrieking, screeching sound, something like fingernails across a blackboard—only a thousand times worse. And the boat was careening about, much like riding a train at high speed through a freight yard, going through switches and crossing "frogs." So on top of being banged and rattled and thrown, I had the sensation of all this noise and screeching of ice against the hull. That went on for three days and three nights, trying to sleep next to the hull that was being scraped. Once the *Sennet* got out into the open water, we looked at the hull, and it was bright and shiny steel, because all the paint had been scraped off. The prow of the submarine was pretty well damaged. I remember it was broken by these towing procedures, and the propellers had bent from being dragged through the ice. Other than that, the submarine was in good shape. There was really not any danger in being pulled, but it was not comfortable.

This was the first time that any of these submariners had ever seen ice or had any experience with it or what it was all about. But then after we got back out in the open sea, we spent the next three weeks or more doing probing experiments where we could submerge. We were all on our own now; we didn't have to worry about anybody else. We could make approaches on icebergs and see what we could do with them with sonar equipment, go under the edges of the ice, and know that we were near open water. We could probe around and get a feel for what we could do. Our first experiences were what the whole problem was about, and about all they did was intrigue us into trying to solve it. I could see that there was much one could do. That was when you just began to visualize what a submarine under ice cover meant.

The commanding officer of the Navy Electronics Laboratory at that time was Capt. Rawson Bennett, who later became chief of naval research, and he's an important part of the story. Way back at the start of the war, he had been one of the main forces to get sonar throughout the Navy properly oriented with the conditions of the sea. All during the war period, in the Bureau of Ships, he had held a key position in electronics and sonar. He recognized the continual need for research and exploratory work and expanding the capabilities of sonar. So coming to NEL as the commanding officer, he was very open about going into anything new.

I should mention that there had been one other attempt to go under the ice by a U.S. sub-

marine. That was the *Atule* in the summer of 1946. It was done in the Atlantic, up in Baffin Bay, but it was done just like submarines that Admiral McCann sent to the Bering Sea in the summer of 1946. The science side wasn't on board, just a fleet operator going ahead with whatever he had. The *Atule* went under the ice for a way, but she did not have the instruments required to avoid ice. She went under, struck ice with the periscope, and came out. The main point is that the Submarine Force was interested in doing things.

It was natural then, in 1947, why we were successful, because we combined the equipment and ideas from the scientists with the operators on board ship, and the combination was very powerful. That year Admiral McCann assigned the *Boarfish* as an experimental submarine. She was another first-class boat, and we equipped her with the QLA scanning system so we could tell what was ahead. And we took with us Art Roshon, who was one of the originators of the QLA system. He could interpret the pictures from the sonar, and he was highly interested in the problem, of course. This was the new challenge of using the equipment for other than minefields. We realized also that we must add something that the *Boarfish* normally would not carry. That was an echo sounder or fathometer, mounted on deck so it could look up. We already had them looking down, to tell how far we were from the bottom, but we didn't have anything to tell us what we were under. And we added a recording thermometer and other devices to try to measure what the ocean was as we went through it.

So after all those preparations, we went with the *Boarfish* up to the Chukchi Sea, north of the Bering Strait, in August of 1947. Admiral McCann always did things in a good way. He meant that we make a study and decided that he would even go himself. So he went along and took the *Nereus*, a submarine tender, and four other submarines. We had quite a task group, but the *Boarfish* was the only one that we intended to go under the ice. When we got there, we decided to have a good look at it first, so we got the *Nereus* to lower her whaleboat. I went

The *Boarfish* moves cautiously in the arctic ice in the summer of 1947. Mounted on deck is an upward-looking echo sounder to measure distance to the bottom of the icecap. *U.S. Navy*

along with Admiral McCann, Art Roshon, Gene LaFond of our oceanographic section, the commanding officer of the *Boarfish*, and some others. We wandered around the ice, just to see what it was all about before deciding whether to go under in the submarine.

The ice was all open toward the outer edge, and at that time of year it was melting, so we could work our way in among the ice floes, probably twenty miles or more. That gave us some idea of the conditions, by seeing what the thickness of the ice was above the water and trying to guess how much it was below the surface. Based on this first trial, which went successfully, it looked like we should try it.

When we got under way in the *Boarfish*, we didn't have any real fear, because on that particular cruise we knew the bottom of the sea. We did have information on that, and it was extremely flat. We had had this look at the ice cover from

above, but we did not know how it would look on the screen of the sonar system. Well, we approached and got a feel of what it looked like on the sonars, and Art Roshon could interpret. We started by being near the surface, looking with the periscope, and relating that to what we saw on sonar. It was a matter of proceeding step by step, and we didn't bump anything. Some thought it was luck, but I think it was just a cautious approach—between two and three knots. At that speed there was plenty of time to become acquainted with what the sonar looked like, make decisions, and make the proper moves.

The depth of water there was probably about 140 feet, which is very shallow. The submarine took up about 50 feet, so we had about 90 feet to play with. I think we usually split that, so there were probably 30 feet of water under the submarine. Then we used the rest for clearing whatever we might run into. Now, we were seeing on the

In August 1958 Lyon keeps track of the overhead ice as the nuclear-powered *Nautilus* makes the first submerged transit under the North Pole. At right is the submarine's skipper, Cdr. William R. Anderson. *Naval Institute Photo Archive*

sonar screen other stuff that looked much thicker, so we'd avoid that and go someplace else where the sea looked pretty clear.

One of the problems we ran into was having room for the equipment. The QLA scanning sonar was in the conning tower, because it was the normal sonar for going through minefields. The only place we had space to put the upward-looking echo-sounding system was in the forward torpedo room. I was watching it, and Art Roshon was in the conning tower watching the sonar. So it was a matter of conversation back and forth over the phone system about what was going on. The commanding officer and Admiral McCann did a lot of running back and forth between the two places to see what was going on and get interpretations from Art and me. You can't say that we were any more expert than they were, but we knew what the equipment could do and had experience with it.

During that first venture, we penetrated about four or five miles under the ice—just a probe to see what it was all about. Then we came out from that, and Admiral McCann went back to the *Nereus*. The other submarines went off doing all kinds of jobs, surveying to see the bathymetry of the ocean, catch biological samples, and drag the bottom—all the things oceanographers do to understand the environment. The *Boarfish* then did some more under-ice runs. I think the longest was twelve miles from open water and then back out again. We had no incidents or any difficulty because we had good information from Sverdrup, who had been in the area on an expedition in the 1920s. Without that, I wouldn't have known what to expect in terms of currents and the thickness of the ice cover. There's a real debt owed Harald Sverdrup, so far as information was concerned— plus he was a believer and pusher of submarines because of his experience with Wilkins and the *Nautilus*.

Altogether, in my recollection, we made maybe four or five dives under the ice; we were only up there on the order of two weeks. Those dives told us that we could go from open sea in a submarine with sonar equipment in the summertime. We could see what we were traveling under, clear the bottom, avoid the ice ahead of us, and come out again. That wasn't sufficient to live in the ice cover or work in it; we recognized that. But it was the first step.

46

Missiles at Sea

VICE ADM. EUGENE P.
WILKINSON, USN (RET.)

During World War II the diesel submarines' only weapons were torpedoes and deck guns. Both were intended primarily for use against ships at sea. In the years following the war, with potential naval enemies largely swept from the world's oceans, the U.S. Navy's Submarine Force was in search of new missions. One of those missions was to attack targets on land. In the late 1940s the development of appropriate weaponry included tests with air-breathing German rockets captured at war's end. Lt. Cdr. Dennis Wilkinson, whom we have heard from in previous chapters of this book, was there at the beginning.

WHEN I LEFT General Line School at Newport I had orders as exec of the *Cusk* (SSG-348), which was the first submarine that fired missiles. We had a very capable officer as skipper, superbly capable and competent, Cdr. Paul "Pete" Summers. But Pete had a hard time delegating responsibility to others. He was so good and so capable that he did a lot of things himself as CO rather than trust other people to do them. He had been unhappy with the performance of his former executive officers and in fact had two of them fired. Then I went as his third executive officer, and the only defense I had was the Bureau of Personnel telling him as they sent me, "Pete, we're sending you an executive officer that we know will be okay." That may be fine in the broader sense, but in the day-to-day context of things it wasn't completely so.

While I was on leave en route to the *Cusk* I was contacted by the ship and told to report in early. So I reported on board late Sunday after-

In this view from 23 January 1948 the stern of the *Cusk* has a hangar and launching rail to facilitate the firing of the Loon. *Naval Institute Photo Archive*

noon to be the exec and navigator. The ship was due to sail the next morning for Hunters Point in San Francisco. We had quarters, stationed the maneuvering watch, made preparation to get under way, sailed out of the harbor, and passed the sea buoy. As the maneuvering watch was secured and the regular section set, the word was passed for me to report to the captain. This was my first minute with him on board when I was not at quarters and maneuvering station.

I went in the captain's room, and then Pete Summers said to me, "What time are we going to pass under the Golden Gate Bridge?"

As good luck would have it, when I had reported on board the afternoon before, because I was going to be navigator I had checked out our track and schedule on up. So I happened to have done it, but certainly I hadn't had any time that morning and I was asked just as the maneuvering watch was secured. I said, "Well, Captain, what

time would you like to pass under the Golden Gate Bridge?"

That slowed Pete down for, oh, fifteen or twenty seconds. He thought about that and said, "What time should we pass under the Golden Gate Bridge?"

I said, "1011, sir." When we passed under the Golden Gate Bridge I was on the bridge navigating. The captain was there, and I called down to the conning tower, "Mark the time."

The quartermaster said, "1011, sir." I'm sure he would have done that if we'd been a couple of minutes off, because the troops were pleased to have a new exec and navigator aboard and were on my side.

Pete liked to check up on everything, and he did things exactly by the book. He kept a list every day of everything that he didn't like, and he'd call me in every morning and go over the items with me one by one. I guess that reached

A cloud of smoke envelops the *Cusk* as she fires a Loon on 20 June 1949. *Naval Institute Photo Archive*

the high point one day of more than ninety items: "I saw the mess cook topside without a hat on, and you know that's against my policy" or "I saw the fireman in the engine room who had a torn sleeve on his dungarees, and you know that's against my policy." That's the right way for the chain of command to work, the captain to go through his exec. On the other hand, there is a timeliness to tell a guy to get down and get his hat on when he's supposed to have a hat on.

I happened to have access to Captain Summers's safe, so I would open it each night. I guess through my entire tour as exec he was never on board when I wasn't there. I met him every morning when he came on board and saw him off every evening, and so afterward I would get out his list and take care of all the items that I could. So the next morning, when he'd go through the list, I'd say, "Well, Captain, that was Jones, and he's gotten rid of that jumper, and he'll never

wear it again," "That dungaree shirt will never go again," or "That was such-and-such, and he'll always wear his hat topside." And this went on item by item.

Or if it was a more important item—like "I think we ought to write a letter to the Bureau of Ships asking about this"—I'd say, "Well, gee, Fred Berry was talking about that, and there might be a draft in your basket." And so after about four or five months Pete stopped keeping a list. Pete Summers was very capable and did a tremendous job as the skipper of the *Cusk* in evaluations of the missiles we had, which were V-1 rockets that had come from the Germans. The *Cusk*'s and *Carbonero*'s performance in that program led on to the Regulus missile program, which led on to Polaris. So Pete Summers deserves his place in history.

We were test firing the Loons, as we called these V-1s. Nearly five hundred of them were captured from the Germans at Peenemünde, and we got them to the Submarine Force. They fired them from Point Mugu, California, and we fired them off the after deck of the *Cusk*. We fired the first one in February 1947. Eventually we had a big, watertight hangar built on the *Cusk*. We could close it up so we could dive with a Loon in there, surface, open it up, pull the Loon out on the launcher, and fire it. Then we would secure the hangar, dive again, and track this bird, which was a pulse-jet rocket. We had a transponder in it so we could get a good echo on it with our radar.

The controls were very rudimentary in that we could give it a signal to put on right rudder or left rudder, or we could cut the engine so it had no more power and would drop into the sea. And just like a crew race making so many strokes, we had a really superior plotting party on the *Cusk*. We would track this bird that we had put in the air, which also was being followed by a jet plane for aircraft safety; the plane could shoot down the rocket if the course was erratic.

We would fire this Loon at a target called Bird Rock, which was some sixty to ninety miles away. We would track it, and we would be taking range and bearing and plotting it every minute. And then we would shift the plots to every thirty seconds and every twenty seconds and every fifteen seconds and every ten seconds. If it wasn't going toward its target, we would apply right rudder for two seconds and then back to amidships, and then we'd plot and see what had happened, and that way we would correct the course toward the target. When we thought it was at the right point, we'd cut the power. The engines would cut off, and naturally the rocket would go down into the sea. I don't think we ever hit Bird Rock, but we came really close.

We fired those Loons from rails on the stern. They were set at a fixed angle that we couldn't vary. So we had no control over the altitude. We steered the missile right or left, and we cut off its engine. They also did shots from the beach. And the *Carbonero*, which didn't have the capability to launch, would also track it. It seems pretty elementary now, but that really was the beginning that led to the Regulus, which was a five-hundred-mile missile that had better control than the Loon.

This testing routine was tough on the crew. We gave the services week after week, and we left San Diego Sunday evening to be up at Point Mugu Monday morning to start work at eight o'clock. So when the other submarines were getting under way on Monday, week after week we were getting under way on Sunday. From a home and liberty aspect, that was tough on our crew. Also our crew for other reasons wasn't the happiest in the world. Now, they didn't get as much liberty.

On the other hand, morale was high, because morale is not really chow and liberty. Morale is pride in unit, and there isn't any doubt that the officers and crew on the *Cusk* had great pride in unit. I could have gone down to the control room as exec and said, "The *Squatfish* thinks they can defeat us playing Parcheesi, and I'd like to bet five hundred dollars." I would have had five hundred dollars instantly, because there wasn't any submarine, in our crew's opinion, that could beat us at anything. But an awful lot of people would've paid the same five hundred dollars to get off the ship. I had people on the *Cusk* say to me, "Commander, there isn't any ship I would rather be on in wartime, but it's not wartime."

47

Fire in the *Cochino*

REAR ADM. ROY S. BENSON,
USN (RET.)

In 1998 authors Sherry Sontag and Christopher Drew created a sensation with their book *Blind Man's Bluff*, the story of covert operations by U.S. submarines during the Cold War. Their first chapter provided an account of an intelligence mission by the *Tusk* and *Cochino* in the summer of 1949. The objective was to pick up signals from Soviet nuclear weapons tests. Alas, things went terribly wrong during that mission, which was commanded by Capt. Roy Benson, who a few months earlier had become the first commander of Submarine Development Group Two. With him during the venture off the Soviet Union was his chief staff officer, Cdr. Richard B. "Ozzie" Lynch. The skipper of the *Cochino* was Cdr. Rafael Benitez, and his exec was Lt. Cdr. Richard Wright.

S OMEONE IN Washington thought of a real bright idea. We had barely gotten started with this new command when a directive came in that the four submarines were to go over across the Atlantic to Londonderry, Northern Ireland, to operate with the British antisubmarine forces. Then we were going on a reconnaissance mission up in the Greenland Sea, the Barents Sea, and up to the north of Norway. This reconnaissance was top secret.

So early in August in 1949 we started across the Atlantic. We did operate with the British forces. Then we proceeded to go up and do some reconnoitering. I divided the submarines into two parts. The *Toro* and *Corsair*, the two that did not have the snorkel and high submerged speed, I put under Commander Lynch. They were not to get east of the line up the center of Norway. They were supposed to stay out of the perhaps more

The sleek-looking *Cochino* is under way on 2 February 1949 after receiving her Guppy conversion. On 25 August of the same year explosions and fires sent her to the bottom of the sea. *Naval Institute Photo Archive, Electric Boat photo*

dangerous areas. The other two, the *Tusk* and *Cochino*, would go into the areas closer to the USSR. The *Cochino* was my flagship, but I went on board the *Tusk* because there were certain reports that I required from my people, and theirs were always slow. I had a chief yeoman, so I took him along to help with the paperwork.

After Ireland we were in Portsmouth, England, for a few days, that being the home port of British submarines. I was planning to go up through the English Channel, but the British said, "No, there are a lot of mines in there. Don't go that way." So we went up between Ireland and Scotland and then around the North Cape of Norway.

We split the submarines into two sections. We were snooping, taking down the characteristics of the radar up in that region. We got the frequencies, the pulse repetition rates, the strength, and tied those characteristics in with locations ashore. We also practiced with our underwater sound equipment, passive sonar—practicing to listen and listen and listen. Of course, we were under strict radio silence. No one was supposed to know where we were. When we left England, we disappeared.

On the morning of the twenty-fifth of August, the *Cochino* and the *Tusk* had both submerged north of the North Cape. We were using the sonars. One of the submarines would try to listen and detect the noises the other one was making. Type of noise has meaning. Naturally, the target would start and stop, turn around, and do all kinds of things that could be recorded, along with the times. Suddenly, over the underwater telephone came a message from the *Cochino*: "We're having a fire! We've got to surface."

In order for someone to understand the *Cochino*'s trouble, I need to explain submarine storage batteries. In our automobiles we have lead-acid storage batteries. They have six cells; each one of these cells is not even as big as an ordinary toaster. The cells at that time in the submarines stood three and a half to four feet high, and they were something like three feet wide and maybe a foot and a half thick. Each one weighed a ton. We had on board the submarine something on the order of 250 of these.

The storage batteries were in two groups, forward battery and after battery. When they converted the submarines to high submerged speed, they had installed higher-capacity cells, and they divided them into two parts. The forward battery was in two parts, and the after one was in two parts. Well, what happened on the *Cochino* was that one half of the after battery had gotten low, so the other half started charging it. When you charge a lead-acid storage battery, you generate hydrogen gas. When you get the proper proportions of hydrogen and oxygen, you don't even need anything to set off an explosion. Generating hydrogen is very, very dangerous. We had hydrogen detectors on our submarines long before my time. We old-timers all experienced hydrogen flashes.

The first indication they had on board the *Cochino* that anything was wrong was when the hydrogen detectors in the after battery showed hydrogen going up. Then they had an explosion, and then they had a fire. The whole living compartment above the after battery was ablaze. So they shut off that compartment, and the people came topside, and some of them had hardly anything on. It was cold, of course; it was in August, but we were up north of the Arctic Circle. There were some people who were slightly burned. The *Cochino* skipper sent word that there was no remote disconnect. In other words, there was no way in which you could flip a switch outside this compartment and take those parts of the battery away from one another. So it would continue to feed on itself.

On the *Cochino* they broke out a rubber boat and sent one of the ship's officers over to explain to me exactly what the situation was. Also, unfortunately, the ship's medical equipment was all in that burning compartment. The pharmacist's mate, an enlisted man, couldn't get to it, and they needed to bring over certain of these things from the *Tusk* to the *Cochino* to treat burns.

The rubber boat arrived, and they got the medical equipment and then went back to the *Cochino*. But about that time a big wave came along, and about twelve men went in the water from the *Tusk*. That became quite an emergency. Six of them were never recovered. Not one of those rescued came under his own power. The people who came aboard did so because their shipmates either jumped into the water and pulled them over or they were close to the submarine and someone was able to help them.

I was on the bridge of the *Tusk* while this was happening. About that time the executive officer of the *Cochino* decided they had to stop this fire, and so he put on a rescue breathing apparatus. He was down in the forward engine room and decided to open the door and go into after battery. He knew exactly where the disconnect switch was. It was near the door that he would open. All he would have to do was open the door and flip the switch, shut the door again, and the fire would subside as soon as the hydrogen burned up. When he opened the door, however, he was overwhelmed by the fire. He was very badly burned.

One of the engines was running slowly at that time. Hydrogen came out of the compartment and into the intake of the engine. The engine then burned hydrogen instead of diesel oil. It speeded up and burst all to pieces. Meanwhile, the exec never got to that disconnect switch, so the fire was still going. When the fire and flames came out of that aft battery room into the engine room, there were several other people there who also had burns, but they weren't anywhere near as bad as the executive officer.

I got a message from the *Cochino*'s skipper that he had two engines running. So I said, "Okay, let's go." Hammerfest, Norway, was about a hundred miles away. We now broke radio silence to say we were under way for Hammerfest and needed medical help. We opened up on our radio, sent out a message, and got a receipt from Naval Station Guam. The message went over the North Pole, apparently. As we were on our way to Hammerfest, all at once there was a tremendous explosion on the *Cochino*. So the skipper sent a message that he thought we'd better start getting his people off.

Meanwhile, I told the skipper of the *Tusk* that I wanted him to get two warhead torpedoes ready. If anybody wanted to interfere while we were trying to rescue, they were going to have a fight on their hands. Then I told the captain of the *Tusk* to put the bow of his ship by the stern of the disabled ship. We got alongside, and it was rough. The wind was blowing, and it was terrible. Someone found a board to use as a gangplank. It was about a foot wide. Naturally, no handrail or any stuff like that. They had to go about six feet to get from one ship to the other. We started taking people off, and we got everybody off, including the exec of the *Cochino*. The captain, Benitez, was the last one to come across. They were abandoning ship, because it was sinking. She sank only about two or three minutes after the skipper came on board. By the time the captain left, approximately two-thirds of the length of the submarine was underwater. As soon as we got everybody off, we put on full speed ahead for Norway.

48

Hot New Guppy

CAPT. PAUL R. SCHRATZ,
USN (RET.)

In the post–World War II period the U.S. Navy drew upon its own wartime experiences and those of German U-boats to enhance the capability of its submarines. The clever acronym Guppy was short for Greater Underwater Propulsive Power. The modifications to the World War II fleet boats in the late 1940s included streamlining by removing topside projections, the addition of snorkels to enable the boats to draw in air while at periscope depth, and an increase in the number of batteries for underwater operation. Lt. Cdr. Paul Schratz determined to show off just what a hot rod he had in his new boat.

IN THE LATE 1940S, when I was assigned to the Bureau of Naval Personnel, I had my morning and afternoon cup of coffee in the submarine detail office. The submarine detailer was my old *Mackerel* skipper, Johnny Davidson, and his assistant was Ebby Bell, a close friend and classmate. But I saw so many people pinging on those poor guys for one job or another that I swore I would never do it. They had my record on file, and I never brought up my future assignment until they mentioned they had me slated for *Pickerel*. Since she was the newest, one of the first Guppy submarines, the best we had and slated for Honolulu duty, all I could say was "Thank you."

Then came a problem—all my old shipmates wrote to get aboard also: "We've done it before, let's do it again." These were fine people, and I would've loved to go to sea with them, but on a small ship, I always thought it was a mistake. The Submarine Force never sent the same skipper and exec together for successive tours for a lot of reasons. A CO and exec who repeat tours together

The *Pickerel* leaps from the water during a high-angle surfacing. *National Archives: 80-G-440604*

know each other's style and won't learn much new.

I sent a letter to the submarine detail officer and said, "I have all sorts of requests from fine officers who want to go to sea with me again. I would prefer that none of them be sent." And I added brashly, "If you send me the worst officers you've got, and if I have anything on the ball as a skipper, I'll make an average crew out of them. If you send me any better than that, I don't have to have much on the ball."

Well, that's egotistic, I realize now, but it's also terribly good psychology, because it put the detailers on record as more than ordinarily responsible for the people they sent. I think they must have looked over the whole Navy list to find the most superb people for *Pickerel*. I had a wonderful group of officers, including Pappy Sims as exec and Snuffy Jackson as engineer and diving officer.

There were several things we did differently in fitting out *Pickerel*. We took liberties with many accepted routines, in the interest of safety—backing down on all man-overboard drills, for example. We could find no way a man could be pulled into the screws and found much hydrodynamic information to justify our position. Contrary to all fleet practice, when in danger of collision at sea, the submarine's best and quickest defense is to dive. In forty seconds no fixed part of the ship is within twenty feet of the surface. On an operational readiness inspection off Pearl a year later, I couldn't seem to make this clear. When the drill came, the officer of the deck thoroughly drenched the inspection team on the bridge when he immediately pulled the diving alarm.

We christened the boat in April 1949 at the Portsmouth Naval Shipyard. On the way around from New England to Pearl Harbor, we stopped at various ports down the Atlantic Coast and the Gulf of Mexico, where we volunteered to take the local Reserve group to sea at every opportunity. Most submarines, when they take Reservists out, tend toward "show and tell" more than putting them on the gear and letting them run the submarine. We were terribly proud of this hot-rod Guppy submarine, and it was really a marvelous piece of gear. After the Reservists rotated through all the ship control stations, helped fire a torpedo or two, my hot-rodders took over to put the ship through all these steep turns, up and down angles, and so forth. It was really thrilling, quite different from any other ship. We always ended our show with what we called an Event Five Hundred, surfacing at a very steep angle, usually about fifty degrees. One of the Reservists in Houston was a newspaperman, and he claimed if he could ever get a picture of the submarine surfacing at a steep angle, his fortune was made.

We started then to get a picture. It isn't easy to get a photographic ship which has sonar gear for tracking and communication while submerged in quiet seas and all that. Just after reporting in to Pearl, we were sent to the Singapore area for a combined fleet exercise with the British. The day before arriving in Manila on the way out, it looked like everything was hunky-dory for a try for a picture. The submarine *Queenfish* was operating with us. They had a cameraman on board, and we gave them the plan. We started at 525 feet—I think test depth was 450—making maximum speed of eighteen knots. We blew the forward tanks, holding the ship on an even keel as long as possible, then threw the planes to full rise. We hit seventy-two degrees on that one—a gorgeous day for photography off

Manila, bright blue sky and everything, a foamy wake all around us. It was quite spectacular, but the camera was a 16-mm movie and we could make only small prints; but they were excellent.

We arrived in Manila the following day, and in my incoming mail was a letter from the force commander, Rear Adm. Babe Brown, commenting on certain of his Guppy submarine skippers using large angles. He didn't want to discourage aggressiveness, but he really did hate to write those eighty-nine letters to next of kin and didn't see what was to be gained by any angle over, say, ten degrees. Well, having just done the stern hinger, we got hold of the camera film and we put it in deep limbo for a while. Babe Brown had been the shipyard commander in Portsmouth when *Pickerel* was built, and there was no question that we were his favorite submarine. We were delighted when he became the new ComSubPac.

He still had the same aide, a classmate of Pappy Sims, who was trying to get the pictures released and kept us advised of the heat on Capitol Hill. A few months later, Admiral Lockwood, who had been ComSubPac in World War II, was going to celebrate some event. Admiral Brown sent for me a few days prior, and we chatted for a while. After much hemming and hawing, he mentioned Admiral Lockwood's big celebration and said he would like to give him "one of those pictures." He suggested how it should be autographed, and I agreed. But something else was clearly on his mind. Finally, placing a great big paw on my shoulders, he asked for one for himself, too: "And I don't care how you autograph that one." So I autographed it "To Admiral Babe Brown, proving that ComSubPac knows all the angles," or something like that.

We took that as permission to release the photo. Because the seventy-two-degree ones were small, we did some others. The one that was so highly publicized, however, was one we were trying to work out with professional photography just as I was detached. My relief gets credit for that one (which was forty-five degrees). Movies of that episode were used in *Silent Service*, the movie about our submarines in World War II, and in many other places.

Admiral Brown was right in discouraging such maneuvers, because there was a risk. You shouldn't start below test depth in any case. When you start up at any time, the bow starts to rise, but the stern goes down quite a distance. The ship pivots about one-third from the bow, so the latter two-thirds may be a lot deeper than you think. At a thirty-degree angle, the stern is one hundred feet below the center of buoyancy. There are always things that can go wrong at that enormous pressure and under maximum speed.

I worried lots about the torpedoes, highly machined surfaces, greased for easier manhandling. If one in the racks should carry away and start thrashing around, the three-thousand-pound air flasks could rupture or the torpedo's engine start a hot run in the room. We had them double and triple chocked down to be sure they couldn't move. Those exercises weren't done haphazardly; it took months of preparation to train people on the planes to the point we thought they could handle it.

Cdr. Ned Beach had pioneered the steep angle in the *Amberjack* in the Atlantic, frequently using thirty to thirty-five degrees. Nobody else in the Pacific was interested. I believe we were the only two. Speed and power were the important advantages we had with the Guppies. You could do thirty-five to forty degrees up in a fleet submarine, but you didn't have the control and other things to pull out in a steep down angle.

We did something else to demonstrate the benefits of this new type of boat, which could pull in air for the diesels through a snorkel. When I got to Pearl with the Guppy submarine, the general attitude in the Pacific was that the snorkel was tested, evaluated, and proven—and therefore need not be used. Quite the contrary. No one had any idea of the strategic and tactical values—and limitations—for snorkel operations. Pap Sims, Snuffy Jackson, and I were inquisitive. We were sure there was much to be learned. For one thing, nobody wanted to snorkel for long periods because it was sometimes hard on the ears. Sec-

ond, at that time there was a problem with the diesels when snorkeling. Operating sixty feet below the surface created heavy back pressures on the diesel exhaust, discharging against sea pressure. Air to the engines was pulled down a narrow tube, and it created a high vacuum in the engine intake blowers.

Operating with a high vacuum on the intake and high pressure on the exhaust sets up stresses in the engine never visualized when the engines were built. The Fairbanks-Morse diesels were the best engines in the world, but they were wiping the heavy aluminum scavenger lobes after less than a hundred hours of snorkeling. Snorkeling puts a doubly heavy load on the engine when starting up. Starting with a cold engine allows a maximum range of expansion, but different expansion of different parts again causes a danger of wiping the blower lobes. Our solution, with the wisdom of Solomon, was to start snorkeling with neither a hot nor a cold but a warm engine, to take the best of both worlds. We also relocated and added thermometers and pressure gauges at critical points not previously protected.

We learned all this just before departure for Hong Kong for the exercise with the British. I asked permission—at no higher a level than the SubPac assistant operations officer—on coming back from Hong Kong to try a long-range snorkel cruise. We weren't sure how far we could go, so I asked only to reduce our speed of advance to ten knots. I don't think anybody higher in the force staff had any idea what we were attempting. Departing Hong Kong with many warm farewells from British units, we started off snorkeling at ten knots rather than the usual fifteen, requiring 100 percent load on the engines, the normal four-hour rate. We left that 100 percent load on for twenty-one days, 16 March to 5 April 1950.

A few problems arose, one potentially serious. *Pickerel* had a new method of spring-loaded cam locks to secure the plating around the conning tower fairwater. On routine dives some had popped loose. When we couldn't get topside to tighten them, they became progressively worse. Soon heavy pieces of sheet metal were tearing

Commander Schratz poses with the ship's plaque after the *Pickerel* arrived at Pearl Harbor to conclude her record-setting run. *National Archives: 80-G-485161*

loose and bouncing down the deck. One or two went through the screws, reducing our speed somewhat for the last four days. They also tore away all of our antennas, so that we couldn't transmit radio messages to ComSubPac. Anticipating the worst, somewhere near Midway I reported to ComSubPac that "because of progressive loss of all transmitting antennas, this may be my last transmission." Just in the nick of time. The average force commander, when a submarine is unreported over twenty-four hours, has a lost-submarine routine to go through.

Adm. Arthur Radford was CinCPac [commander in chief, Pacific] at the time, and when we were unreported for forty-eight hours, he said, "Order her to the surface." Admiral Brown, our great friend, asked for a delay, assuring the big boss of his great faith in the ship. He couldn't be sure we were still able to receive messages, however, and sent out an air-search team. They couldn't find us, so the second day he ordered us to broach enough to show running lights and fire flares. Although they knew our track accurately, unfortunately, they couldn't find us. The running lights had grounded out. We

were four days unreported before they finally found us a day out of Pearl.

Because somebody had claimed that a French or German submarine had been submerged for five hundred hours, we asked by short-range VHF radio to be allowed to stay off Pearl Harbor in the operating area just long enough to pass five hundred hours. On surfacing at the entrance to the channel, we had covered 5,187 miles in twenty-one days—505 hours—continually submerged, with two engines continually on propulsion.

Lots of small problems greeted us. We lost topside grease lines, fittings, cabling, the entire conning tower fairing, the whip antenna, some deck plating, and the periscope protection. Of major logistic significance, we found that fuel consumption was about 60 percent higher than for normal cruising, which meant that the range of a snorkeling submarine was reduced very seriously. Granted, we were at 100 percent load, but nobody realized the difference. Even with the nuclear submarine just over the horizon, the reduced fuel endurance was an important logistic factor.

The Bureau of Ships was delighted, however, that we had succeeded without wiping an engine blower. By then we had sixteen hundred snorkeling hours on each of the four engines. They were still trying to get one to run for one hundred. Curious to learn the secret of our engine endurance, they first asked for a fuel analysis. Their theory was that the fuel we got in Hong Kong made the difference in engine performance. We sent a sample for a routine analysis. The report: excessive sediment, excessive moisture, insufficient flash point, insufficient pour point, does not meet submarine standards, do not use. Clearly this would have only increased our difficulties.

I forwarded this report to the Bureau of Ships without comment and waited for their next reaction as to the secret of our success. They sent two engineers out to see for themselves. The crew had been alerted beforehand that our secret—adding a few gauges at critical points to monitor performance better and always starting a warm rather than a hot or cold engine to snorkel—would stay with us unless they were willing to give us full credit for it. If they insisted on snooping around to find out for themselves and then invented the idea when they got back to Washington, no go.

Well, their first shock came when they found we had disconnected the snorkel safety circuits which cut out the engines if the men on the diving planes lost depth control and ducked the air intake under water. These were over-engineered and oversensitive, many times operating when they weren't supposed to. When you duck the head valve under water, three spark plugs trigger a system to shut the valve and keep the ocean out. Those big diesels then pull all the air out of the boat unless shut down quickly. It's quite painful on the eardrums, a questionable add-on for engine shut-down.

Our men dreamed up a better idea. At the maneuvering controls, they had an ordinary milk bottle—this was back in the days when milk came in glass bottles—in front of the controllermen and put a condom over the top of the bottle, with the head painted red. Well, when the sea breaks

over the head valve, it slams shut. The vacuum rises, and the condom gets rigid right in front of their noses. Well, these youngsters' minds were on sex as much as engineering, and they immediately responded to pull the engines off the line. That was *our* snorkel safety circuit; the model designed by old men was bypassed.

This didn't impress the BuShips people very much. With some doubts, I had decided to include our modification in my patrol report. Admiral Brown also deliberated before passing it along to CinCPac, Admiral Radford; he didn't think Radford would appreciate it. We learned later that he broke up laughing over it. He said he wanted to come down to congratulate us—and obviously to get a firsthand look. It's the first time CinCPac had personally visited a submarine since the Nimitz days during the war—all because of a contraceptive. But BuShips never learned the secret. The diesel submarine era in the United States is a thing of the past, and I suppose the secret died with it.

Navigation submerged offered another problem. Bowditch, who wrote the gospel of seamanship, disposed of the problem in a single sentence: "When long-range submerged cruises of the future become possible, the means of navigation will be at hand." We had Loran, but Pap Sims and I wanted to stimulate new ideas on navigation for the watch officers. They took turns for two days at a time as navigator, using any conceivable means: soundings, celestial transits by periscope for longitude lines, sun sights by measuring the altitude in the periscope crosshairs, and so forth. Despite the limitations, we knew our position accurately throughout. At a constant speed of 10.2 knots, before the screw damage from topside plating reduced speed somewhat, and with no steering loss from sea action on the hull, navigation was far more accurate than normal. Our landfall was exactly as predicted.

When the story broke after our arrival in Pearl, the public reaction throughout the United States and internationally was unbelievable. We received messages of congratulations from the secretary of defense, SecNav [Secretary of the

Because her initial arrival at Pearl Harbor in April 1950 wasn't photographed, the *Pickerel* had to go out and come in again for this picture to be taken. *National Archives: 80-G-485143*

Navy], CNO [chief of naval operations], and numerous public officials. The media went ape over it, creating one immediate problem: Nobody had thought to photograph our surfacing and arrival in Pearl. So three days later, we got under way, went to sea, turned around, and snorkeled back to the entrance buoys for our "official" welcome. All photos were carefully air-brushed to hide the loss of plating and collateral damage to the periscope fairwater plating.

49

Those Disastrous Pancake Diesels

ADM. HAROLD E. SHEAR,
USN (RET.)

Hal Shear was a blunt, aggressive naval officer who served in the destroyer *Stack* and submarine *Sawfish* in World War II. When the Korean War began in 1950, he was in the Bureau of Naval Personnel and was involved in providing manning for ships and shore stations as the Navy went to a wartime footing. In 1951, as he relates, he went back to sea as the Navy was commissioning its first new postwar submarines, the fast attack boats of the *Tang* class. He served in the *Trigger* as executive officer to Cdr. Edward L. "Ned" Beach. Years later, when Beach delivered the eulogy at Shear's funeral, he described his former exec as the finest naval officer with whom he had ever served.

ONE DAY I was called over to the submarine desk in OpNav. The head of the submarine desk was one Chick Clarey, then a commander, and his assistant was Jim Calvert. Both of them became flag officers, both of them great guys. They hauled me over there one morning and said, "Shear, you're about ready to go back to sea again. How'd you like to put the *Trigger* in commission?" I couldn't believe it. Best damn job I could possibly have gotten. They said, "Ned Beach is going to be skipper, and we want you to go up there and be exec. We think you can hold Beach down." I never told Beach that.

So I was ordered to the *Trigger*, and the first thing I did was go off to advanced prospective commanding officer school for about a month, six weeks. Then I reported to the *Trigger* in the summer of 1951. She was then about two-thirds or maybe three-quarters of the way through new construction at Electric Boat in Groton, Connecticut. We built three *Trigger*s at Electric

Cdr. Ned Beach was first skipper of the new fast-attack boat *Trigger* after having served in the fleet boat *Trigger* during World War II. *Naval Institute Photo Archive; courtesy of Ingrid Beach*

Boat and three *Tang*s at Portsmouth Naval Shipyard. They were essentially the same class of submarines, but they had some minor differences. They were the first new submarines built since the end of the war, and the first new submarines since the fleet boat. The Guppies were just versions of the fleet boat.

These fast attack boats had many changes in them. The first thing we had to do was qualify in the new submarine and find out what she was all about, what made her tick, what was new and different in the systems. There were many differences. Probably the principal difference was the power plant. The three ships built by Electric Boat had the General Motors pancake diesel engine, and that engine became a disaster. It should never have come off the test stand. It was mounted vertically with the generator hanging under it, if you can imagine a generator hanging under an engine dripping oil. The engine looked like one of the old rotary aircraft engines with

the pistons going out around the rotary crankshaft that went out the top and bottom. The pancakes were very high speed, almost three times the speed of a good old heavy-duty diesel, Fairbanks Morse engines of World War II fame which ran forever—magnificent engines.

The pancakes were disasters almost from the start; even on sea trials we knew we had big problems. They would chew up the gears. Sometimes we'd have to go into the crankcase and just rake out the chewed-up gears and valves and bearings with a hoe. We had four of those engines, and if you could keep one of them running you were lucky. We got through our sea trials, and then we had a period of operating up and down the East Coast before the ship went on shakedown cruise. We got the engines halfway settled down so we could keep at least half of them running.

Beach was just raising hell everywhere about the problems with those engines, as well as some of the other things in the ship he wanted changed. I had to sort of hold Beach down from going a little bit too far, and I was senior enough and with experience enough so that I could do that. Beach had had a great combat record during the war. He was with Roy Benson on the earlier *Trigger*, with George Street in *Tirante*, and Ned commanded the *Piper* at the end of the war. So Beach was really a great naval officer.

He was smart as hell, enthusiastic, and very competent. He liked to get the most out of a submarine that he possibly could. But sometimes he got a little bit too enthusiastic and got a little bit critical, not of juniors but of his seniors. So I had to be strong enough to say, "Goddamn it, Ned, you can't do that." I had to be the balance wheel. So it was a good thing that I was with Beach at that period. With those engines he'd have gone really half-cocked if I hadn't held him down. As it was, we had enough trouble. Sometimes I had to hit him over the head with a two by four, but he listened to me. He had great respect for me, and I had great respect for him.

When we got to operating, we took the secretary of the navy out. Beach was going to show him everything his new submarine could do, and she could do a lot, even with her bad engines. He

The Electric Boat shipyard lowers a lightweight General Motors "pancake" diesel engine into the hull of the *Trigger*. The new engine, which had a vertical crankshaft, caused many problems for the *Trigger* and her sisters in the *Tang* class. *Naval Institute Photo Archive*

would put her into thirty-degree dives and angles and dangles and really show the ship off. And I must say the secretary was very impressed. We had the secretary aboard a couple of days, I believe. I think we took him from New London to Norfolk, Virginia.

One of the things we did was take the ship to Washington; we brought it up the Potomac River. The *Trigger* drew nineteen feet, and that Potomac River has only about a twenty-foot channel. I was navigator and I was kind of nervous going up there, but we took her up without a pilot, no problem. We brought her up there to show her off to Congress and show her off to the Pentagon.

When we had a bunch of congressmen on board, one of them was Carl Vinson, sort of a big

daddy to everybody in the Congress in those days—big daddy as far as the military goes, the navy in particular. We showed him the ship in great detail and took his picture with the periscope and gave him a big dinner, and he was just like a kid. We told him it was the greatest submarine in the world when we knew damn well it wasn't, particularly with those engineering problems, although it had many other good features. Some electrical features and some of the torpedo tube improvements were excellent. But overall, that class was not the greatest class we ever built.

In the spring of 1952, just after we brought the ship back from Washington, I got orders to my first command. In the *Trigger* Ned Beach was

The new *Trigger*, commissioned in 1952, was part of the first class of new diesel submarines that went into service following World War II. She was a step beyond the Guppy conversions and was able to travel faster submerged than on the surface. *Courtesy of Rickart Connole*

As part of the commissioning ceremony for the new *Trigger* in March 1952, Vida Connole Benson presents a painting to Cdr. Ned Beach, the first commanding officer, depicting the surfacing of the new fast-attack boat with a ghostly image of the wartime *Trigger* in the sky. The boy just to the left of the painting is Rick Connole, son of David Connole, the last skipper of the World War II *Trigger*. His mother, who married submariner Roy Benson after the war, is making the presentation. *Courtesy of Rickart Connole*

still captain, and the chief engineer, Flag Adams, relieved me as exec. They went off on a real shakedown cruise to Rio de Janeiro, Brazil.

Well, when they went off on that long cruise, I knew they were going to have trouble. They barely staggered down to Brazil, keeping one out of four engines going, sometimes two if they were lucky. They got into Brazil, and they had to use every spare part they had on board to get the engines back together, just one continual problem with those engines. They started home after a period in Brazil, and Ned kept getting madder and madder. He was firing off one dispatch after another, castigating the manufacturer, castigating the naval architects, castigating the Submarine Force for ever accepting those engines. He sent all this stuff back to ComSubLant [commander, Submarine Force, Atlantic Fleet], and it didn't go over well. I was then CO of the *Becuna*, operating out of New London, and the ComSubLant headquarters were right there at the submarine base. So I was aware of all these messages coming back from the ship, and I suspected that Ned would get a little bit wild because of the problem with engines.

Flag Adams was a hell of a good man, but he couldn't hit Ned over the head the way I could. So the stuff that he sent off in dispatches was just a diatribe—deserved, but not the way to do things. When Ned got back, ComSubLant wasn't sure he was the greatest skipper in the world. I don't think there was any thought of relieving him, but there was much great unhappiness about Ned Beach and those engines in the *Trigger*. And I knew this was coming because I had gotten wind of it, knowing the staff and having been around that staff.

So I went down to be the first guy aboard the *Trigger* when Ned got back. I just forced myself aboard and I grabbed him and sat him down in the wardroom and said, "Ned, you're in deep trouble and you'd better face up to reality." I told him everything that was going on and the way his messages had been received as a lead balloon. He then realized that he had far overstepped things. He's been forever grateful to me that I got down there and got to him first, before the staff did, because at least it gave him a little bit of alert time to get his thoughts in order.

50

Photo Reconnaissance

VICE ADM. JOE WILLIAMS JR.,
USN (RET.)

For someone who eventually became commander, Submarine Force, Atlantic Fleet, Joe Williams had an unusual background. He enlisted in the Navy in 1940 as an apprentice seaman, advanced quickly during wartime to chief motor machinist's mate, and then got a commission. Before the war was over he was involved in a number of amphibious operations in the Pacific theater. After the war he served in a destroyer and then went to Submarine School so he could qualify for the higher pay that went with service in the boats. In 1950, when he was a lieutenant, he reported to the *Ronquil* as the officer third in seniority in the boat but completely new to submarines. His skipper was Cdr. Harry Fischer. By the time the boat deployed to the western Pacific, Williams had gotten his submarine sea legs under him.

WHILE ON DEPLOYMENT we operated out of Yokosuka, Japan, and we went on photographic and intelligence-gathering missions up off the Soviet Union—Sakhalin Island and the port of Vladivostok. We monitored the ship movements out of Vlad and recorded by sonar all the signatures of the ships. It was rather routine, because usually all we saw were merchant ships, but we photographed them faithfully. Occasionally we would get some warships to photograph.

I was the photographer and shot through the periscope. The Navy had sent me to photographic school. I would shoot them with the 70-mm camera and a 35-mm camera. I would develop the 35-mm to see what we had, and then we would write up our intelligence reports. There was a lot of attention paid to them. I don't know what real value they turned out to be, other than it sure kept them updated on what was going into Vlad and what was coming out. And, of course, we were there to monitor any Soviet warship movements. This was during the Korean War, so if they headed south, we immediately notified commander, Naval Forces Far East, based in Japan.

One day we saw about five of them that came out to exercise. We patrolled most of the time right off of the twelve-mile-limit approaches to Vlad. Sometimes we patrolled in the strait between Hokkaido and Sakhalin. There we encountered the sharpest thermocline—that is, layer of temperature difference—I ever ran into. We dove the boat one morning off the southeast tip of Sakhalin. When we got down to sixty feet, we just stopped, as though we had hit bottom. I started flooding the boat, and I flooded and flooded. I took on several tons of water, and then I thought, "What the hell? Who compensated this boat?" I looked up at the bathythermograph trace that recorded sea temperature. I should have looked at it previously, but I didn't. The stylus had traveled twenty-eight degrees in a straight line across the chart. The change in temperature makes a great difference in buoyancy, which was why we had such a hard time getting submerged.

Harry Fischer was having a fit, because the boat was hanging up there with the periscope shears bobbing in and out of the water and daylight coming in. I said, "Captain, we can get through it. We can drive through it, but it's also going to take a lot of water." We finally made it. I don't know how many tons of ballast I took on to get through that thing. At full speed, with a twenty-degree down angle, we drove her under that thermocline. It's remarkable how a change in temperature can reduce or increase the density of the ocean that you're working in.

I've forgotten now how many tons of ballast we took on board that boat for, say, a one-degree change in temperature. I don't know whether it's a fraction or not, because it just escapes me. But it's quite a complex medium in which submarines operate. One has to know and understand how to exploit it, because it's ever changing. That thermocline didn't exist five miles away.

Lt. Joe Williams pulled a fast one when he and a friend put together a panoramic mosaic that wasn't quite what it seemed. *Courtesy of Susan Williams*

Once we got squared away, we took a photograph of a merchant ship, about a ten thousand tonner, maybe fifteen thousand. It was a big ship with one stack. We couldn't find it in our intelligence manuals, and so in a few days Fischer said, "Let me look at these things. Let me look at the ship." After studying the pictures and ship data we were given prior to patrol, he said, "You see this ship here with two stacks?"

I said, "Yes, sir."

"Could they have modified that ship to be the ship we photographed?"

I was busy and didn't pay much attention to him. I said, "I don't think that's very feasible."

"I think it is."

"Well, I don't think so."

So we got back to Yokosuka. We turned in the photographs, but we didn't mention the possibility in our patrol report. Sure enough, Naval Intelligence came back and said, "You got the first photograph of such and such that has been in Vladivostok Shipyard being converted to a new propulsion plant with one stack." Harry would never let me forget that. That was one-upmanship, and he drove it home.

While we are on the subject of photography, I want to tell you about a photoreconnaissance exercise we conducted for grade in the Submarine Force competition before we departed San Diego for that deployment in 1951. We photographed about three miles of shoreline north of La Jolla. There were white beaches and rocky promontories backed up by sheer, rugged, serrated cliffs with undulating heights—a dramatic scene. We photographed it on 70-mm film. The run went as smooth as silk, and I immediately developed and printed the pictures on board as required. The photographs were spectacular.

The format required us to make a panoramic photo mosaic to accompany the report. You made the mosaic by cutting each print in succession with a razor blade and then fitting the pictures together on tacky paper. In the cutting, compensation had to be made for the difference in distances to the objects appearing in the print. The waterline of the beach was always the closest point to you, but the tops of the bluffs might be a mile or so farther away than the bases. There was no perfect solution, but a good cutter could produce a good product that would clearly present the features of most interest to a commander planning a landing.

This mosaic, which I did not have to make on board, was to turn out to be about five feet long. We got in about noontime, and I took all of my prints and tacky paper home. I spread them out on the table and every other flat surface in the dining room and went to work. By 6:00 PM. I had about three feet of it completed, and my wife Margaret said, "Stop, wash up, fix us a drink, and then we will eat in the breakfast nook." I was complying when the doorbell rang. There was Lt. (jg) Bob Metzger, an old sub school buddy, still a bachelor, and just in from a six-month deployment to the western Pacific. He was loaded with gifts for Margaret and our children and some booze for me—and for him. So we had a few drinks, much laughter and talk, and ate dinner.

Then I had to get back to the mosaic, because the report was to be in the submarine division commander's hands by noon the next day. Bob Metzger said, "I'll help. We will be through in an hour." Well, we started cutting these pictures and tacking them down. We would drink a little and cut and paste and giggle. At midnight Margaret went to bed in disgust, leaving us to giggle along the beach and up the bluffs. It really, surprisingly, went extremely professionally until we got to the last three hundred yards at the southern end of the beach. I could not find the last four photographs of the run. I had made two prints of everything, but those four were missing. I looked at the mosaic and realized that the height of the bluff on the north end was very similar to the height at the southern end, so I took the spare first four photographs from the north end and used them at the south end. It looked good, and who would notice that the two trees with boulders around them on the north end were identical to the trees and boulders on the south end? Bob and I really giggled as I pasted that together. We had a final drink to it and went to bed.

The next day I handed Harry Fischer the finished report, copies of all the photographs except for four, and the five-foot-long mosaic. He was ecstatic. He took it directly to the division commander. It won the squadron competition. I was now dismayed because it was going out to Sub-Pac intelligence for evaluation. They didn't notice the doctoring. It won the SubPac competition, and I received a letter of commendation from the force commander. I guess because in 1951 the submarine forces were looking for any mission to justify their existence, it was sent to the director of Naval Intelligence for evaluation and, incidentally, as a first-rate example of how well submarines could collect intelligence. I was now scared to death. If the deception was discovered, Harry—along with ComSubPac—would hang me high.

Lo and behold, I received a glowing commendation from the director of Naval Intelligence, via ComSubPac, ComSubRon Three [commander, Submarine Squadron Three], and ComSubDiv Thirty-Two, all of whom had very nice things to say. I heaved a sign of relief. But my family knows me as a lousy photographer, even with a modern camera that does it all for you—my commendations notwithstanding.

51

The Whale-Shaped *Albacore*

CAPT. HARRY A. JACKSON,
USN (RET.)

During the first half of the twentieth century, the submarine was essentially a submersible surface ship. The fleet boats of World War II were good for about twenty knots when their diesels were driving them along the surface of the water. Once submerged, they switched to their electrical batteries and could make about nine knots—and then only for an hour or so. As the nuclear power came along, so also came the promised ability to be able to spend extended periods underwater and thus the need for a hydrodynamic hull shape that would permit increased speeds submerged. The test vehicle for the teardrop or whale-shaped submarine was a diesel boat, the *Albacore*, which was commissioned on 6 December 1953. The lessons learned from her operation were later incorporated in the *Skipjack* class and subsequent nuclear submarines. In the 1950s Cdr. Harry Jackson was a naval architect whose fascination with submarines dated from the 1920s, when he practiced salvaging toy submarine models he had made of wood and lead.

THE *Albacore* WAS in the same congressional authorization as *Nautilus*, the first nuclear submarine. I had a lot of to do with the design and development of the *Albacore*. The *Albacore* was conceived in the National Academy of Science at the direction of Rear Adm. Charles Momsen in OP-31. It was created by a team made up of, among others, several retired officers—Rear Adm. Paul Lee, Rear Adm. Andy McKee, Vice Adm. Ned Cochrane—and Ken Davidson, who was the chairman of the Davidson Laboratory down at Carnegie Tech. They came to the conclusion that there were many things that not only could be but should be explored. They proposed to make an attack submarine with a streamlined body, a single propeller, and modified control surfaces.

They proposed this to the CNO's office, and OpNav said, "Hey, that's too far advanced. We can't make that kind of step."

So under the leadership of Paul Lee, who was working for Gibbs and Cox, the naval architecture firm, they said, "Hey, if you don't like what we're doing, you'd better disband the committee. If you persist in just duplicating what we have, there's no need to have us, and we'll all quit."

There was some debate and controversy, and someone in OpNav said, "Well, we will make an experimental ship. Therefore you guys can go play with it and do what you want, and we won't lose a submarine in our fleet." So it was decided that it would be an experimental ship. Well, the David Taylor Model Basin in Carderock, Maryland then took over, and they really developed the concept design from a hydrodynamic point of view. Streamlined body of revolution, a sail that had low drag, would go fast. It was made with bow planes up forward, and they considered different configurations of stern control surfaces. They also originally considered counter-rotating propellers. The main reason that the *Albacore* was so fast was her small size—about two hundred feet long.

The model basin reps proposed this design, and there were some comments by the Bureau of Ships (BuShips). BuShips had to get their axe in, and they made some changes to it. But it was approved for construction at the same time *Nautilus* was approved for construction. Then the Portsmouth Naval Shipyard was given the job of the contract design and detail design. When I went to Portsmouth, first I was a ship superintendent on the waterfront, and then I went up to the design division, and I was designated design project officer on *Albacore*.

The model testing first started out in Ken Davidson's tank up at the Stevens Institute of Technology, in Hoboken, New Jersey, and he did a lot of work up there, and good work. The model basin took his data and refined it because they had a bigger tank and better instrumentation. At that time the model basin had a lot of

good hydrodynamicists who developed all the coefficients for the equations of motion, and that really changed our ability to design submarines with assurance that you could control them. Before that it was sort of like a trial and error.

When they had fleet boats that could only make nine knots for a short time, control was really not very important because as long as you kept your balance of buoyancy and weight, that was the major thing you worried about. Once we got to higher speed submarines, we had to understand the control better.

We tried all kinds of new concepts on *Albacore*. Fortunately, we didn't have any weapon systems to worry about, so that made it pretty easy. For instance, we went to an aircraft-type hydraulic system, and so it was much lighter and faster operating. I can't say it was more reliable, but it was using fly-by-wire electronic-controlled control surfaces. When we had the first sea trials, the ship ran real well, and then we started making modifications in the after control surfaces.

When we first designed the ship, we wanted to put the control surfaces forward of the propeller and the general consensus of opinion was negative. Actually, Admiral McKee was part of this. He said, "Hey, we tried that once and it didn't work." Well, it was tried on the first *Holland* fifty years earlier. It was also tried on the *S-3*. But instead of trying to find out why it didn't work and doing something about it, they just said, "Hey, it didn't work. We'll never try it again."

So the first stern surfaces on the *Albacore* had to be behind the propeller. In order to support them, we had to have huge big arms out there. The hydrodynamic loads in high-speed turns with vibrations were so high that the factor of safety if all those arms happened at the right time was about .8, and that didn't look very prudent. But still the maximum stresses if you got them all at once would cause them to crack, and if they cracked they'd probably fall off. So we never did really exercise the ship to its maximum. But then we made the next step, where we put the control surfaces forward of the propeller. This was the cruciform tail arrangement—a tail in the shape of a cross.

The *Albacore* sits in a bowl to demonstrate her revolutionary hull shape to those who come to see her in Portsmouth, New Hampshire. At right is the visitors' center. *Naval Institute Photo Archive*

We also put a real good high-aspect ratio on them and made them long enough so they got outside the boundary layer to obtain lots of force on the planes. We took it to sea, and it worked fine. No problems at all. We weren't sure whether it was going to work or not, but Kenny Gummerson, who was the first commanding officer of the *Albacore*, made us pull the ship with tugs into the middle of the river. Then he started slow ahead because he wasn't sure that you could control it, but it controlled all right. The faster you went, the better the control got.

I remember being with Commander Gummerson on sea trials. It was a beautiful moonlight night, and the bridge was so small we could only put two people on there. He invited me to come up on the bridge, and he said, "But you've got to be the lookout." So I was the lookout.

He got a message: "Permission to dump garbage?"

He really didn't give it much thought. He said, "Permission granted." Pretty soon we heard a big clatter in the trunk coming up there, and here

came the garbage can up, and the only guys up there to take it were the captain and me. So we reached down and hauled it up. We looked at one another, and I said, "I guess we throw it over the side." We dumped it over, and it went all over the sail.

When we sent it down, we said, "Gee, there's got to be a better way," so the next day we started designing a trash disposal unit.

There were obviously more important issues. We still had bow planes, but in the trials we wanted to see what it would do if we took the bow planes off. Someone on the Atlantic Fleet Submarine Force staff said, "Hey, you can't do that."

We said, "Well, we think it's all right. We just want to try it."

After long debate they said, "Okay, you can take it off for one of the sea runs, but they've got to go right back." We took them off, but they never went back on because you could control the ship fine. But we only could get away with that on *Albacore* because she was a high-speed submarine and she ran around at high speed and could get enough dynamic lift on the hull that she didn't need the bow planes. The trim could be changed, and the angle, and we could drive it up and down with the propeller. Worked fine. We finally got permission to put the X-stern on it, which we did. It turned out fine, and the ship behaved marvelously. Most of the foreign submarines have adopted it.

The turning diameter of the *Albacore* was about one half that of an ASW (antisubmarine warfare) ship operating with it. The next thing we did was put on counterrotating propellers, and that increased the speed almost 20 percent. We tried different kinds of combinations of propellers and number of blades, the pitches and so forth, because we were learning, and we did all that on there.

When a submarine is going through the water, it creates a wake and drag behind it. That wake has got energy in it. If you put the propeller on the axis, some of that energy can be recaptured and transferred into thrust. Or if you have two propellers, then they are outside the boundary layer, and there is no opportunity to recover the other. That's the reason that counterrotation is good. One propeller is behind the other one, and the first one puts rotational energy in the wake, and the second one takes it out, so you recapture that energy that would normally be lost, going downstream. So it's pretty straightforward when you look at the hydrodynamics, but if you're just looking at it through a periscope or from the bridge you don't see all those things.

The maneuverability of the *Albacore* was really fantastic, particularly with the X-sterns. As a matter of fact, it was so great that ComSubLant got concerned about the fact that these crews were doing too much hydrobatics. Instead of saying, "Gee, isn't it wonderful that they can do all those things?" he said, "Hey, you guys are going to kill yourselves." And that philosophy also held back the development of the *Albacore*. They thought it was too risky to operate.

That disturbed me, because they should have said, "Find out why they can do these things" and

"Do we need to make other ships like them?"

During that time, Lord Mountbatten, who was the First Sea Lord of the British Navy, came to visit Adm. Arleigh Burke, who was CNO, and one of the things he wanted to do was see the *Albacore*. So Burke said, "Good, we'll take my plane and fly down and see it." Admiral Burke didn't know much about the *Albacore*, so he thought he'd like to have somebody on board who did. They asked around who knew about the *Albacore*, and I said, "Gee, I do."

So they said, "Well, we want you to go with Admiral Burke down to ride the *Albacore*, and he's going to take Mountbatten with him."

I said, "Gee, that's fine." I jumped at that chance.

So we got in the admiral's plane, and pretty soon the steward came and said, "The admiral would like you to come back in the cabin and talk to him." So I met Mountbatten and shook hands and so forth, and he started asking me questions about the *Albacore*, and I was able to answer most of them. We had a great time. This was just the three of us all the way from Washington to Key West. I could see that Admiral Burke was getting kind of fidgety, because he wanted to talk about other things probably far more important than the *Albacore*. But Mountbatten wanted to talk about the *Albacore*. He wanted to know about why we adopted the shape we did. He wanted to know about the power plant. He wanted to know about the hydraulic systems. He wanted to know about the hydrodynamics of the control surfaces. He was very, very knowledgeable, and I was quite impressed with the questions he asked. He had a good technical grasp, and he wasn't really a submariner. He was a surface ship driver, but he asked all the right questions.

The *Albacore* probably has had more influence on the navies of the world than any submarine since the *Holland*, and we don't recognize it in this country. A perfect example of that is the wife of one of the senior naval officers up at Portsmouth, where they have it on exhibit. She said, "Why do they have that awful old thing sitting out there? It doesn't even have a war record."

52

Firing the Regulus

REAR ADM. NORVELL G. WARD,
USN (RET.)

In the 1950s, while the U.S. Navy was getting into the era of antiair missiles by mounting them in the cruisers *Boston* and *Canberra*, it also had Regulus 1 surface-to-surface missiles. These were fired by both surface combatants and surfaced submarines. As commander, Submarine Squadron Five in 1956–57, Captain Ward supervised tests of the missiles. The experience stood him in good stead, because he subsequently served as commander, Submarine Squadron Fourteen, the first group of nuclear submarines equipped to fire the Polaris ballistic missile.

W E HAD the Regulus missile coming into operation in the submarines, and Port Hueneme and Point Mugu were the center of the missile range for the Navy. There were several missile operations off of southern California. The Regulus had a very elementary inertial platform in it, primarily a two-dimensional one. One part was to keep it on the level flight and to keep it from rolling, and the other was a vertical gyro to give it direction. The guidance was provided by electronic signals from an external source. For short ranges after firing, the firing submarine could provide necessary guidance. For the longer ranges, we had to have another submarine at a certain distance from the firing submarine and from the target, to provide what was designated as terminal guidance. In other words, the second submarine would put the missile over the target and key it for detonation.

In early 1957, we conducted a cold-weather missile firing in the Aleutians. The guidance

The hangar aft of the *Tunny*'s conning tower could accommodate two Regulus 1 missiles. *Naval Institute Photo Archive*

submarine went up to the Aleutians. The concept of the operation was to fire a five-hundred-mile missile and have it destructed deliberately over one of the uninhabited islands in the Aleutians. We had the USS *Wilkinson*, one of the large frigates, as the observing ship near the target.

I was the officer in charge of conducting the operation, since it was one of my submarines. The submarines went up independently. I flew up and boarded the *Wilkinson* in Kodiak. Then we went down the Aleutian chain to the target island, just off of the target island, and at the designated time, the Regulus was fired. It was tracked successfully by the guidance submarine, and we think it detonated over target. There were some high clouds that day, and we just didn't see it from the *Wilkinson*. But according to the tracking data, it was a fairly successful run. The purpose was to evaluate performance of a Regulus missile under cold conditions.

I first found out about the future Polaris system in the spring of 1957, when Rear Adm. William F. "Red" Raborn, with his traveling team, came out to San Diego and put on a show in Air-Pac's (Air Force, Pacific Fleet) big auditorium of what was going to be done with Polaris. I believe when Red Raborn went to Washington to head up the Navy's long-range missile program, the concept was that they would use Jupiter missiles in surface ships as the Navy's contribution to missile warfare.

The new program had two important differences from Regulus. One was that it didn't require terminal guidance. The other one was that in order to launch Regulus, the submarine had to be on the surface. The concept as expounded by Rear Adm. Red Raborn and his team in the spring of 1957, was that the Polaris, as it became known, or the solid-propellant missile, would be launched from a submerged platform and would have its

The *Tunny* fires the Regulus 1 during tests in 1958. *Naval Institute Photo Archive*

own built-in guidance system. In other words, it would be a ballistic missile. We had Regulus, but before Regulus was really proven and became fully operational, it was out of date, overcome by developments in missilery. I know it was retained in the Submarine Force for an additional few years, but then it was phased out. Polaris became the vehicle.

53

Tangling with the Soviets

VICE ADM. JOE WILLIAMS JR.,
USN (RET.)

After his initial submarine service in the *Ronquil*, recorded in an earlier chapter, Joe Williams served as executive officer of the *Icefish* and *Bashaw*. In mid-1957 he got command of his own diesel boat, the *Bluegill*, homeported in Pearl Harbor. As in his previous submarines, Williams's boat had the Cold War mission of collecting intelligence on the Soviets.

B Y THIS TIME, we had better-equipped ships. Our electronic gear was state of the art; we could intercept and faithfully reproduce signals to the point where they were some use to the intelligence community. Sonar was the same way, and we did a lot of recording. We photographed the Soviets during their exercises. The results of our efforts went to the Office of Naval Intelligence.

When I was near the end of about a fifty-day patrol, I received a message that the boat that was up north to pick up a convoy coming around through the Arctic had damaged his periscopes in the ice. So I was to go up there and relieve him. The message directed, "Stay until you have only enough fuel to permit you to reach Adak [Alaska]. Refuel at Adak and proceed to Yoko-suka [Japan]."

So we went up there, and I think that patrol lasted some seventy or eighty days. I was moving north into the Bering Sea for the first time, and it was an interesting patrol. I thought the Soviet ships were not going to come around, but we got them and did a good job. Then we went into Adak, and the people there did not know of the possibility of our coming in.

Lieutenant Commander Williams is shown in close-up and in front of the sail of his Guppy-type submarine *Bluegill* on the occasion of an inspection held on 15 May 1958. With him and his sailors are the commanders of the submarine squadron, Capt. Paul Stimson, and submarine division, Cdr. Frank Andrews.
Courtesy of Susan Williams

We sent a logistics requisition to Adak. It said we needed fresh provisions, fuel, and laundry services for the bedding and uniforms of nine officers and eighty-seven men who were on a long patrol. When they got that message, the laundry at Adak had already loaded the machines for the dependents and everybody else that lived there on the island. So they unloaded all their big washers, and they met us on the pier. We were low on fuel at that point. We were probably running on the fumes from those dirty clothes. They smelled so bad after that many days at sea.

On a diesel/battery submarine, you don't take a lot of showers, particularly on a long patrol. You water the batteries, you start the evaporators, and you fill up the battery water tanks. Then you make sure all the rest of the tanks are filled. Then the captain takes a shower, and then everybody else takes a shower. If the captain doesn't take a shower, they don't take a shower, and we didn't do a lot of showering. You know, forty days is one thing. Fifty days is something. Eighty days is something else. That's a long time. When the people from the laundry started off-loading our clothes, they became ill—some vomiting because of the odors. So I said to the chief of the boat, "Have our people load it and take it down to the laundry. You handle loading that clothing and bedding into those laundry machines." That's what they did, because it was really bad. My wife remembers the mail that we sent from Adak. Our son Clark walked in from school one afternoon, sniffed the air, and said, "Got mail from Dad."

We made another interesting patrol, and I can't recall for sure whether it was on that deployment or the next one. We went back up off the Kamchatka Peninsula again, and there I experienced something very unusual. Mount Shipunski is an active volcano just off the peninsula. It was one of the navigational features we used, and it rumbled frequently. We'd get a bearing on it to help fix our position and ensure we were still outside the twelve-mile limit. I'm sure it was the source of what I'm about to tell you.

We had had a pretty exciting week, and we were all tired. On Sunday I pulled up north of Point Shipunski, kind of out of the way, for a rest. It was a beautiful day, flat, glassy sea, and we were at periscope depth. I was sitting in the wardroom talking with the executive officer, Lt. Lou Nockhold. All of a sudden, all the dishes flew up in the air. There was a tremendous shock to the submarine. I stepped up and immediately fell down out in the passageway. I could look down through the submarine with all the watertight doors open, all the way back to the maneuvering room. I thought, Collision? No. Runaway electric motor? No.

Everything was going through my mind, and then a second shock wave hit, then a third shock wave hit. As I was looking down through the hull, the whole boat was undulating. This hull with half-inch steel plate was very limber. What I saw was a standing wave. We were at the epicenter of an earthquake, which I'm sure originated from that active volcano. It was a pretty exciting period of time. It lasted a few minutes but seemed like ages. I finally crawled into the control room and looked at the depth gauge. It was bouncing between a thousand feet and zero as the shock waves pegged it in both directions. I had no idea, so I said to the exec, "Can you see anything?"

He said, "Both periscopes are out of commission." So I checked the pressure gauges to see how deep I was, and, there again, they were all going from one end of the scale to the other. Then it quit, and we were right at periscope depth, right where we started, hadn't moved a bit. But I noticed on the bathythermograph that the temperature of the water had increased in that instrument by about fourteen degrees, which indicates a lot of energy. Well, I know it was a lot of energy.

We had a problem. One periscope was beyond fixing; the other could be used only on low power. All of the equipment in the ship, particularly anything with fine gear teeth, had vibrated and bounced enough that the gearing was now out of timing. That included our automatic depth control and fire control equipment. I had to assume that there was no structural damage to the hull. There were no leaks, so we went about our business, but it was a very scary time. It took us a couple of days to get things put back together to where we could go in and play with the Soviets some more.

Our operating rules at the time: "Don't get detected. Shoot if shot at or to avoid being rammed. Stay outside the twelve-mile limit unless authorized otherwise." The Soviets had a very interesting operation going on during one patrol. I got my nose right in the middle of that, and I was detected. I'm sure they saw my scope while I was making an observation near Point Shipunski, so here came the destroyers. The Soviet ships chased me for three days, which kind of convinces you that they know where you are.

In my efforts to get away, I headed east, away from the Soviet coast. I went down under the thermocline. It was down around 290 feet, and I was on a boat with a test depth of 312 feet. So I went down to 312, and the temperature layer was a pretty good blanket for me. But the Soviets were not dumb. They just said, "Well, where's the guy going to go normally if he's been detected?" I'm sure they knew that I knew they'd detected me. So they just kept easing out toward the east, which was toward Point Shipunski. Now, whether they had me at that point was difficult to tell. You cannot really decipher echo ranging because of that darn thermocline.

I went to bed that day, because I knew it was probably going to be a sleepless night. Then I got up. The executive officer came in and said, "The air's getting pretty bad."

I said, "Well, we've got some more time." So we went about another fifteen hours, I guess. I cleared Point Shipunski, and they were still with me. So I eased up to periscope depth, and the minute I broke through the thermocline, they had me, and here they came. So down I went

again. We had already spread out lithium to reduce the carbon dioxide level, but we were running now close to forty-eight hours.

While we were looking at these guys, the very-low-frequency radio antenna picked up enough of the fleet broadcast that we got a little bit of communications. When they decoded one message, it just said, "To *Bluegill*, remember the avoidance of detection is paramount to the collection of intelligence." That was not a really uplifting message to get from the force commander at that time.

That night I finally came up, and the Soviet surface ships were quite a ways astern. I could not really make sure they were back there, but I lit off an engine and started snorkeling. I had no sooner done that than the sonar with the big ears said, "Captain, I have Skoryy destroyers at high speed astern." So I put on the other two engines and snorkeled at max speed away from then until they got within close range, and I pulled the plug and went down again. By this time I had a full bag of air in there; we could breathe.

The Soviets had some very good ASW forces out there. The *Gudgeon* had just been up there before me, and she had been forced to surface. My boss was very sensitive about that, and I sure didn't want to surface. I ended up surfacing at night. I wasn't quite sure where they were, and we came up with the outer torpedo doors open. If one of those ships had made a run at me, I would have fired.

We surfaced, and it was just pitch black. They were there, but we stole out from among them. We got out and waited three or four days and then went back in. By this time they'd calmed down, but those patrols in a diesel boat could get very exciting.

54

Angles and Dangles

ADM. HARRY D. TRAIN II,
USN (RET.)

From the beginning, the Navy was a principal ingredient in Harry Train's heritage. His dad was Rear Adm. Harold Train. His brother-in-law, Lt. Spence Wilson, was lost in the sinking of the *Tullibee* in World War II. Wilson's example of undersea service led Ens. Harry Train to volunteer for Submarine School, which he entered in the spring of 1951. By then, the U.S. Navy was already on the path toward nuclear-powered submarines. The keel for the world's first, the *Nautilus*, was laid in June 1952, when Train was serving in the *Wahoo*, one of the first of the new post–World War II diesel boats. By the early 1960s Train, as a lieutenant commander, was involved in the assignment of submarine officers in the Bureau of Personnel. For reasons he explains in this chapter, Train chose not to get into Adm. Hyman Rickover's nuclear program. In the meantime, Train was assigned to command of the USS *Barbel*, a member of the final class of diesel submarines built for the U.S. Navy. She was commissioned in January 1959, and Lieutenant Commander Train became skipper in July 1962.

I WANTED COMMAND of a *Barbel*-class submarine in the worst way, because they were the newest nonnuclear submarines in the Navy. And since I was in the bureau, I was sitting right there at the left hand of the guy who was going to make the decision. Over the course of endless conversations on what was good and what was the best and what I'd really like to do, I made it clear that I wanted one of those boats.

When I found out I'd go to *Barbel*, it was then homeported on the East Coast. It had suffered a major casualty when it had a five-inch saltwater

The *Barbel* cruises on the sun-washed surface of the sea off the island of Oahu. Her hull shape and sail resemble those of nuclear-powered submarines of the era. *Naval Institute Photo Archive*

line carry away at test depth while operating out of Norfolk. The boat was saved because the engineer was down in the lower flats of the machinery space, sitting on the sea valve, making some notes and doing some work when the line failed. He stood up and spun the valve shut, by which time he was totally underwater. It took in twenty-nine tons of water in about thirty seconds, the time it took him to shut the valve. They were quite lucky in getting the boat on the surface, and were lucky not to hit a destroyer when they emergency surfaced.

They put it back in the yard, and they welded all the silver-brazed fittings in those copper-nickel pipelines. So, in effect, the *Barbel* ended up being the first sub-safe submarine in the United States Navy. It was not long thereafter, in April 1963, that we lost the *Thresher*, probably due to a sil-braze fitting. *Thresher* was built about the same

time *Barbel* was built, and her loss led to the official sub-safe program to correct the vulnerable pipes. Up to the loss of *Thresher*, *Barbel* was the only submarine in the Navy with a welded salt-water system. We never had another inkling of a problem.

At the time I got orders, *Barbel* had just come out of the yard after eleven months of repairs because of the flooding. When I received my orders, I fully expected to be based out of Norfolk. By the time I was detached, the boat had just been ordered to San Diego. It was proceeding to San Diego as I drove across country to join it. *Barbel* had just arrived in San Diego as I arrived there. I checked into a motel and went looking for a house. I was almost ready to sign a lease when the current skipper, Lt. Cdr. Joe Meyer, got word to me that *Barbel*'s home port was changed to Pearl Harbor. So our household effects, en route to San Diego, had to be diverted to Hawaii.

Once I took over command, I was so happy and so confident that I was smiling from dawn till dusk every day. I had a reasonably good group of officers. Through my BuPers connections, I did put one gentleman in the wardroom who was important to me. Lt. (j.g.) Dick Marlin was a limited duty officer who, as an electrician's mate first class, had been the main power electrician on *Wahoo* when I was engineer. Dick Marlin had pulled my chestnuts out of the fire so often as a first class electrician, as the guy in charge of the main power gang on the *Wahoo*, that I had total confidence in him. Having been a submarine engineer as long as I had been, I really wanted a submarine engineer that I would not be fighting with all the time. It was great, never had to worry about the engineering plant. Never had an engineering problem the whole time I was on board.

Command at sea really defies description. You can write about it all you want, but it means different things to different people. To some it means importance, and the authority is more important than the accountability. To others it means loneliness. I never found it to be a lonely role, but other commanding officers I've known very closely sort of detached themselves mentally and emotionally from the people around them.

There's really a fine line. In previous wardrooms I had enjoyed being one of the boys, and it was no longer possible to do that all the time. So it was important to pick those occasions when you wanted to be one of the boys. These would be beer ball games and wardroom parties and the wardroom participation in, say, Submarine Force events, which were submarine birthday balls and other social events, where you participate as a wardroom and everybody sits at the same table with a unit esprit and identity. That's relatively important. You can't be too stuffy on those occasions.

The boat operated like a Swiss watch. It went fast. Each of those three submarines in the *Barbel* class had some differing characteristics. We had clamshell doors on the top of the sail, just like modern nuclear submarines do. They gave you a completely flat fairing on top of the sail when the periscopes and the masts were down. The other submarines didn't have clamshells. We also did not have the things that turned out to be a problem on the other boats. They called them rat traps. These were doors on the fairings for the ballast tanks that would have enabled you to close off and fair the ballast tanks. Even nuclear submarines today don't have those. They didn't work very well, and we were blessed by not having them.

We were about four knots faster than the other two submarines in the class, for reasons no one has ever adequately explained. The *Barbel* handled like a dream. We were still in the process of learning how to handle the teardrop hull shape that later became standard in nuclear submarines. We were, as a crew, virtually in the position of being test pilots for that hull form. In very high-speed operations, it would do things that all your previous submarine experience didn't condition you for. For instance, when you were at high speed and put the rudder on, instead of the bow coming up, the bow would go down. Well, it's common knowledge in submarines today that at high speed the bow does something different than it does at low speed.

One day we had Rear Adm. Chick Clarey, who was then the Pacific Submarine Force commander, out with a bunch of civilian guests. He asked us to do what they call hydrobatics, very high-speed maneuvering. We were doing twenty-three knots and changing depths and making course changes. The boat would roll thirty-seven degrees—what's called snap roll at a max-speed, max-rudder turn. On one occasion we were turning and changing depth at the same time. The bow went down instead of up, and all the inclinometers and the gauges went off the scale, so I have no idea of what angle we achieved, but somewhere in excess of a fifty-degree down angle.

The more the planesman pulled back on the yoke, to put more stern planes on it, the tighter the turn became, the more the roll. We were in what the aviators call a graveyard spiral. The stern planes became the rudder, the rudder

Rear Adm. Bernard "Chick" Clarey, commander of the Pacific Fleet Submarine Force, has his binoculars at the ready while atop the *Barbel*'s sail on 16 August 1962. He was in the open air again after the crew nearly lost control of the submarine during underwater hydrobatics.
Courtesy Adm. Harry D. Train II

became the stern planes, and we were turning tighter. That right rudder was driving us down, and we didn't know what to do. So we let go of all the controls, and the boat pulled itself out. It was a very stable boat. But our downward vertical component was in excess of a thousand feet a minute. We didn't have much time to pull out. The experience was a startling sensation for Admiral Clarey, who had been in submarines for many years. He was a little wild-eyed after it was all over.

I thought very highly of Chick Clarey; he ran a very good show. When the *Thresher* was lost, someone told him that the *Barbel* had had a similar problem. Around that time, the *Barbel* was alongside the pier getting ready to go over to West Loch in Pearl Harbor to pick up some torpedoes. We had a brand-new executive officer, Lt.

Cdr. Pete Conrad. As we singled up mooring lines to get under way, the phone on the pier rang. One of the line handlers answered it and said the admiral's flag secretary wanted to talk to me. So I answered the phone and learned that Admiral Clarey wanted to talk. I said, "Okay, I'll be right over." Then I told Pete Conrad to take the boat over to West Loch, since I had confidence in him.

I went up to the admiral's office, and Admiral Clarey was pacing while we were talking. He was asking about the piping system in *Barbel* and what had been done to it after the casualty. As he was pacing he was looking out the window, and he said, "Harry, what's the number of *Barbel*?

I said, "Five-eighty."

"What's it doing out there?"

I had to tell him that it was en route to West Loch to pick up torpedoes. Since I wasn't on

Angles and Dangles | 249

board, he didn't think that was a very good decision, but it worked out all right. It wasn't a difficult boat to handle. The pivot point was back right under the after capstan, so the whole bow swung. It was almost the classic length-to-beam ratio for a teardrop hull. All subsequent classes have gotten longer and longer and longer and don't have that classic teardrop shape that the *Barbel* had.

I was able to satisfy the admiral's concerns about our piping. Although they did not officially put us in a category of being a sub-safe submarine, we were not one of their problem children. The test depth for the *Barbel* was not reduced until after I left. They had reduced the other submarines' test depths long before that. The first thing I did when I went to sea after the *Thresher* was lost was take it down to test depth and drive it around at max speed for about an hour to build up my own confidence and to build up the confidence of the crew. Then we went to work doing the things we would normally do.

A couple of years later we became the guinea pig for the first nuclear submarine overhauls at Puget Sound Naval Shipyard, which up to then hadn't done any. They wanted to overhaul the *Barbel* to see how to do a nuclear submarine, because the only way we differed from a nuclear submarine was that we didn't have the reactor. At that time they sub-safed the *Barbel* fully, put the emergency blow systems in. They were just developing the infrastructure to do these overhauls. It was a good yard. It had always been a good yard, and they really took good care of us.

My immediate superior in the chain of command was the division commander, a gentleman named W. E. White, and he was later succeeded by Cdr. Lloyd Yeich. The division commander's role, of course, was not an operational one. It was purely training and maintenance, but they were a pretty active part of our world. Sometimes the division commander would take all the ships in the division to Lahaina Roads, off the island of Maui, because that was such a beautiful calm area to conduct torpedo shoots for the training of our crew, as well as the prospective commanding officers' school.

During my time in command, we deployed twice to the western Pacific. When the Cuban Missile Crisis occurred in the autumn of 1962, the *Barbel* had just arrived in Yokosuka, Japan. We drew so much water, about twenty-eight feet, that we tied up at wet dock number six. Also, the Japanese, who remembered the atomic bombs dropped in World War II, tended to think *Barbel* was a nuclear submarine. The Japanese people wanted to demonstrate. So the base put us somewhere where we were sort of hidden from sight.

We arrived about eleven or twelve at night, and Capt. Sunshine Aubrey, who was the chief staff officer of Submarine Flotilla Seven, asked all of the skippers to come up to the subflot headquarters early that morning. That included Don Whitmire, Tom Bigley, Buck Dietzen, myself, and one other CO whose name I can't remember. We were all sitting around trying to figure out what to do in response to the Cuban situation. We finally decided that the best thing for the Submarine Force to do was to provide a screen north of Task Force 77, which was the Seventh Fleet aircraft carrier force. Task Force 77 would be stationed outside the entrance to Tokyo Bay and north toward the Tsugaru Strait between the islands of Honshu and Hokkaido. We would form a submarine barrier north of Task Force 77 to detect and report any Soviet submarine activity in the vicinity or to the north.

We got under way, submerged as soon as we got into deep water, and snorkeled the rest of the way up to station. During that time, I found one of the little nuances that we hadn't predicted during our planning sessions. The result was that both *Bream*, Lt. Cdr. Tom Bigley's submarine, and *Barbel* were in the same transit lane. I was doing about fourteen knots and, of course, Bigley could only do about seven or eight at max speed, because the *Bream* was an old boat, built in World War II. I passed him like he was tied to a post, but I didn't know it was him. So I called over on the UQC underwater telephone and asked, "Tom, is that you?"

He called back, "Yes."

But we learned a little that way—those little refinements you never think about. It never occurred to me that I was so much faster than the *Bream* that, on a snorkel transit, I was going to pass him like he wasn't there.

The mission we were on was a precautionary thing, because the Cuban situation caught us right out of the blue. The submariners felt they ought to be doing something, and commander, Naval Forces Japan felt that it would be useful to have the submarines out there. We didn't know what we were supposed to be doing. We stayed out there for thirty days. In that time we managed to get cross-threaded with the Japanese Maritime Self-Defense Force.

When I was in my patrol area, I was right under a Japanese maritime air patrol area. We had not told the Japanese our submarines were there. I'd get up and try to snorkel at night, and the Japanese P2V patrol planes would be up there dropping sonobuoys, not because they knew I was there, but because that's what they did in their area. So they were picking me up. They would start getting all agitated and then start making runs, and then I'd have to shut down the snorkel and go down and go someplace else and come up where I could snorkel some more. It was the same thing every night, but we weren't in position to tell them we were friendly. In those days you didn't transmit anything. In fact, you took the fuses out of your radio transmitters when you got under way.

Later we went on a surveillance operation out of Yokosuka, to a patrol area off Vladivostok and the following year one out of Pearl Harbor to a patrol area off Petropavlosk. We did very well in those surveillance patrols off the Soviet Union— never had any equipment problem the entire time. During the Petro surveillance patrol—I'm not sure, but I think we broke the longest time submerged record. We didn't do it consciously. We were submerged from the time we left Pearl until the time we returned. It was about sixty-four days, if I remember it correctly. Being underwater that long didn't appear to bother anybody. The crew got into a routine, not unlike the routine that submariners get into today. They eat, sleep, work, and stand watch. At the time it was a new routine for submariners.

During one of those deployments, we had a very exciting close encounter with the aircraft carrier *Kitty Hawk*. We were operating as the aggressor force against Task Force 77, and we were detected by two *Dealey*-class destroyer escorts and a destroyer, the *Brinkley Bass*. Those three escorts held us down for quite a while. We were at the low end of our battery cycle, so we couldn't do any high-speed maneuvers to get away. Finally it came time when I thought it was prudent to get back up and do some battery charging, so I hollered "Uncle" and told them that I needed to come up. The senior ship, which was the *Brinkley Bass*, brought me up to one hundred feet. The procedure at that point is that you fire a yellow flare. If it looks clear to the destroyer, then he tells you on the underwater telephone, "Roger, yellow, all clear, surface." He doesn't really mean surface; he means come up to periscope depth.

So I fired the yellow flare, and he said, "Roger, yellow, all clear, surface."

When I came up to periscope depth, it was blacker than hell outside. I had the ability to wheel the periscope around awfully fast and see everything in one sweep and then get it down fast. I took a real fast sweep, and I spotted the destroyer and the two destroyer escorts. And I saw a red light very high in the sky, and I asked the destroyer, "What is that helicopter doing up there"?

He said, "What helicopter"?

"I see a red light at [such-and-such a bearing]."

"Oh, that's the *Kitty Hawk*."

I was seeing the red sidelight of the aircraft carrier, but I didn't hear the *Kitty Hawk* at all. It is difficult to hear an aircraft carrier's screws when it's going fairly slowly and you're masked by the hull of the aircraft carrier. So I flooded everything and took the *Barbel* down and had the privilege of hearing that big threshing machine come thumping overhead. You really cannot hear it from dead ahead. Those types of things happened every now and then, and they certainly got your attention.

It was after these two deployments that the *Barbel* went to Bremerton, Washington, for the sub-safe overhaul.

While we were there I was called back to

Of this photo taken on board the *Barbel* in 1963, the now-white-haired Train wrote puckishly, "Just to show that I was not born with gray hair and I did work hard enough to sweat." *Courtesy Adm. Harry D. Train II*

Washington to be interviewed for the nuclear program. I ended up in Vice Adm. Hyman Rickover's offices, along with Bill Crowe—future chairman of the Joint Chiefs. Bill Crowe was CO of the *Trout* at the time, and both of us were non-volunteers. It didn't make any difference that we didn't want to be in the nuclear program. We went through the whole day of preliminary interviews with Rickover's deputies—Bill Wegner, Dave Leighton, Ted Rockwell, and a fourth guy whose name I've forgotten. They asked us technical questions about things that we should have forgotten about long ago but for some reason I still remembered from my Naval Academy days.

At the end of all these interviews, I kept telling Bill Wegner and Dave Leighton that I was not a volunteer for the program. I would do anything, would go anywhere the Navy sent me, but it was important for them to recognize that I was not volunteering for this program. Even so, I would execute any orders that were given to me. I presume Bill Crowe was saying something of the same thing.

But Rickover called me in and said, "Train, why don't you want to come and enter the nuclear power training program?"

I said, quite frankly, "Because although I ad-

mire the things that you've accomplished, I don't like your leadership techniques, and I do not want to be a part of the community that has to follow your technique." He didn't get mad.

He said, "Well, suppose that I were to make an arrangement with you where I could treat you officially and never have any personal contact with you and you were to then exercise command without ever having me visit your ship and without ever having me personally involve myself in the way you run things?"

I said, "No, that would not solve my problem, because I would still be in your milieu of leadership, where I could not bestow that faith upon my people that I feel is important to my form of leadership."

He said, "Okay, go away and I will talk to Admiral Smedberg about it."

I thought I'd better sure as hell get to Vice Adm. William Smedberg, the chief of naval personnel, before Admiral Rickover called him. I knew from years of experience that Rickover made his phone calls like that along about six o'clock, just before he shut up his office. So I got on the shuttle bus and hotfooted it over to the Bureau of Naval Personnel and went up and told Admiral Smedberg about what had happened.

About that time Bill Crowe walked in. Sure enough, Rickover called Smedberg while I was sitting right there.

Admiral Smedberg was listening and listening and listening. Then he said, "He's sitting right here, I'll tell him." He said, "Admiral Rickover says to tell you that he's going to order you to nuclear power training anyway. What do you want me to do?"

I said, "I want you not to issue the orders."

"Okay." Then he turned back to the phone and said, "I understand what you're saying, Rick, but I'm not going to do it."

Then Smedberg said, "Okay, get out of here, go back to your ship." So I went back to my ship.

Years later Rickover told Vice Adm. Steve White, who was then ComSubLant, that I was the only guy who had ever turned him down successfully. He was wrong because Bill Crowe turned him down too.

When I got back to the West Coast, something interesting had happened. They were having morning quarters on the *Barbel* when I arrived, so I went to the submarine living barge. There was no one up there, which is normal during quarters. I went into my office, sat down at the desk, and the phone rang.

I picked the phone up, and it was the base commander. He said, "Okay, Harry, where is it?"

I said, "Where is what?" I swung around in the swivel chair just at that point, and there, behind my desk, I saw this big old antique ship steering wheel with a plaque on it. I recognized that it had come from the officers' club. And I said, "Oh, God. You are undoubtedly talking about the steering wheel, aren't you?"

"Yes, I am. If you get it back here before noon, I will forget about it."

So I walked out to the window over where the XO was holding quarters, and I said, "Conrad, get your ass up here." He came hot-footing it up to the office, and I said, "Get it back."

He said, "Have you tried to lift that thing?"

"No, I haven't tried to lift that thing."

"Try it."

So he got on one side and I got on the other, and we couldn't even get it off the deck. How those inebriated wardroom officers ever got that thing up there from the officers' club unseen, I have no idea.

55

A Few Days in October

CHIEF SURFACE ORDNANCE
TECHNICIAN, CWO-4,
JERRY E. BECKLEY, USN (RET.)

At the beginning of the 1960s, when the Cold War was filled with wintry blasts in the relations between the global superpowers, the U.S. Navy's big public splash in the nuclear weapons field arrived with the Polaris-armed nuclear-powered submarines. They deployed from their base in Holy Loch, Scotland, to go on deterrent patrols on the periphery of the Soviet Union. They were poised to strike in retaliation if the USSR initiated a nuclear strike. But the Polaris submarines were not alone in making deterrent patrols with nuclear weapons. Some of the diesel boats had been armed with Regulus missiles that had a maximum range about one-third the distance the Polaris could fly. That meant they had to get that much closer to the intended target areas than did their Polaris counterparts. They also required a surfaced submarine close to the target area to provide terminal guidance for the missiles. When the Cuban Missile Crisis of 1962 threatened global incineration, the Regulus submarines *Tunny* and *Barbero* were on station in the western Pacific. The *Grayback* left the submarines' base at Pearl Harbor to join them. On board was Gunner's Mate Technician 1st Class Jerry Beckley. In the 1950s he had been one of the last gunner's mates to join the submarine service; in 1962 he was in position to arm a weapon with far more power and range than the deck guns that had once been installed on board diesel submarines.

I HAD ORIGINALLY departed Submarine Base Pearl Harbor in 1959 after a two-year tour at Guided Missile Unit Number 90 (the predecessor of GMU-10) as a gunner's mate second class (submarine service). I was headed for

The missile-equipped submarine *Grayback* is shown with a Regulus 1 on her launcher, forward of the sail and aft of the missile hangar. *Naval Institute Photo Archive*

From 1957 to 1961 the Navy had a rating titled nuclear weapons man. Depicted here is a badge for a chief petty officer in that rating; it shows a bomb superimposed on the whirling electrons of an atom. *Courtesy of Jerry Beckley*

Nuclear Weapons School. While doing my tour in Nevada, I was frequently asked the question, "What is a sailor, and more especially a submarine sailor, doing in the desert anyway?"

I'd usually reply, "We are building a submarine in Lake Mead and will float it down the Colorado River." Some bought the response; others didn't. It wasn't much of a cover story, but it was all I could come up with to distract from the distinctive rating insignia I wore as a nuclear weapons man—a bomb dropping through a helium atom. The petty officer "crow" attracted so much attention that the rate was changed in 1961 to gunner's mate technician and the insignia changed to crossed guns.

When I returned to Pearl after school, I soon became a member of the very restricted and unique group of warhead technicians who rode the "Reg boats," the Regulus submarines. We were the people who, in time of war, would arm the warheads in keeping with the "two-man rule." This protocol simply stated that "two men of equal knowledge, each capable of detecting an unauthorized act by the other," must be within proximity of the nuclear weapons at all times. And to arm the weapon, both would have to turn the switch. (To launch a Regulus, the captain would also have to turn a key located on a separate console; this was an added safeguard.)

I was assigned duty aboard the USS *Grayback* in August 1962. Even though I was a former crew member of a conventional, hangar-equipped submarine, the USS *Perch*, and familiar with the Guppy conversion boats, still I wasn't prepared for what I saw tied up at the Sierra Piers. This was the ugliest submarine I had ever laid eyes on. For those who never saw the USS *Grayback* or her sister ship, USS *Growler*, imagine two grain silos secured side by side with the domes facing aft on the forward deck, about twenty feet forward of the sail of a *Swordfish*-class submarine. The large forward superstructure was designed to cover two missile hangars, each capable of storing two Regulus 1 missiles or one Regulus 2. The Regulus 1 was a transonic cruise missile powered by J-33A turbojet engine. It was capable of delivering a thermonuclear warhead to a target five hundred miles distant at a speed of 550 knots.

The ugliness of the *Grayback* notwithstanding, this boat—and the other four Regulus subs—were the only submarine nuclear deterrent strike force in the Pacific Fleet. Polaris was not yet a reality in the Pacific. The Soviet submarine fleet sailed from a warm-water port to cover targets in Hawaii, Japan, Philippines, and the continental United States without anyone—other than us, that is—threatening their front door. In fact, in 1962 submarines had not yet received the Mark 45 antisubmarine torpedo, and SubRoc, the antisubmarine rocket, was still on the drawing board. So there was very little except a lot of ocean between the guys wearing white hats and those wearing black hats.

The diesel Reg boats carried a 120 percent crew. We dubbed ourselves the "Black and Blue Crew" (as opposed to the Polaris boats' rotating "Blue and Gold" crews) because we didn't rotate and had a never-ending stream of responsibilities, maintenance and otherwise. When we deployed, we always tried to leave a few selected people at home. The selected people were crew members with emergencies or schools, or any manner of problems that could have been impacted by their absence.

There were also those who would never be part of the stay-at-home crew, and I was one of them. The captain explained that to me as soon as I was introduced to him. During my short conversation with Lt. Cdr. John J. Ekelund, he mentioned the 120 percent and the stay-in crew. Then he also told me that any time the *Grayback* got under way with Blue Birds (tactical missiles) aboard that he, the warhead officer, the cook, the hospital corpsmen, and myself would be on board under any and all circumstances. The warhead officer and I were joined at the hip as far as the two-man rule was concerned.

There was no doubt in my military mind that this was going to be "long and arduous sea duty," because from what I could tell we would no sooner get into port, have a short refit, and shoot Red Birds (fleet training missiles) before we'd deploy again. I found out that the average in-port period for a Reg boat was around three months, and during our deployments we'd have to travel to some pretty severe parts of the world. The

In this shot a Regulus 2 is out of the *Grayback*'s port hangar and on the launcher. Regulus 2 was test fired, but the program was canceled before the missile could be deployed. *Naval Institute Photo Archive*

This is a close-up of the *Grayback*'s twin-cell missile hangar in the bow. It could accommodate four Regulus 1 missiles or two Regulus 2s. *Naval Institute Photo Archive*

voyages could last months, especially if another boat broke down, a situation that might necessitate a "back to back out of Adak"—a trip to the refueling base at Adak, Alaska, and then right back to the teeth of the deployment zone.

A few weeks after reporting aboard, I was notified that I would be interviewed for the Personnel Reliability Program (PRP), which was really a screening process for those of us who had responsibilities for the missiles and warheads. I was called into the wardroom with the commanding officer, executive officer, missile division officer, and chief of the boat. These folks comprised the PRP screening process. Considering I was the only person authorized to make up the two-man rule with the warhead officer, I was asked questions pertaining to how I felt about the mass destruction and death a nuclear detonation would bring to the population of our target area. My response was simply that when I was in the Army during the Korean War as an infantryman, death was individualized and personal. But in wartime it makes little difference if you kill one

or a million. One must keep it in perspective. They seemed to be satisfied. So I was now part of the *Grayback* PRP.

On 7 October 1962, after a refit and missile training, we slipped our moorings at Pier S-9 in Pearl and headed out for my first, and *Grayback's* sixth, deterrent missile patrol. We had been on station only a short period when again I was called into the wardroom with the same folks who were present for the PRP screening. This time the captain and the XO were a little more stern-faced than before, and for what I was soon to learn, good reason. The steward was asked to step out of the forward battery, and both hatches were put on the latch—closed by not secured.

Captain Ekelund stated that we had received a message that the defense posture had increased to Defense Condition 2 (DefCon 5 was normal) and he was going to open the sealed emergency war orders. The content of those orders, which for the sake of the security oath I swore as far back as the 1950s and 1960s, as well as the one I still serve under, will not be revealed by me. I will say that some of them were directed to the warhead officer and myself. We were to prepare the nuclear warheads for arming, and, if necessary, missile launch.

My task was to remove more than sixty Philips-head screws securing an access panel on the underside of each of the four Regulus 1 missiles, exposing the front of the W-27 warhead where the high-voltage thermal battery (HVTB) pack was bolted in the inverted (stored) position. This was part of the safety mechanism. I then removed the four bolts securing the HVTB, turned the battery around to the potential-use position, reinstalled it, and torqued the bolts. In a launch sequence, the very last task for me, while the warhead officer was putting the settings into the fuzing and firing panel, would be to insert the static boom into the nose of the missile, turn to lock it in place, and insert and tighten the cannon plug. I would then drop down to where the war-

head officer was and check his settings. If this had actually been done, I would have closed the latch and kissed the world good-bye, because that would have been the end of it.

Fortunately, when the order came, it wasn't a launch order. Instead, the next day, thankfully, we were told to relax the DefCon and restore the warheads to their safe war-reserve condition. Few people alive today have a full appreciation of how close this country and the Soviet Union came to what was later to be termed mutually assured destruction (MAD). In addition, few people, except for those of us who rode those old Regulus submarines—some of which were held together with baling wire and prayers—have a full appreciation for the sacrifices made by these Silent Service officers and men, whose usual patrol period was ninety-plus days and occasionally a back to back out of Adak.

56

A Submariner's Memories

WAYNE L. MILLER

In the early 1960s the Cold War was in full swing, and the United States was still a decade away from the all-volunteer force for military service. Healthy male citizens had to register for the draft when they reached their eighteenth birthdays. If they did not volunteer for service or qualify for a deferment, they could count on being in the Army for a two-year hitch of active duty. Wayne Miller enlisted in the Naval Reserve in the spring of 1963, when he was seventeen. He was in what was known as the two-by-six program, which meant he signed up for a six-year overall obligation, including two years of active duty in the Navy and four years of drilling in the Naval Reserve.

A S I WAS GROWING UP, I had an interest in the service. I had four uncles who were in World War II, and my Dad was a Marine. When I was a boy, Dad took me to see Navy ships when they came into port. I joined the Naval Reserve to avoid being drafted; I didn't want to go into the Army. My home was in Baltimore; a friend and I enlisted at the Fort McHenry Naval Reserve Center, near the old fort that inspired the National Anthem. Then my friend talked me into volunteering for submarines, even though I didn't know much about them at that point.

For a few months before I went to boot camp at Great Lakes I drilled at the reserve center. Once a month we did two eight-hour days on a Saturday and Sunday. I was an E-1, a seaman recruit, and in the beginning I was just scared of everybody, basically. We got some classroom work, and at a pier behind the center were a reserve destroyer and a submarine. We had a school-of-the-boat-type deal on board the *Guavina*. She had been a regular submarine, but after the war she was redesigned. She had additional tanks on the outside that carried aviation gasoline so she could refuel seaplanes at sea.

Those diesel boats had a particular smell, which later became very familiar to me. The *Guavina* was kind of cramped, but it wasn't as bad as it was in regular boats, because it was a school boat. It had been decommissioned, so it was gutted out and made into a training-type facility. The tubes were still there, but no torpedoes, just the compartments. The forward battery was basically still there, and the officers' quarters and stuff like this, but in the after battery they just had the galley and the head and the eating area. The berthing area was all open—no bunks. And the engine rooms were there and maneuvering and so forth.

The instructors were TARs, active-duty Reservists. They were qualified submarine sailors. They taught you some of the stuff on the boat because you didn't really have to go to the full Submarine School to go through the program. In the fall of 1963 a group of Reservists and I went through two weeks of Submarine School in New London, and later I went out two weeks on the *Sarda*. That qualified me as an SG, which was basically a submarine graduate. And it was equal to going through the Submarine School.

The only thing I missed at the time was going through the escape tank. I had to do that later on, and that was fun. I didn't know how to swim at the time and still don't. We used the Stenke hood rather than the old Momsen lung. I wore a life jacket with a Stenke hood attached over the top of it. It had a window in the front so I could see out. A group of us went into a compartment filled with water. As the water level came up, I tried to keep my head above water to keep from drowning because I'm short. I was treading water for a while, and finally it was my turn. I did as told—ducked down underneath the hatch and into the tall escape trunk. There were divers throughout the tank to pull someone over to the side if he had any trouble.

The idea was that the life jacket would provide the buoyancy to carry us up, and you had to exhale air from your lungs as you went up. If someone didn't, the divers would punch him in the stomach to make sure he did it. The instructors told us to extend our arms straight up and put our hands together. If there was any debris on the surface of the water in a real situation, your hands would push it out of the way. We did have a little entertainment as distraction while we were going up; there were pictures of mermaids painted on the inside of the tank. I developed some momentum as I went up, and when I finally broke the surface, about three-quarters of my body popped above it. The whole ascent took about twenty-five or thirty seconds at the most. The experience included real protection in terms of safety, and it gave you some peace of mind on your ability to get out if something happened to your submarine.

During my time in Submarine School I was planning to be an electronics technician because I had done well on the aptitude tests. But then it turned out I couldn't make the ET rating in submarines because both ETs and sonarmen stand the sonar watches, and the hearing test indicated that my ears weren't up to it. So instead of going right to a submarine, I was sent back to the Naval Reserve center in Baltimore. I talked to a yeoman who was connected with the *Guavina*, and as a result I applied for the basic A school for interior communications (IC) electrician at Great Lakes, Illinois. That started my two-year active duty obligation in May of 1964, and the school ran through October of that year.

After A school I had two weeks' leave and came home and got married to my girlfriend, Donna Ward. Since I was not yet a petty officer at that point, my pay—even with the dependent's allowance—was only a couple of hundred dollars a month. Donna and I couldn't afford to live together yet, so after the honeymoon she went back to live with my parents in Glen Burnie, near Baltimore, and I went back up to New London and reported to the *Piper*. I spent close to four years serving in that boat. I was only eighteen when I reported aboard, and there wasn't much I

Before the era of deep-submergence rescue vessels, a free ascent from a downed submarine required learning the breathing techniques. The escape tower at New London was a challenge for many a fledgling submariner. *Naval Institute Photo Archive*

could do on liberty, because I couldn't go out drinking in town. So I spent most of my off-duty time on the base.

When I was first on board I stood seaman watches—on the stern planes and bow planes and as a helmsman and lookout. The chief of the boat was Master Chief Torpedoman Joe Negri, who was of Italian descent. He was in charge when I helped take care of maintenance on the topside of the boat, including chipping paint. One night some of us were on watch in *Piper*'s control room, and people started telling ethnic jokes. The chief was getting frustrated; you could see him moving around. Finally he came out with a joke that said, "What's black and blue and rolls around on the deck?"

About five or six guys were standing the watch, and they looked at each other. "We don't know, Chief."

"The next one of you guys who tells a guinea joke." That shut us all up.

Negri was a very good chief—stern but good. And he was fair. He respected the guys, and the guys respected him. When he said something, we listened. He expected you to do your job, and as long as you did your job, he took care of you. He also took care of you when you didn't quite measure up.

When the submarine was in New London, I came home on weekends to see Donna. (Later, when the *Piper* was in a shipyard in Maine, she moved up there for a while until she got pregnant. But we just couldn't afford it, so she moved back with her parents. It was a tough way to start a marriage.) I came home to see Donna one holiday weekend, but I didn't realize there was a different train schedule on holidays. Normally the train came back and got into New London about six o'clock. The conductor would wake the guys up, because he knew where we were going. This particular train didn't get in until a few hours after the regular time. When I got to the submarine base, I hustled down the pier, and there was Chief Negri. He saw me and said, "You're late, ain't you?"

"Yep."

"It looks like you owe me some time, don't you?"

"Yeah, chief, how much?"

"How about a few hours in the bilges tonight?"

"Okay, no problem." It was clear that I had made a mistake, and both the chief and I knew it. Chief Negri knew that it wasn't on purpose, but he wanted to remind me what the rules were without my getting sent to captain's mast and getting something in my official record. So I spent about three or four hours in the bilges, which were spaces down below decks, cleaning up the water and spilled diesel fuel, and that was it.

The big emphasis once I got aboard was to get qualified as a submariner and earn my dolphins. That meant learning practically everything there was to know about the submarine. I tried to learn one system a week and get checked off by petty officers. Included were such items as compartmentation, air systems, trim and drain systems, electrical systems, main power, communications systems, vents, main ballast tanks, doors on the special safety tanks, and the communications gear that was in each compartment. The various hydraulic systems were probably the most complicated. They really drilled things into me so I would learn the boat, but it still took a long time. For one thing, I had to spend some time mess cooking. Then, in 1965, the *Piper* went to the Portsmouth Naval Shipyard in Maine, for about six or seven months. I wasn't able to qualify on some systems because they were torn out. It was

supposed to take only eight or nine months to qualify, but it took me about fifteen, even though I was never behind.

I qualified in submarines on the *Piper* in January of 1966. I drank my dolphins from the bottom of a pitcher of beer in Guantánamo Bay, Cuba. What a great feeling it was to put those on my uniform; it was like living in a different world. After that, for example, I was able to sit with the crew and watch the movies that were shown at night in the after battery room. Before that, sometimes they'd let me watch if I was a couple of weeks ahead of schedule, but most of the time they wouldn't let me in there. It was a big relief when I got qualified. There was a sense of belonging. It was the culmination of a lot of hard work. After you qualified, people seemed to trust you more. In May of 1966 I enlisted for six years in the regular Navy—no longer a Reservist.

During my time on board, the *Piper* operated in the Caribbean several times on Springboard exercises, but the main job was being a training boat for officers in the Submarine School at New London. Being a school boat, we were up and down like a porpoise. The *Piper* had over thirteen thousand dives during her career, and that included close to three thousand in my time in the crew. When we went out on the training periods the instructors from Submarine School would go out with the students. The idea was to get the boat in trim fore and aft so that it would maintain a one-degree down bubble, basically inert. As part of the training the instructor would have about ten or fifteen crew members go forward in the boat, and all of a sudden it got heavy. To compensate the student would have to pump water from the forward trim tank to the after trim tank. As soon as people heard that, then they would move aft. The instructor wanted to see how the officer handled the situation. We called it a "trim party."

In 1967 the *Piper* was supposed to go on a north Atlantic run. In about February or March of that year they did a test discharge of the battery while tied to the pier with steel cables fore and aft. The idea was to run on the battery at the six-hour rate to see how long it would last. Every submarine had to do that every once in a while. The boat had had battery problems, which was one reason for the test. They wanted to make sure the battery was good enough to go up to the North Atlantic, because it was necessary to stay submerged while patrolling on the lookout for Soviet submarines. The battery crapped out after about three hours. There was a plan to put her in for a battery job, but the decision was made to decommission her instead. She was sent to the shipyard at Portsmouth, Virginia, to be inactivated.

She was officially put out in the middle of June and later went to Detroit to be a floating classroom, as the *Guavina* had been for me in Baltimore. A couple of the former skippers came to Portsmouth for the *Piper*'s decommissioning. One of them was retired captain Ned Beach, author of *Run Silent, Run Deep*. I had read the book and seen the movie, so I enjoyed meeting him. He was friendly, and I enjoyed going through the boat with him as he told me what he remembered from being skipper in World War II. Captain Beach told me that the normal complement of torpedoes was twenty-four—ten in the tubes and fourteen in the racks. But in the last war patrol in 1945 he was carrying a few extras strapped down on the deck in the torpedo rooms. He was one of the last ones to come off war patrol in 1945.

I had the honor of standing the last below-decks security watch in the *Piper* as she was decommissioned. I was kind of disappointed not to be topside, but I had to do my part. After that I joined the IC gang in the *Clamagore*, which was in better condition. We went on the sort of North Atlantic patrols like the one the *Piper* was scheduled for but couldn't make. We also operated in the Mediterranean with the Sixth Fleet.

By this time I was old enough to go ashore and have a drink. I developed a number of good friends on board the *Clamagore*. There were guys that I would go on liberty with. A bunch of us would get drunk; that was the main thing at the time. That was the older Navy, different than it is now. I remember one time when we went ashore in Palma, Mallorca, probably in 1967. One of the electrician's mates was a third class petty officer. He was a real small guy, and his nickname was

"Twiggy," which is what they called one skinny British fashion model back then. We had a lot of nicknames for guys. Our Twiggy probably weighed about 110 pounds soaking wet, and he was short.

Electricians used to get an extra allotment of dungarees because they used to go into the battery wells to water batteries, and acid would make holes in the dungarees. The electricians got about three sets of dungarees a quarter. As I remember, the smallest size dungarees available had a twenty-eight-inch waist, and Twiggy had to have them cut down so they'd fit. That's how small he was. He qualified for his dolphins about the time the boat went into Palma. Just as I had in Guantánamo, it was time for him to drink his dolphins. We went into one bar, and someone passed the hat to pay for Twiggy's drink. Everybody chipped in a buck or two. Someone got a martini shaker that was probably about fifteen or twenty ounces in capacity. People were pouring in a shot of this and a shot of that, and then someone dropped the dolphins in and gave the shaker to Twiggy. He drank it straight down. We couldn't believe it, because most guys couldn't get it down. When he got to the bottom, he pulled out the dolphins with his teeth the way he was supposed to. Then he said, "That was good; I'd like to have another one."

Someone said, "We can't afford another one." Then we hung around in the bar for another twenty minutes or half an hour. Twiggy started getting a little woozy, so a couple of guys decided they'd better get him out of there. We took him for a walk; our mistake was that we walked him away from the boat. He got only about three or four blocks before he started getting sick. He got sick all over himself and partly on the guys helping him. It was tough trying to hold up a 110-pound guy with rubber legs. We finally got a taxi and took him to the pier. There was a destroyer next to the pier, and we managed to get him across to the *Clamagore* on a stretcher. The regular hatch wasn't big enough, so we got permission from the officer of the deck to open up the torpedo room hatch and lower him through it to get him below. Our corpsman and our skipper checked to make sure he was okay. Twiggy was put to bed, and they got the guy standing torpedo room watch keep an eye on him all night. That's probably the closest I've ever seen anybody come to alcohol poisoning, but he was okay the next day.

One time when the *Clamagore* went to the Med I took seventeen pairs of dungarees and stored them under my mattress. Each bunk had about a three- or four-inch foam pad as a mattress and a sheet over the top of it. There was also a sort of vinyl cover that was put on to keep the bedding dry. I did laundry only twice while we were in the Med for a four-month period. When we'd go into port, I'd stuff my clothes into a laundry bag with my name on it, and the cleaners would take the stuff and bring it back clean a couple of days later. The uniforms were pretty ripe by that time. We wore them more than a couple of days. Everything smelled so bad; diesel fuel got into everything, so you smelled like diesel fuel. Showers were normally available only for the cooks and mess cooks when the boat was at sea. You could wash up, but that was about it.

In the Med the *Clamagore* operated as part of the Sixth Fleet. A lot of the time was spent being a target for antisubmarine warfare ships. We did that in the Atlantic also, playing with the P-3 Orions out of Brunswick, Maine. The planes would drop sonobuoys into the water and try to find the submarine. We also worked with destroyers out of Newport. One time on the underwater telephone came a message, "War shot in the water." The destroyer accidentally fired a war shot at the *Clamagore*, instead of one that was designed to miss deliberately. It hit the submarine three times and put some dents in the hull. We heard that the destroyer skipper got in trouble.

In 1968 the boat had to go above the Arctic Circle to listen for Russian submarines. A Soviet boat would come out of the Med and would be passed off to the *Clamagore* for tracking. The idea was to get sound signatures from different types of boats and to keep track of where they were. We spent about forty-seven days underwater during that patrol. We snorkeled seven, eight, ten times a day, a little at a time to charge the batter-

ies. At the end of one patrol in 1968 the *Clamagore* went into Portsmouth, England, and was pretty low on food, fuel, and so forth. This was about the time that the nuclear submarine *Scorpion* was reported missing in the Atlantic. There was an effort to get our boat under way to look for her, but the captain said she needed three or four days to reload food and fuel and water. We never did go look for her.

Eventually, after having started out as a mess cook in the *Piper*, I made petty officer first class in 1969. I was pleased to sew the rating badge on my jumper and pleased also with the increase in pay, especially since I had a family. I became the leading IC electrician on the *Clamagore*, and we continued to have a lot of interesting operations, including the overseas deployments.

In the late summer of 1970 the *Clamagore* headed for another trip to the Mediterranean. Our itinerary was pretty well mapped out. We were due to pull into Rota, Spain, to take on stores and fuel, and then to Crete to hook up with the rest of the task force we would be with in the Med. The boat picked up six or seven chiefs who were supposed to go to Naples. They had to ride a submarine a certain amount of time to collect their submarine pay. The chiefs came aboard in Rota, and then the *Clamagore* went to Malta to drop off all but one of the chiefs. He still needed to get more time, so he figured he'd ride the boat over to Crete.

While we were en route from Malta to Crete in early September, a bunch of Palestinian commandos hijacked some airplanes and blew them up in the desert in Jordan. The U.S. Navy responded with an increased number of ships in the Eastern Med. This involved the *Clamagore*, but a lot of us in the crew didn't know what was going on. The officers knew, but they didn't tell us. All of a sudden, we got orders to go to the Suez Canal and to make torpedoes ready for war. We didn't know what the hell was going on. The boat carried some exercise torpedoes and a Bravo load of war shots—maybe six or eight. They were armed and ready to go and loaded in the tubes. So we patrolled off the north entrance to the Suez Canal, waiting for anything to come out.

We were submerged for a long time, probably two to three weeks, snorkeling at night. We couldn't leave until we were relieved by a nuclear submarine that had to get under way from New London and come over to the Med.

While all this was happening, our wives knew where the submarine was supposed to go, but they didn't know where we really were. And that was tough, because we couldn't send or receive mail except when we pulled into port. Donna was writing letters to me all this time, and I finally got a bunch from her when the boat arrived in Naples after we were relieved out by Suez. She numbered her letters. I started by reading the last one or two and was glad to find that everything was okay. Then I started reading them in sequence from the beginning. After a couple of them, they started getting unpleasant. She complained that I wasn't writing, and she wondered what in the world I might be doing. She was really mad.

Unfortunately, no one had told the wives what was going on. The women were all in the same boat. Finally, after about three weeks, the cap-

tain's wife got the women together and explained what was going on, that the submarine was on some special operations. I called Donna when we got to Naples, even though it was difficult and expensive. You had to go to a special phone exchange in Naples to place an overseas phone call. She was glad to hear from me when I finally got through.

My four years in the *Clamagore* came to an end in September 1971. I got my first shore duty when I reported to the Naval Photographic Center in Anacostia, just across the river from Washington, D.C. At that time I expected to do two years of shore duty and then report to another submarine, because by then I was a career Navy man. But things don't always work out the way you plan. When it came time to leave, we had some illness in the family, and it just wouldn't have worked to be away on sea duty for extended periods. So I left active duty then but took with me a lot of memories of the boats and my shipmates.

57

Last of the B-Girls

MASTER CHIEF MACHINIST'S
MATE CHARLES E. WORMWOOD
III, USN (RET.)

The U.S. Navy's last class of diesel-powered attack submarines were nicknamed the "B-Girls." They were the *Barbel*, *Blueback*, and *Bonefish*—all commissioned in 1959. As it happened, the *Blueback*, which joined the fleet in October of that year, was the last to be commissioned, and she was also the last to be decommissioned, which happened on 1 October 1990. She thus had the distinction of being the final full-fledged diesel-electric attack submarine to serve on active duty in the Navy. In the closing years of the submarine's career, Wormwood was her chief of the boat, the crew member who was the chain-of-command link between the top officers and the rest of the enlisted crewmen. Before he reported to the *Blueback*, Wormwood served in nuclear submarines, beginning as an engineman and later converting to become a machinist's mate.

THE USS *Will Rogers* (SSBN-659) was my first boat, the last of the "Forty-one for Freedom" missile submarines. I kind of stepped backward from there. I went to the USS *Permit* (SSN-594), and that's where I really got my maintenance wings wet. I never worked so hard at being an A-ganger in my life. Because we had the auxiliary diesels there, I got highly trained on the Fairbanks-Morse engines. I got selected for fleet diesel inspector and went to Submarine Squadron Three; all the boats in the squadron were in the 594 class.

I filled in for the squadron command master chief a few times, so when the opportunity came up for the *Blueback*, I jumped on it. I had not served in any diesel boats before her, but when I was the diesel inspector my sea daddies were all

diesel-boat sailors, and they had told me stories and showed me the ropes as they were grooming me. So I had some good information going in; I didn't walk in completely blind. This was something I always wanted, and, boy, I loved it. It was just a natural place for me to go. I had about two years on board before she was decommissioned.

We had great camaraderie in that crew. They'd kill each other in a heartbeat, but nobody else better touch them. My welcome aboard came when I hadn't even stepped on the boat yet. I was invited to a function at the chief engineman's house. I'll never forget, there was a little second class electrician's mate there. He caught me off guard, and he picked me up and threw me through a closet door as a little bit of hazing for a nuke sailor. That was my initiation. When I did get to the *Blueback* herself, for a little while I was the new guy, walking around on eggshells. They were doing a double take on me, because I hadn't been on a diesel boat before, but it didn't take me long to win them over. We developed a mutual respect that I'll never forget.

As chief of the boat I was the commanding officer's liaison with the crew. I was the senior enlisted advisor, battle stations diving officer, watch bill coordinator for the enlisted, first lieutenant—kind of a jack of a lot of things. The skipper and I got the job done. We took care of business, took care of the troops. When I got on there, the biggest problem I saw in the crew had to do with captain's masts, the punishments for various offenses. I thought that things should be handled at a lower level. I didn't think everything should be in front of the captain. My view was that the chiefs were supposed to take care of things on their own. I made it a point of making that happen. We went from two or three masts a week to maybe one a month or every other month. I was raised by dinosaurs, I guess, but we took care of stuff on the deck plates.

Before I came, the *Blueback* had bounced through a couple of COBs (chiefs of the boat) in rapid succession. There was no consistency, so I tried to provide that. I won over the crew because I held my ground with the wardroom. The chiefs were back out on the deck doing what they needed to do, supporting the crew and getting the job done. When things were supposed to be done and didn't get done, there was hell to pay. By the same token, I stood up for them with the wardroom when that was necessary. I was straight up with them, and I wasn't afraid to get down and get dirty with them either.

We didn't have very many nonrated men in the crew, because there was such an abundance of diesel-boat sailors and so few diesel boats to go to, so most everybody on board was a petty officer. I only had a handful of nonrates, really. About 90 percent of the enlisted were already qualified submariners by the time they reached the boat.

We used to do a lot of stuff together—football, baseball, basketball. Crew parties were the norm. There wasn't a lot of room for recreation on the old B-girls, so recreation under way involved tormenting each other. One of the tricks was to run fore and aft to torment the diving officer while he was trying to hover the boat at periscope depth. They used to have trim parties quite often, more than we did on a nuclear boat. You could get a trim party going in a heartbeat. We'd wait for the diving officer to start pumping, and then run back to the other end. We had a lot of cribbage players. I learned bridge, which I had never played before in my life. We had spades and hearts and pinochle—a lot of pinochle players, good ones. Acey-deucy was popular. We had movies, of course. The chow was excellent. We were very, very fortunate. We had a first class cook. That guy believed in his job, and he could take an old sock and make it taste like roast beef.

Besides working with the crew, another part of the appeal for me in that boat came from those three screaming Fairbanks-Morse engines. In this job I had nothing to do with nuclear power. The requirements for nuclear power are pretty stringent and so are the inspections that go with it and the work and the maintenance to keep up with the standards. A diesel boat had high standards, but things were still not as hard as on a nuke boat. You didn't dive as deep, you didn't have as many certifications to jump

through. Most of the guys on the diesel boat took care of their own stuff, whereas on a nuke boat you had to get a lot of outside "assistance." So a diesel boat, you really felt like it was yours; you were a lot more independent.

The *Blueback* was a sweet boat on operations. Just before I came aboard she did a war op with either the *New Jersey* or the *Missouri*. My shipmates told me that our CO did the old diversion maneuver, where he strung fishing boat lights on the sail, and he had the decks awash, running on one diesel. They said he was able to sneak in close and hit her with torpedoes. I remember hearing that the CO of the battleship was very upset about that.

A regular event for the boat during my time on board was providing ASW services for surface ships on a weekly-type basis. On a diesel boat it was so darn quiet when you were down there that we really had the advantage at the time. So it was pretty good training for the destroyers—if they could find us, which they rarely did. Usually we had to make some kind of noise. She was already a very old boat when I got to her, but there was still some life in the old girl.

She was a good boat—tired but good. We still had teak decking that the crew had covered with nonskid paint for whatever reason. So we made it a regular upkeep thing to strip a portion of the deck back to the teak and paint it with a flat black paint like it was supposed to be. I was very proud of those deck planks when I saw them. I couldn't believe they had them all covered up. I made it a point to get them uncovered and back in the condition they should have been.

We had some fun when we were recruited into the filming of *The Hunt for Red October*. The producers picked the *Blueback* because we were the only boat with six torpedo tubes. So they filmed all the Russian torpedo scenes on our boat. They used our torpedomen, who all got paid a pittance to get their hair cut short and learn Russian songs. The movie people did a couple of days filming them in Russian uniforms while they were topside loading torpedoes on and off the boat. They also took some action shots of people running down the passageway into the torpedo

In this overhead view of the *Blueback* the boat's teakwood decking is visible fore and aft of the sail; the wooden deck was a throwback to diesel submarines of an earlier time. *Naval Institute Photo Archive; Ingalls Shipbuilding*

room. I wish they had used more of those scenes in the movie or director's cut or something. But all the Russian torpedo-firing sequences in the movie were actual torpedomen off the *Blueback* in our torpedo room. The weapons officer on the *Houston*, which played the nuclear submarine *Dallas* in the movie, was actually our weapons officer off the *Blueback*.

My old boat, the *Permit*, was the one they filmed in dry dock at the beginning of the movie, so two of my boats were in the movie. I'm kind of proud of that. They did things right in that show. Sean Connery was a pretty good guy. He did a lot of research. They worked a lot with the chief of the boat on the *Houston* to get him away from some of the Hollywood touches and make him more realistic, which I thought was good. They put a lot of work into that movie on the military side, getting the facts right. And they did a stand-up job of sending us personalized invitations to the premiere in San Diego. I thought that was outstanding. They invited just about the whole submarine community in San Diego, where we were based. Anybody that had anything to do with the movie sat in the front, from the CO on down to the crew. We filled the theater to the max.

Maybe it was because of the *Blueback*'s age, but we probably spent more time in port than at sea. By the time I arrived, she had already made her last deployment to the western Pacific. So we spent our time on the West Coast. In Alaska we did some testing, but mainly it was a port visit. We had to be up that way anyway, so the CO managed to finagle a port call for us. We were the first submarine to hit Juneau, Alaska, in many, many years. We went in there among the cruise ships and just had a heck of a good time. During our travels we were a regular at the Portland Rose Festival. That's why Portland fought so hard to get the *Blueback* down there after she was eventually decommissioned.

She caught the summer SeaFair in Seattle. In Seattle one time we had the Disney characters on board. I think Donald Duck and Goofy were topside. Somebody brought them out in a small boat and transferred them over on top of us, and they rode us in. It was a bit strange, because Green Peace was there at the same time, trying to protest us carrying nuclear materials. We kept yelling at them, "We're a diesel boat. We don't have anything nuclear on board." And, on top of that, we had the Disney characters, for crying out loud. We used to tie up at Pier 70 there in Seattle; they always treated us well.

In keeping the boat going, spare parts were not a problem after the *Bonefish* incident. She had a fire in her battery compartment in April 1988, and there was so much damage that she had to be decommissioned. Her hull was still available for most exterior and main component parts. So we pretty much got whatever we needed from her and, later, the *Barbel*. The enginemen we had on board were just outstanding. Most of them had been on board all three of the B-girls. They had so much experience and "McGyverism" that they could keep anything going. They could make it work. God bless them, they were good at it.

For instance, we lost our bat wings. On top of the snorkel mast there was a set of flaps that dropped down when you raised the mast. Their purpose was to keep the diesel exhaust from coming back in the intake. We had a problem snorkeling there for a while because the diesel exhaust would come back into the boat, and that wasn't at all pleasant. So we had to get the bat wings off one of the boats that was already decommissioned.

Actually, because of my role as chief of the boat, I didn't do too much hands-on work when I was on *Blueback*. I served in a couple of technical meetings and stuff, especially when we had a generator flooding incident up around San Clemente, California. That was during our last underway period. I remember the personnel transfer of the squadron group that came up to check us out when we had that generator problem. We were in a terrible, terrible storm. They must have sent out about every expert they could find from the squadron staff on a torpedo retriever. I can remember that the biggest enlisted guy we had on board was a second class sonarman. He and I tied ourselves topside, to the deck runner up there. We had to time the personnel transfer to

Now that she is retired, the *Blueback* is open for visitors at the Oregon Museum of Science and Industry in Portland.
Courtesy Oregon Museum of Science and Industry

when the two keels were even, and we just kind of grabbed people off the bow of the torpedo retriever and threw them on deck and then shuffled them down the hatch. They immediately went to berthing, because they were all so seasick they couldn't do anything for about six hours.

We had to be towed back to San Diego. That casualty was definitely the contributing factor in her being decommissioned. We were in a testing program that should have kept us on line for probably another year or so. We were testing different communications devices and various pieces of equipment. As it turned out, we had the ability to finish most of that in port.

At the decommissioning ceremony for the *Blueback* a huge crowd attended—a lot of old salts, a lot of tears, a lot of speeches. Unfortunately, I couldn't stand up with the crew at the decommissioning because I had been in a khaki-

versus-blue shirt basketball game and they took my knee out. So Senior Chief Roy Booth took my place at the ceremony. That was kind of upsetting, because I really wanted to be there. I was in the audience. I've never seen so much hoopla for a boat. I saw a lot of decommissionings in San Diego, and that had to be one of the biggest. There were more flags and admirals and retired people than I had seen in years. It was a pretty big event.

Following her decommissioning she sat there in San Diego for quite some time afterward. Some of the crew that was attached to the squadron used to go down and check on her, look in the bilges and stuff like that. She was eventually towed up to the Puget Sound Naval Shipyard in Bremerton, Washington. I remember when they brought her up they didn't get one of the hatches battened down right, so she suffered some leakage and flooded a little bit. I was stationed there at the shipyard when she arrived, so I was there to meet her. She got some minor cosmetic work there at the yard to be ready for mothballing.

In May of 1994 the *Blueback* opened up for visitors down at Portland OMSI—the Oregon Museum of Science and Industry. When I finally left the Navy that same year, my retirement party in July lasted for about a week. It started in Bremerton, near where I live, and there were two vans of us, because a lot of my buddies from the *Blueback* came with me. A bunch of us just jumped in the vans and went on a road trip. We wound up down in Portland visiting the old girl, and then we went and bought ourselves some live crabs for the return trip to Bremerton. We had a good time during that week; I had a lot of good shipmates on there.

When I hear, see, or say the letters DBF, they always bring a swelling of pride and a flood of memories to me. The new submariners scoff, laugh, or ask, "Where are they now?" But DBF means more to me than "Diesel boats forever." To me it is the essence of pride, camaraderie, honor, and tradition—and one of the best families I ever had the privilege to be a small part of.

58
End of an Era

CDR. ANDREW WILDE, USN

Just over a century after President Teddy Roosevelt took his ride on board the gasoline-fueled, 149-ton *Plunger*, the Navy operated its last diesel-electric submarine. Submariners wear dolphin insignia when they qualify in their craft, so perhaps it is fitting that the last diesel boat in commission bore the name *Dolphin*. A decade and a half after the final diesel attack submarines were decommissioned, the *Dolphin* remained in service as a test platform for new equipment. She left the active roster on 22 September 2006. In her final months of duty, the boat's commanding officer described his submarine and her crew.

IT'S BEEN QUITE A WHILE since the Navy had a separate career path for diesel submariners, so those of us in the crew of the *Dolphin* have all gotten our experience in nuclear submarines, both the attack types and the Tridents. I got to be skipper the same way one gets to any submarine. After I got an engineering degree in college, I went through six months of nuclear engineering training, six months at a prototype, Submarine School, and then a series of nuclear-powered ships.

As I became more senior, I was executive officer of the USS *Maine*, an SSBN, and then was deputy commander of Submarine Squadron Eleven, and this opportunity for command opened up when I was ready to transfer. I was fortunate to be picked for the *Dolphin*. First and foremost, it was the chance to command a submarine at sea. And I liked the unique aspect that it was a research and development submarine and deep-submergence vehicle. It does a lot of science and technology missions that really appealed to me.

The enlisted crew is made up of regular submarine ratings, including some nuclear-qualified electrician's mates, only because we don't have conventional electrician's mates in the Submarine Force. Everyone else is in a submarine rating. We have yeomen, sonarmen, auxiliarymen, quartermasters, radiomen, and nonnuclear machinist's mates. We don't have any torpedomen or fire controlmen, because the boat doesn't have any weapon systems at all. The *Dolphin* is a niche submarine in terms of its mission, but the crew is mainstream in terms of their assignments. There's no diesel-specific training required to run the equipment on board. The machinist's mates operate the Detroit diesel engines, which are reasonably similar to the Fairbanks-Morse auxiliary diesels in nuclear submarines. The *Dolphin* is smaller, so we have just a couple of four hundred-horsepower diesels, similar to bus engines.

We do get a few enlisted men who are not already qualified in submarines, but the crew is top-heavy because we don't have many officers. The executive officer and I are the only two line officers, and then I have two limited duty officers in engineering and supply. We have a higher proportion of chief petty officers, senior chiefs, and master chiefs than in almost any crew since we have only fifty-two men altogether. The chiefs are basically fulfilling officers' roles. If you believe that chiefs run the Navy, that's especially true on board the *Dolphin*, because the chiefs really do run my boat. And there is a lot of camaraderie among the crew, since we do missions that a lot of other submarines don't.

The *Dolphin* rolls to port as a tugboat pulls her away from a pier in her homeport at Point Loma, San Diego. *Courtesy USS Dolphin*

The chief of the boat, my liaison with the enlisted crew, is Joe Eller. His rating is missile technician, and he has spent his career in *Trident*-class nuclear-powered missile submarines. He's a larger-than-life character, and now he is somehow cramming himself into the *Dolphin*, which doesn't even have torpedoes anymore. With his personality, he has trouble fitting into the boat sometimes. He is a great guy, very energetic. He is the classic chief of the boat. When I was going up through the ranks, I thought of what I might someday want in a COB, and I was really lucky in getting him. He is always out with the crew, talking with guys, keeping them pointed in the right direction, and making sure he knows what the men's concerns are, especially when rumors are flying. He is truly a heartfelt advocate for the crew.

We're based in San Diego, and typically we go out to the science and technology community and just look for things to do. We have both research and tactical applications. For instance, we have oceanographic work for the University of Texas Applied Physics Lab. One of our base missions on the tactical side is to act as a target for the newest air-dropped lightweight torpedo. For the operational evaluation of the Mark 54 torpedo, the Navy needed a bottom submarine. The boat has been fitted with equipment so we can actually anchor on the bottom of the ocean. That requires some training, because it's certainly not a trivial evolution. The *Dolphin* has the capability to go deeper than three thousand feet and has done so

on a number of occasions, but we don't do that anymore. The latest equipment on board is so sensitive that it can't go below one thousand feet.

The submarine really has a juxtaposition of the very old and the very new. We have the same main-frame sonar that was on the "Forty-one for Freedom" ballistic missile submarines that were commissioned in the 1960s. Ours is the last one in existence in the Navy. It sits right next to our obstacle-avoidance sonar, a very advanced bottom-mapping sonar, which benefits us tremendously in doing our bottom-mooring mission, because you want a very good view of what's on the bottom. We test and evaluate new equipment for the entire submarine fleet, such things as towed-array sonars and a floating-wire antenna for communicating with Trident submarines. The *Dolphin* had the first e-mail that submarines ever used at sea, and now submarines use that as a matter of course.

The great thing about the *Dolphin* is that because we don't have any set deployment cycle, we can do modifications to the boat relatively inexpensively and without interrupting an operating schedule. Our operational tempo is perhaps 30 percent at sea and 70 percent in port because we spend a lot of time getting modified to do our special missions. Typically we go out for a week at a time. We have forty-five bunks, so with a crew of fifty-two we sometimes have to hot-bunk, that is, have men using the same bunk in shifts. Other times we leave a few of the crew behind when we go to sea to make room for the visiting scientists we often have on board.

There are no staterooms on board. Our wardroom is basically a small office with three bunks in it. I get the middle bunk, the exec gets the lower bunk, and the engineer gets the top one. We have one table that seats six in the crew's mess. That's where all of us eat. It's a challenge to fit in for meals, especially when we're operating and with such limited space. My motto when I first came aboard was that the troops eat first; I borrowed that from the Marine Corps. The chow line forms, and as soon as one guy is done, another one moves in and takes his seat. I tell the officers that as soon as the troops have finished, they can sit down and eat too. After everyone else is done, the exec, chief of the boat, and I sit down for a meal.

We used to have a rating in the Navy called "mess management specialist." Now it's called "culinary specialist," so the food tastes better. The Navy has gone to a prime vendor concept, so now a submarine will order food from the same contractors that restaurants order from. Our mess is so small that we just order through a local food chain in San Diego. So our guys go online with a computer, pick out what they want, and once a week a truck comes down and drops off our food. We have the best food in the Navy, and particularly in the Submarine Force. I've been told that by many people.

The *Dolphin* is like any other submarine, only smaller—nine hundred tons, 165 feet long, 18 feet in the beam. At that size, if one guy goes from forward to aft, it changes the boat's angle by two degrees. When you're just walking around inside,

Machinist's mates Josh Alkire and Justin Newsome work on an air manifold in the upper level of the boat's engine room. *Courtesy USS Dolphin*

Culinary Specialists Dwayne Larkee and Seth Target prepare lunch for the crew in the submarine's compact galley. *Courtesy USS Dolphin*

the spaces are the same size you would experience on any submarine; it's just that there are fewer of them. You walk forty feet, and you're at the bow; and you walk back another hundred feet, and you're at the stern. It's not really cramped inside per se, although the crew members do get a lot less personal space than in a fleet submarine.

I spend most of the underway time on the bridge, because we're on the surface most of the time, and I love it up there. For normal operations we can go about eight hours submerged, and if we really stretch it we could probably spend up to twelve hours underwater. Our batteries are state of the art, completely sealed units.

Still, our boat is thirty-eight years old, which by any measure makes it late in life. We have a lot of old direct-current electric motors, which frequently will have some level of commutator arcing. Our main motor has two squirrel-case cooling fans inside. Soon after I took command, we got down to two thousand feet—this was before we had the new equipment installed. We had about two and a half hours left on the battery and were going about a knot and a half. One of those blower motors started arcing very badly, and I thought, "Boy, this is a really interesting situation that they didn't train me about in prospective commanding officers' school." I love my diesel-electric submarine, but I sure miss the horsepower that the nuclear reactor provided in my previous experience. We weighed getting

up there fast versus running the battery out. Being concerned about battery endurance was old hat to World War II submariners but new to me. Fortunately, we were able to make it to the surface without a fire starting. It took about twenty minutes—a pretty long twenty minutes.

One of the things I've worked on is getting the crew together following a long overhaul the *Dolphin* went through. She had to be repaired after a serious flooding casualty. The only way to get inside the submarine is through a watertight door in the sail, and that leads to a hatch down into the boat herself. Back in 2002, because of some design flaws, that door came open while the *Dolphin* was at sea. Water got in through the door and down the hatch, which is inside the sail, and filled up the pump room. She got in trouble very quickly but didn't sink. The valves needed to dewater the boat were in the area that was flooded. CPO John D. Wise Jr. received a Navy and Marine Corps Medal for his heroics, because he dunked down into fifty-five-degree water, in the dark, to operate valves that got the water out and saved her. Afterward it took years to fix her up, and the result is that the boat is now probably in better material condition and more seaworthy than at any time since she was built.

But another result of that long shipyard period was that we had a crew that hadn't spent much time with each other. One of the things I'm working really hard on is getting submarine traditions instilled back in the boat—things like playing cribbage after meals and all those things we've taken for granted as submariners through our careers. When I got on board and found we weren't playing cribbage, I almost had a heart attack. It's challenge because there is only one table in the mess, and guys are generally trying to sleep when they're not on watch.

Part of that emphasis on crew unity goes back to when I was on the staff of commander, Submarine Squadron Eleven. I got to go to San Francisco to speak at a Memorial Day ceremony for the old *Pampanito*, a World War II boat. I had heard the submarine stories and read some books, but I really hadn't closely connected with the most important part—the people associated with our diesel submarines. For the past couple of years I've really had a chance to connect personally with the veterans from that submarine in par-

ticular, because I've been there several times. So I was even that much more excited when I got orders to come to the *Dolphin*.

As much as I've enjoyed this command, the end is in sight for our boat. She is on the block for decommissioning because she is almost forty years old. I'm personally disappointed that the Navy didn't decide to keep the *Dolphin* around even longer, but I realize that the Navy is making a lot of very difficult fiscal decisions. One of my priorities as we move forward is that when we have a decommissioning ceremony for the USS *Dolphin*, the Navy's last diesel-electric submarine, by golly, it's going to be a party worthy of her rich diesel submarine heritage. On the one hand, it is an honor to be the last skipper, but it's also sad at the same time, because she is the end of a long, long line.

Sources of Chapters

"Parks and the *Pompano*" is taken from Naval Institute oral history interviews of Captain Cutter, conducted on 30 November and 1 December 1982 by Paul Stillwell. An article similar to this chapter appeared in the premier issue of *Naval History*, 1987, 72–76.

"The President Takes a Plunge" is taken from Roosevelt's letter of 28 August 1905 to Secretary of the Navy Bonaparte. The material is reprinted by permission of the publisher from *The Letters of Theodore Roosevelt*, vol. 4, *The Square Deal, 1901–1905*, ed. Elting E. Morison (Cambridge: Harvard University Press), 1324–25. Copyright © 1951 by the President and Fellows of Harvard College.

"World War I" is taken from oral history interviews of Admiral Foster, conducted on 15 February and 23 March 1966 by John T. Mason Jr. The material appears in the "Reminiscences of Paul F. Foster," 107–53, in the Columbia University Oral History Research Office Collection.

"Submarine School" is taken from Naval Institute oral history interviews of Admiral Murray, conducted on 3 May and 13 June 1970 by Etta-Belle Kitchen.

"Beginning of the S-Boats" is taken from a Naval Institute oral history interview of Admiral Dyer, conducted 29 April 1969 by John T. Mason Jr.

"Building the Submarine Base at Pearl Harbor" is taken from a Naval Institute oral history interview of Admiral Murray, conducted on 13 June 1970 by Etta-Belle Kitchen.

"Early Command" is taken from Naval Institute oral history interviews of Admiral Bauernschmidt, conducted 20 August and 16 September 1969 by John T. Mason Jr.

"Loss of the *S-51* and *S-4*" is taken from a Naval Institute oral history interview of Admiral Dennison, conducted 8 November 1972 by John T. Mason Jr.

"Far East Duty" is taken from a Naval Institute oral history interview of Admiral Eller, conducted 15 June 1973 by John T. Mason Jr.

"R-Boat Service" is taken from a Naval Institute oral history interview of Admiral Walker, conducted 11 September 1984 by Paul Stillwell.

"Oddball S-Boat" is taken from a Naval Institute oral history interview of Admiral Irvin, conducted 11 August 1978 by John T. Mason Jr.

"Developing the Fleet Boats" is taken from a Naval Institute oral history interview of Admiral Murray, conducted on 15 August 1970 by Etta-Belle Kitchen.

"Submarine Tender" is taken from a Naval Institute oral history interview of Admiral Bauernschmidt, conducted 16 September 1969 by John T. Mason Jr.

"Submarine Detailing" is taken from a Naval Institute oral history interview of Admiral Davidson, conducted 28 August 1985 by Paul Stillwell.

"Developing the Torpedo Data Computer" is taken from a Naval Institute oral history interview of Admiral Walker, conducted 11 September 1984 by Paul Stillwell.

"The *Squalus* Rescue" is taken from a Naval Institute oral history interview of Chief Badders, conducted 22 September 1971 by John T. Mason Jr.

"Encounters with Corpses" is taken from a Naval Institute oral history interview of Admiral Curtze, conducted 1 June 2000 by Paul Stillwell.

"Another View on the *Squalus*" is taken from a Naval Institute oral history interview of Captain Evans, conducted 15 May 1989 by Paul Stillwell.

"Grandstand Seat at Pearl Harbor" is taken from a Naval Institute oral history interview of Admiral Ramage, conducted 27 August 1973 by John T. Mason Jr. A similar version appeared in *Air Raid Pearl Harbor! Recollections of a Day of Infamy* (Annapolis: Naval Institute Press, 1981).

"Disaster at Cavite" is taken from a Naval Institute oral history interview of Admiral Ward, conducted 10 September 1986 by Paul Stillwell.

"Escape from the Japanese" is taken from a Naval Institute oral history interview of Chief Ship's Clerk King, conducted 4 August 1986 by Paul Stillwell.

"Reservists at Submarine School" is taken from a Naval Institute oral history interview of Admiral Wilkinson, conducted 17 January 1998 by Paul Stillwell.

"*Drum* at War" is taken from an oral history interview of Admiral Rindskopf, conducted on 11 November 1999 by Dan Struble, and from an earlier unpublished memoir written by Admiral Rindskopf. Both are available from the Naval Historical Foundation, Washington, D.C.

"Breakers Ahead!" is taken from an article by Captain Beach in *Naval History*, April 1999, 42–44. That article is an excerpt from Beach's memoir *Salt and Steel* (Annapolis: Naval Institute Press, 1999).

"Battle of Midway" is taken from a Naval Institute oral history interview of Admiral Benson, conducted 18 March 1980 by John T. Mason Jr.

"Peril at Fifty Fathoms" is taken from an article by Mr. Grieves in *Naval History*, Fall 1988, 18–22.

"Sub Sailors' Liberty" is taken from an article by Mr. O'Meara in *Polaris*, published by the U.S. Submarine Veterans of World War II.

"Surface Action" is taken from a Naval Institute oral history interview of Captain Schratz, conducted 30 November 1984 by Paul Stillwell.

"Stern Skipper" is taken from a Naval Institute oral history interview of Admiral Burke, conducted 14 March 1997 by Paul Stillwell.

"Special Missions" is taken from a Naval Institute oral history interview of Admiral Ward, conducted 11 September 1986 by Paul Stillwell.

"Scouting the Gilbert Islands" is taken from a Naval Institute oral history interview of Admiral Irvin, conducted 17 August 1978 by John T. Mason Jr.

"Saga of a *Sculpin* Survivor" is taken from a post–World War II account by Chief Petty Officer Rocek. The full version appeared in the December 1979 issue of *Polaris* and the January 2004 issue of the *Submarine Review*. It is also available on the Internet at http://donmac.org/590files/191.htm.

"Aide to Admiral King" is taken from a Naval Institute oral history dictated by Captain Dornin on 10 May 1982.

"Crossing the Equator" is taken from a Naval Institute oral history interview of Admiral Burke, conducted 14 March 1997 by Paul Stillwell.

"Black Submariner" is taken from an oral history interview of Chief Petty Officer Mays, conducted for this book on 1 March 2005 by Paul Stillwell.

"Wolf Pack Operations" is taken from a Naval Institute oral history interview of Admiral Ramage, conducted 16 October 1973 by John T. Mason Jr.

"Rescuing POWs" is taken from a Naval Institute oral history interview of Admiral McNitt, conducted 31 December 1997 by Paul Stillwell.

"Enemy Rescue" is taken from an article by Mr. O'Meara in the November 1996 issue of *Polaris*, published by the U.S. Submarine Veterans of World War II.

"New Bride, New Boat" is taken from an unpublished family history written by Commander Alden.

"Abandoning the *Darter*" is taken from a Naval Institute oral history interview of Admiral Wilkinson, conducted 17 January 1998 by Paul Stillwell.

"Dodging Mines and Praying" is taken from a Naval Institute oral history interview of Admiral Burke, conducted 20 March 1997 by Paul Stillwell.

"Not Enough Fish" is taken from Captain Calkins's article "Down to the Sea in Ships'—Names," *U.S. Naval Institute Proceedings*, July 1958, 28–34.

"SubPac Operations" is taken from a Naval Institute oral history interview of Admiral Ward, conducted 11 September 1986 by Paul Stillwell.

"The Postwar Naval Reserve" is taken from an article by Captain Laning in *U.S. Naval Institute Proceedings*, October 1984, 54–55. That article was excerpted from Naval Institute oral history interviews of Laning, conducted 24 and 25 April 1984 by Paul Stillwell.

"Submarines and Ice" is taken from a Naval Institute oral history interview of Doctor Lyon, conducted 30 January 1971 by Etta-Belle Kitchen.

"Missiles at Sea" is taken from a Naval Institute oral history interview of Admiral Wilkinson, conducted 18 January 1998 by Paul Stillwell.

"Fire in the *Cochino*" is taken from a Naval Institute oral history interview of Admiral Benson, conducted 8 April 1980 by John T. Mason Jr.

"Hot New Guppy" is taken from a Naval Institute oral history interview of Captain Schratz, conducted 30 November 1984 by Paul Stillwell.

"Those Disastrous Pancake Diesels" is taken from a Naval Institute oral history interview of Admiral Shear, conducted 9 September 1992 by Paul Stillwell.

"Photo Reconnaissance" is taken from a Naval Institute oral history interview of Admiral Williams, conducted 5 October 1995 by Paul Stillwell.

"The Whale-Shaped *Albacore*" is taken from a Naval Institute oral history interview of Captain Jackson, conducted 1 September 1998 by Paul Stillwell.

"Firing the Regulus" is taken from a Naval Institute oral history interview of Admiral Ward, conducted 16 September 1986 by Paul Stillwell.

"Tangling with the Soviets" is taken from a Naval Institute oral history interview of Admiral Williams, conducted 5 October 1995 by Paul Stillwell.

"Angles and Dangles" is taken from a Naval Institute oral history interview of Admiral Train, conducted on 16 July 1986 by Paul Stillwell.

"A Few Days in October" is taken from a memoir of *Grayback* duty in Chief Warrant Officer Beckley's web site: www.geocities.com/jerry_beckley/. A version appears in a broader web site: http://hometown.aol.com/periscopefilms/Regulus-MissileCuba.html. The memoir also appeared in the *American Submariner*, 2001.

"A Submariner's Memories" is taken from an oral history interview of Mr. Miller, conducted for this book on 1 November 2004 by Paul Stillwell.

"Last of the B-Girls" is taken from an oral history interview of Master Chief Petty Officer Wormwood, conducted for this book on 30 March 2006 by Paul Stillwell.

"End of an Era" is taken from an oral history interview of Commander Wilde, conducted for this book on 29 March 2006 by Paul Stillwell.

Index

A-1, USS (SS-2), renaming of *Plunger* to, 191

A-2, USS (SS-3), renaming of *Adder* to, 191

A-boats, 40

ABDA (American-British-Dutch-Australian) Command, 101–2

Abele, Mannert L., 106

Abemama, *Nautilus* scouting of, 141–43

Adams, Alden W., Jr. "Flag," 231

Adams, Arthur S. "Beanie," 26

Adder, USS (SS-3), renaming as *A-2*, 191

AL-1 (USS *L-1* [SS-40]), 19

AL-2 (USS *L-2* [SS-41]): command by Foster, Paul F., 19–24; German submarine sinking credited to, 24

Albacore, USS (AGSS-569): 235–38; command by Gummerson, Kenneth C., 237; commissioning of, 235; design changes in, 236–38; influence of, 238; visit by Lord Mountbatten, 238; whale shape of, 235–38

Alden, Ann (Buchholz), 177–82

Alden, John D.: as author, 181–82; marriage of, 177–82; service in *Cachalot*, 179–80; service in *Lamprey*, 179–82; service in *Pike*, 177–79; at Submarine School, 177–79

Aleutian Islands, 141, 239–40, 242, 244, 258–59

Alkire, Josh, serving in *Dolphin*, 277

Alton, USS (IX-5), *Chicago* name change to, 39, 60

Amberjack, USS (SS-522), 193, 223

American Steel Navy (Alden), 181–82

Amoy, China, visit of *S-33* to, 54

Anderson, William L., command of *Thresher*, 96, 120

Anderson, William R., command of *Nautilus*, 211

Andrews, Frank A., 243

Arashi (Japan), 118

Arctic Submarine Laboratory, 205

Argonaut, USS (SM-1), 72, 141

Arizona, USS (BB-39), 76, 108

Arkansas, USS (BB-33), 43

atomic bombs, 198–99

Atsuta Maru (Japan), 7

Atule, USS (SS-403), 162, 209

Aubrey, Norbert E. "Sunshine," 250

Australia: escape from Philippines to, 101–3; stop between war patrols for U.S. submarines, 111, 120, 140, 156–57, 159–61, 181, 185; treatment of black submariners in, 159–60

Azores, in World War I, 16–19

Azusa (Japan), 171–72

B-17 bombers, 138, 139

B-29 bombers, 198

B-boats, 40

"B-girls," last of, 267–73

Back from the Deep (LaVO), 93

Badders, William: Medal of Honor awarded to, 84; in *Squalus* rescue, 80–84

ballistic missiles, 240–41

Bang, USS (SS-385), wolf pack operations of, 163–65

Barb, USS (SS-220), in rescue of Allied prisoners from sea, 170–73

Barbel, USS (SS-580): accident of, 246–47; among last diesel-engine submarines, 267; clamshell doors of, 248; command by Train, Harry D., III, 246–53; in Cuban Missile Crisis, 250–51; decommissioning of, 271; hydrobatics of, 248–49; Soviet surveillance by, 251; sub-safe program for, 247, 249–50, 251; teardrop shape of, 248

Barbero, USS (SSG-317), Regulus missiles in, 254

Bashaw, USS (SS-241), 242

Bass, USS (SS-164), 71, 193

Bates, George J., 202–3

Bates, William H., 203

Battle of Leyte Gulf, *Dace* and *Darter* in, 183

Battle of Midway, 117, 118–19

Battle of Savo Island, 111

Battle of Sunda Strait, 101

Bauernschmidt, George W.: command of *R-2*, 44–46; design changes sug

Bauernschmidt, George W. *(cont'd.)*
gested by, 46; early command opportunity of, 42–46; service in *R-
3*, 43–44; service in *R-5*, 43; service in Supply Corps, 42, 72–74;
service on *Beaver*, 72–74; at Submarine School, 42–43
Bauernschmidt, Maude, 42, 44, 46
Beach, Edward L. "Ned": books by,
113, 264; command of fast-attack
Trigger, 227–31; high-angle surfac-
ing of in *Amberjack*, 223; service
in *Piper*, 228, 264; service in
Tirante, 228; service in wartime
Trigger, 113–17, 228
Beard, Donald C., 96
Beaver, USS (AS-5), 72–74; in building
of Pearl Harbor base, 36–37;
service of Bauernschmidt,
George W., on, 72–74; service of
S-33 with, 51–57
Beckley, Jerry E.: in Cuban Missile
Crisis, 254, 258–59; in Personnel
Reliability Program, 258; service
in *Grayback*, 254–59; service in
Perch, 256
Becuna, USS (SS-319), 231
Bell, C. Edwin "Ebby," 220
Bemis, Harold M., 17–19
Benitez, Rafael C., command of
Cochino, 216, 218–19
Bennehoff, Olton: clashes with Rick-
over, Hyman, 64–66; command
of *S-48*, 64–66; in development of
torpedo data computer, 77
Bennett, Rawson II, 209
Ben's Busters (submarine wolf pack),
170–71
Benson, Roy S.: command of *Trigger*,
116, 228, 230; on fire in *Cochino*,
216–19; as lecturer at Submarine
School, 179; in *Nautilus* action at
Midway, 118–19; service of
Beach, Edward L., with, 228
Benson, Vida Connole, 230
Benson, William S., 16
Bering Sea, 206, 209, 242
Bessac, Norman B., 131
Besugo, USS (SS-321), 162
Biesecker, Charles, 179
Bigley, Thomas J., 250
Bikini atomic bomb tests, 200
"Black and Gold Crew," 256
black submariners, 158–62; liberty ex-
periences of, 159–60; postwar
Navy opportunities for, 162; treat-
ment in Australia, 159–60
Bland, Jud, 152
Blind Man's Bluff (Sontag and Drew),
216
Block Island, 48
"Blue and Gold Crew," 256

Blue Birds (tactical missiles), 256
Blueback, USS (SS-326), 181
Blueback, USS (SS-581): commission-
ing of, 267; decommissioning of,
267, 272–73; generator flooding
incident, 271; in *The Hunt for Red
October*, 269–71; as last of "B-
girls," 267–73; at Oregon Mu-
seum of Science and Industry,
273; service of Wormwood,
Charles E. III, in, 267–73; teak
deck planking, 269–70
Bluegill, USS (SS-242/SSK-242): Cold
War reconnaissance by, 242–45;
service of Mays, Hosey, in, 162
Board of Inspection and Survey, 33–34
Boarfish, USS (SS-327), under-ice oper-
ations of, 209–11
Bombay Shoal, 183–85
Bonaparte, Charles Joseph, 10–12
Bonefish, USS (SS-223), 190
Bonefish, USS (SS-582), 267, 271
Bonita, USS (SS-165), 193
Booth, Roy, 272
Bordeaux, France, 20
Boston, Massachusetts, 201–02
Boston and Maine Railroad, 70
Boston, USS (CAG-1), 239
Bougainville Island, landings on, 136,
139
Bowfin, USS (SS-287), black sub-
mariner in, 160–61
Brazil, 231
Bream, USS (SS-243), outpaced by *Bar-
bel*, 250–51
Brinkley Bass, USS (DD-887), 251
Brisbane, Australia, 156–57, 159
Brockman, William H. Jr., 118
Brown, John H. "Babe," 222–25
Brown, George E., Jr., 147, 151
Brunswick, Maine, 265
Buchholz, Ann, 177–82
Buchholz, Art, 178–79
Burgan, William W., 133
Burke, Andy, 188
Burke, Arleigh, 238
Burke, Betty, 132–33, 187
Burke, Julian T., Jr.: Donaho, Glynn
"Donc" as stern skipper of,
132–35; equator crossings of,
156–57; in minefields of Sea of
Japan, 186–90; service in *Flying
Fish*, 133–35, 156–57, 186–90
Burke, Tina, 187
Busch-Sulzer diesel engines, 32–33
Bushnell, USS (AS-2), 16, 17–19, 21,
23–24

Cachalot, USS (SS-170): command by
Comstock, Merrill, 67, 70, 75; design and construction of, 67–69;
service of Alden, John D., in,

179–80; service of Davidson, John
F., in, 75
Calcaterra, Herbert A. "Chainfall," 6
California, USS (BB-44), 4
Calkins, William F., boats named by,
191–94
Callaway, William F., 17
Calvert, James F., 112, 227
camouflage of *Parche*, 163
Camp Dealey, Guam, 196
Camp Ofuna, 150–52
Canberra, USS (CAG-2), 239
Canopus, USS (AS-9), 51, 100
Canton, China, visit of *S-33* to, 54
Carbonero, USS (SS-337), in missile
program, 214–15
Carey, Ed, 177
Carlson, Evans F., 141
Carpender, Arthur S., 24
Cavite Navy Yard: bombing of,
98–100; as *SS-33* base, 51
Chaumont, USS (AP-5), 57
Chicago, USS (CA-14/CL-14), 38–41,
44, 60
China, service of *S-33* in, 53–57
Chub, USS (SS-329), 193
Chuyo (Japan), 147–50
City of Rome, collision with *S-51*, 48
Clamagore, USS (SS-343), service of
Miller, Wayne L., in, 264–66
Clarey, Bernard A. "Chick," 227,
248–50
Clytie, USS (AS-26), 162
Coale, Griffith Bailey, 161
Cochino, USS (SS-345), fire in,
216–19
Cochrane, Edward L. "Ned," 235–36
Coco Solo, Panama, *S-48* service at,
62–64
Cold War: Cuban missile crisis in,
47, 250–51, 254, 258–59; fire in
Cochino, 216–19; *Gudgeon* forced
to surface during, 245; recon-
naissance by *Barbel*, 251; recon-
naissance by *Bluegill*, 242–45;
reconnaissance by *Clamagore*,
264; reconnaissance by *Ronquil*,
232–34; Regulus-armed sub-
marines in, 254–59
Cole, Cyrus W., 83–84, 88
Colorado, USS (BB-45), 107
Comstock, Merrill: at Portsmouth
Navy Yard, 67; command of
Cachalot, 67, 70, 75; on detail
duty, 75; *Pompano* qualifications
observed by, 2–3; on surface reloading, 168
Conger, USS (SS-477), 193
Congress, U.S., 202, 229
Connery, Sean, in *The Hunt for Red October*, 271
Connole, David R.: command of

wartime *Trigger,* 230; duty in *Pompano,* 1–3, 7, 8–9

Connole, Rickart, 230

Conrad, Peter C., 249, 253

"Convoy College," 166

Corbus, John, 160

Cornell underwater listening tests, 16–17

Corregidor Island, Philippines, 53, 108–9

Corsair, USS (SS-435), in Cold War reconnaissance, 216

Crandall, Orson L., 84

Crete, 265

Crevalle, USS (SS-291), black submariners in, 158–60

Cromwell, John P., 146

Cross, John H., 64

Crowe, William J. Jr., 252–53

Cruzen, Richard H., 208

Cuban Missile Crisis, 47, 250–51, 254, 258–59

Curts, Maurice E., "Germany," 96

Curtze, Charles A., and *Squalus:* analysis of accident, 88–90; in recovery and repair, 85–90, 93

Cusk, USS (SSG-348), missile firing from, 212–15

Cutter, Slade D.: antics ashore in Hawaii, 8–9; command of *Seahorse,* 1, 153; on Dornin, Robert E., 153; Navy Crosses awarded to, 1; respect for, 1; service in *Pompano,* 1–9, 132; training and qualification of, 1–3

D-3, USS (SS-19), command by Dyer, George C., 35

D-boats (dog-boats), at Submarine School, 28

Dace, USS (SS-247): in Battle of Leyte Gulf, 183; rescue of grounded *Darter* crew by, 183–85

Dakar Maru (Japan), 169

Dana, George, 60

Danhoff, Joseph B., 64

Daniels, Josephus, 24, 26

Darter, USS (SS-227): in Battle of Leyte Gulf, 183; grounding and abandonment of, 183–85

Dauntless, USS (PG-61), 155

David Taylor Model Basin, 236

Davidson, John F.: as detail officer, 75–76, 220; service in *Cachalot,* 75

Davidson, Kenneth, 235–36

Davidson Laboratory, 235

Davis, William S. G., 200–202

Dennison, Robert L.: in Cuban Missile Crisis, 47; early command opportunity of, 47–48; on loss of *S-4* and *S-51,* 47–50, 80; service in *S-8,*

48–50; service in *S-50,* 48; at Submarine School, 48

depth charges: against *Crevalle,* 159; *Drum,* 109; *Flying Fish,* 156; *Pompano,* 5; *Sculpin,* 146; *Thresher,* 121–23; *Trigger,* 119

detailing of personnel, 75–76, 220

Detroit, Michigan: base for *Piper,* 264

Devilfish, USS (SS–292), 193

Dewey dry dock, 52

Deyo, Morton L., 203

Diablo, USS (SS–479), 193

diesel engines: *Dolphin* as last submarine in commission with, 274–79 ; final class of submarines with, 246; of fleet boats, 67, 69–70; of Guppy boats, 223; last of "B-girls," 267–73; pancake, in fast attack boats, 228–31; of R-boats, 40–41, 61; of *S-2,* 32–33; Submarine School course in, 29–30; in whale-shaped boats, 235

Dietzen, Walter N., Jr., "Buck," 250

Distinguished Service Medal, to Foster, Paul F., 24

Disney Studio, cartoon images of submarines, 192

Dolphin, USS (SS-169), 67

Dolphin, USS (SS-555), as last diesel boat in commission, 274–79Donaho, Glynn R. "Donc": Navy Crosses awarded to, 132; as stern skipper to Burke, Julian T., Jr., in *Flying Fish,* 132–35

Doolittle raid, 120, 149

Dorado, USS (SS-248), 129

Dornin, Robert E. "Dusty": as aide to King, Ernest, 153–55; command of *Trigger,* 153; Cutter, Slade D. on, 153; intercession on behalf of Cutter, Slade D., 9; service in *Gudgeon,* 153

Doyle, William T., 92, 93

Drew, Christopher, 216

Drum, USS (SS-228): arrival in Pearl Harbor, 108; command by McMahon, Bernard, 110–11; command by Rice, Robert H., 108–10; command by Rindskopf, Maurice H., 111–12; command by Williamson, Delbert, 111; erroneous report of sinking, 109; first war patrol of, 109–10; memorial, 111; second war patrol of, 110; service of Rindskopf, Maurice H., in, 107–12

Dunbar, Palmer H., Jr. "Crow," 89

Duncan, Max C., 172

duration-of-war (DOW) enlistments, 37–38

Dyer, George C., on beginning of S-boats, 31–35

e-mail, first used at sea, 276

early command opportunities, 42–46, 47–48

echo sounder, in under-ice operations, 209

Edison, Charles (secretary of the navy): presented Medals of Honor for *Squalus* rescue, 84

Eel, USS (SS–354), 193

Ekelund, John J., command of *Grayback,* 256, 258–59

Electric Boat Company, 26–27, 40, 69, 99, 227–29

Eller, Agnes, 51, 54–55, 57

Eller, Ernest M., 51–57

Eller, Joe, 276

Empress Augusta Bay reconnaissance, 136–37, 139–40

endless-chain system, 27, 28

engines, diesel. See diesel engines

Enijun Pass, *Thresher* actions at, 120–21

Enterprise, USS (CV-6), 4

equator crossing, 156–57, 159

Evans, Robert L., and *Squalus:* analysis of accident, 92–93; in recovery and repair, 88–90, 91–93; as shipbuilding superintendent, 85–86

Event Five Hundred, 222–23

Experimental Diving Unit, *Squalus* rescue by, 80–84

Fairbanks-Morse diesel engines, 223, 228, 267–68, 269, 275

Falcon, USS (ASR-2): in *S-4* salvage, 49-50; in *Squalus* rescue, 80–84, 88

Fanning, USS (DD-37), 24

Far East, service of Eller, Ernest M., in, 51–57

fast attack boats: construction of, 227–28; pancake diesel engines of, 228–31; Shear, Harold E. in *Trigger,* 227–31

fathometer, in under-ice operations, 209

Fenno, Frank W., Jr. "Mike," 7, 130

Ferrall, William E. "Pete," command of *Seadragon,* 98–99

Fife, James, Jr., 28

Fischer, Harry F., Jr., command of *Ronquil,* 232–34

Fishers Island, *G-4* service off, 15

five-patrol rule, 125, 198

fleet boats: development of, 67–71; mockup of, 70; Rindskopf, Maurice H., as youngest CO of, 111; "spit" planning method for, 68

Fluckey, Euene B., 166, 170, 171–72

Flying Fish, USS (SS-229): command by Donaho, Glynn R. "Donc," 132–35; command by Risser, Robert, 188, 190; equator cross

Flying Fish, USS *(cont'd.)*
ing of, 156–57; Japanese prisoner in, 189; in minefields of Sea of Japan, 186–90; misbehavior of crew, 134; reunions of, 157; service of Burke, Julian T., Jr., in, 133–35, 156–57, 186–90; sinkings in Sea of Japan, 189

Flynn, Jack, 173

FM sonar, 186–90, 207

Fore River Shipbuilding Company, 31–32

Forrestal, James V., 201, 203

Fort McHenry Naval Reserve Center, 260

"Forty-one for Freedom," 276

Foster, Paul F.: command of *AL-2,* 19–24; command of *G-4,* 15–17; Distinguished Service Medal awarded to, 24; on establishment of submarine base, 13–14; German submarine sinking credited to, 24; listening devices tested by, 16–17; service in *G-4,* 14–17; service in K-boats, 13–14; service on *Bushnell,* 17–19; Sperry gyroscope tested by, 15–16; on World War I submarine service, 13–24

Freeman, Mark, 122

Friedell, Wilhelm L., 18

Fuso Maru (Japan), 169

G-2, USS (SS-27), 28

G-4, USS (SS-26): Italian design of, 14; listening devices tested in, 16–17; metacentric height problems of, 14; reversibility feature of propellers, 14–15, 17; service of Foster, Paul F., in, 14–17; Sperry gyroscope tested in, 15–16

G-boats: at Submarine School, 28. *See also specific submarines*

Galas, Al, 110–11

Gallaher, Antone R., command of *Bang,* 163–64

Gato, USS (SS-212), 107, 108

Gea Pass, *Thresher* actions at, 121–23

General Dynamics, 26–27

General Line School, 212

General Motors Corporation, 69–70, 229

Geneva Convention, 151

German submarines, World War I: *AL-2* action against and sinking of, 22–24; operations off U.S. East Coast, 28; surrendered, examination and analysis of, 31

German submarines in World War II220

Gilbert Islands, scouting by *Nautilus,* 141–45

Gilmore, Howard W., 65, 106

Graf, Frederic A., 64–65

Grayback, USS (SSG-574): command by Ekelund, John J., 256, 258–59; in Cuban Missile Crisis, 254, 258–59; firing safeguards in, 256; 120 percent crew of, 256; Personnel Reliability Program in, 258; Regulus missiles in, 254–59; service of Beckley, Jerry E., in, 254–59; stay-in crew of, 256; ugliness of, 256

Great Lakes, Illinois, site of Navy boot camp, 162, 260; training schools, 261

Great White Fleet, 10

Greater Underwater Propulsive Power. *See* Guppy boats

Gregory, Joseph "Nino," 52

Grenadier, USS (SS-210), 150–52

Grenadier, USS (SS-525), 162

Grenfell, Elton W., "Joe," 96

Grieves, Billy A., service in *Thresher,* 120–23

Groton, Conn., site of Submarine School, 26, 178

Growler, USS (SS-215), 106, 170–71

Growler, USS (SSG-577), 256

Grunion, USS (SS-216), 106

Guam: as ComSubPac headquarters, 132, 187–88; 195–99; *Flying Fish* stop en route to Sea of Japan, 187–88; liberty stop for submarines between patrols, 124, 198

Guardfish, USS (SS-217): command by Ward, Norvell G., 136–40; lifeguard duty of, 138–39; sinking of *Kashu Maru,* 137–38; special missions of, 136–40

Guavina, USS (AOSS-362), as training boat, 261, 264

Gudgeon, USS (SS-211), 96, 153

Gudgeon, USS (SS-567), 245

Guided Missile Unit Number 90, 254

Guillot, James C., 52

Gummerson, Kenneth C., command of *Albacore,* 237

Guppy boats: high-angle surfacing of, 222–23; modifications in, 220; reconnaissance by *Bluegill,* 242–45; record-setting submerged journey of, 223–26; Schratz, Paul R., in *Pickerel,* 220–26; snorkels of, 220, 223–26

Gygax, Felix Xerxes, 36–41

Hale, John I., 91

Halsey, William F., Jr., 5

Hammerhead, USS (SS-364), wolf pack operations of, 165–69

Hancock, Joy Bright, 35

Hancock, Lewis: absence of, 33–35;

command of *S-2,* 32–35; death in dirigible service, 35

Hardhead, USS (SS-365), 193

Hart, Thomas C., 17–19, 98, 101

Hartley, Henry, 49

Hawes, Richard E. "Spittin' Dick," 100

Hawkbill, USS (SSN-666), 205

Hazlett, Edward E., Jr. "Swede," 75–76

Headden, William R., 65

Head Hunters, 166

Henderson, USS (AP-1), 51

Henderson, Richie, 133

Hensel, Karl G., 105–6, 134

Hickam Field, air base in Hawaii, 38

High Jump to Antarctica, 206–9

Hiroshima bombing, 198–99

Holland, USS (AS-3), 46, 175, 187, 195

Holland, USS (SS-1), 10, 236, 238

Holland-type submarines, 41

Hopping, Hallstet L., 4

Houston, USS (CA-30), 101, 103

Houston, USS (SSN-713), 271

Howard W. Gilmore, USS (AS-16), 161–62

The Hunt for Red October (film), 269–71

Hunter, Samuel H., Jr., 99

Hydeman, Earl T., 188, 190

hydrobatics, 248–49

hydrodynamic hulls, 235–38, 248

hydrogen, and potential for fire, 217–19

ice, operations in and under, 205–11

Icefish, USS (SS-367), 242

Ireland, U.S. submarines in World War I, 19–24; U.S. submarines in the Cold War, 216–17

Irex, USS (SS-482), 193

Irvin, William D.: command of *Nautilus,* 141–45; in ComSubPac operations, 195; relationship with Rickover, Hyman, 64–66; scouting of Gilbert Islands, 141–45; service in *S-48,* 62–66; at Submarine School, 62

Irvin, Carolyn, 63–64

"is-was," 2, 60

Ives, Norman S., 3

Jack, USS (SS-259), 193

Jackson, Harry A., work on *Albacore,* 235–38

Jackson, Ralph F. "Snuffy," service in *Pickerel,* 221, 223

Japanese Maritime Self-Defense Force, 251

Japanese Navy: antisubmarine actions against U.S. boats, 121–23, 167; in the Battle of Midway, 115, 118–19; near Rabaul, 138; near

Shetland Island, 137; transportation of prisoners of war, 147–49; visit to Hawaii in the 1920s, 44–45

Japanese prisoners: in *Flying Fish*, 189; *Pompano* transport of, 7–8; rescue from sea by *Seahorse*, 174–76

Japanese surrender, 25, 199

Johnston Island, refueling stop for *Nautilus*, 143

Jordan, captured planes blown up, 265

Julihn, Lawrence V., 121

Jupiter missile, 240

K-boats, 13–14, 18–19

Kachidoko Maru (Japan), 170

Kamchatka Peninsula, 244

Kampia (Japanese secret police), 151

Kashu Maru (Japan), 137–38

Keeler, Doc, 175

Kempff, Clarence S. "Pluvy," 70

Kimmel, Husband E., 94, 95, 97, 107

Kimmel, Manning M., 107, 110

King, Cecil, escape from Philippines, 101–3

King, Ernest, Dornin, Robert E. as aide to, 153–55; supervised salvage of *S-4*, 49

King, Florie, 154–55

King Neptune ceremony, 156–57, 159

Kirkpatrick, Charles, 154–55

Kitty Hawk, USS (CVA-63), close encounter with *Barbel*, 251

Koei Maru (Japan), 169

Korean War, *Ronquil* reconnaissance during, 233

L-boats, 17–19

La Guardia, Fiorello, 49–50

LaFond, Gene, 209–11

Lake, Simon, 32–33

Lake Torpedo Company, 31–33

Lamprey, USS (SS-372): command by Nelson, William T., 180–81; commissioning of, 180–81; decommissioning of, 181; service of Alden, John D., in, 179–82; surface duel of, 181; war patrols of, 181

Laning, Richard B., postwar Reserve organization by, 200–204

Larkee, Dwayne, serving in *Dolphin*, 277

Lawver, Rowland C., 178

Lee, Paul F., 235–36

Legion of Merit, awarded to Irvin, William D., 145

Leighton, David T., 252

Lewis, Jack H., 113–15

Leyte Gulf, battle of, *Dace* and *Darter* in, 183

liberty, 124–27; for black submariners, 159–60

lifeguard duties, 138–39, 198

lights, shock-resistant, 46

Lipes, Wheeler, 99

Litchfield, USS (DD-336), 2, 7

Lockwood, Charles A.: congratulations to wolf pack commanders, 168; Dornin, Robert E., told of assignment by, 153–54; entry into Sea of Japan promoted by, 186–87; high-angle surfacing photo for, 222; at Japanese surrender, 199; as Pacific Fleet Submarine Force commander, 134, 186–87, 195–99; visit to *Flying Fish*, 186–87; Ward, Norvell G., on, 196–98

Loons (V-1 rockets), firing from *Cusk*, 213–15

Louisville, USS (CA-28), 104

Lurline (U.S. passenger ship), 36

Luzon, Philippines, escape from, 101–3

Lynch, Richard B. "Ozzie": in Cold War reconnaissance, 216; scouting of Gilbert Islands in *Nautilus*, 141–45

Lyon, Waldo K.: death of, 205; under-ice operations of, 205–11

MacArthur, Douglas, 111

Mackerel, USS (SS-204), 128, 220

Maine, USS (SSBN-741), 274

Makin, *Nautilus* actions and scouting at, 141–45

Maloelap, *Thresher* actions at, 120–21

Manitowoc, Wisconsin, boats built in, 179–81

Manko Maru (Japan), 169

Mann, Stephen S. Jr., 113–14

Marblehead, USS (CL-12), 101

Mare Island Navy Yard: destroyer construction in 1918; inactivation of *Lamprey*, 181; *Sculpin* work at, 147; *Pompano* work at, 3; submarine command at, 134

Mariposa (U.S. passenger ship), 36

Mark 1 fire control system, 77–78

Mark 2 fire control system, 77–79

Marlin, Richard E., 248

marriage, during World War II, 154, 177–82

Marshall Islands: *Drum* stop at, 111; *Pompano* actions at, 5–6; *Thresher* actions at, 120–23

Matsuta Maru (Japan), 2

Mayrant, USS (DD-402), 58

Mays, Hosey: as black submariner, 158–62; equator crossing of, 159; liberty experiences of, 159–60; postwar Navy career of, 162; service in *Bowfin*, 160–61; service in *Crevalle*, 158–60; service on ten

ders, 161–62; treatment in Australia, 159–60

McCann, Allan, in ice operations, 206, 209–11

McCann rescue chamber, 47, 49, 80–84

McClintock, David H., 183–85

McDonald, James H., 84

McFarland, USS (AVD-14), 3

McGrath, Thomas Patrick, 4

McKee, Andrew I., 92–93, 235–36

McLean, Heber H., 71

McLean, Ridley, inspections by, 45–46

McMahon, Bernard F. "Barney," command of *Drum*, 110–11

McNitt, Robert W., in rescue of prisoners, 170–73

McQuiston, Edward I., 58

McWhorter, Ernest D., 14–15

Medal of Honor: to Cromwell, John P., 146; to Fluckey, Eugene B., 170; to Foster, Paul F., 13; to Ramage, Lawson, P., 169, 170; to rescuers of *Squalus*, 84

Mero, USS (SS-378), 193

Merrick, USS (AKA-97), in ice operations, 207

Metcalf, John T. "Red," 64

Metzger, Robert L., 234

Midway, battle of, 113, 117, 118–19

Midway Island: *Drum* stop at, 108–9; *Flying Fish* stop at, 135; *Parche* stops at, 164–66; *Pompano* stop at, 7; *Seahorse* visits to, 124, 126; *Trigger* patrol and accident off, 113–17

Miers, Anthony C. C. "Tony," 129

Mihalowski, John: Medal of Honor awarded to, 84; in *Squalus* rescue, 82–84

Miller, Donna (Ward), 261–62, 265–66

Miller, L. V., 162

Miller, Wayne L., 260–66; encounter with Beach, Edward L., 264; qualification as submariner, 263; service in *Clamagore*, 264–66; service in *Piper*, 261–64; in Soviet reconnaissance, 264; at Submarine School, 261; in Suez Canal patrol, 264–65

Millican, William J.: command of *S-18*, 120; command of *Thresher*, 120–23

Milwaukee, USS (CL-5), 70

minefields: *Scorpion* laying of, 129; Sea of Japan, 186–90

missiles: ballistic, 240–41; Blue Birds, 256; *Cusk* firing of, 212–15; Polaris, 239, 240–41, 254, 256; Red Birds, 256; Regulus, 239–41, 254–59; safeguards for, 256; submerged firing of, 240–41, 254; surface firing of, 212–15, 239–41, 254

Missouri, USS (BB-63): 1980s, 269; World War II surrender, 25, 199

Mitsuma, Seiza, 175–76

Mizuho (Japan), 109–10

Momsen, Charles B. "Swede," 82, 83, 235, 261

Momsen lung, 47, 49, 179, 261

Moore, Dinty, 149

Moray, USS (SS–300), 193

Mount Olympus, USS (AGC-8), in ice operations, 207

Mount Shipunski, 244

Mountbatten, Louis, visit to *Albacore*, 238

Murray, Clive, 25

Murray, Stuart G. (son of Stuart S.), 70

Murray, Stuart S.: as aide to Kempff, Clarence, 70; assignment of Burke, Julian T., Jr., by, 133; duty at Portsmouth Navy Yard, 67-71; in building of Pearl Harbor submarine base, 36–41; command of *Porpoise*, 71; command of *R-17*, 40–41; in fleet boat development, 67–71; *G-2* training of, 28; at Japanese surrender, 25; Marine Corps requested by, 25–26; Navy commission ordered for, 25–26; R-boat crossing to Pearl Harbor, 36; service in *R-20* ordered, 30; seven-foot bunk for, 71; at Submarine School, 25–30; submarine service selected by, 26; "Sunshine" nickname of, 25; "vulnerable tail" accident of, 41

N-boats, 48

Nagano, Osami, 44–45

Nagasaki bombing, 198–99

naming of submarines, 191–94

Naquin, Oliver F., command of *Squalus*, 80, 82, 83, 88, 90–91, 93

Narwhal, USS (SS-167), 141

National Industrial Recovery Act of 1933, 69

Nauru, *Nautilus* scouting of, 141–43

Nautilus (Wilkins's submarine, ex-*O-12*), under-ice attempt by, 205–6, 211

Nautilus, USS (SS-168): combat insignia awarded to, 145; command by Brockman, Bill, 118; command by Irvin, William D., 141–45; role in Battle of Midway, 118–19; scouting of Gilbert Islands, 141–45; sinking of *Soryu* by, 119

Nautilus, USS (SSN-571): authorization of, 235; command by Wilkinson, Eugene P., 112, 183; keel laid for, 246; under-ice transit of North Pole by, 205, 211

Naval Forces, Far East, 233

Naval Institute Proceedings, 171

Naval Institute's General Prize Essay Contest, 51

Naval Photographic Center, 266

Naval Research Laboratory, 46

Naval Reserve, post–World War I, departure of officers, 38

Naval Reserve, post–World War II: enlistment of Miller, Wayne L., in, 260; organization by Laning, Richard B., 200–204; submarines acquired for, 202–4; tour in *Pickerel*, 222

Naval Reserve, World War II, experiences at Submarine School, 104–6

Naval Reserve Officer Training Corps (NROTC), 104

Navy and Marine Corps Medal, to Wise, John D., Jr., 278

Navy Cross: to Cutter, Slade D., 1; to Donaho, Glynn R. "Donc," 132; to Parks, Lewis S., 6; to Rindskopf, Maurice H., 112

Navy Day, 10

Navy Electronics Laboratory (NEL), 205, 206–7, 209

Negri, Joe, 262–63

NELSECO engines, 40–41

Nelson, William T., 180–81

Nereus, USS (AS-17), in ice operations, 209–11

New Jersey, USS (BB-62): operations in the 1980s, 269

New London, Conn.: base established at, 13–14; escape tower at, 179, 261–62; Submarine School at. *See* Submarine School

New London Ship and Engine Company, 26–27

New Mexico, USS (BB-40), 42

Newsome, Justin, 277

New York Navy Yard (Brooklyn), 16, 33, 205

Nimitz, Chester W.: in building of Pearl Harbor submarine base, 38; command of Submarine Division Fourteen, 40–41; detailing duties of, 75–76; Dornin, Robert E. told of assignment by, 153–54; on early command opportunities, 42, 44; method of operation, 41; as Pacific Fleet commander in chief, 6, 51, 134, 153–54, 196, 225; service of Eller, Ernest M., under, 51; support for postwar Naval Reserves, 203; technical knowledge of, 40–41

Nimitz, Chester W. Jr., on Submarine School staff, 112

Nockhold, Louis W., 244

Norfolk Naval Shipyard, Portsmouth, Virginia, 264

North Carolina, USS (BB-55), 132

North Pole, first under-ice transit of, 205

Northwind, USCGC (WAGB-282), in ice operations, 207–9

nuclear power program: refusal of Crowe, William J. Jr., to join, 251–53; refusal of Train, Harry D., III to join, 246, 251–53; Rickover, Hyman, and, 62, 251–53; submarine overhauls in, 250. *See also specific nuclear submarines*

nuclear weapons program, Beckley, Jerry E., in, 254–56

O-12, USS (SS–73), under-ice attempt of as *Nautilus*, 205–6

O-boats, 29, 48, 179

Ocean Island, *Nautilus* scouting of, 141–43

O'Kane, Richard H., 166

Oklahoma, USS (BB-37), 76, 108

O'Meara, James B.: in rescue of enemy from sea, 174–76; service in *Seahorse*, 124, 174–76; on World War II liberty, 124–27

one-dollar houses, 38–40

120 percent crew, for Regulus-armed submarines, 256

Ono, USS (SS–357), 193

Operation Barney, 187

Oregon Museum of Science and Industry, 273

Ozark, USS (LSV-2), freed American prisoners on, 151–52

P2V Neptune, 251

P-3 Orion, 265

PBY Catalina, 4

Pace, Leo L., on death of Raymond, Reggie, 130–31

Palau Islands, *Drum* action off, 111; *Flying Fish* patrol off, 135

Pampanito, USS (SS-383): Memorial Day ceremony for, 279; naming of, 193; in rescue of Allied prisoners from sea, 171; wolf pack operations of, 170–71

Panama, *Crevalle* visit to, 159; *S-48* service in, 62–66; *Snapper* service in, 77

pancake diesel engines, 228–31

Parche, USS (SS-384): camouflage of, 163; command by Ramage, Lawson P., 163–69; Parks, Lew, in, 165–66; Peterson, George, in, 164, 165–66; sinkings by, 164–65, 167–69; surface reloading of, 164–66; wolf pack operations of, 163–69

Parker, Isaiah, 70

Parker Ranch, Hawaii, 73

Parks, John, 9

Parks, Lewis S.: antics ashore in Hawaii, 8–9; attack techniques of, 7; command of *Pompano*, 1–9, 165; early sinkings of war by, 7; in *Parche* wolf pack operations, 165–67

Parks's Pirates (submarine wolf pack), 166

Paulding, USCGC (CG-17), collision with *S-4*, 48

pay, submarine: for enlisted personnel, 12, 43–44, 50; La Guardia's law on, 50; for officers, 46, 50

Pearl Harbor: base for submarines in the 1920s, 36-41, 43–46, 59–61; in the 1930s, 72–74; in the 1940s, 108–10, 117, 118, 120, 125, 130, 133–34, 142, 145, 161, 163, 168, 176, 187; in the 1950s, 222–26, 242; in the 1960s, 247–48, 251, 254, 256, 258; black submariners in, 161.Pearl Harbor attack: communications in, 96–97; news reaches *Pompano*, 3; news reaches Rindskopf, Maurice H., 107–8; Ramage, Lawson P., as witness to, 94–97; submarines at sea during, 96

Peary, USS (DD-226), 101

Pelias, USS (AS-14), 161

Pennyman, Timothy, 158–59, 160

Perch, USS (SS-173), 151

Perch, USS (APSS–313), 256

Permit, USS (SSN–594), 267, 271

personnel detailing, 75–76, 220

Personnel Reliability Program (PRP), 258

Peterson, George E., 164, 165–66

Peto, (SS–265), 181

Petropavlosk, reconnaissance of, 251

Philadelphia shipyards, *G-4* construction at, 14; *O-12* conversion at, 206

Philippines: Battle of Leyte Gulf, 183–85; Cavite Navy Yard disaster in, 98–100; *Drum* action in, 111–12; escape of King, Cecil, from, 101–3; service of *S-33* in, 51–53

photo reconnaissance, 141–45, 232–34

Pickerel , USS (SS-524): christening of, 222; command by Schratz, Paul R., 220–26; diesel engines of, 223; high-angle surfacing of, 221–23; record-setting submerged journey of, 223–26; Reserve tour in, 222; snorkeling of, 223–26

Pigeon, USS (ASR-6): in Cavite Navy Yard disaster, 100

Pike, USS (SS–173): design and construction of, 69, 71; service of Alden, John D., in, 177–79; torpedo data computer in, 179

Pilotfish, USS (SS-386), 200

Piper, USS (SS-409): decommissioning of, 264; service of Beach, Edward L., in, 114, 228, 264; service of Miller, Wayne L., in, 261–65; as training boat, 263–64

Plaice, USS (SS-390), cartoon image, 192

Pleatman, Ralph S., 7

Plunger, USS (SS-2): renaming as *A-1*, 191; Roosevelt, Theodore, ride in, 10–11, 274;

Plunger, USS (SS–179): in company of *Pompano* during Pearl Harbor attack, 3, 96

Point Mugu, California, missile control from, 215, 239

polar icecap, surfacing through, 205

Polaris missile: as ballistic missile, 240–41; "Blue and Gold Crew" for, 256; first submarines equipped to fire, 239; Regulus surpassed by, 240–41; submarines deployed with, 254; submerged firing of, 240–41, 254

Pollack, USS (SS–180): in company of *Pompano* during Pearl Harbor attack, 3, 96

pollywogs, 156–57

Pompano, USS (SS-181): 1–9; commanded by Parks, Lew, 1–9, 165; early sinkings of war by, 7; first war patrol of, 4–6; Japanese prisoner transported by, 7–8; naming of, 193; at sea during Pearl Harbor attack, 3, 96; training in, 1–3

Porpoise, USS (SS–172): command by Murray, Stuart S., 71; design and construction of, 68–71; keel layers for, 70; launching of, 71; mockup of, 70; propeller shaft alignment for, 70

Portland, Oregon, *Blueback* at, 271, 273

Portsmouth Navy Yard/Naval Shipyard: *Albacore* work at, 236–38; construction of fast attack boats, 228; conversion of submarines for Reserve use, 204; development of fleet boats at, 67–71; news of Pearl Harbor reaches, 107–8; *Pickerel* christening at, 222; *Piper* repairs at, 263; *S-4* and *S-8* modifications at, 48; *S-3* construction at, 31–32; *S-48* repairs at, 63; *Scorpion* construction at, 128; *Sculpin and Squalus* construction at, 146; *Squalus* recovery and repair at, 85–90;

Presidential Unit Citation, awarded to *Guardfish*, 137, 139

Prewett, Biven M., 32, 33, 34

prisoners, allied: rescue from sea, 170–73

prisoners, Japanese: in *Flying Fish*, 189; *Pompano* transport of, 7–8; rescue from sea, 174–76

prisoners, U.S.: captured from various submarines, 93, 146–152

prostitution, 125–27

Proteus, USS (AS-19), command by Laning, Richard B., in, 200

Puget Sound Naval Shipyard, *Barbel* overhaul at, 250–51, 253; *Blueback* arrival after decommissioning, 272–73

QLA sonar, in under-ice operations, 207, 209–11

Queenfish, USS (SS-393): operation with *Pickerel*, 222; in rescue of Allied prisoners from sea, 170–73; sinkings by, 171–72

Queenstown, Ireland: base for U.S. submarines in World War I, 19–21

Quigley, William M., 35

Quincy, Massachusetts, *S-1*construction in, 31–32

R-1, USS (SS-78): part of Submarine Division Nine, 59

R-2, USS (SS-79): command by Bauernschmidt, George W., 43–46; inspection by McLean, Ridley, 45–46; rated depth of, 45; sick battery of, 45–46

R-3, USS (SS-80), service of Bauernschmidt, George W., in, 43–44

R-4, USS (SS-81): part of Submarine Division Nine, 59; service of Rindskopf, Maurice H., in, 107

R-5, USS (SS-82), service of Bauernschmidt, George W., in, 43

R-8, USS (SS-85): accommodations in, 60; diesel engines of, 61; maximum speed of, 60; service of Walker, Edward K., in, 58–61; versatility of crew in, 61

R-17, USS (SS-94): command by Murray, Stuart S., 40–41; post–World War I switch of personnel to regular Navy, 38; vulnerable tail and accident of, 41

R-20, USS (SS-97), Murray, Stuart S., ordered to, 30

R-boats, 36, 58–61; diesel engines of, 40–41, 61; iceboxes in, 45, 60–61. *See also specific submarines*

Rabaul, *Guardfish* lifeguard duty off, 138–39

Raborn, William F. "Red," Polaris missile development, 240

radar, 166, 189, 217

Radford, Arthur W., 224, 225

Rakuyo Maru (Japan), 170–73

Ramage, Lawson P. "Red": command of *Parche*, 163–69; Medal of Honor awarded to, 169; surface reloading innovation of, 164–66, 168; witness to Pearl Harbor attack, 94–97; wolf pack operations of, 163–69

Raymond, Reginald M.: death of, 130–31; as *Scorpion* executive officer, 128–31

Red Birds (fleet training missiles), 256

Reed, Russell, 3–4

Regulus missiles, 239–41; 120 percent crew for, 256; cold-weather firing of, 239–40; firing safeguards for, 256; in *Grayback*, 254–59; guidance of, 239; Personnel Reliability Program for, 258; precursor of, 214–15; stay-in crew for, 256; surface firing of, 239–41, 254; surpassed by Polaris, 240–41; two-man rule for, 256

The Reminiscences of Paul F. Foster (Foster), 13–24

rescue chamber, McCann, 47, 49, 80–84

Reservists. *See* Naval Reserve

Rice, Robert H.: assignment of Rindskopf, Maurice H., by, 112; command of *Drum*, 108–10

Rice, Eunice, 110

Richmond, USS (CL-9), 94

Rickover, Hyman: clashes with commander, 64–66; contributions to nuclear Navy, 62; criticism of leadership techniques, 252; recruitment rejected by Crowe, William J. Jr., and Train, Harry D., III, 246, 252–53; relationship with Irvin, William D., 64–66; service in *S-48*, 62, 64–66; at Submarine School, 62

Rindskopf, Maurice H.: command of *Drum*, 111–12; first war patrol of, 109–10; Navy Cross awarded to, 112; service in *Drum*, 107–12; service in *R-4*, 107; on Submarine School staff, 112; as torpedo data computer operator, 109

Rindskopf, Peter, 110, 112

Rindskopf, Sylvia, 107, 110, 112

Risser, Robert D., 187–89

Risser's Bob Cats (submarine wolf pack), 188

Robeson, Paul, 179

Rocek, George, as *Sculpin* prisoner and survivor, 146–52

Rockwell, Theodore, 252

Ronquil, USS (SS-396): command by Fischer, Harry, 232, 233; photo reconnaissance by Williams, Joe, Jr., in, 232–34

Roosevelt, Franklin D., 86, 169

Roosevelt, Franklin D., Jr., 58

Roosevelt, Theodore: advocacy of submarines by, 10–12; ride in *Plunger*, 10, 274

Roshon, Art, 209–11

Ross Sea, under-ice operations in, 207–9

rotation system, 125

Royal Hawaiian Hotel: haven for submariners, 8, 58, 124, 161

Royal Navy (British): operations in the Cold War, 216–17, 222–23; World War I, 19–20, 24; World War II, 129

Run Silent, Run Deep (Beach), 113, 264

Runner, USS (SS-275), 130–131

S-1, USS (SS-105), construction of, 31–32

S-2, USS (SS-106), 31–35; acceptance tests of, 32–33; active service of, 35; command by Hancock, Lewis, 32–35; commissioning of, 35; construction of, 31–32; diesel engine of, 32–33; motor room fire in, 33; service of Dyer, George C., in, 32–35

S-3, USS (SS-107), construction of, 31–32, 236

S-4, USS (SS-109), engine room, 34; loss of, 31, 47–50, 83

S-8, USS (SS-113), service of Dennison, Robert L., in, 48–50

S-9, USS (SS-114), service of Rickover, Hyman G., in, 62

S-18, USS (SS-123), command by Millican, William J., 120

S-28, USS (SS-133), loss of, 161

S-33, USS (SS-138): accommodations in, 52–53; atmospheric changes in, 56–57; main induction valve of, 56; service in China, 53–57; service in Philippines, 51–53; service of Eller, Ernest M., in, 51–57

S-44, USS (SS-155), prisoners from, 151

S-45, USS (SS-156): control room in, 57

S-48, USS (SS-159): command by Bennehoff, Olton, 64–66; as oddball S-boat, 62–66; service of Irvin, William D., in, 62–66; service of Rickover, Hyman, in, 62, 64–66

S-50, USS (SS-161), service of Dennison, Robert L., in, 48

S-51, USS (SS-162), loss of, 31, 47–50, 60

S-boats: beginning of, 31–35; completion of last, 31; construction of first, 31; oddball, *S-48* as, 62–66. *See also specific submarines*

Sailfish, USS (SS-192): crew reunion, 152; service during World War II, 93; sinking of Japanese ship carrying *Sculpin* prisoners, 93, 147–49; *Squalus* recommissioned as, 85, 88, 93, 146, 148

Sakhalin Island, reconnaissance of, 232–34

Salmon, USS (SS-182), 193, 200

Salt and Steel (Beach), 113

San Diego, USS (ACR-6), sinking of, 30

San Francisco, USS (CA-38), 111

San Pedro, California, 30

Sarda, USS (SS-488), 193, 261

Saunders, Harold E., 49

Savo Island, battle of, 111

Sawfish, USS (SS-276), 227

Schneider, Earle C. "Penrod": service in *Pompano*, 1–3; service in *Trigger*, 114–15

Schofield Barracks, Army post in Hawaii, 38

Schratz, Henrietta, 128

Schratz, Paul R.: in Bureau of Naval Personnel, 220; command of *Pickerel*, 220–26; on death of Raymond, Reginald, 130–31; high-angle surfacing of, 222–23; record-setting submerged journey of, 223–26; service in *Scorpion*, 128–31; snorkeling methods of, 223–26

Schratz, Regina, 131

Schreiber, George, 129

Scorpion, USS (SS-278): 264; command by Wylie, William N., 128–31; death of Raymond, Reginald, on, 130–31; first war patrol of, 128–29; minefield laid by, 129; service of Schratz, Paul R., in, 128–31

Scorpion, USS (SSN-589), commissioning of, 131; loss of in the Atlantic, 265

Scotland, submarines deployed at Holy Loch, 200, 254

Scripps Institute, 206

Sculpin, USS (SS-191): attack on, 146; building of, 85; crew reunion, 152; prisoners from, sinking of ship carrying, 93, 147–49; scuttling of, 146; *Squalus* and fate of, 93, 146; in *Squalus* rescue, 82, 91, 146; survivors of, capture and fate of, 146–52

Sea Dog, USS (SS–401), in minefields of Sea of Japan, 188–90

Sea of Japan, U. S. submarines in, 186–90

Seadragon, USS (SS–194), in Cavite bombing, 98–100

Seagull, USS (AM-30), 60

Seahorse, USS (SS-304): cartoon image, 192; command by Cutter, Slade D., 1, 153; command by Wilkins, Charles W., 174–76; liberty for sailors of, 124–27; in rescue of enemy from sea, 174–76; service of O'Meara, James B., in, 124, 174–76

Seal, USS (SS-183), Reserve acquisition of, 204

Sealion, USS (SS-195): in Cavite disaster, 98–100

Sealion, USS (SS-315, sinking of ship carrying Allied prisoners, 170–71

Searaven, USS (SS-196), 85–86

Seattle, Washington, 271

Seawolf, USS (SS-197), 85–86

Seawolf, USS (SSN-575), 200

Second Marine Raider Battalion, 141

segregation, of black submariners, 158–60

Sennet, USS (SS-408), under-ice operations of, 207–9

Shafter, Fort, Army post in Hawaii, 38

Shanghai, visits of *S-33* to, 53–56

Shark, USS (SS-174), 69, 193

Shear, Harold E. "Hal," service in fast-attack *Trigger*, 227–31

shellbacks, 156–57

Shenandoah, USS (ZR-1), 35

Shinso Maru (Japan), 121

Sibitsky, Martin, 82

Sieglaff, William Bernard "Barney," 187

Sims, William E. "Pappy," service in *Pickerel*, 221–223, 225

Sirago, USS (SS-485), 193

Sixth Fleet, U.S., 264–66

Skate, USS (SSN-578), 112

Skipjack (SSN-585) class, 235

Small, Walter L., 134, 135

Smedberg, William R. III, 252–53

Snapper, USS (SS-185), 77

Solomon Islands, reconnaissance of, 136–37

sonar: in Cold War reconnaissance, 217, 232, 242; of *Dolphin*, 276; in minefields of Sea of Japan, 186–90; in salvage of *S-4*; in under-ice operations, 206–7, 209–11; used by *Thresher, 121;* used by *Trigger* at Midway, 119

Sontag, Sherry, 216

Soryu (Japan), 119

Soviet Union, Cold War with. *See* Cold War

Soviet Union, reconnaissance of: by *Barbel*, 251; by *Bluegill*, 242–45; by *Clamagore*, 264; fire in *Cochino* during, 216–19; *Gudgeon* forced to surface during, 245; by *Ronquil*, 232–34

Sperry, Lawrence, Sr., 15–16

Sperry gyroscopic stabilizer, 15–16

Spinax, USS (SS-489), 193

Squalus, USS (SS-192): accident analysis by Curtze, Charles A., 88–90; accident analysis by Evans, Robert L., 92–93; recommissioning of, 85, 88, 93; recovery and repair, Curtze, Charles A. in, 85–90, 93; recovery and repair, Evans, Robert L. in, 88–90, 91–93; removal of bodies from, 85, 93; rescue of, 80–84; *Sculpin* and, 82, 91, 93, 146; World War II service as *Sailfish*, 93, 146, 147–49

Stack, USS (DD-406), 227

Steelhead, USS (SS-280): sinkings by, 167–69; wolf pack operations of, 165–69

Stenke hood, 261

Sterlet, USS (SS-392), 162

Stevens Institute of Technology, 236

Stimson, Paul C., 243

Stormes, Max C., 52–53

Street, George L., 228

Stokowski, Leopold, 179

Sturgeon, USS (SS-187), escape from Java in, 102–3

sub-safe program, 247, 249–50, 251

submarine(s): advocacy by Roosevelt, Theodore, 10–12; black men in, 158–62; casualties in World War II, 110, 120; chances of survival in World War II, 120; early command opportunities in, 42–46, 47–48; naming of, 191–94; postwar acquisition for Reserve, 202–4; U. S., first combat action for, 13; under-ice operations of, 205–11; in World War I, 13–24. *See also specific incidents, personnel, and submarines*

Submarine Development Group Two, 216

Submarine Division Fourteen, 36–41, 60

Submarine Division Nine, 43, 59–60

Submarine Division Sixteen, 51

Submarine Division Thirty-two, 234

submarine pay: for enlisted personnel, 12, 43–44, 50; La Guardia's law on, 50; for officers, 46, 50

Submarine Flotilla Seven, 250

Submarine Force Atlantic Fleet: concern about *Albacore* development, 237–38; received messages on

pancake diesels, 231; Williams, Joe, Jr., as commander, 232

Submarine Force Pacific Fleet: headquarters at Pearl Harbor, 133, 143, 145, 168, 171, 222, 224 ,248–49; headquarters in Guam, 186–87, 195–99; operating procedures, 195–99; photo review, 234; under-ice research, 206; welcome for returning prisoners, 152

Submarine School: Alden, John D. at, 177–79; aptitude marks at, 104–6; Bauernschmidt, George W., at, 42–43; black submariners at, 158; Cutter, Slade D., at, 1, 3; D-boats (dog boats) at, 28; Dennison, Robert L., at, 48; diesel engine course of, 29–30; electrical engineering course of, 30; endless-chain system of, 27, 28; first classes of, 28–29; G-boats at, 28; influenza epidemic and quarantine at, 30; Irvin, William D., at, 62; Miller, Wayne L., at, 261, 263; Murray, Stuart S., at, 25–30; notebooks required in, 43; orders for, 76; Reservists at, 104–6; Rickover, Hyman, at, 62; Rindskopf, Maurice H., on staff of, 112; signaling course of, 43; Walker, Edward K., at, 58; Williams, Joe, Jr., at, 232

Submarine Squadron Eleven, 274, 279

Submarine Squadron Five, 239

Submarine Squadron Four, 72

Submarine Squadron Fourteen, 239

Submarine Squadron Thirty, 161–62

Submarine Squadron Three, 234

submerged firing of missiles, 240–41, 254

Suez Canal, *Clamagore* patrol at, 264–66

Summers, Paul E. "Pete," command of *Cusk*, 212–15

Sunda Strait, battle of, 101

Supply Corps, service of Bauernschmidt, George W., in, 42, 72–74

surface firing of missiles, 212–15, 239–41, 254

surface reloading, 164–66, 168

Sverdrup, Harald, 206, 211

Swatow, China, visit of *S-33* to, 54

Swinburne, Edwin R., 94, 171–2

Swordfish, USS (SSN-579), 256

Tai Sing Loo, 73

Tang, USS (SS-306), prisoners from, 151

Tang (SS-563) class, 227; construction of, 227–29 Shear, Harold E., in *Trigger*, 227–31

Tarawa, *Nautilus* scouting of, 141–43

Target, Seth, serving in *Dolphin,* 277

Tarpon, USS (SS–175), design and construction of, 69

Task Force 77, 250–51

TDC. *See* torpedo data computer

teardrop shape, 235–38, 248

tender, 72–74

Texas University Applied Physics Lab, 276

Third Naval District, 33

Thomas, Raymond "Roaring Bull," 33–34

Thomas, Willis M. "'Tommy," 8–9

Thompson, Robert R., 40–41

Thresher, USS (SS–200): actions at Enijun Pass, 120–21; actions at Gea Pass, 121–23; grappling hook ensnaring, 122–23; at sea during Pearl Harbor attack, 96; service of Grieves, Billy A., in, 120–23

Thresher, USS (SSN–593), loss of, 247, 249–50

Thunder Below (Fluckey), 170

Tiburon, USS (SS–529), 193

Tinosa, USS (SS–283), wolf pack operations of, 163–65

Tirante, (SS-420), service of Beach, Edward L., in, 228

Tjilatjap, Java, 101-3

Tokyo Bay, *Scorpion* action in, 129

Tokyo Maru (Japan), 7

Tokyo Rose, erroneous report of sinking of *Drum,* 109

Toro, USS (SS–422), in Cold War reconnaissance, 216

torpedo data computer (TDC): development of, 64, 77–79; use of in attack approaches, 5; 109, 134, 179

Train, Harold C., 246

Train, Harry D., II: command of *Barbel,* 246–53; criticism of Rickover, Hyman, by, 252; in Cuban Missile Crisis, 250–51; hydrobatics of, 248–49; nuclear program avoided by, 246, 251–53; service in *Wahoo,* 246, 248; Soviet reconnaissance by, 251

Trepang, USS (SS–412), 193

Triebel, Charles O., 162

Trigger, USS (SS–237): command by Benson, Roy S., 228, 230; command of Dornin, Robert E., 153; reef struck by, 114–17; service of Beach, Edward L., in, 113–17, 228

Trigger, USS (SS-564): command by Beach, Edward L, 227–31; construction of, 227–28; pancake diesel engines of, 228–31; service of Shear, Harold E., in, 227–31

Trout, USS (SS-202), 7, 193

Truk Atoll: destination of *Pompano,*

4–5; destination of *Thresher,* 123; *Drum* under attack, 110; *Sculpin* survivors imprisoned at, 146–47, 151

Tsingtao (Qingdao), China, visit of *S-33* to, 55–56

Tulagi, *Guardfish* actions out of, 136–40

Tullibee, USS (SS–284), 246

Tuna, USS (SS–203), 193

Tunny, USS (SS–282 / SSG–282), 170, 193, 239–41, 254

Tusk, USS (SS–426), in Cold War reconnaissance, 216–19; rescue of *Cochino* crew, 218–19

Tusler, Floyd A., 86–88

Twelfth Naval District, 134

two-by-six program, 260

two-man rule, for missile firing, 256

UB-65 (Germany), *AL-2* action against, 22–24

Ulmsted, Scott, 22

Ultra messages, 110, 146

Ulua, USS (SS–428), 193

under-ice operations, 205–11

U.S. Submarine Attacks during World War II (Alden), 182

Unyo (Japan), 171–72

Urakaze (Japan), 149

Utah, USS (BB-31), 13, 16

V-7 (Dolphin), design and construction of, 67

V-8 engines, 69–70

V-1 rockets, firing from *Cusk,* 213–15

V-boats, 67–68, 191

Veterans of Foreign Wars, 202

Vinson, Carl, in fast-attack *Trigger,* 229

Vladivostok, Soviet Union, reconnaissance of, 232–34, 251

Vlattas, John, serving in *Dolphin,* 278

Voge, Richard G. "Dick": command of *Sealion,* 98–99; in ComSubPac operations, 195–99

vulnerable tails, in Holland-style submarines, 41

Wahoo, USS (SS-238), Burke, Julian T., Jr. reassigned from, 133–34; lost with all hands, 133–34; naming of, 193

Wahoo, USS (SS-565), service of Train, Harry D., II, in, 246, 248

Wake Island, *Pompano* actions at, 4, 6

Walker, Edward K.: command of *Mayrant,* 58; in development of torpedo data computer, 77–79; service in *R-8,* 58–61; at Submarine School, 58

War Surplus Administration, 201

Ward, Donna: See Miller, Donna (Ward)

Ward, Norvell G.: in bombing of Cavite Navy Yard, 98–100; command of *Guardfish,* 136–40; in ComSubPac operations, 195–99; frustration and missed opportunities of, 136, 140; lifeguard duty off Rabaul, 138–39; on Lockwood, Charles A., 196–98; in Regulus missile operations, 239–41; sinking of *Kashu Maru,* 137–38; special missions of, 136–40

WAVES (Women Accepted for Volunteer Emergency Service), 35

Wegner, William, 252

West Virginia, USS (BB-48), equator crossing of, 156–57

Wetmore, Alexander, 193–94

whale shape, 235–38, 248

Whangpoo (Huangpu) River, *S-33* in, 54

Wheaton, Albert J., 32, 33–34

White, Steven A., 253

White, W. E., 250

Whitmire, Donald B., 250

Wichita, USS (CA-45), 128

Wilde, Andrew, command of *Dolphin,* 274–79

Wilkin, Warren D., 92–93

Wilkins, Charles W. "Weary," 174–76

Wilkins, Hubert, 205–6, 211

Wilkinson, Eugene P. "Dennis": command of nuclear *Nautilus,* 112, 183; as executive officer to Summers, Paul, 212–15; in grounding and abandonment of *Darter,* 183–85; in missile firing from *Cusk,* 212–15; poker playing of, 183, 185; as Reservist at Submarine School, 104–6; on Submarine School staff, 112

Wilkinson, Janice, 185

Wilkinson, USS (DL-5), in Regulus missile tests, 240

Will Rogers, USS (SSBN-659), 267

William Cramp shipyards, *G-4* construction at, 14–15

William H. Bates, USS (SSN-680), 202

Williams, Clark, 244

Williams, Joe, Jr.: Cold War reconnaissance by, 232–34, 242–45; command of *Bluegill,* 242–45; service in *Ronquil,* 232–34; at Submarine School, 232; unusual background of, 232

Williams, Margaret, 234, 244

Williamson, Delbert F., command of *Drum,* 111

Wilson, David Spencer, 246

Winton diesel engines, 69–70

Wise, John D., Jr., 278

Withers, Thomas, Jr., 94

wolf packs: in minefields of Sea of Japan, 188–90; Ramage, Lawson P. on, 163–69; in rescue of Allied prisoners from sea, 170–73

World War I: duration-of-war enlistments in, 37–38; submarine service in, 13–24. *See also specific incidents, personnel, and vessels*

World War II: black submariners in, 158–62; courting and marriage during, 177–82; liberty in, 124–27; submarine casualties in, 110, 120; submarine chances of survival in, 120. *See also specific incidents, personnel, and vessels*

Wormwood, Charles E. III: on DBF ("diesel boats forever"), 273; on filming of *The Hunt for Red October,* 269–71; service as chief of the boat in *Blueback,* last of "B-girls," 267–73; service in *Permit,* 267; service in *Will Rogers,* 267

Wotje Atoll, *Pompano* actions at, 5

Wright, Richard, executive officer of *Cochino,* 216, 218–19

Wylie, William N., command of *Scorpion,* 128–31

Wyoming, USS (BB–32), 205

X-stern, of *Albacore,* 238

Yancey, USS (AKA-93), in ice operations, 207

Yangtze River, *S-33* in, 54

Yawata (Japanese), 5

Yeich, Lloyd G., 250

Yokohama, Japan, 149

Yokosuka, Japan, 232–33, 242, 250–51

Young, Cassin, 111

Young, Charles M., 111

Zandam (Dutch), 101–2

Zollars, Allen M., 87–88, 93

About the Editor

PAUL STILLWELL, who lives in Arnold, Maryland, with his wife Karen, is an independent historian. He has a bachelor's degree in history (1966) from Drury College, Springfield, Missouri, and a master's degree in journalism (1978) from the University of Missouri. From 1962 to 1992 he participated in the Naval Reserve, retiring with the rank of commander. He spent thirty years, from 1974 to 2004, on the staff of the U.S. Naval Institute in Annapolis, Maryland. He was the first editor-in-chief of *Naval History* magazine and for more than twenty years ran the organization's oral history program. He turned one series of interviews into *The Golden Thirteen: Recollections of the First Black Naval Officers,* which was recognized by *The New York Times* as one of the notable books in the field of history for the year 1993.

In the late 1960s, as a naval officer, Stillwell served on board the USS *Washoe County* in Vietnam War action. His subsequent service in the USS *New Jersey* led to his interest in battleships. He has written books on the histories of three battleships, the *New Jersey, Missouri,* and *Arizona.* He edited the book *Air Raid: Pearl Harbor! Recollections of a Day of Infamy* and wrote the coffee-table book *Battleships,* which was published in 2001. This is his second book on submarines; in 1993 he was coauthor, with Vice Adm. Robert Y. Kaufman, of *Sharks of Steel.* In 1994 Stillwell was awarded the Naval Institute author of the year award, based on the publication of *The Golden Thirteen* and *Sharks of Steel.* Later that year he received the Navy League's annual Alfred Thayer Mahan Award for Literary Achievement. Stillwell has made numerous television appearances on various aspects of naval history. He has been on NBC, CBS, ABC, CNN, A&E, the Discovery Channel, and the History Channel.